A Catholic Response
in Sixteenth-Century France
to Reformation Theology—
The Works of Pierre Doré

Front cover:
A depiction of "The Mother of Sorrows"
Illustration from the first edition of Pierre Doré's *Dyalogue instructoire des chrestiens en la foy, esperance, et amour en Dieu*, published in 1538 by Jean Real in Paris.

A Catholic Response in Sixteenth-Century France to Reformation Theology— The Works of Pierre Doré

John Langlois

Roman Catholic Studies
Volume 18

The Edwin Mellen Press
Lewiston•Queenston•Lampeter

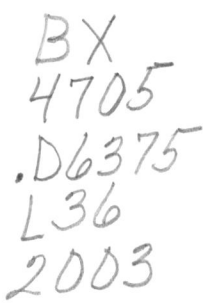

Library of Congress Cataloging-in-Publication Data

Langlois, John, 1963-
  A Catholic response in sixteenth-century France to Reformation theology : the works of Pierre Doré / John Langlois.
    p. cm. -- (Roman Catholic studies ; v. 18)
  Includes bibliographical references and index.
  ISBN 0-7734-6697-5 (hc)
  1. Dorâ, Pierre, 1500?-1569. 2. Justification--History of doctrines--16th century. 3. Lord's Supper--Catholic Church--History--16th century. 4. Catholic Church--Doctrines--History--16th century. I. Title. II. Series.

BX4705.D6375L36 2003
230'.2'092--dc21
                                                                    2003051034

This is volume 18 in the continuing series
Roman Catholic Studies
Volume 18 ISBN 0-7734-6697-5
RCS Series ISBN 0-88946-240-X

A CIP catalog record for this book is available from the British Library

Copyright © 2003 John Langlois

All rights reserved. For information contact

The Edwin Mellen Press   The Edwin Mellen Press
Box 450   Box 67
Lewiston, New York   Queenston, Ontario
USA 14092-0450   CANADA L0S 1L0

The Edwin Mellen Press, Ltd.
Lampeter, Ceredigion, Wales
UNITED KINGDOM SA48 8LT

Printed in the United States of America

*For my parents,
in gratitude for their example and
unwavering love*

TABLE OF CONTENTS

ABBREVIATIONS.. iii

PREFACE... v

FOREWORD... ix

ACKNOWLEGEMENTS... xi

INTRODUCTION... 1
   Pierre Doré's Historiographical Reputation... 3
   Doré's Place in the Institutional Response to the Reformation in France........... 21

**CHAPTER 1: DORÉ AND THE FRENCH DOMINICANS IN THE EARLY
   SIXTEENTH CENTURY** 39
   Doré's Religious and Intellectual Formation... 40
   Doctor, Preacher, Writer, and Spiritual Director in Turbulent Times 49
   The French Dominicans and the Reformation 60

CHAPTER 2: AN OVERVIEW OF DORÉ'S WORKS 75
   The Works and Subsequent Editions... 76
   Theological Instruction with an Appeal to the Heart................................... 82
   The Dedications... 89
   Doré's Sources and Pedagogical Methods.. 98
      The Primacy of Scripture.. 101
      The Fathers and Aquinas.. 109
      Traces of Humanism.. 112
      The Extensive Use of Metaphors and Images..................................... 117
      The Art of Polemics 122

CHAPTER 3: JUSTIFICATION, GRACE, MERIT AND FREE WILL 131
   Sola Fide: Refuting the Cornerstone of the Reformation............................. 132
   "...And the greatest of these is love": The Necessity of Formed or Living Faith...138
   "Blessed are you...": A Discussion of Merit and Free Will 147
   The Woman at the Well: A Living Image of How Justification Takes Place......... 155
   Conclusion 162

CHAPTER 4: THE EUCHARIST: TRANSUBSTANTIATION AND "DEIFICATION"..165
Transubstantiation Resoundingly Affirmed.. 170
The Problem of Local Presence.. 183
A Defense of the Ministerial Priesthood and the Eucharist as Sacrifice............... 190
Practical Counsels: Preparing to Receive the Eucharist............................. 205
An Encouragement to Frequent Communion... 209
Deification: The Principal Effect of the Eucharist...................................... 215
Conclusion.. 222

CHAPTER 5: THE VIRTUOUS LIFE AND MARY ITS IMAGE 225
The "Rock of Virtue": A Keynote and Herald of the "Doréan" Project.............. 228
Mary, the Mirror of Virtue.. 233
In Defense of the Immaculate Conception... 236
Mary's Triumph and Ours... 246
The Struggle to Live Virtuously: Fanning the Flames of Divine Love............... 251
Conclusion.. 258

CONCLUSION 261

APPENDICES
1. *Chronological Listing of Doré's Works and Number of Subsequent Editions*.. 269
2. *List of Editions of Doré's Works* 271
3. *Editions of Doré's Works Arranged According to Library*........................ 279
4. *List of Dedications* 289

BIBLIOGRAPHY 291

INDEX 301

ABBREVIATIONS

AGOP	Archivio Generale Ordinis Praedicatorum, Rome
BA	Bibliothèque de l'Arsenal, Paris
Benoît	Benoît, J.-D., ed. *Institution de la religion chrestienne* (critical edition)
BL	British Library, London
BM	Bibliothèque Municipale at Amiens, Bordeaux, Châlons-en-Champagne, Dijon, Lyon, Marseilles, Rouen, Toulouse, Troyes, and Versailles
BMJ	Bibliothèque Méjanes, Aix-en-Provence
BMZ	Bibliothèque Mazarine, Paris
BNF	Bibliothèque Nationale de France, Paris
BPU	Bibliothèque Publique et Universitaire, Geneva and Neuchâtel
BR	*Biographical Register of Paris Doctors of Theology 1500-1536*
BRA	Bibliothèque Royale Albert Ier, Brussels
BRBL	Beineke Rare Book Library (Yale), New Haven, Connecticut
BS	Bibliothèque du Saulchoir (Couvent S. Jacques), Paris
BSB	Bayerische Staats Bibliothek, Munich
BSG	Bibliothèque Sainte-Geneviève, Paris
BUG	Bibliothèque de l'Université de Gand, Ghent
CRL	Center for Research Libraries, Chicago
CTSA	Bibliothèque du Couvent Saint-Thomas d'Aquin, Toulouse
CUL	Cambridge University Library, Cambridge
Denz.	Denzinger, H., ed. *Enchiridion symbolorum definitionum et declarationum de rebus fidei et morum*
DTC	*Dictionnaire de théologie catholique*
Dupuy	Dupuy, Pierre. *Preuves des libertez de l'église gallicane*
FSL	Folger Shakespeare Library, Washington, District of Columbia
HAB	Herzog-August-Bibliothek, Wolfenbüttel

HES	Theodore Hesburgh Library (Notre Dame), Notre Dame, Indiana
HOU	Houghton Library (Harvard), Cambridge, Massachusetts
IC	Institut Catholique, Paris
LC	Library of Congress, Washington, District of Columbia
McNeill	McNeill, John, ed. *Calvin: Institutes of the Christian Religion*
MLA	Médiathèque Louis Aragon, Le Mans
MOPH	*Monumenta ordinis fratrum praedicatorum historica*
PL	Migne, J.-P., ed. *Patrologiae cursus completus. Series Latina*
QE	Quétif, J., J. Echard, eds. *Scriptores ordinis praedicatorum*, vol. 2
RCFT	*Regestum conclusionum sacrae facultatis theologiae in universitate parisiensi*, 1 (1505-1533); 2 (1533-1549); 3 (1552-1574)
RSPT	*Revue des Sciences Philosophiques et Théologiques*
RSV	*New Oxford Annotated Bible* (Revised Standard Version)
UEL	University of Edinburgh Library, Edinburgh
UMI	University of Michigan Library, Ann Arbor, Michigan
Weimar	*D. Martin Luthers Werke, Kritische Gesamtausgabe* (Weimar, 1883)

Preface
By Guy Bedouelle, O.P.

In a reference to the translation of the Scriptures into the vernacular, one of the great points of debate in the sixteenth century, Pierre Doré exclaims in his *Le college de sapience* (1539), "the Faculty of Theology in Paris does not at all wish to keep the Sacred Scriptures from the people, as some slanderous Calvinists are wont to say." However, in his mind, such translation of the Word of God is like medicine which needs to be taken at the direction of a physician. Herein is summed up the perspective of our Dominican friar: he praises the Bible as a means to salvation, for this is the source of good theology, but not without issuing precautions for its proper use, indicating the need for a good pastoral approach.

We are thus invited in this present work by John Langlois to rediscover a figure of great interest who is today virtually unknown after centuries of neglect or at the very least indifference. This is paradoxical for in the first half of the sixteenth century, Pierre Doré, doctor of the illustrious Faculty of Theology at the University of Paris, was one of the most prolific writers of the time. Among his contemporaries, only John Calvin could boast of a greater number of editions of his works in French. But who in our own day has ever heard of Doré, except perhaps for a few specialists of the Reformation? The author attempts here to understand the success enjoyed by Pierre Doré and what this could have meant for this period in history, fertile in theological challenges and controversies of all sorts.

If the Master d'Oribus of chapter XXII of Rabelais' *Pantagruel* is indeed a reference to our friar, as the prudent demonstration of John Langlois seems to indicate, and if Protestants continued to refute him even towards the end of the sixteenth century, the name Doré afterwards seems to fall into oblivion. We must wait for the *Scriptores ordinis Praedicatorum* of Quétif and Échard in the eighteenth century to bring him and his work once again to light. Then, it is solely those specialists of the Parisian Faculty of Theology or of the Dominican

Order in France who have any knowledge of him. Yet, most recently, the work of James Farge, Denis Crouzet, Marie-Madeleine Fragonard, Francis Higman and others have helped to resurrect Doré and his place in the history of sixteenth-century France.

After providing a detailed description of Doré's *milieu* and his works, John Langlois ably demonstrates that the friar's manner and style are characteristic of the Catholic pre-Reformation. Doré loves to cite authorities, both patristic and scholastic, especially St. Thomas Aquinas. Yet his manner of presentation has little in common with scholasticism, even if the doctrine remains solidly Thomistic. Also discernable in his work are "traces of humanism," a fact which calls into question the opinion, spread far and wide at the beginning of the sixteenth century, particularly by Hutten, of an absolute cleavage between "illustrious men" and "obscure men," an opposition which has since been oft repeated. Doré's abundant use of metaphors and images, particularly in the devotional works, can prove disorienting to the modern reader. Some are frankly ridiculous or out of place, such as those we find scattered throughout the *Anatomie et mystique description de members et parties de nostre saulveur Jesuschrist*, published in 1546. At the same time, we should note as the principal characteristics of Doré's work his decision to produce most of it in French as well as the related fact that many of the books are dedicated to women. Both are indications of his target audience.

Francis Higman has already shown that Doré had corrected and amended an anonymous text which was actually a previous translation of a small work by Luther. John Langlois demonstrates here, with texts at hand, that Doré incorporated word for word in his *L'arche de l'alliance nouvelle* of 1549 several paragraphs of Calvin's *Petit traicté de la saincte Cène*, published in 1541. What this indicates is not only a sense of literary ownership other than our own but also Doré's interest in the truth wherever it might be found. It is also surprising to discover that our friar does not hesitate to illustrate Catholic doctrine by making use of those scriptural texts most often cited by the Reformers, particularly those which seem to support the idea of justification by faith alone: the faith of Abraham, for example, or that of the "good thief." In an ingenious if not always convincing way, Doré finds in these scriptural figures illustrations of the good works that must accompany faith and thus overturns the perspective. Other examples he points to include Mary Magdalene and the Samaritan woman whom Jesus encounters at the well. The latter figures prominently in the *Dialogue de la justification chrestienne* published in 1554. Here, Doré interprets Christ's request of the woman for a drink of water as the image of grace calling forth and demanding good works on the part of the believer. We are thus given very interesting insights into the history of exegesis in the sixteenth century. Finally, the notion of merit is reaffirmed by Doré's interpretation of the Beatitudes in which he links each beatitude to the recompense attached to it as a promise.

What comes to the fore in this study is how Doré conceives his role as theologian first of all in terms of controversial theology. This is evident in the *Anti-Calvin* of 1551, of which there seems to presently remain only one extant copy. The most crucial question is that of the Eucharist. Doré does not hesitate to reaffirm the sacrificial aspect as well as the ministerial priesthood which the notion of sacrifice implies. At the same time, Doré is a proponent of more frequent access to the sacrament by believers, recalling the practice of the early Church. This is particularly interesting in light of the use of the historical argument in controversy, as exposed in Polman's classic work. What we can discern, then, in Doré is a certain freedom of judgment which makes of him a theologian who is neither purely reactionary nor conservative.

Finally, we have Doré as spiritual and devotional writer. Here, John Langlois defends a thesis which seems quite accurate: both forms, that of the devotional work and that of the polemical work, are two aspects of the same project: a defense of the Catholic faith. The primary example is one of Doré's top best-sellers, *Les allumettes du feu divin*, which was edited fourteen times (including two Latin editions) throughout the sixteenth and into the seventeenth century with the last edition being published in Cologne in 1691. Yet Doré's theology of the virtuous life grounded in divine love is announced from his very first work appearing in 1525. The image of fire is also a recurring theme.

In *L'image de vertu* (1540), Doré puts forth the Virgin Mary as the mirror of the virtuous life and exemplar for all Christians. His Marian theology is accompanied by a defense of the Immaculate Conception. It is clear that Doré is not a partisan of the commonly held position of the Dominicans at the time and he must also attempt to explain Aquinas' teaching on the matter. In fact, he tries to demonstrate that St. Thomas actually defended the doctrine at a certain point in his career. He also makes reference to the teaching of the Council of Basel and its definition of the doctrine. It is less a question here of a gallican spirit than of an allegiance to the royal court whose religious politics took up the defense of the acts of this council, considered schismatic by the papacy. From this perspective, Doré, like many of the doctors of the "Sorbonne," did not have much choice in the matter. But to return to the point at hand, the strong suit of this study is the solid knowledge of Aquinas' thought which John Langlois brings to his analyses of Doré's works, for St. Thomas is Doré's most important source.

In summary, this work, by clearly pointing out Doré's innovations and attempting to identify the audience for which he wrote, confers on the Dominican theologian the remarkable role which historiography until now has passed over. Knowledge of such a figure of the Catholic pre-Reformation, though he was not a genius but nevertheless highly gifted and possessing an incredible zeal, helps us to understand the preparatory steps leading to the great work which would be accomplished by the Council of Trent, both in terms of its theological determinations and its pastoral application. For these reasons, this book, harmoniously written and presented, should be a tremendous help to all who believe that the Catholic reform of the sixteenth century should be considered under all its aspects and through all its various stages.

Foreword

When I shared with a colleague my desire to research the Dominican response to the Reformation in sixteenth-century France, his reaction was "good luck finding something worthwhile to write about." He went on to explain that, in his mind, this period was not one of the more illustrious in the long history of the Order of Preachers. Fortunately, I did not allow myself to be deterred in my quest by his pessimistic outlook. And while there is some truth to his negative assessment of Dominican activity in the post-Reformation period, it nevertheless betrays what is a general and widespread ignorance of the intense work of some sixteenth-century friars who were actually significant players in the unfolding of the Catholic response to the Reformation. It is my hope that this present study will serve as a corrective to such misleading generalizations.

This monograph is an exposition of the life's work of Pierre Doré (1497-1569), Dominican doctor of theology at the University of Paris. It is the first such study of perhaps the most significant Catholic spiritual writer in France in the aftermath of the Reformation. The reader will find here an examination of the major themes of Doré's works and how they formed the basis for his program of theological instruction for the French laity in response to the new teaching being propagated in the vernacular by the Reformers. Particular attention is given to his sources and pedagogical methods. What emerges is the portrait of a man imbued with zeal for sharing the riches of Catholic faith and piety with the "little ones" whose eternal salvation he saw as threatened by those who had rejected basic tenets and devotional practices of the traditional faith in the name of reform.

Because Doré's works offer an important window not only into the Catholic reformation in France but also into the kind of literary style which appealed to a wide reading public in the sixteenth century, I have decided to offer here the citations from his works in the original sixteenth-century French. For those readers who may be at a disadvantage as a result of this editorial decision, I strive to summarize within the text the main threads of the thought expressed in the citations. Thus, even those unfamiliar with sixteenth-century French should nevertheless be able to profit from this study.

Over the centuries, bibliographers and historians have portrayed Pierre Doré in terms as diverse as hero and champion of the faith, saint, religious fanatic, or even an eccentric worthy of derision. The reader will doubtless arrive at his or her own conclusions in this regard. Yet no matter what opinion one may come to have of the man, it is incontestable that he was among the leading Catholic figures in the France of his day. Indeed, it would be difficult to fully appreciate the nature of the Catholic reformation in France apart from him.

Acknowledgements

I am indebted to several scholars whose assistance and encouragement made this monograph on Pierre Doré possible. In the first place, I would like to thank Prof. Guy Bedouelle, O.P., for his fraternal mentorship throughout the writing of this work and for graciously accepting to contribute the preface to the present edition. His expertise in the field of Dominican history and the Reformation period in particular proved to be an invaluable resource for me.

Special thanks also to Prof. Francis Higman, himself a Doré enthusiast, who provided much encouragement in the early stages of this project and who willingly shared with me the fruits of his extensive bibliographical research which became the foundation of my own work. I also wish to acknowledge the helpful comments he offered as I was preparing the text for publication.

I am similarly indebted to Prof. Marie-Madeleine Fragonard for sharing with me her as yet unpublished research on the literary output of French Dominicans in the sixteenth century. Her work has been critical in highlighting the important contribution of Pierre Doré among his contemporaries.

Finally, I gratefully acknowledge the invaluable assistance of Prof. James Farge whose close reading and critique of an early draft helped to improve the present work in significant ways.

In the category of technical assistance, I would like to extend a special word of thanks to David Mott, O.P., for his help in preparing the cover illustration of this book.

More remotely, the following people contributed to this project in a special way through their friendship and moral support. In particular, I wish to thank Romanus Cessario, O.P., for his fraternal encouragement over the years and for the model of scholarship he has been to me. I am also deeply grateful to Peter Girard, O.P., and to Dr. Paul Gondreau and his wife Christiana for the moral support they have provided me throughout this endeavor.

Finally, a word of thanks to my Dominican brothers at the Albertinum in Fribourg, Switzerland and at the Annunciation Priory in Paris for the warm welcome and fraternity they extended to me during my years of research and writing in Europe.

INTRODUCTION

If one were to make a list of the great Catholic spiritual writers of the sixteenth and early seventeenth centuries, that list would surely include the Spanish mystics Teresa of Avila and John of the Cross, as well as the reforming bishop of Savoy, Francis de Sales, to name but the most prominent. Their works are considered classics precisely because they have transcended the period in which they were produced and have a continuing appeal to readers who are seeking to grow in the spiritual life. Among the numerous spiritual writers of the same period whose works never achieved the status of classics is the French Dominican and doctor of theology at the University of Paris, Pierre Doré (ca. 1497-1569). While his name might be somewhat familiar to connoisseurs of sixteenth-century France, particularly those who are interested in Reformation history, his fame and appeal as a spiritual writer have long since vanished. Yet in his time, Doré was a very successful, even best-selling author. In fact, he has the distinction of being the most edited Catholic writer in France during the first half of the sixteenth century. Only the Genevan Reformer, John Calvin, can claim a greater number of editions of his works in the same period.[1] Clearly, we are dealing here with a man who exercised a certain amount of influence on his contemporaries through his literary production in what was a religiously fervent

---

[1] See Francis Higman, *Piety and the People: Religious Printing in French, 1511-1551* (Aldershot: Scolar Press, 1996), p. 5.

but also very turbulent period in French history. Thus, although the works of Pierre Doré have since lost their appeal as devotional literature, they are nevertheless an important means of coming to a greater understanding of the religious culture of sixteenth-century France, in particular the Catholic response to the challenges posed by the advent and spread of the Reformation.

The fact that a good portion of this French Dominican's writings has an unmistakably polemical tone to it makes a study of Doré and his work within the context of Reformation-era France even more pressing. While the substance of these works is devotional and catechetical, it is nevertheless clear that the spiritual counsel and theological instruction offered in them are ordered to a very specific objective—keeping the ordinary faithful from being deceived and falling prey to heresy. Indeed, the works are occasioned by the appearance in the first half of the 1500s of heterodox ideas—principally those of Luther and Calvin—being disseminated by means of the printed word thanks to the fairly recent invention of the printing press. In making good use of this new invention himself, Doré turns out to be one of the major figures in the Catholic response to the Reformers in France. Most interesting is the fact that he is engaged in the battle for orthodoxy a full quarter-century before the close in 1563 of the Council of Trent, the Church's official doctrinal and disciplinary response to the challenge of the Reformation. Fighting fire with fire, or more properly speaking, heterodox books with orthodox books, the Dominican theologian represents more of a grass-roots response to Reformed theology in France, one which preceded the official magisterial response of a general council. If the doctrinal definitions and reform measures of Trent were a principal, and one might say indispensable, factor in stemming the tide of Protestantism in Europe, the role played on a smaller scale by Catholic writers such as Doré should not for that reason be overlooked or downplayed. On the contrary, in the absence of a concerted effort on the part of the papacy and even local bishops to make a serious response to the ideas of the Reformers in the early years of the Reformation, the work of Pierre Doré and of others like him answered a most pressing need for a reasoned defense of the traditional faith.

Pierre Doré's Historiographical Reputation

Although no comprehensive study of Pierre Doré and his work has ever been done, he is by no means a complete unknown in the world of Reformation historiography. His name and the titles of his writings show up in numerous bibliographical sources of sixteenth-century works. These entries usually contain some basic biographical data as well. He also receives at least a mention, and sometimes a bit more than that, in some older, general works on the history of the Dominican Order. More recently, our friar has figured in a fair number of publications by sixteenth-century scholars, notably Denis Crouzet, James Farge, Marie-Madeleine Fragonard and Francis Higman. A good place to begin this study then is to examine briefly Doré's already existing historiographical reputation. What kind of picture emerges of him from what bibliographers and historians have already written? What has been their assessment of the man and his work?

We begin with one of the oldest evaluations of both Pierre Doré's personal character as well as the significance of his writings. This documentary evidence comes from neither a historian nor a bibliographer but from one of the Dominican's publishers. The 1586 edition of one of Doré's best-selling works, *Les allumettes du feu divin*, contains a letter in which the publisher, Jean Pillehotte, recommends both the book and its author to his readers. At the time that this edition appears, Doré has been deceased for seventeen years already. Nevertheless, Pillehotte's letter provides one of the earliest testimonies of the reputation that the friar enjoyed among his contemporaries:

> *Or combien que je te pourrois faire un long & ample discours de l'utilité du present livret, comme aussi des excellentes & rares vertus de ce bon*

> & devot religieux Frère Pierre Doré. Neantmoins j'ayme mieux, que lisant ce livret, tu cognoisses par effect le bien & proffit qu'il t'apportera, que si tu l'entendois par mes paroles seulement, & touchant à l'auteur je crois que par la lecture de ses aultres beaux & devotz livres tu en as telle cognoissance, que sans que je le te presche tu le recognois pour un singulier miroir de toute saincteté & devotion, lequel nostre Seigneur, qui en tout temps faict reluire le Soleil de sa grace sur les hommes, a faict apparoistre en nostre france, voire de nostre temps.[2]

While not discounting the "sales-pitch" factor here, that the primary motivation behind this letter is undoubtedly to promote sales of the book, we cannot simply reduce the publisher's praise of Doré to a crass ploy for increasing profits. There is a genuineness to his comments and if his words are taken at face value, it would seem that the Dominican theologian with his "excellent and rare virtues" had a reputation among his contemporaries for sanctity of life—a rather rare quality among the often worldly clergy of the early sixteenth century. Whether or not he was in reality the "singular mirror of sanctity and devotion" which Pillehotte paints him out to be, his writings certainly give evidence of a deeply spiritual, prayerful man who was a serious religious. How then might we account for the polemical spirit and intolerance towards the "heretics" of his day which is also clearly evident in his books? Is Doré a man of contradictions? Perhaps this fiery spirit can be interpreted as a manifestation of a holy zeal for the Christian faith at a time and in a culture where society at large cherished neither freedom of conscience nor the separation of church and state. In other words, Doré's moral character should not be judged by our contemporary standards, which had no relevance in his day.

While Pillehotte is full of praise concerning the Dominican theologian's sanctity of life, he goes on to offer a more critical assessment of his literary skills. In addition to correcting the numerous typographical errors from the previous printing of *Les allumettes* in 1548, the publisher informs his readers that because

---

[2] See "Le libraire au lecteur," in *Les allumettes du feu divin* (Lyon: Jean Pillehotte, 1586). **[Dijon, BM—584]**.

the book contains diction and many sentences that are far removed from the candor and purity of the French language, he has corrected it and made it "speak French" more properly.[3] His stated purpose in doing so is to assure that the reader will be taken in by the beauty of the content rather than be distracted or amused by the stylistic faults. Criticism of Doré's long-windedness and the labyrinthine style of "Doréan" phrases are most definitely a commonplace in the historiography that has followed.

However, before taking a look at that historiographical reputation, there remains yet another critical appraisal of Doré by one of his contemporaries which must be examined. The problem is that there is no consensus among scholars as to whether or not the Dominican is actually the object of this particular reference. The passing remark appears in Chapter XXII of Rabelais' *Pantagruel* where mention is made of a certain Master d'Oribus which some have maintained is a satirical reference to Doré.[4] This point has been much debated by bibliographers and historians alike and this present study is unlikely to bring a definitive end to the matter.[5] Nevertheless, an opinion will be offered.

The *Pantagruel* was first published in 1532, the same year that Doré was admitted as a doctor in theology at the University of Paris. While he certainly

---
[3] Ibid., "...*je l'ay faict parler françois un peu plus proprement qu'il ne faisoit au paravant.*"
[4] As the story goes, Panurge revenges himself on a Parisian lady by scenting her dress with bitch odors because she has spurned his love. So perfumed, the lady attracts all the dogs in town who, in heat, proceed to wet her without stop. Even when she regains her house, the dogs continue to urinate outside the door to such an extent that a veritable stream of urine begins to flow "...*et c'est celluy ruysseau qui de present passe à Sainct Victor, auquel Guobelin tainct l'escarlatte, pour la vertu specifique de ses pissechiens, comme jadis prescha publicquement nostre maistre d'Oribus.*" Citation taken from *Rabelais: Oeuvres complètes*, tome I (Paris: Éditions Garnier Frères, 1962), p. 335. The edition used by the publisher for this presentation was the definitive edition of François Juste, Lyon, 1542.
[5] These are a sampling of the varying opinions. The nineteenth-century bibliographer, Jacques-Charles Brunet, *Manuel du libraire et de l'amateur des livres*, vol. 2 (Geneva: Slatkine Reprints, 1990), p. 819 is among those who think that Rabelais is definitely refering to Doré. Jean Plattard, *Oeuvres complètes de Rabelais* (Paris: Société les belles lettres, 1946), p. 203 among others, suggests that the reference is to the Dominican preacher and later inquisitor, Matthieu Ory. André Duval, "Doré, Pierre" in *Dictionnaire de Spiritualité*, p. 1645 takes the position that Doré's career was not yet sufficiently established for the reference to be to him. James Farge, *Biographical Register of Paris Doctors of Theology* (Toronto: Pontifical Institute of Mediaeval Studies, 1980), p. 138, while taking note of the preceding two opinions, nevertheless believes it more plausible that the attribution is to Doré rather than to Ory.

would have engaged in public preaching since the early 1520s, the approximate time of his priestly ordination, it is highly questionable that he would have achieved such renown among the intellectual elite by 1532 as to merit this rather burlesque and unflattering portrayal by the French master of satire. Presumably, Rabelais would have spent his barbs on someone of more prominent standing than an ordinary mendicant preacher with no academic distinctions or reputation to speak of at the time of the *Pantagruel*'s writing. Yet, this is in fact a moot point because the reference to Master d'Oribus is actually not to be found in the first edition of 1532. Indeed, the reference only appears a decade later, an addition made by Rabelais in what is considered to be the definitive edition of 1542 published in Lyon by François Juste. This fact throws new light on the whole question because by this time, Doré's literary career had taken off and his reputation was well established. Thus it is certainly more plausible that he would have attracted the attention of the famous satirist, who may have been familiar with some of Doré's early works or had perhaps heard the theologian in the pulpit. Furthermore, that Rabelais would have found something in the Dominican's preaching at which to poke fun is not very hard to imagine. Subsequent chapters will give examples of the at times odd and amusing metaphors that Doré uses to illustrate his point. It is then quite likely in my estimation that Master d'Oribus and his sermon on the origins of the infamous "stream" passing by Saint-Victor[6] is meant to be a caricature of Doré's preaching and writing. At the same time, while the reference is far from flattering, it does indicate that Doré had achieved a certain renown among his contemporaries, even the master satirist of the period.

What seems to be the first bibliographical reference to our friar and his works is a short notice found in the *Chronicum Fratrum Ordinis Praedicatorum* (1585) by the Lusitanian Dominican Antonio Senensi. The *Chronicum*, a "Who's Who" type of compilation of famous Dominicans and their writings going back to

---

[6] See note [4].

the foundation of the Order, is basically a forerunner of the *Scriptores Ordinis Praedicatorum* (1721), to be discussed shortly, with the exception that the biographies and bibliographical listings of the former are much less complete than those of the latter. In the *Chronicum*'s notice on Doré, a compact biography highlights his connection with the ducal house of Guise along with the fact that he composed most of his works in French. This information is followed by a listing of merely a handful of his known titles. The nine titles mentioned are not even given in the original French but have been translated by the author into Latin. Nevertheless, Doré's inclusion in this bibliography, which was published only sixteen years after his death, is indicative of his having achieved recognition within the Order as a friar of stature.

The oldest French Dominican source on Doré is the *Histoire des saincts, papes...& autres hommes illustres qui furent superieurs ou religieux du couvent de S. Jacques de l'Ordre des FF. Prescheurs à Paris* by Antoine Mallet and published in 1634. Mallet provides little in terms of bibliographical information on Doré's works, citing only his Lenten conferences to the duke and duchess of Guise published in two volumes under the title *Les collations royales* and another work, *Le directoire de salut*. He is the only source to mention the existence of this latter work—no other bibliographer since seems to have had any knowledge of it. Yet perhaps of greatest interest here is Mallet's presentation of Doré as spiritual director to the house of Guise as well as to numerous other princes of the realm. In fact, he points to the exemplary moral standing of the Guise family members as evidence of Doré's own piety and virtue saying, "...*s'il faut juger de l'adresse d'un directeur, par les effects de sa conduitte, quand je voy que la maison de Guise estoit une escholle de vertu, dont leurs ames estoient les temples, il nous sera aisé de conjecturer quel estoit nostre Pierre Doré.*"[7] In describing the particular virtue of Claude de Guise, Mallet cites his ardent desire to defend

---

[7] Antoine Mallet, *Histoire des saincts, papes, cardinaux, patriarches, archevesques, docteurs de toutes facultez de l'Université de Paris, & autres hommes illustres, qui furent superieurs, ou religieux du couvent de S. Jacques de l'Ordre des FF. Prescheurs à Paris* (Paris: Jean Branchu, 1634-45), p. 233.

the Catholic faith by combatting heretics. The implication then is that the zealous Doré exercised a certain influence in stirring up and promoting this ardor in his spiritual son. For Mallet, the influence here is a positive one but future bibliographers will offer a much different perspective.

It is J. Quétif and J. Échard in their *Scriptores Ordinis Praedicatorum* who provide the real foundation upon which all subsequent research on Doré has been based. In addition to an extensive biographical sketch, they include a complete listing of his works in their original titles along with indications of later editions. According to their enumeration, Doré has a total of thirty-six published works to his name, two of which are in Latin and the remainder in French. They also note the existence of a manuscript that was never published. However, their list of subsequent editions is not complete. I have found later editions of certain works that they do not mention. At the same time, they mention editions and even a few titles of which there no longer seem to be any extant copies. It is quite possible that the copies which existed during their time have since been lost or destroyed. In Chapter 2, I will discuss the results of my own research on the works and subsequent editions in greater detail. Suffice to say that the *Scriptores* is an indispensable source for gaining a basic knowledge of Pierre Doré and his work.

In the *Dictionnaire bibliographique, historique et critique des livres rares* (1791), we have proof that some of Doré's works continued to be much sought after well into the eighteenth century, if not for their content at least for their value as a collector's item in one's personal library. The dictionary, anonymously compiled, has the stated goal "...*de faciliter en peu de mots, la connoissance exacte & certaine, avec leur juste appréciation, des Livres rares & précieux, soit Manuscrits, soit Imprimés.*"[8] This buyer's guide lists six of Doré's books as worthy collectibles: *Le college de sapience, Les allumettes du feu divin, L'image de vertu, Oraison panegyrique, La tourtrelle de viduité,* and *La caeleste pensée*. It should be noted that the first three mentioned in this listing were among Doré's

---

[8] *Dictionnaire bibliographique, historique et critique des livres rares* (Paris: Cailleau et fils, 1791), pp. viii-ix.

best-sellers. Although no reason is offered here for why these particular works by the sixteenth-century French Dominican are to be sought after by eighteenth-century collectors, the dictionary does help to confirm that Doré's writings had a significance beyond the time period in which they were produced.

A much more important bibliographical source produced in the nineteenth century is Jacques-Charles Brunet's *Manuel du libraire et de l'amateur des livres* (1860). Although much of the information here is basically a recapitulation of Quétif and Échard, Brunet's list does include a few editions not mentioned in the *Scriptores*. In contrast, however, to the glowing appraisal of Doré given by the Dominican bibliographers, Brunet offers a much different assessment in a few lines of biting commentary. For example, in his notice on *Les allumettes du feu divin*, he comments that it is a book no different from many others of the same genre and whose only originality lies in its distinctive title.[9] Becoming even more caustic, he goes on to say of Doré's books that "...*ils se distinguent tous par leur style ridicule, et presque toujours par la singularité des titres.*"[10] While acknowledging, and one gets the impression almost grudgingly so, that some of these works have been re-published several times, Brunet ends his commentary by saying that if copies of the other works are now practically impossible to find, this is not to be lamented for it is no great loss to the literary world.

We have already noted that the Lyonese publisher Jean Pillehotte mentioned having to "correct" Doré's style in order to make *Les allumettes* more comprehensible and appealing to readers in the latter portion of the sixteenth century. Thus it is easy to see how that style might be even less appreciated by readers in the nineteenth century. Yet, despite an apparent consensus on the limitations of Doré's literary skills, there is a world of difference between Pillehotte's and Brunet's assessments of the author's significance. Whereas Pillehotte sees something of merit in Doré's work despite its stylistic faults and devotes himself to its propagation, Brunet is much less convinced that there is any

---

[9] Brunet, *Manuel*, p. 818.
[10] Ibid., p. 819.

value at all to be found in it and does not regret in the least the fact that much of Doré has become hard to find in the nineteenth century. Modern-day researchers can nevertheless be grateful that Brunet did not let his evident prejudices prevent him from providing very useful and accurate bibliographical information on an author for whom he seems to have had little use or appreciation.

A similar yet noticeably more balanced appraisal of Doré is found in volume 2 of *La faculté de théologie de Paris et ses docteurs les plus célèbres* (1901) by abbé Pierre Féret, himself a doctor of theology from the same faculty. Féret's tomes consist of biographical notices with references to the works of the authors he treats. In the case of Doré, he lists the titles in order of publication including in most cases a brief abstract of the work. Drawing almost exclusively from the biographical information in Quétif and Échard, the abbé paints Doré as an ardent champion of the Catholic cause, waging combat against the Protestants through his writing and his preaching. Commenting on his writings, Féret nevertheless falls in line with Brunet's point of view when he says that the Dominican "*eût dû produire moins et mieux.*"[11] From Brunet he also borrows the adjective *singulier*, using it in a pejorative way to describe Doré's writings. However, he then goes on to make an admission with which Brunet could never have agreed when he writes:

> *Pierre Doré s'etait fait connaître, en même temps, par un grand nombre d'ouvrages qu'il avait publiés. Les titres de plusieurs sont* **singuliers** [emphasis mine] *et souvent le contenu ne l'est pas moins. Par-ci par-là, cependant, se révèle une originalité qui n'est pas de mauvais goût.*[12]

Not only do we have here a somewhat fairer assessment of Doré, but Féret has hit upon a key to understanding the evident success which several of Doré's works enjoyed—there is a certain originality to them which is not always in bad taste! What exactly this originality is, Féret never really explains. This will be one of

---

[11] Pierre Féret, *La faculté de théologie de Paris et ses docteurs les plus célèbres—Époque Moderne*, vol. 2 (Paris: Alphonse Picard et fils, 1901), p. 276.
[12] Ibid., p. 277.

the goals of this present study, to bring out some of the original elements that made the writings of Doré appealing to his contemporaries, elements in fact that even the modern reader can find engaging despite our different sensibilities.

Notwithstanding this fairly positive insight, Féret's concluding statement leaves a more negative impression. Siding with the general opinion that the Master d'Oribus of *Pantagruel* is in fact a reference to Doré, he begins by pointing out that Rabelais' caricature of the preacher is a bit excessive and forced. Nonetheless, he concludes his article with this comment, "*Sans prendre à la lettre ce qu'a dit Rabelais, il n'est pas téméraire de penser que le prédicateur ne se montrait pas moins excentrique que l'écrivain.*"[13] Judging that Rabelais' satire, while perhaps excessive, would have had some factual basis to it, Féret ends finally by categorizing Doré as an eccentric. Indeed, it seems that eccentricity and irrelevance sum up well the appraisal of Doré to be found in nineteenth- and early twentieth-century historiography.

The notable exception to this overall unfavorable judgment, and this is no great surprise, is the brief mention that Doré receives in the writings of Dominican historian D.A. Mortier. Although the title of his eight-volume masterwork, *Histoire des maîtres généraux de l'ordre des frères prêcheurs* (1911), indicates a rather restricted subject matter, it nevertheless goes beyond a mere accounting of the administration of each Master of the Order and includes a good deal of the larger history of the Order as well as the general history of the Church. Thus it is in the chapter on Master Vincent Justiniani (1558-1570) that we find a brief mention of Pierre Doré in the context of preachers who went into battle against the Protestant Reformation. Like Mallet a few centuries earlier, Mortier here highlights the theologian's relations with the house of Guise and how he would have certainly influenced the ultra-Catholic family in its struggle to rid France of the scourge of Protestantism.[14] He presents Doré himself very

---

[13] Ibid., p. 288.
[14] "*On sait combien les Guise luttèrent en France contre les calvinistes. Leur confesseur et ami [Doré] eut certainement une part très grande dans l'énergie qu'ils déployèrent pour défendre la*

favorably as an ardent defender of the Catholic faith. This question of what kind of a role Doré may have played in encouraging or even inciting the Guise in their virulent persecution of French Protestants is one that will be taken up later in this study. As far as Mortier is concerned, the influence is unquestionable. But neither is it a cause for shame—in his eyes, Doré conducted himself as a true son of St. Dominic in rousing others in defense of the faith at a time when the Church was rife with heresy.

From Mortier at the beginning of the century, we jump to more recent years where several contemporary scholars have taken more than simply a passing interest in Pierre Doré. Mention must first be made, however, of an encyclopedia article on Doré that appears in the *Dictionnaire de spiritualité* (1937). Written by Dominican historian and archivist, André Duval, the article is marked by balance and solid facts supported by documentation in attempting to reconstruct Doré's career, which is no easy task given the relative paucity of such documentation. In his conclusions, Duval, like several others before him, makes a point of calling into question Doré's "literary taste." He also brings out that the originality of his works "...*s'y manifeste beaucoup plus dans la langue, les images, les métaphores systématiquement développées, que dans les idées.*"[15] Duval is right here—Doré is a master of image and metaphor, sometimes a bit forced, but more often than not very beautiful and spiritually moving. If he is not an original thinker, he is an author of significance nonetheless precisely because of his ability to present the faith to the common people with the help of appealing images and metaphors.

Among the contemporary historiographers, James Farge of the Pontifical Institute of Mediaeval Studies in Toronto provides a very important biographical summary and bibliography of Doré in his *Biographical Register of Paris Doctors of Theology, 1500-1536*. While the bibliography depends in large measure on the *Scriptores*, it is more complete because it combines information from several

---

foi catholique." D.A. Mortier, *Histoire des maîtres généraux de l'ordre des frères prêcheurs*, vol. 5 (Paris: Alphonse Picard et fils, 1911), p. 551.
[15] Duval, "Doré," p. 1644.

other sources. Like Duval, Farge presents a very objective and balanced image of Doré, one based solely on documented material. The facts are allowed to speak for themselves with very little commentary offered to color one's judgment. While allowing that "Doré's works appear bizarre to the modern reader,"[16] Farge acknowledges that the Dominican's literary production along with the numerous editions of several of his works is a clear sign that his writings were not so off-putting to the reader of the sixteenth century.

In a later work related to the *Biographical Register*, his *Orthodoxy and Reform in Early Reformation France: The Faculty of Theology of Paris, 1500-1543*, Farge provides some impressive statistics confirming Doré's significance within his time period. According to his findings, Pierre Doré, with thirty-four titles to his name, turns out to be the third most prolific author among the graduates of the faculty of theology during the period 1500-1536. Only the famous humanist scholar Josse Clichtove and the Scottish doctor John Mair out-produced him with fifty-seven and thirty-nine titles respectively.[17] When Farge then divides the works of the Paris doctors into different categories, Doré comes out in first place in the category of devotional works with a total of twenty-five titles, which amounts to twenty-seven percent of the total.[18] Though "works of piety" is perhaps a bit too general of a description for much of Doré's writings, as will be shown in Chapter 2, nevertheless it serves the purpose here in Farge's attempt to classify and quantify Doré's work broadly speaking. These statistics certainly begin to call into question some of the remarks leveled against our friar by previous historiographers concerning his eccentricity and irrelevance. In light of Farge's findings, it becomes more and more difficult not to maintain that the man commonly portrayed as an overzealous defender of the traditional faith was actually a rather important figure in sixteenth-century France and not simply an irrelevant eccentric.

---

[16] BR, p. 138.
[17] See James K. Farge, *Orthodoxy and Reform in Early Reformation France: The Faculty of Theology of Paris, 1500-1543* (Leiden: E.J. Brill, 1985), p. 100.
[18] Ibid., p. 102.

For Denis Crouzet, professor at the University of Lyon, Doré's significance goes far beyond his literary output. In a monumental work on the wars of religion in France, *Les guerriers de Dieu: La violence au temps des troubles de religion, vers 1525 - vers 1610* (1990), Crouzet describes our friar as "*...un mystique dont toute l'oeuvre consiste en l'élaboration d'une stratégie de lutte contre l'hérésie, construite sur l'image sublimante du feu divin.*"[19] That Doré had a mystical side to him and that he had a definite strategy for combatting the Protestant heresy in France is certainly a well-founded assessment. However, Crouzet goes on to assert that Doré's anti-Protestant strategy is intimately related to his mysticism, a claim that is not so evident. In order to fairly present his position, a bit of explanation is therefore in order.

Crouzet, like several of the historiographers we have already discussed, sees a causal link between Doré and the religious fanaticism that characterized the ultra-Catholic house of Guise. However, the tone here is much different from that of Mortier, for example, who spoke of Doré's influence in this regard with a certain pride. For Crouzet, the extraordinary influence wielded by the Dominican spiritual director of this important ducal family led to dire consequences for the French nation with the eventual outbreak of violence and civil war in the name of God. Calling into question the prevailing interpretation of the wars of religion as being a result not only of strongly-held religious convictions but of personal and dynastic rivalries as well, he cites Doré's close connection with the Guise as proof that the religious motive in fact superseded all others:

> *Cette présence de Pierre Doré autour des Guise ne relativise-t-elle pas le stéréotype interprétatif des conflits de lignages en tant que luttes pour le contrôle du pouvoir ou guerres de clans aristocratiques à arrière-plan de rivalités personnelles et de vendettas? Le religieux n'est-il pas premier? L'intransigeance intégriste des princes lorrains ne s'enracine-t-elle pas dans l'émotion et l'illumination de l'Un en soi de la mystique eucharistique qu'enseignait simplement Pierre Doré, 'car nostre*

---

[19] Denis Crouzet, *Les guerriers de Dieu: La violence au temps des troubles de religion, vers 1525 - vers 1610*, vol. 1 (Seyssel: Champ Vallon, 1990), p. 374.

15

> *seigneur nous communique ainsi son corps, qu'il est entierement faict un avec nous, et nous avec luy'?*[20]

What is most interesting here is that Crouzet does not attribute the warrior spirit of the Guise to an explicit call to arms by the Dominican (though Doré, as will be shown, certainly did make such statements). Rather he contends that it is Doré's highly mystical teaching on the Eucharist which is to blame.

The link between Eucharistic mysticism and religious warfare, which is hardly self-evident, is explained by Crouzet as follows. Several devotional writers of the period, (Doré was not alone), when writing on the Eucharist spoke in terms of the transformation that occurs within the believer at the moment of communion with the body and blood of the Lord. A recurring theme was that after receiving the real presence of Christ in the Eucharist, the believer could truly echo what St. Paul says in his letter to the Galatians (2:20), "…it is no longer I who live, but Christ who lives in me." Crouzet goes on to develop the idea that there was a *glissement* or slippery slope from this notion of mystical metamorphosis in Christ to a fanatical violence against the adherents of the Reformation who among other things denied the real presence. He reasons that by promoting Holy Communion as a real participation in Christ's own eschatological victory over sin and death, mystic writers of the period gave the faithful a spiritual basis for justifying violence against heretics because such righteous combat was a way for the believer to actualize that eschatological victory over evil which had been mystically experienced through communion. Commenting on a leitmotif in Doré's writings that the believer is actually "deified" or divinized through his union with Christ in the Eucharist, Crouzet sums up his argument concerning the dangers inherent in the Eucharistic mysticism being promoted by the Dominican and others:

> *Pierre Doré va peut-être plus loin encore dans l'idée d'une métamorphose mystique dans un texte curieux qu'il publie en 1549,*

---

[20] Ibid.

> *L'arche de l'alliance nouvelle, et testament de nostre Saulveur Jesus Christ, contenant la manne de son precieux corps, contre tous sacramentaires heretiques. L'union d'amour, plus qu'elle fait vivre l'homme saint dans une présence sacrale, plus qu'elle le dépossède de sa condition finie de pécheur, devient, par le Mystère de la communion eucharistique et de sa puissance sacralisante, déification ou apothéose: 'Nostre Dieu, dict l'escripture [en marge Deut. 4], est comme un feu qui consume: Or le feu, de sa force et condition, il convertist tout en sa nature, tout ce qu'on luy applicque, pareillement, quand nous recepvons dignement ce sainct sacrement (...), il nous allume et embrasse du tout, et nous convertist en luy. Par ainsi l'homme déifié peult dire avec S. Paul: aux Galatiens Vivo ego, iam non ego, vivit vero in me Christus.' Chacun devient victoire virtuelle de la Vie sur la mort, de l'Esprit sur la chair, et là, de cet imaginaire d'un avènement eschatologique en soi et par soi, se déduit le sacral de la violence des guerres de religion.*[21]

To enter into a debate on the validity of Crouzet's reasoning concerning a possible link between Eucharistic mysticism and religious warfare is beyond the scope of this study. However, regardless of whether one agrees with Crouzet's position or not, one cannot accuse Pierre Doré of consciously trying to imbue his readers with a spirit of violence against heretics by promoting their mystical union with Christ in the Eucharist. He was much more blunt than that, explicitly stating more than once that the Reformers and their adherents should be burned at the stake for their defection from the true faith. There is no need, therefore, to "read into" Doré's devotional writings and particularly his teaching on the Eucharist a kind of spiritual or mystical justification for religious warfare. Although there was a definite anti-Protestant strategy behind his attempts to stir up the spirit of devotion of the laity, as will be shown in subsequent chapters, violence was most certainly not the intended end.

A much more nuanced view of Doré's strategy for combatting the Reformation comes across in a yet-to-be-published colloquium paper and a recently published article of Marie-Madeleine Fragonard, professor of French literature at the University of Paris III: "Les publications des dominicains entre innovation et réaction 1500-1560," Colloque de Göttingen (March, 1992) and

---
[21] Ibid., pp. 375-376.

"Pierre Doré: Une stratégie de la reconquête," appearing in *Calvin et ses contemporains* (1998). In the first place, she presents Doré as somewhat of an original among his contemporaries in the Order in terms of how he dealt with the reality of the Reformation. She writes:

> *Alors que l'ensemble des Dominicains français adopte un comportement silencieux, puis vivement polémique (le rôle d'Inquisiteur y est pour quelque chose), Pierre Doré adopte un comportement atypique: une écriture presque exclusivement française, orientée vers la piété plutôt que sur la dogmatique ou la polémique...*[22]

For Fragonard, the polemical aspect of Doré's work, while undeniably present particularly in the later writings, is nevertheless secondary to his main purpose, which is to respond not to the heretics themselves, but rather to the faithful who risk being led astray by the new ideas of the Reformers. She describes Doré as adopting more of a defensive position in regards to points of controversy, saying that what he does is not so much to refute as to affirm, teach, and lead his readers along the path of Truth as traditionally propounded by the Church.

More than anything else, Doré's writings, according to Fragonard, reflect a desire to educate the laity in the basics of the faith, in all those things which are essential for salvation. As she puts it:

> *Pour ses livres de dévotion et contre les erreurs curieuses, Doré construit une théologie de l'essentiel, tant sur le dogme que sur l'incorporation essentielle de la foi dans la conscience des croyants; il effectue une sorte d'élagage et de recentrage sur ce qui est essentiel au salut.*[23]

What we see emerging in Fragonard's discussion is more of an emphasis on Doré as theologian rather than simply as a devotional writer or anti-Protestant polemicist. It is a more accurate and well-rounded presentation, one that neither caricatures nor whitewashes the Dominican as we have seen in some of the other

---

[22] Marie-Madeleine Fragonard, "Pierre Doré: Une stratégie de la reconquête," in *Calvin et ses contemporains*, ed. Olivier Millet (Geneva: Droz, 1998), p. 179.
[23] Ibid., p. 191.

historiographies. She establishes Doré as having a definite strategy for opposing Protestantism, but one that was directed to the lay faithful, not to the heretics themselves, with the intention of keeping the laity from being seduced by the errors being propagated through the printed text.

Another important point which is made in both of Fragonard's articles is the fact that a good number of Doré's books are written at the request of and for the spiritual nourishment of women, particularly noblewomen or nuns. Fragonard is the first to highlight this "woman factor" which is present in the dedications of several of the devotional works and she interprets it as Doré taking seriously the spiritual yearnings of "...*les femmes instruites, assez pour lire, pas assez pour être savantes.*"[24] The dedications also reflect a very close connection between Doré and the upper classes of French society. Although the works themselves are meant for general consumption, nevertheless they are first and foremost directed to the elite of society. Fragonard explains:

> *Tant par les dédicaces que par les formes stylistiques, Doré écrit pour une élite sociale qui ne sait pas simplement 'lire,' et qui raisonne dans un cadre où l'action (autoritaire), la culture (lettrée) et la piété ne se séparent pas. Il lui faut opérer une reconquête sociale et protéger les puissants, parce qu'ils sont des modèles et les garants de l'ordre physique du monde.*[25]

This is a further elaboration of Doré's strategy, not only to theologically educate the laity, but more particularly to ensure that the upper classes do not become infected with the virus of heresy. Again what comes across most strongly in Fragonard's presentation is that there is a double aspect to Doré's work; a concern to provide the laity with a spiritual nourishment which is theologically based for their own personal growth within the larger context of a strategy to combat the errors of Protestantism and restore unity of faith in sixteenth-century France.

---
[24] Marie-Madeleine Fragonard, "Les publications des dominicains, entre innovation et réaction (1500-1560)," in *Actes du Colloque de Göttingen, Changements religieux, genèse de l'État moderne et transformations sociales. Place, fonction et images des clercs, France et Empire (1500-1650)*, March 1992. Publication forthcoming.
[25] Fragonard, "Stratégie", pp. 185-186.

It has already been noted that the recent bibliographical work of Francis Higman, former director of the Institut d'histoire de la Réformation at the University of Geneva, has helped bring to light Pierre Doré's literary significance as a best-selling author in his time. In his recently published *Piety and the People* (1996), Higman seeks to provide a working research list of all religious books printed in French in the period 1511-1551. His principal aim is to bring into focus "...not so much the Reformation of the theologians, as the Reformation of the people: what was available to the public at large, what forms of piety were promoted, what mental processes are invoked?"[26] Perhaps the most surprising result of his research is the emergence of Doré as one of the top five edited writers in France in the period under study—in the same league with and even ahead of the much more famous Luther, Erasmus and Rabelais and just behind John Calvin. It is not without reason that this discovery brings Higman to comment, "On purely statistical grounds, his [Doré's] place in the history of the Reformation conflict has clearly been seriously undervalued."[27] What is more, Higman breaks with the long-standing tradition of historiography on Doré when he goes on to say that:

> These five authors constitute what must be called the first division. It is noteworthy that four of them are among the most admired *writers* [italics his] of their age, with an aesthetic sense of language which sets them apart. In fact the fifth, Pierre Doré, is also a brilliant stylist, but in a manner alien to modern taste (see the titles of his books). His highly florid and metaphor-filled style was clearly more appreciated by contemporaries than it is today.[28]

Higman's point here is well taken. Although Doré's style has not aged as well as that of the other great writers of the period, historiographers until now have judged him a bit unfairly on this matter. In light of his popularity with the reading

---

[26] Higman, *Piety*, p. 2.
[27] Ibid., p. 5.
[28] Ibid., p. 6.

public of the sixteenth century, this fairer appraisal of his stylistic qualities is long overdue.

A few years prior to the publication of *Piety and the People*, Higman produced an article on the *Dyalogue instructoire des chrestiens en la foy, esperance, et amour en Dieu*, a catechism composed by Doré in 1538. This article, which appeared in *Aux origines du catéchisme en France* (1989), is significant on the grounds that it is the first exposé of any of Doré's writings. As Higman points out in the article, the *Dyalogue* was written as a response to or refutation of a catechism written two years earlier by the Bernese pastor Gaspard Megander. Higman's analysis of Doré's refutation brings out some interesting aspects of the Dominican's approach to his task. Perhaps most interesting is the fact that Doré attempts in this work to base his doctrinal exposition solely upon scriptural references. Higman comments:

> *L'érudition biblique de Doré est considérable, et comprend l'Ancien Testament aussi bien que le Nouveau. Il semble bien que, dans le contexte d'une réponse à un écrit réformateur, il a choisi de se baser exclusivement sur le seul texte qu'acceptera l'adversaire lui-même, la Bible.*[29]

But while Doré makes no explicit references in his catechism to other sources, such as the Fathers of the Church, Higman notes that "*...son exposé se base (naturellement) sur une formation très poussée en théologie.*[30] One detects here a certain appreciation for Doré's biblical and theological formation. In the end, Higman is led to the conclusion that the *Dyalogue* is not so much a catechism limited to the basics of the faith as it is a manual of theology which seeks to provide a broad-based instruction in Catholic doctrine. According to his research, it is the first such serious instruction to appear in French. While more extensive examination of the *Dyalogue* itself will be given in several subsequent chapters of this present study, the important point to be made here is once again that Pierre

---
[29] Francis Higman, "La réfutation par Pierre Doré du catéchisme de Megander" in *Aux origines du catéchisme en France*, ed. Pierre Colin (Paris: Desclée, 1989), p. 62.
[30] Ibid.

Doré can no longer be ignored or pushed aside as an irrelevant eccentric who is of little significance in the history of the Reformation period in France.

There is, of course, an element of truth in everything that has been said about Doré in the historiography since his death. Some historians have been overly critical of the friar, others all too laudatory, while still others have managed to keep a more balanced perspective. My hope is to build on the work and insights of those who have given us this present picture of the French Dominican, with a particular focus on *why* he consecrated his life to writing works of piety and theological instruction for the laity, *what* was the substance of his teaching and *how* did he attempt to communicate his message. I do not pretend here to be producing the definitive work on Pierre Doré, but what I hope will be a general introduction to the work and significance of this man who was a key figure in the Catholic and Dominican response to Reformation theology in a France which was bitterly divided by questions of faith in the sixteenth century.

Doré's Place in the Institutional Response to the Reformation in France

While Pierre Doré's refutation of the principal tenets of Reformation theology is at the heart of this present study, his efforts to stem the tide of Protestantism in France must first be placed in context with a brief discussion of the broader institutional reaction to the outbreak of heresy in the first half of the sixteenth century. What I call the "institutional" response to the new teaching is made up of three principal components: the monarchy, the episcopate, and the celebrated Faculty of Theology at the University of Paris. Of the three, it is the Faculty of Theology which early on and most consistently opposed the new ideas. The episcopate on the other hand seems to have been by and large rather indifferent, a collection of distracted shepherds more concerned with worldly affairs than with preserving the flock in doctrinal purity. There were of course a few notable exceptions to this rule. A handful of French bishops actively opposed the Reformation while others became avid promoters of the new movement. Most, however, seem to have gone on with the day-to-day business of being a Renaissance prelate as if nothing were really wrong. Finally, the monarchy, and here we are basically considering Francis I who reigned from 1515 to 1547, was initially rather sympathetic to the humanist movement with its calls for reform in the Church but became more repressive as this reform became more and more equated with the rejection of traditional doctrine. It is clear, then, that there was by no means a unified institutional response to the advent of the Reformation in France, at least in the early stages.

The reasons for this ambiguity in the institutional response during the initial decades of the Reformation's progress are manifold. However, one of the principal factors is that the relationship between various reform movements and the Reformation *per se* was itself quite ambiguous. The humanist reformers belonging to the circle of Meaux are a prime example of the blurred distinctions between reform and Reformation in the France of the 1520s. The main inspiration behind the formation of this group was Guillaume Briçonnet, bishop of Lodève, and from December 1515 onwards, bishop of Meaux.[31] While bishop of Lodève, he was also named abbot of the prestigious abbey of Saint-Germain-des-Prés outside of Paris where, from 1507 until 1515, he labored to reintroduce a spirit of observance and evangelical living among the monks. Upon his arrival in Meaux in 1516, he quickly took steps to imbue his diocese with the same spirit of renewal and reform based on the Gospel through a program of pastoral visitations and the promotion of evangelical preaching. His project soon attracted others, humanists and like-minded intellectuals intent upon reforming the Church in France from within based on what would come to be called the notion of *évangélisme*. Thus was born in 1521 the school of Meaux, among whose ranks was found the celebrated French humanist Jacques Lefèvre d'Étaples as well as Guillaume Farel who would later play an active role in the reform of Geneva and

---

[31] For a detailed presentation on Briçonnet's life and work, see Michel Veissière, *L'évêque Guillaume Briçonnet, 1470-1534* (Provins: Société d'histoire et d'archéologie, 1986).

Neuchâtel. All in the group were intent on reform, but between Briçonnet's unflagging loyalty to the Roman Church and its magisterium of which he was a part and Farel's eventual whole-hearted embrace of the Protestant cause lay a very wide spectrum of ambiguous positions which at times rendered judgments concerning the heterodoxy or orthodoxy of the circle of Meaux a matter of intense disagreement, particularly between the king and the Faculty of Theology.[32]

A word must be said here on the close link between Christian humanism and the Reformation. While it is true that not all humanists became Protestants, the humanist emphasis on Scripture and a return to the sources of the Christian faith along with calls for the reform of abuses in the Church did lay the groundwork for Luther and the other radical reformers. Nonetheless, Luther can rightly be considered the "father" of the Reformation because his personal rejection of the authority of the Roman church unleashed a veritable tidal wave of defection in the name of reform well beyond the German borders. At the same time, his influence on the development of the Reformation in France is a subject of debate among scholars of the period precisely because of the practically concurrent reforming activities of French humanists such as Lefèvre d'Étaples.[33] In fact, in his monumental study of the origins of the Reformation, Imbart de la Tour unhesitatingly affirms that it is Lefèvre who is more properly speaking the "father" of the Reformation in France, not Luther:

> *Luther est Allemand; Érasme, universel. Ni l'un ni l'autre ne pouvaient se flatter d'entraîner la France dans les voies de l'évangélisme: le premier trop 'national' pour agir d'une façon durable sur un autre peuple que le sien; le second trop lettré pour conquérir d'autres adeptes que l'élite. Dans cette diffusion de 'l'Évangile,' il fallait donc que la*

---

[32] For further discussion of the Faculty's pursuit and condemnations of the Meaux intellectuals, of whom some nevertheless enjoyed royal protection, see Farge, *Orthodoxy*, pp. 170-185.

[33] In *La diffusion de la réforme en France: 1520-1565* (Geneva: Labor et Fides, 1992), p. 19, Francis Higman mentions two schools of thought on this issue. The "German" school gives Luther all the credit for the early diffusion of the Reformation in France, whereas the "French" school insists on the prior existence of the humanist movement within France, onto which Luther's ideas were eventually grafted, leading to the protestantization of humanism. On this same issue, see also Lucien Febvre, "Les origines de la réforme française et le problème des causes de la réforme" in *Au coeur religieux du XVIe siècle* (Paris: SEVPEN, 1957), pp. 3-70.

France eût son ouvrier propre. Cette réforme française, un homme d'abord l'a rêvée, l'a tentée, qui, depuis 1509, s'était mis à la tête de notre humanisme chrétien: Lefèvre d'Étaples.[34]

A more contemporary and circumspect assessment of Lefèvre's role in the movement towards full-blown reform in sixteenth-century France is given by Dominican historian Guy Bedouelle who points out that the celebrated humanist never broke with the Church of his time. Bedouelle emphasizes that though there are many points of convergence to be found between Lefèvre's theological positions and those of the Reformers, the humanist maintained a certain discretion and "voluntary silence" in regard to the developing divisions, never explicitly taking sides.[35]

My purpose here is not to enter the fray over the precise role played by Lefèvre d'Étaples in the evolution of reform movements in France. Rather, the point is to contextualize the Faculty of Theology's eventual pursuit of the humanist and his associates at Meaux. There is in fact an important link between the advent of Lutheran literature in France and this negative reaction to Lefèvre. Despite Imbart de la Tour's attempt to give Lefèvre the pre-eminent place in the French Reformation, he goes on to observe that Luther's writings were quickly disseminated in France beginning in 1519, citing a claim from Froben, Luther's publisher in Basel, that he had sent 600 copies of his works to Paris.[36] Such dissemination of the German Reformer's thought was certainly not without significant effect, particularly among the intelligentsia. Clearly then, we can speak of a convergence between the advent of Lutheran ideas in France and the activities of French humanists who were promoting similar views on the

---

[34] Pierre Imbart de la Tour, *Les origines de la réforme*, vol. 3 (Paris: Librairie Hachette, 1914), p. 110.

[35] Guy Bedouelle, *Lefèvre d'Étaples et l'intelligence des Écritures* (Geneva: Droz, 1976), p. 235 writes *"Il demeure que Lefèvre ne s'est pas engagé pour tel ou tel 'parti': il lui a semblé possible—et ce l'était alors—de ne pas se prononcer publiquement. Lefèvre n'a jamais, comme d'autres, rompu avec l'Eglise de son temps. Sans minimiser l'importance de la situation politique et religieuse de la France d'avant l'Affaire des Placards pour expliquer une telle attitude, il nous importe surtout de constater que Lefèvre n'a pas **voulu** [emphasis his] choisir."*

[36] Imbart de la Tour, *Les origines*, p. 170. See also Higman, *Diffusion*, p. 19.

interpretation of the Scriptures and other "reform" issues. Given this convergence, it is hardly surprising that in the eyes of the Faculty of Theology, the official watchdog of orthodoxy in the French church, there was little difference between Luther and Lefèvre, between the radical ideas emanating from Wittenberg and those emanating from Meaux. In fact, it is precisely beginning in 1521 when it condemned the German Reformer that it also began to take a closer look at the works being published by the humanists who until then had gone relatively unchallenged.[37] The introduction of Luther's works into France, then, while not exactly a point of departure for the reform of the French church, can be seen as a catalyst which provoked an initial response of opposition to reform movements on the part of the ecclesiastical institution.

To begin to give here a detailed account of the Faculty's attempts to suppress Lutheranism, and by extension humanism, in France is beyond the scope of this introduction. My concern, rather, is to paint in broad strokes not only the Faculty's reaction to the Reformation but also that of the king and the French bishops in order that Pierre Doré's contributions may be better understood and contextualized. By far the weakest opposition to the new ideas being disseminated from the pulpit and through the printing press was that shown by the hierarchy, at least taken as a whole.[38] There were some exceptions, of course, notably the Dominican bishop of Troyes, Guillaume Petit, whose efforts to stem the spread of heresy early on will be discussed in greater detail in the following chapter. Guillaume Briçonnet for his part, although hounded by the Faculty of Theology because of his humanist connections and evangelical reforms at Meaux, nevertheless took strong measures against preachers who had imbibed the "venom" of Luther, solemnly decreeing, "*vous defendons expressément, sous*

---

[37] Farge, *Orthodoxy*, p. 170 states that, "Prior to the condemnation of Luther the Faculty assemblies had largely ignored the academic squabbles between scholasticism and humanism." Opposition to Lefèvre and others was limited to certain individuals on the Faculty, notably the doctors Marc de Grandval and Noël Beda.

[38] For a contemporary study of the state of the French episcopate in the sixteenth century, see Frederic Baumgartner, *Change and Continuity in the French Episcopate: The Bishops and the Wars of Religion, 1547-1610* (Durham: Duke University Press, 1986).

peine d'Excommunication et Anathème, que vous permettiez de prescher en vos Chaires ces detestables Lutheriens, et tous autres...faisans profession de leur doctrine."[39] However, Briçonnet and Petit were most definitely in the minority. Few other bishops reacted so strongly to the outbreak of heresy. By and large, the episcopate in France suffered from the same abuses that were prevalent throughout the hierarchy in the pre-Tridentine Church—absenteeism, pluralism, a disregard for the office of preaching, a Renaissance preoccupation with patronizing the arts, the desire to accumulate personal wealth, and sexual incontinence. A good number of the French bishops in the sixteenth century were tainted by at least some if not all of these vices. There is little surprise, then, in Frederic Baumgartner's assessment that "...few bishops were involved before 1560 in the efforts to counter the Reformation."[40] Yet, a word of caution is in order here, for personal weakness and moral decadence were not always associated with a lack of interest in extirpating heresy, as the case of Cardinal Charles de Lorraine clearly demonstrates. A member of the ultra-orthodox Guise family who was named bishop at the tender age of nine, the cardinal was among the staunchest defenders of the faith in the French hierarchy, even while holding several dioceses, fathering a number of illegitimate children, spending 400,000 écus in 1550 for a library of Greek manuscripts and protecting humanists such as Rabelais whose writings could be sharply critical of the Church![41] Other prominent prelates who actively opposed the Reformation include Cardinal François de Tournon of Bourges, to whom Doré dedicated his polemical *Paradoxa...ad profligandas haereses* (1543) and Cardinal Antoine Du Prat of Sens. But these were among the exceptions in an episcopal body that was amazingly indifferent to the dangers of the new teaching in the realm.

The question arises of how men with such little concern for the spiritual exercise of their office could have ever received the appointment in the first place.

---

[39] Decree against Lutheran Preachers, 13 December 1523. See Veissière, *Briçonnet*, p. 258.
[40] Baumgartner, *Change*, p. 122.
[41] Ibid., see p. 119 ff.

Part of the answer lies in the Concordat of Bologna signed between Pope Leo X and Francis I in 1516 which gave over to the French king the right to fill all but a few of the episcopal vacancies in his kingdom. Although the Concordat outlined rather stringent criteria for potential candidates, including a minimum age of twenty-seven, the possession of at least a licentiate in theology as well as having demonstrated good moral character, a loophole in the agreement permitted the king to appoint members of the nobility who did not necessarily meet the stated qualifications.[42] In effect, the bishops were civil servants more than they were shepherds, very often friends of the king who could be counted on to support his domestic policies and to uphold the rights of the French church vis-à-vis the Apostolic See. Given the circumstances, it is easy to understand why the reaction of the French episcopate as a whole to the spiritual threat posed by Reformed theology was rather insipid. But if the shepherds failed miserably in their duties towards the flock, the Faculty of Theology more than made up for their lack of vigilance with a series of measures clearly aimed at preserving the church in France from the errors of Luther and subsequent Reformers.

James Farge notes that the Faculty of Theology, which was considered to be the *concile permanent des Gaules*, was at the forefront of the "counter-Reformation" movement in France, a good twenty-five years before the opening of the Council of Trent in 1545.[43] Beginning with its condemnation in April 1521 of 104 propositions drawn from Luther's writings,[44] the Faculty took a consistent approach of responding to heresy both by censure and eventually by a positive declaration of orthodox doctrine. This is not to imply, however, that all the members of the Faculty were of one mind and heart concerning the impertinence

---

[42] It should be mentioned that the pope maintained the right to reject a nomination, in which case the king would have to submit another name within three months. If the second name were also rejected, then the pope would gain the right to fill the vacancy. Baumgartner points out, however, that while there are numerous examples of first-round rejections, no second candidate ever seems to have been rejected. Ibid., p. 12.

[43] See James Farge, *Le parti conservateur au XVIe siècle: Université et Parlement de Paris à l'époque de la Renaissance et de la Réforme* (Collège de France, 1992), p. 31.

[44] The condemned propositions are presented in Charles-Joseph Hefele, *Histoire des conciles d'après les documents originaux*, vol. 8, pt. 2 (Paris: Letouzey et Ané, 1921), pp. 758-773.

and heterodox nature of the new ideas. In fact, several Paris doctors were among the early promoters of "Lutheranism" in France. Thus the Faculty had to be concerned with purging its own ranks of those who had become infected with the new theology. The result was that a good portion of its anti-Reformation activities was directed against its own members. Among the doctors condemned or censured early on in 1523 were Martial Mazurier and Pierre Caroli, both members of the school of Meaux, for their criticism of prayers to the saints and prayers for the dead. The Dominican doctor Aimé Maigret was condemned the following year. More will be said concerning his case in the next chapter. These condemnations were not purely an academic affair, an internal disciplinary matter of consequence only to the Faculty. On the contrary, the censures were intended to have ramifications well beyond the halls of academia, for they fell upon men who were spreading their unorthodox views through preaching, teaching and writing. Thus the Faculty's pursuit of its own members for heresy was not merely in view of maintaining its reputation for orthodoxy in a pristine state but was also directed to silencing those doctors who were sowing seeds of dissent among the faithful particularly by means of the pulpit.

Although this inquisitorial activity of the Faculty of Theology was principally directed to its own members, it also encompassed those outside its ranks, as has been already mentioned. Nonetheless, whether it was pursuing fellow doctors or various other humanists and Lutherans, the Faculty could not be content merely to silence the "voice" of heresy. It also had to find an effective way of dealing with the silent dissemination of heterodox teaching through the printed text, a much more difficult medium to control. The Faculty thus turned to the censorship of books as yet another method by which to stem the tide of the Reformation in France.[45] Farge points out that although the Faculty had long

---

[45] The censorship activities of the Faculty of Theology are discussed in the following: Francis Higman, *Censorship and the Sorbonne: A Bibliographical Study of Books in French Censured by the Faculty of Theology of the University of Paris, 1520-1551* (Geneva: Droz, 1979), Higman, *La diffusion de la Réforme en France, 1520-1565* (Geneva: Labor et Fides, 1992), pp. 149-158, J.M.

claimed the prerogative of reviewing and approving texts produced in the realm by manuscript copyists and later by printers, it in fact made very little use of this privilege prior to the influx of Luther's texts in Paris in 1519.[46] This was the alarm which brought the privilege out of dormancy.

However, a very important fact to be noted here is that the Faculty had no juridical authority whatsoever to enforce its decisions concerning heretical texts. For this it depended upon the cooperation of the Parlement of Paris which alone had the authority to enact the censures along with punitive measures against unsubmissive publishers. Soon after the Faculty's condemnation of Luther, the Parlement followed suit by prohibiting in June of 1521 the publication or sale of any work touching on Scripture or the Christian faith without having obtained the prior seal of approval from the Faculty.[47] Yet despite this affirmation by the Parlement of the theologians' power and duty to censure, the Faculty in fact made surprisingly little use of the privilege prior to 1540. Francis Higman distinguishes between the sporadic censorship of this initial period, where only eleven printed books and twelve manuscripts were condemned, and the more systematic approach to censorship adopted after 1540 leading up to the Faculty's first edition of the *Catalogue des livres censurez* in 1544.[48] In stark contrast to the mere twenty-three texts censured in the twenty-year period between 1520 and 1540, the *Catalogue* of 1544 lists a total of 233 titles, among which are included some of the books censured earlier. Publications emanating from both Geneva and Neuchâtel figure prominently among the condemned works, indicating that a good portion of the heretical texts were being imported from outside of France. Censorship alone, however, was not enough to ensure that tainted books would not reach the French reading public. A condemnation from the Faculty had to be accompanied by searches for smuggled books in bookshops with the subsequent

---

De Bujanda, ed., *Index des livres interdits*, vol. 1 (Geneva: Droz, 1985), pp. 51-76, and Farge, *Orthodoxy*, pp. 213-219.
[46] Farge, *Orthodoxy*, p. 213.
[47] Ibid., p. 168.
[48] See Higman, *Censorship*, pp. 49-61.

prosecution of both booksellers and traders caught with the contraband. An ordinance of Parlement in 1542 decreed that booksellers could not display books for sale until the bales had been opened and inspected by four officials who would in turn submit any suspect material to two specially appointed doctors of the Faculty of Theology for definitive judgment.[49] This attempt to regulate the importation of books into the realm and their sale was once again reinforced by a joint action of king, who at this time was Henry II, and Parlement in the Edict of Chateaubriant (1551), which stipulated that bales of imported books must be unpacked under the surveillance of two delegates from the Faculty of Theology.[50] All of these measures, particularly from 1540 onwards, certainly hampered the dissemination of heretical literature in France. However, despite all the censures, book burnings, house searches and inspection of imports, there is little doubt that heterodox texts continued to slip through the cracks of suppression, inspiring an ever-growing number of *réformés* in an increasingly divided France.

As important as censorship was in the Faculty's program for stemming the tide of heresy, perhaps the most significant of all its anti-Reformation measures was the publication of the Articles of Faith in 1543. Farge explains their significance:

> ...the articles highlight those doctrines and practices of the Church which the Faculty, after closely monitoring the rise of heterodoxy in France for twenty-five years, regarded as integral to the essential deposit of faith. Moreover, this articulated statement of belief manifests the evolution in the Faculty from general statements about orthodoxy at the beginning of the century, through ad hoc refutation of objectionable doctrines, and finally culminating in specific exposition of essential tenets.[51]

Like the later decrees of the Council of Trent, the Articles of Faith clearly demarcated the boundaries between heterodox and orthodox belief by dissipating all ambiguity and formally defining the fundamental truths which the Reformers

---

[49] See James Farge, *Registre des conclusions de la faculté de théologie de l'université de Paris*, vol. 2 (Paris: Klincksieck, 1994), Appendix 2, pp. 449-450.
[50] Article XV of the Edict. See Higman, *Censorship*, p. 65.
[51] Farge, *Orthodoxy*, p. 208.

had called into question.[52] In the absence of effective leadership on the part of the bishops whose primary duty as shepherds was to teach the faith and defend it, the Faculty's twenty-nine articles filled an important gap in the institutional response. Meant principally to serve as guidelines for preachers, they were also published for the benefit of the general public by royal decree throughout France. A kingdom-wide standard of orthodoxy was thus established. But perhaps most importantly of all, the Articles were a positive statement of the faith in response to heresy, a formal articulation of the truth to be believed rather than merely a condemnation of the error to be avoided.

The consistent opposition of the Faculty of Theology to the new ideas of humanists and Reformers alike and the measures it took to prevent their spread were nevertheless often thwarted, particularly in the beginning, by the monarchy. His most Christian majesty, Francis I, was a man completely taken with the spirit of the Renaissance and deeply committed to the humanist movement. This penchant of his, coupled with the influence of his sister Marguerite de Navarre, who herself was very sympathetic to the humanist cause, often put the king at odds with the much less tolerant attitude of the Faculty towards all aspects of the reform. For example, to the consternation of the venerable theologians, he had the humanist Louis de Berquin twice released from prison, despite the fact that both Faculty and Parlement had condemned him for his translations of Luther's works.[53] Others who enjoyed royal favor over and against the Faculty were Lefèvre d'Étaples, Michel d'Arande and Gérard Roussel, all members of the Meaux circle. In the case of Roussel who was condemned by the Faculty in 1533 for preaching the errors of Luther, not only did he receive the protection of the court but his patroness Marguerite even prevailed in having her brother the king banish from Paris Roussel's leading opponent on the Faculty, the syndic Noël Beda. This is not the place to give a full-fledged review of the various instances

---

[52] For the complete text of the Articles see Farge, *Le parti conservateur*, Document IX, pp. 141-149.
[53] Taking advantage of the king's absence from Paris, the Parlement eventually got its way with Berquin and had him executed in 1529.

where Francis I opposed the Faculty's pursuit of certain doctors or humanists for heresy. Suffice to say that had royal authority supported the Faculty of Theology's inquisitorial activities from the beginning, the reform movement might have been nipped in the bud and unity of faith could possibly have been preserved in France.

Was Francis I, then, a crypto-protestant? Hardly. Francis was a shrewd politician, not a religious reformer. If he openly supported the Lutheran princes of Germany, it was not because of a secret attraction for Luther's doctrine, but rather to de-stabilize his Hapsburg archrival, Charles V. In his own realm, his fairly tolerant attitude towards reform had everything to do with humanist scholarship and nothing to do with the revolution in doctrine being proposed by Luther and others. The normally tolerant monarch, for example, reacted strongly to the famous *affaire des placards* in 1534 when the real presence of Christ in the Eucharist was severely derided in a series of broadsheets that were posted in cities throughout France, with one even appearing on the king's bedroom door! Arrests and executions followed, indicating the extent of the king's displeasure over the incident. The reform party had clearly gone beyond the limit of what he was willing to tolerate. And it was in fact at Francis' insistence that nine years later the Faculty drew up the Articles of Faith, in order, as the king wrote, "to provide a much needed remedy for the many scandals and schisms which have heretofore come about...and that such novelties and pernicious enterprises bring no inconveniences and irreparable damages to our religion."[54] Although the king on several occasions thwarted the Faculty's attempts to suppress those whom it had determined to be heretical, he was never a supporter of Reformation theology *per se*. His tolerance of reform evaporated when essential doctrines of the faith, particularly those concerning the Eucharist, were called into question.

It must be acknowledged that the preservation of the traditional faith in France was in the king's interest for several reasons, not the least of which was

---

[54] Letter of Francis I adopting the Articles of Faith. See Farge, *Orthodoxy*, p. 209.

the income and political power deriving from his authority to nominate candidates to the episcopacy according to the terms of the Concordat of Bologna. He had nothing to gain from the type of radical reorganization of ecclesiastical structures being promoted by the Reformers who wanted to do away with bishops. Yet, at the same time, to reduce Francis I's increasingly repressive actions towards the Reformation over the years to nothing more than blatant self-interest would be unfair to him and inaccurate. While he certainly favored certain types of reforms being promoted by the humanists, and while he was thoroughly Gallican in asserting his rights over the church in France, he nevertheless did hold two things sacrosanct: the belief in the real presence of Christ in the Eucharist, and the belief in the unity of the Church, at least within his kingdom. These were fundamental dogmas which, as defender of the faith, he was unwilling to compromise. Francis' response to the Reformation, then, is best understood as a complex combination of political concerns, self-interest and religious conviction. Politics and self-interest dictated that he support Lutherans abroad as a way of weakening Hapsburg power. Self-interest and religious conviction, however, dictated that he be much less tolerant of heresy in his own kingdom. As a humanist, he gave frequent support to the cause of reform in the early years, much to the chagrin of the Faculty of Theology. However, as the lines between reform and Reformation became more distinct, royal policy became more consistently opposed to the new theology with the result that king and Faculty joined forces in 1543 in clearly defining the difference between orthodoxy and heterodoxy with the Articles of Faith.

This brings us now to Pierre Doré and where he stands in relation to the institutions of monarchy, episcopate and Faculty of Theology, each of whose responses to the Reformation in France varied greatly. First of all, it should be observed that he was in some way associated with all three of these important institutions—as a doctor of the revered Faculty, as a priestly member of the hierarchy and as confessor to the ducal family of Guise with its important political connections. These associations meant that he was well-placed to exert a good deal of influence if he so chose, and that is precisely what he did. As theologian, religious priest and confessor to the nobility, Doré was a significant player in the institutional response to the Reformation. At the same time, perceiving the inadequacy of that response, he did not hesitate to put into motion his own strategic plan to keep France in the Catholic faith.

It is interesting to note the decidedly different stance which Doré adopted in relation to each of the institutions of which he was part. In regard to the Faculty, which he often refers to as "mother" in his writings, he portrays himself as the loyal son who ardently defends "her" methods to check the spread of heresy. So convinced is he of the value of censorship in particular that he willingly submits his own work to the scrutiny of his colleagues on the Faculty. In a letter entitled *"Submission de l'aucteur à la disposition de l'eglise"* found at the end of the 1539 edition of his fourth book, *Le college de sapience*, he writes, *"En tous les dessusdictz opuscules, ou il y auroit faulte, car qui est l'homme sur la terre qui ne faille, me submetz à toute censure, correction, & obeyssance de l'eglise."*[55] This letter is followed by a notice that the book has been certified to be free of doctrinal error by his colleagues, the doctors Thierry, Divollé, Corrigie and de Bolo. The communion of spirit with the Faculty of Theology which such submission indicates is confirmed throughout Doré's writings, for whenever he mentions the Faculty it is to praise the faithful mother, guardian of truth, who is setting the example for all those who would enter into battle against the heretic reformers.

As regards the hierarchy, however, Doré adopts a rather critical stance quite unlike the reverential affection he manifests for the Faculty. Although in his writings he defends the hierarchical nature of the Church as divinely instituted, he does not hesitate to castigate unworthy clergy who are failing to live up to the

---

[55] *Le college de sapience, fondé en l'université de vertu* (Paris: Antoine Bonnemere, 1539), fol. Niii v°. **[Paris, BA—8° T 6955]**.

demands of their calling. Lamenting that the prelates and clerics of the Church of his time are far from the example of Christ in their personal lives, he writes:

> Jesus a esté pauvre & ilz sont riches, il a esté humble & ilz sont orgueilleux, il a fuy gloire & ilz la cerchent, il a demandé l'honneur de son pere & ilz demandent leur propre, il a esté fidele à son pere & ilz sont infideles, il a labouré & travaillé & ilz vivent en oysiveté & à leur ayse, vacans a volupté.[56]

He also readily admits that in the body of Christ, "...*depuis la plante des piedz, jusques au sommet de la teste, il n'y a point de santé, l'eglise a bon besoing de reformation.*"[57] It is clear that Doré sees the hierarchy of which he is part as being in large measure responsible for the Protestant problem. Not only has their style of life occasioned the legitimate criticisms of the Reformers, but their worldliness has also prevented them from taking the necessary action to answer the doctrinal challenge posed by the same Reformers who have rejected the traditional church as hopelessly corrupt. Thus Doré does not fail to call the shepherds to task for failing in their duty towards the flock.

At the same time, it must be admitted that Doré's criticisms of the shepherds evaporate into thin air when it comes to Cardinal Charles de Lorraine, whom he extols with the following, "*y a il Prelat aujourdhuy, en toute la France (sans deroger a personne) qui pour l'aage soit plus adressé en bonnes meurs, & lettres tant humaines, que divines, ne plus grand zelateur de la foy, tenant en cela de ses ancestres, vrays tuteurs, & propugnateurs d'icelle foy, que Charles monseigneur l'Archevesque de Reims?*"[58] The cardinal, as mentioned earlier, was hardly a model prelate and was in fact guilty of many of the faults which Doré excoriates in other bishops. Perhaps the Dominican turned a blind eye in this case because of his very close association with Charles' parents, the duke and duchess

---

[56] *Le cerf spirituel, exprimant le sainct desire de l'ame, d'estre avec son Dieu* (Paris: Jean Ruelle, n.d.), fol. 83v°. **[Paris, BA—8° T 6959]**.

[57] *La premiere partie des collations royales* (Paris: René Avril, 1546), pp. 251-252. **[Paris, BNF—Inv. A 6838]**.

[58] Dedication to Antoinette de Bourbon, *La seconde partie des collations royales* (Paris: René Avril, 1546), p. 7. **[Paris, BNF—Inv. A 6838]**.

of Guise. Or perhaps the cardinal's personal life could be excused because when it came to the defense of orthodoxy in doctrine, he stood out as a shining light in the French church. In any case, aside from this present example, Doré seems to have been a willing critic of the French episcopate in general, calling the bishops to task for their scandalous behavior and chastizing them for their lethargy in preaching against the doctrinal errors of the Reformers. Since it was evident that the hierarchy with a few exceptions would be of little help in the battle against heresy, Doré concentrated his efforts instead on arousing the monarchy to second the anti-Protestant measures being advanced by the Faculty of Theology.

Precisely what kind of relations Doré maintained with the monarchs Francis I and his son Henry II is difficult to determine from the available sources. However, it is not improbable that his close association with the powerful Guise allowed him at least some kind of access to the royal ear. Even if that were not the case, Doré certainly attempted to curry favor with the court by dedicating some of his works to members of the royal family. Whether in the dedications or within the works themselves, the Dominican often inserts laudatory comments commending the monarchy for its vigilance in maintaining orthodoxy in the kingdom. For example, the following praise is offered to Francis I for his firm response to the monstrous *affaire des placards* in which the Holy Eucharist was defamed:

> ...nous avons le bon roy Francois, qui vous en fera bonne justice: comme avez veu par experience, es sacramentaires bruslés, comme ils avoient bien desservy en ceste ville de Paris & aylleurs, pour leurs blasphematoires plaquars: O que dieu a faict beaucoup pour la chrestienté, quand en ce calamiteux temps, nous a donné ung tel prince, de nom & de faict treschrestien.[59]

Although Francis I's repression of the new ideas was not always so firm as in this instance, Doré never criticizes the king for at times being too soft on the crypto-reformers who find protection at the royal court. He is ever the king's humble

---

[59] *Le college*, fol. lxi v°.

servant and prefers instead to encourage the king on the right path by praising his majesty when he takes the appropriate measures to quash the religious rebels.

Ultimately, however, Doré's objective is to see that the monarchy follow the lead of the Faculty of Theology in the matter of defending the faith, that it lend the force of its authority in support of the Faculty's program of censorship and inquisition. Thus, he offers this advice to Henry II, to whom is dedicated *L'arche de l'alliance nouvelle* (1549):

> *C'est certainement le moyen pour corroborer ton throne & sceptre amplifier, que de zeler l'honneur de Dieu, & la foy maintenir, mettre le coeur en la loy divine, & la faire en ton royaume estroictement observer & garder, en extirpant ou corrigeant blasphemateurs du nom de Dieu, & heretiques sacramentaires: A quoy s'employe de toutes ses forces ta fille tresobeissante, la sacrée faculté de Theologie de Paris, ma mere.*[60]

There is somewhat more of a lecturing tone here than Doré was ever wont to use in regard to Henry's father. Nevertheless, the overall tenor of the advice remains appropriately respectful of the royal authority, to which the Faculty of Theology remains a most obedient daughter. Yet, Doré makes it clear that in order for the daughter's efforts to curb the spread of the Protestant heresy to be successful, she must be seconded by her father the king who alone has the authority to mete out the punishment which the heretics deserve for their crimes against God and the state. The Dominican is anxious to do what he can in order to forge closer ties between the monarchy and the Faculty, and thus create a more unified institutional response to the Reformation.

As already mentioned, repression, even if the result of a coordinated effort between two powerful institutions, can only produce very limited results. The burning of heretics and their books is not enough to stifle the spread of ideas which inspire men's hearts. What is needed is an argument, a response to these ideas which will show them to be empty and false, unworthy of the mind's

---

[60] Dedication to Henry II, *L'arche de l'alliance nouvelle, et testament de nostre Saulveur Jesus Christ, contenant la manne de son precieux corps, contre tous sacramentaires heretiques* (Paris: Benoît Prevost, 1549), fol. Avii r°. **[Paris, BNF—Inv. D 21877]**.

consideration. As Francis Higman so aptly remarks, "*La censure peut rendre dangereuse la circulation des livres interdits; elle ne peut pas les supprimer. La seule réponse valable à un mauvais livre est un bon livre.*"[61] The Faculty of Theology took a step in this direction by drawing up its Articles of Faith in 1543. These Articles marked the first time the Faculty went beyond a mere condemnation of errors and actually defined the fundamental doctrines which were being challenged. But it must be admitted that a published list of dogmas is hardly an attractive medium for conveying the truth. It is here that Pierre Doré creates a special niche for himself within the larger institutional response to the Reformation. His writings fill a definite gap in that institutional response which was preoccupied with silencing and refuting error more than with a positive proclamation of the truth.[62] In the catechetical works he provides his readers with the fundamental instruction they need to understand the heart of the faith. In the polemical works, he takes up some of the key issues of the Reformation debate and argues the Catholic understanding to his readers. Finally, in the devotional works, which are the majority, he seeks to draw the reader to a more loving union with Christ in faith, hope and love. His purpose is indeed to fight a bad book with a good book, one filled with the solid doctrine of the Church explained in a way that the ordinary believer can understand. Herein lies Pierre Doré's specific contribution to the Catholic response to the Reformation in France.

---

[61] Higman, "Le domaine français (1520-1562)" in *La réforme et le livre—l'Europe de l'imprimé (1517-v. 1570)* (Paris: Éditions du Cerf, 1990), p. 153.

[62] Mention should be made here of a recent monograph on François Le Picart (1504-1556) who was a contemporary of Doré and his colleague on the Faculty of Theology. Larissa Taylor, *Heresy and Orthodoxy in Sixteenth-Century Paris: François Le Picart and the Beginnings of the Catholic Reformation* (Leiden: E.J. Brill, 1999) presents him as one of the forerunners of the Catholic response in France to the ideas of the Reformation through his popular preaching from the mid-1530s to his death. Although collections of his sermons were published posthumously beginning in the late 1550s, he himself never produced any written works in response to the Reformers. Doré remains unique in terms of an early and prolific communication of orthodox teaching through the printed text. Nevertheless it is clear that Le Picart and Doré shared a common strategy for trying to preserve the faith of the laity in France and touched upon very similar themes in their respective modes of communication.

Chapter 1
DORÉ AND THE FRENCH DOMINICANS
IN THE EARLY SIXTEENTH CENTURY

The rather long life of Pierre Doré, spanning over seventy years, coincides with the reigns of no less than five French kings, from Louis XII (d. 1515) to Charles IX (d. 1574), with perhaps the height of his career occurring during the reign of Henry II (1547-1559). While his writings are the principal focus of this study, they are by no means the sum of his life's work. Documentary evidence, though neither abundant nor complete, points to a quite varied and active career of preaching, teaching, occupying positions of authority both within the Order and without, and offering spiritual counsel to prominent members of the French aristocracy. Indeed, given this intense activity, it is quite extraordinary that somewhere in the midst of it all, the Dominican theologian found time to produce thirty-five works, many of which are of substantial length.

It has been noted in the previous chapter that several of the existing biographical notices on Doré already provide us with a basic sketch of the theologian's life. The most complete information in this regard is found in the *Scriptores* of Quétif and Échard, in Duval's entry in the *Dictionnaire de spiritualité*, and finally in Farge's *Biographical Register of Paris Doctors*. Building on this foundation, I will attempt in the present chapter to more amply fill out the basic sketch found in these works by first of all relating the principal moments of Doré's life and career to the larger historical context. At the same time, two important issues that none of the sketches has yet fully examined, Doré's intellectual formation at S. Jacques in Paris and the significance of his later relationship with the house of Guise, are discussed here. Finally, in the second half of this chapter, I will focus on Doré's relationship to his fellow Dominicans, particularly in terms of how the friars in France responded to the Reformation. It is important to determine whether his work was part of a concerted effort among French Dominicans to contain heresy or whether it was a totally unique enterprise, one in which Doré stands out as a model.

Doré's Religious and Intellectual Formation

Virtually nothing is known of Doré's early years, including his date of birth. He did have at least one sibling, Marguerite, an only sister to whom he dedicates *La croix de penitence* (1545). In the dedication, he makes reference to having visited her recently in the town of their birth, Orléans. That is the extent of any solid factual information concerning his origins and family. Quétif and Échard, and every one since, place his approximate date of birth as being around the beginning of the sixteenth century. However, it is possible to come to a closer approximation of his birth date by combining two other known facts. First of all, we know that Doré received his licentiate in theology from the University of Paris in February 1532.[63] Secondly, one of the requirements for receiving the license was that the candidate, in addition to being of legitimate birth and having already been ordained, also be at least thirty-five years of age.[64] Therefore, with the help of a little basic arithmetic, we can be fairly certain that Pierre Doré was born in the vicinity of 1497 or perhaps even a bit earlier.

If Doré's childhood years remain shrouded in mystery, so too do the details of his vocation to the Dominican life. Quétif and Échard date his entrance

---

[63] BR, p. 137.
[64] See Farge, *Orthodoxy*, p. 24.

to the Order around the year 1514, thus at the approximate age of seventeen and only three years before Martin Luther posted his 95 Theses against indulgences on the chapel door at Wittenberg, heralding, though unknowingly at the time, the start of the Reformation. Although this momentous event in its unfolding would have a profound effect on the future course of Doré's life and career, he was initially shaped as a young religious in the Order of Preachers by the unfolding of another kind of reform movement, this one occurring within the Order itself.

It is at the Dominican priory of Blois, a little distance farther down the Loire from Orléans and also the royal residence in the early sixteenth century, that Pierre Doré was received as a novice in 1514. His entrance at this particular priory is of profound significance because it happened to be a house of strict observance where the rule and constitutions of the Order were kept in their entirety. The Dominicans were not alone among the religious Orders of the period in having such reformed houses. In fact, this reform of religious life in the Church, sometimes referred to as the observant movement, had been going on throughout the fifteenth century in an attempt to restore the spirit of observance in monasteries and convents which had become corrupted by the spirit of the world or had departed too much from the ideals of the founders. Luther himself belonged to a reformed monastery of the Augustinian Hermits. While corruption and decadence were still rampant in the Church particularly among the hierarchy and the secular clergy when he and other reformers broke with Rome, there is no question that there was a great deal of reform occurring among the religious clergy who in turn were working to bring about authentic renewal within the rest of the Church.

The particular reform movement in the Dominican Order which shaped Pierre Doré in his initial formation actually dates back to the mastership of Raymond of Capua (1380-1400) who was the spiritual director but also a disciple of the tireless mystic-reformer, Catherine of Siena. His idea for instituting reform was quite simple, to separate those friars interested in observing the rule in its fullness from those who preferred the *status quo* by setting up a house of strict observance in each province. Ironically enough, this idea of reform through separation is not much different from the approach later taken by the Protestant Reformers who believed that reform of the Church from within was impossible and that the only thing left to do was to separate from the diseased body and begin anew. Yet, the Dominicans found a way of preserving at least a minimal sense of unity between the observants and the conventuals (or the un-reformed) with the establishment of the system of congregations existing side by side with the already established system of provinces. Like the province, the congregation was a territorial grouping of priories, specifically those of the strict observance, with the ability to govern itself under the Master of the Order. Both provinces and congregations sent representatives to the General Chapters which determined certain matters for the Order as a whole. Thus, unity was maintained even while a distinctly different way of living the Dominican life was being promoted in the congregations of observant houses. It should also be noted that the division between the congregations and the provinces had nothing to do with doctrine or theology, unlike the later division between the Reformers and the Church of Rome.

Though begun at the end of the fourteenth century, this Dominican reform movement made its way into France at a snail's pace so that it was not until the beginning of the sixteenth century that a significant number of priories there were actually won over to observance. By far one of the most important catalysts, if not the initial point of entry for the observant movement in the north of France, was the reform of none other than the celebrated *studium generale* of the Order at S. Jacques in Paris. It is not that the Jacobin friars had finally been overcome by the spirit of renewal which was making great progress throughout the rest of the Order. On the contrary, reform was imposed on S. Jacques in 1501 by edict of Master Vincent Bandelli who was unwilling to let the most important general *studium* of the Order continue along the path of laxity in the religious life. In a bold move, he removed the priory from the jurisdiction of the Province of France and placed it under the jurisdiction of the Congregation of Holland which had been formally erected in 1457.[65] Although resistance to reform among the Jacobin friars was initially fierce, the strong will of Jean Clérée, the man chosen by Bandelli to reform S. Jacques, coupled with the use of a little brute force eventually won the day.[66] With the Jacobins having submitted even if very reluctantly to the life of discipline as prescribed by the constitutions, it was not long before the spirit of reform spread, though in a more peaceful manner, to other French priories including that of Blois. Upon embracing the life of strict observance, a priory was then immediately removed from the jurisdiction of the Province of France and placed under the Congregation of Holland in order that the newly planted seed of reform might be properly nurtured and maintained.

Around the time of Doré's entrance into the Order in 1514, the priory of Blois, while remaining a house of strict observance, became part of a new jurisdictional entity, the Gallican Congregation. Political considerations were the driving force behind this development, the result of a concession to the French king, Louis XII, who loathed the idea of French subjects being under the

---

[65] For further details on the Congregation of Holland and the Dominican observant movement in general, see Albert De Meyer, *La Congrégation de Hollande ou La réforme dominicaine en territoire bourguignon 1465-1515* (Liège: Imprimerie Soledi, 1946).

[66] The following extract from the *Registres du Parlement* dated 10 March 1501 describes how Parlement had to authorize a detachment of soldiers to assist Clérée in taking possession of the convent which was being held by force by a rather large group of recalcitrant friars. *"Ce jour à l'apresdisnée la Cour a esté advertie que aujourd'huy matin tantost aprés la prononciation de l'Arrest d'entre Frere Jean Maigny sous-prieur, & autres Religieux de l'Ordre des Jacobins de Paris, & Frere Jean Clerée, & autres Religieux reformez dudit Ordre, & ou contempt d'iceluy Arrest, & irreverence de la Cour, lesdits Clerée & Religieux reformez auroient esté mis hors dudit Convent, & y estoient entrez grand nombre de gens en armes qui tenoient ledit Convent par force, & doutoit l'en que de ce survint grand inconvenient: pour ouquel obvier, & à ce que au Roy demeure la force, & l'authorité de la Cour soit gardée, a esté ordonné que les Lieutenant Criminel, Examinateurs, Sergens de Chastelet, Archers, Arbalestriers, & gens de guet, & autres qui ont accoustumé defendre la force & voye de fait en cette ville, en la compagnie du Gouverneur de Paris, en tel & si grand nombre que souffise, iront audit Convent, & y donneront telle provision que inconvenient n'en advienne, & à leur obeyr & donner confort & ayde contraindront ceux qui verront estre à faire, tellement que force & authorité demeure au Roy & à Justice: & fera cry parmy la ville que nul ne soit si osé de donner confort ou ayde à ceux qui tiennent ledit Convent par force, ne à leurs complices & adherens, sur peine d'estre desobeissans au Roy & à la Cour..."* Cf. Dupuy, pp. 1213-1214.

jurisdiction of a congregation based in a foreign land, in this case the Congregation of Holland. Acceding to the king's desire to nationalize the Dominican reform movement in the north, Pope Leo X charged Cajetan, the Master of the Order, to reorganize the French observant priories into a separate congregation.[67] In order to distinguish it from the already established Congregation of France located in the Midi (not to be confused with the unreformed "province" of France in the north), Cajetan chose to name the new entity the Gallican Congregation and issued the decree of erection on 3 November 1514.[68] Doré had most probably already begun his novitiate by this point, making him among the youngest members of the new congregation. The spirit of reform, relatively new and fresh at the priory of Blois, certainly left its mark on the young novice who, as we have seen, would later in life lament the general state of the clergy as a veritable plague upon the Church.

Upon completion of his novitiate, Doré, according to Quétif and Échard, continued on to Paris for his theological studies. For what it is worth, they describe him as a very talented and disciplined student with a reputation for piety.[69] Although no source is cited as the basis for this character profile, it is a description consistent with the type of person that is revealed by his later writings. The profile also fits someone who would have been judged by his religious superiors as having the requisite qualities to pursue advanced studies leading to the doctorate. Restrictions placed on the religious orders by the Paris Faculty of Theology limited the number of candidates they could present for the license, which was conferred only every two years. The Dominicans were allowed as many as four candidates for each license class but usually only presented two or three.[70] Doré's being selected then to pursue the license and doctorate is evidence

---

[67] In this reorganization, the Congregation of Holland lost twenty-two priories in French territory. See De Meyer, *Congrégation*, p. xcviii.
[68] See Mortier, *Histoire*, pp. 171-173.
[69] "...*egregia indole, pietate non fucata, disciplinae regularis cura diligentiori, eruditione a studio indefesso...*" QE, p. 203.
[70] See Farge, *Orthodoxy*, pp. 56-57.

both of his intellectual gifts and of a disciplined character well-adapted to serious academic work.

Normally, a candidate for the doctorate in theology had to undergo a rigorous minimum of thirteen years of study proceeding through six successive stages in order to obtain the coveted prize of the title "doctor."[71] If Doré arrived at S. Jacques after completing his novitiate in Blois sometime in 1515, that leaves a gap of seventeen years, not thirteen, between the beginning and end of his studies since we know that he received the doctorate in 1532. It is possible to account for the extra time by presuming that he would have spent the first three and one-half years or so doing his preparatory studies in the arts. Thus he would not have commenced theological studies until 1519. We also know that in 1525, Doré received an assignation by the General Chapter of Rome to teach *in parvis scholis*.[72] This assignment corresponds exactly to what would have been Doré's period of apprenticeship as *biblicum* (normally occurring after the sixth year of theology) when he would have lectured on the Scriptures under the tutelage of a master.

More important than delineating the various stages of Doré's formation, however, is the attempt to discover the character of the intellectual formation which he received in Paris, for this is what will give us insight into his later work. By and large, the Dominican students from different provinces and congregations assigned to the *studium generale* in Paris either by the General Chapters or by the Master of the Order himself followed the Faculty's prescribed course of studies based on two primary texts, the Bible and Peter Lombard's *Sentences*. However,

---

[71] Ibid., pp. 11-28. The course of studies was as follows: 1) As *studens*, the candidate attended lectures on the Bible and the *Sentences* of Peter Lombard for a period of six years, 2) the student was then admitted to the *primus cursus* (*biblicum* for mendicants) for a period of three years, during which time he lectured on the Scriptures as an apprentice teacher under the direction of a *magister*, 3) after successfully passing the *tentativa* or disputation, the candidate was received as a *baccalarius sententiarius* and spent one year lecturing on the *Sentences*, 4) then began a three-year period as *baccalarius formatus* during which time the candidate was required to participate in one academic disputation per year, 5) upon successful completion of the disputations and a review by the Faculty, the license was conferred, 6) the *licentiatus* became a doctor by completing two final disputations, the *vesperia* and the *magisterium*, usually within the year.
[72] MOPH, 9, p. 208.

for the Friars Preachers, these studies were done within their own house, S. Jacques, and under Dominican *baccalaurii* rather than at the university itself under the seculars.[73] At the time, the Jacobin priory was the Order's pre-eminent *studium generale* to which were assigned among the brightest and most promising of Dominican students from all over Europe. A record from 1530 puts the number of friars in residence at about 400![74] The international character of the house was certainly an important formational influence on all who studied there.[75] At the same time, such cultural diversity coupled with the fact that the students came from both the un-reformed provinces and the reformed congregations meant that there was a constant struggle to maintain the spirit of observance which had been brought to the priory at the turn of the century by Jean Clérée. In fact, there is evidence that the Parlement continued to intervene in the matter, as the following ordinance of 19 October 1521 makes clear:

> *Sur les plaintes alleguées par les Religieux escoliers estudians au Convent de Jacobins de cette ville de Paris...la Chambre de Parlement ordonnée par le Roy au temps des vacations, a ordonné & ordonne, qu'en ensuivant le dernier Arrest donné par la Cour entre lesdites parties, que la reformation audit Convent tiendra, & sera entretenue & gardée selon sa forme & teneur, & à ce seront contraints tous ceux qui pour ce feront à contraindre, par toutes voyes & manieres deues & raisonnables, & par detention de leurs personnes...*[76]

Despite the almost constant struggle to maintain observance at S. Jacques, it nevertheless continued to be a reformed house of the Gallican Congregation

---

[73] James Farge, "Les Dominicains et la Faculté de Théologie," *Mémoire Dominicaine*, 12 (1998/1): p. 22.

[74] Ernest Coyecque, *Recueil d'actes notariés relatifs à l'histoire de Paris et de ses environs au XVIe siècle*, vol. 1 (Paris: Imprimerie nationale, 1905, 1923), p. 230 § 1155.

[75] However, it seems that in 1525, the Parlement of Paris passed an ordinance forbidding Parisian religious houses from accepting foreign students. When the Carmelites were found to be in violation, two councilors were appointed to inspect the convents, including S. Jacques, and insure compliance: "*...commet ladite Cour ledit Dorigny, & M. Nicole le Cocq aussi Conseiller en ladite Cour, pour aller visiter ledit Convent des Carmes, **ensemble les Convents des Jacobins** [emphasis mine], Augustins, & Cordeliers de cette dite ville, & les Convents de saincte Croix, des Blanc-manteaux & des Billettes, & leur faire reiteratives defenses de ne loger ne recevoir aucuns Religieux estrangers de leur Ordre, sur peine d'amende arbitraire, & de privation de leurs privileges.*" See DuPuy, p. 1165.

[76] Ibid., p. 1224.

throughout Doré's student years and later regency. It is most probable, however, that the regular life was not as strictly observed as what he would have experienced as a novice at Blois.

Nevertheless, the renewal which occurred at S. Jacques at the beginning of the sixteenth century involved not only a renewed appreciation for regular observance but also the rediscovery of an appreciation for the teaching of the Order's greatest theologian, Thomas Aquinas, thanks largely to the influence of a nominalist turned Thomist, Pieter Crockaert.[77] Crockaert had been a Master of Arts at the College of Montaigu when in 1503 he experienced a double conversion to both the Dominican religious life and to the thought of Thomas. After making profession in the Order, he was strongly influenced by the Dominican master, Gilles Charronelle who was "reading St. Thomas" in his lectures, though it is not known if this means he was actually teaching from the *Summa Theologiae* or, what is more likely, that he was commenting the *Sentences* from a Thomistic perspective.[78] It seems, however, that inspired by the example of Charronelle, Crockaert went a step further when he began teaching at S. Jacques and actually used the *Summa* "...*como base de su enseñanza y texto oficial de sus lecciones.*"[79] Both Ricardo Villoslada and M.D. Chenu, in their respective studies on the University of Paris and S. Jacques, assert that the master from Brussels actually "substituted" Aquinas' *Summa* for Peter Lombard's

---

[77] See both M.D. Chenu, "L'humanisme et la réforme au collège de Saint-Jacques de Paris," *Archives d'histoire dominicaine*, 1 (1946): pp. 146-148, and Augustin Renaudet, *Préréforme et humanisme à Paris pendant les premières guerres d'Italie, 1494-1517* (Geneva: Slatkine Reprints, 1981), pp. 693-694.

[78] See Ricardo Villoslada, *La Universidad de Paris durante los estudios de Francisco de Vitoria, O.P. (1507-1522)*, Series Facultatis Hist. Ecclesiasticae, vol. 14 (Rome: Aedes Universitatis Gregorianae, 1938), pp. 267-268.

[79] Ibid., p. 261. Villoslada reaches this conclusion based on what Francisco Vitoria writes of his master Crockaert in the prologue to his edition of the *Secunda secundae* (1512): "*Cum enim iam lusculis annis scribendo, docendo, ac disputando insumptis, posses iure tuo quietioribus curis vitam agere, tamen pro tua in sanctum doctorem fide et observantia hanc secundam secunde sancti Thome partem, quam priore anno interpretari inceperas, ad finem usque deducere instituisti, nec laboris neque rationem habens, modo ne sancti Thome doctrina iacturam faceret,*" cited on pp. 279-280.

Sentences, an obligatory text in the University's curriculum.[80] In a recent publication on Dominican education in the first hundred years of the Order's history, M. Michèle Mulchahey lends support to this claim when she writes:

> The *Summa theologiae* would eventually win out as the friars' standard textbook of theology, the object of Dominican commentaries in its own right. But this would not happen until the early sixteenth century, and then not in the order's convent schools, but in its *studia generalia* and from university chairs.[81]

Although curiously enough she makes no mention of the Thomistic renewal occurring in Paris under Crockaert, she does point to various other universities and *studia* where the same thing was happening. If, then, the *Summa* was in fact replacing the *Sentences* as the standard theological textbook in Dominican intellectual formation beginning in the sixteenth century, that is not to say that the Lombard's work was therefore completely disregarded. It is certain that the Dominican students would have had to study the *Sentences* at some point in order to pass on to the stage of *baccalarius sententiarius*. Nevertheless, a new breed of students who would be well-versed in the thought of Aquinas was most definitely being formed.

To appreciate Crockaert's legacy at S. Jacques, one has only to look as far as his most famous disciple, Francisco de Vitoria, the great Spanish commentator of the *Summa*, particularly the *secunda secundae*. Though Crockaert died prematurely in 1514 after less than a decade of teaching at S. Jacques, he nevertheless had time in those few short years to inspire several disciples such as Vitoria who not only continued to study Thomas, but also went on to form others in the thought of the scholastic theologian. It is in the midst of this Thomistic renaissance that Pierre Doré was formed intellectually when he began his theological studies at S. Jacques approximately five years after Crockaert's death.

---

[80] See Ibid., p. 279, and Chenu, "L'humanisme," p. 147.
[81] M. Michèle Mulchahey, *"First the Bow is Bent in Study"—Dominican Education before 1350* (Toronto: Pontifical Institute of Mediaeval Studies, 1998), pp. 165-166.

In fact, it is highly probable that he studied Thomas early in his formation under the great Vitoria himself before the master went on to Valladolid in 1523.[82] Without a doubt, then, Doré not only received a solid grounding in the scholastic theology of Aquinas, but he in all probability received it at the hands of one of the brightest lights of the time.

Doctor, Preacher, Writer, and Spiritual Director in Turbulent Times

The years immediately following Doré's reception of the doctorate in 1532 are, in Farge's words, "generally acknowledged to be the most crucial period for the history of the Reformation in France...[and] for the Faculty of Theology in Paris."[83] As we have seen, the Faculty's attempts since the early 1520s to preserve France from heresy by swiftly condemning theologians, preachers and writers who embraced and propagated evangelical ideas were at times frustrated by the monarchy. Several of the leading humanists and reformers found refuge from the Faculty's inquisitorial pursuits in the court of the Renaissance king, Francis I. This initial royal benevolence towards reform movements, however, gave way to a much more repressive posture after the *affaire des placards* of October 1534. The reform party, in so blatantly attacking the Eucharist, had gone beyond the limit of what Francis I was willing to tolerate. Repression of heterodoxy intensified in the 1540s as the Faculty began to make full use of its authority to censure and also, at the king's insistence, produced in the Articles of Faith a clear statement of fundamental truths to be adhered to by

---

[82] This conjecture is based on the following line of influence which Villoslada, *Universidad*, p. 277, establishes between Crockaert and Jean Benoist through the mediation of Vitoria: "*Los que más brillo regentaron la cátedra del maestro, fueron Pedro F. de Nimega, Francisco de Vitoria, Mateo Ory, Juan Benoît. De los demás hubo algunos cuyo paso por París fué demasiado fugaz para dejar huella de su enseñanza. Ni Ory, ni Benoît es probable que alcanzasen a Crockaert en Santiago, ni fueron por tanto discípulos suyos inmediatos, pero bien pudieron serlo de Francisco de Vitoria en Teología.*" Since Doré received his doctorate the very same year as Benoist, it can thus be assumed that he too would have been a disciple of Vitoria.
[83] Farge, *Orthodoxy*, p. 200.

all true Christians. The battle lines between orthodoxy and reform-thinking, initially ambiguous and difficult to distinguish, were becoming much more clearly drawn.

Doré's activity during this early period of hardening positions in the mid-1530s is virtually unknown. About the only solid evidence we possess is a record of his participation at one of the Faculty's meetings in 1533. In addition to teaching and presiding over academic disputations, one of the privileges and duties of a doctor in theology was to participate in regular convocations on different matters concerning the faith. Shortly after the Roussel affair[84] the Faculty at one of its meetings allowed a poem written by Marguerite de Navarre, *Miroir de l'âme pécheresse*, to incur a censure. It comes as little surprise that this censure, which seemed to call into question the orthodoxy of the king's sister, caused quite a stir in the royal court. In an attempt to placate the royal temper over the affair, the Faculty at three subsequent meetings denied that it had formally condemned the poem. Doré is recorded as participating in the meetings of 27 October and 8 November and joining in the denial.[85] There are only three other recorded appearances of Doré at these convocations and they will be discussed in the appropriate place in this chronological presentation. By any accounting, it is a rather poor record of attendance. It seems, however, that the Dominican theologian was not alone among his colleagues in this regard.[86] Yet, the fact that much of his time was not only spent away from Paris but was also consumed by an intense writing activity might serve to explain why he did not make greater use of this doctoral privilege.

Doré's first major work, *Les voyes de paradis*, appeared in 1537, a full five years after the completion of his doctorate. But if it took him some time to first put ink to paper, this initial work served to unleash a flurry of literary

---

[84] See Introduction, p. 31.
[85] BR, p. 138, based on RCFT 1, fols. 267v°, 269r°. For the text of these meetings, see James Farge, *Registre des procès-verbaux de la faculté de théologie de l'université de Paris, (de janvier 1524 à novembre 1533)* (Paris: Aux Amateurs de Livres, 1990), pp. 302-306.
[86] See Farge, *Orthodoxy*, p. 96.

activity. Indeed, he produced three more books by 1539, the year he received his first major appointment to an official post within the Gallican Congregation. At the chapter of the congregation gathered in Dinan, Doré was named regent of studies at S. Jacques, an appointment which was confirmed on 2 June by the curia of the Order in Rome.[87] It seems that at the time of the chapter, Doré was residing at Blois. In fact, the 1538, 1539 and 1540 editions of *Les allumettes du feu divin* all mention that Doré is a friar of the priory of S. Avoye in Blois. Apparently, then, he continued to reside there even after his appointment as regent of studies at S. Jacques for a term of at least three years. It also seems that Doré had actually been the prior of Blois before 1539 because in *Le college de sapience*, which appears that year, he speaks of having tried to re-institute the confraternity in honor of Mary Magdalene during his priorship there.[88] Thus, Doré probably left Paris and became prior of Blois for the first, but not the last time, around 1535 and it was there that his initial works were produced.[89]

In the later part of 1540, a rather unusual incident seems to have taken place, one that is out of character for Doré. Our friar is recorded as having been imprisoned for a time along with fellow Dominicans Henri Gervais and Jean Fabry "*...pour les patentes rebellions, desobeyssances, & contradictions par eux faites au Roy.*"[90] According to the notice, their time of confinement was served at the priory of S. Martin-des-Champs. The entry in the *Registres du Parlement* is unfortunately no more specific than that in detailing exactly in what way or why Doré and the others disobeyed his majesty Francis I. It is indeed hard to imagine him as ever rebelling against royal authority given the glowing terms in which he normally presents the monarchy in his writings. In any case, whatever the cause for Doré's brief imprisonment, it does not seem to have lasted very long nor does

---

[87] AGOP, IV. 25. *Registrum Augustini Recuperati*, 2 June 1539, fol. 508r°.
[88] *Le college*, fol. cxxxvi r°.
[89] J.D. Levesque, "Le couvent des frères prêcheurs de Blois," *Documents pour servir à l'histoire de l'ordre de Saint-Dominique en France* 28 (Ier trimestre 1993): p. 13, says that Doré was elected prior of Blois in 1534 but gives no source for this information.
[90] Dupuy, p. 1167.

he seem to have harbored any ill feelings towards the king, for he went on to dedicate his *L'arbre de vie* to Francis I in 1542.

The first evidence of Doré being a renowned preacher comes in 1543 when he was chosen to deliver the eulogy on 7 June for the deceased Admiral, Philippe de Chabot.[91] By this point, he had authored eight or nine books and had clearly established a solid reputation for himself, particularly among the elite of French society. It goes without saying that the honor of preaching at the funeral of an admiral of France would not have been given to just anyone. Doré, now approximately forty-six years old, had come into his own. The sermon appears in print, bound with that same year's edition of *La deploration de la vie humaine*, as well as with all the subsequent editions of this work. In the text itself there are hints that Doré enjoyed a very close relationship with the Chabot family. Near the end, for example, he addresses words of consolation to the widow using the familiar "*tu*." He also recounts having had conversations with the Admiral's only son, mentioning in particular a meeting in Dijon. It would seem then that Doré had begun in the early 1540s to develop connections with the rich and powerful of French society.

Doré's second recorded appearance on the Faculty also takes place in 1543, this time for the signing of the Faculty's Articles of Faith.[92] Their significance has already been discussed in the previous chapter and it is no surprise that Doré would have made an effort to be present for this important articulation of orthodox belief. What is most interesting, however, is that Doré goes on to borrow this idea of articulating essential tenets of the faith and basically incorporates the Faculty's twenty-nine articles into his first explicitly polemical work, *Paradoxa Fratris Petri Aurati, doctoris theologi, ordinis*

---

[91] Paul Guérin, ed., *Registres des délibérations du Bureau de la ville de Paris*, vol. 3 (Paris: Imprimerie Nationale, 1886), p. 26, contains this notice of the event: "...*puis fut faict une belle predication par ung docteur en theologie, nommé Deaurati, jacopin, à la louenge dud. seigneur, lequel print pour son thesme les deux versetz du prophete David: 'In pace in idipsum dormiam et requiescam, quoniam tu, Domine, singulariter in spe constituisti me,' lesquelz il exposa bien au propos.*"
[92] BR, p. 138, based on RCFT 2, fol. 80r°.

prædicatorii, ad profligandas hæreses, ex divi Pauli apostoli epistolis selecta, ineluctabilibusque sanctorum patrum firmata testimoniis, which appears the very same year. But whereas the Articles of Faith respond only to the particular issues of debate raised by the sixteenth-century Reformers, the *Paradoxa* is a set of 100 theses, arranged in alphabetical order, which refutes certain errors of the past as well as those of his time. It is a kind of compendium of Catholic teaching on essential points of faith that have been challenged by the likes of more ancient heretics such as Pelagius and Arius to name but a few. The implication Doré is making in his *Paradoxa* is clear: this is the company in which Luther and Calvin now stand.

It would be a mistake to think, however, that the Faculty of Theology and theologian-writers like Doré were the only ones involved in combatting the Reformation at this time. Certain members of the nobility also felt a responsibility in conscience to preserve the integrity of the faith in France. Among these was the Duke of Guise, Claude de Lorraine. It is not known how he came to meet Pierre Doré, but in 1544, the duke asked the friar if he would be his confessor. This marks the beginning of a very close relationship between Doré and one of the most important families in sixteenth-century France. Among Claude's twelve children were 1) Marie, the eldest, who became the wife of King James V of Scotland and then mother of the ill-fated Mary Stuart, Queen of Scots, 2) François, the father's successor as duke and the perpetrator of the Massacre of Wassy in 1562, 3) Charles, archbishop of Reims, Cardinal de Lorraine, one of the most powerful prelates of the French church who, despite the decadence of his personal life, actively worked for the reform of the Church, and 4) Louis, archbishop of Sens, Cardinal de Guise. Finally, it is Claude's grandchildren, notably Henri, the third duke of Guise, who would be at the forefront of the wars of religion and the formation of the Catholic League in the final decades of the century. Doré's close association with such a politically powerful family is a clear indication of the prestige he had himself achieved by mid-life.

In asking Doré to be his confessor, it is evident that the first Duke of Guise saw in this theologian a man of like mind and spirit. The two were nearly the same age, with Claude having been born in 1496. Upon the duke's death in 1550, Doré composed a tribute in his honor in which he tells of the prince's great zeal for the faith. Here the Dominican recounts how the duke invited him to join forces with the house of Guise in defense of Catholic orthodoxy:

> ...allons mon pere en Bourgogne, dont je suis gouverneur, pour la foy batailler. J'auray l'espée & le glaive materiel, & vous le glaive spirituel de la parolle de Dieu, par ainsi combaterons tous heretiques & adversaires de la foy, & seront ou convertis ou punis.[93]

If Doré is to be taken at his word here, and there is no reason why he should not be, then it seems that Claude de Lorraine had his own sense of vocation in regards to rooting out heresy in his lands even before he met the Paris theologian. What he saw in Doré was a fellow combatant, a preacher, teacher and writer who could wield great influence over the people by clearly exposing for them the truths of the faith. If and when such persuasion might fail, the duke would then assure submission to the truth by means of the sword. Perhaps Doré has here embellished the recounting of his association with the duke by inserting this allusion to the two-sword theory of the division of powers in a Christian kingdom. But there is no reason to doubt that the sentiment, if not the language in which it is expressed, is authentically that of Claude de Lorraine.

It has been pointed out in the Introduction that some of the existing biographical sketches have presented Doré's appointment as confessor to the Duke of Guise as an explanation for the family's fanatical zeal in persecuting French Protestants. However, this claim is too exaggerated and does not take into account the already ultra-Catholic leanings of the family even before Doré's contacts with them, not to mention their political aspirations which were also a

---

[93] *Oraison panegyrique pleine de consolation, pour hault et puissant prince, Claude de Lorraine, Duc de Guyse, per de France, decedé ceste presente année, 1550* (Paris: Jean de Brouilly, 1550), fol. 14r°. [**Le Mans, MLA—B.L. 8° 1098**].

significant factor in their rivalry with the houses of Montmorency and Bourbon. In fact, when Francis II succeeded to the throne at the age of sixteen upon his father Henry II's death in 1559, it is the Guise who in fact came to power, for the year before, the young prince had married the young princess of Scotland and niece of the powerful Duke of Guise, Mary Stuart. Poor in health and weak in character, the adolescent king handed over practically the entire administration of the kingdom to his wife's uncles, Duke François I and the cardinal, Charles de Lorraine.[94] Though this virtual rule of the Guise over France came to a quick end with the young king's death but a year later, their political ambitions were in no way diminished. In this period of French history where rival noble families embraced different religious faiths, it is extremely difficult to separate political motivation from religious zealotry in the turbulent events that took place. Therefore, as regards the ultra-Catholic fanaticism of the Guise, it would be more accurate to say that Doré confirmed and encouraged the family in their sentiments rather than that he was the major inspiration behind their anti-Protestantism. Had the theologian never come into contact with Claude de Lorraine, it is highly unlikely that the subsequent history of the wars of religion would have been any different.

At the time that Doré accepted the invitation of the Duke of Guise to become his confessor, it seems that he was once again the superior of the friars at Blois, for in 1545, he attended the chapter of the Gallican Congregation at Le Mans in virtue of his being prior of S. Avoye. At the chapter, he was elected a definitor or councilor.[95] Of course the year 1545 is highly significant for the history of the Reformation because it marks the opening of the long-awaited council meant to respond to the Protestant challenge. Yet it took almost a quarter-century after Luther's excommunication in 1521 before the Council of Trent was

---

[94] Dividing between themselves the role of first counselor, the duke oversaw military affairs while the cardinal took charge of finances and religious affairs. See Lucien Romier, *Le Royaume de Catherine de Médicis: La France à la veille des guerres de religion* (Geneva: Slatkine Reprints, 1978), p. 57.
[95] AGOP, IV. 28. *Registrum Francisci Romei de Castiglione*, 12 March 1545, fol. 211r°.

finally convoked by Pope Paul III. The papacy's fear of conciliarism since the days of Constance and Basel as well as Franco-German or more precisely Valois-Hapsburg rivalry contributed to the rather long delay in convoking this badly needed reforming council of the Church. But the delayed convocation serves to highlight even more the importance of Doré's earlier efforts as well as those of the Faculty of Theology to propagate orthodox teaching in France in response to the dangerous doctrines of the Reformers. In many ways, Doré was ahead of his time, taking action not only to stem the spread of heterodoxy but also to promote authentic reform in the Church long before a general council was convoked as the magisterium's official response to the problem. Nevertheless, although the Dominican's anti-Protestant strategy had little connection with Trent, his later works do contain occasional references to the council's determinations, particularly concerning the issue of justification by faith. It is clear that Doré recognized the crying need for this official teaching on the part of the magisterium and sought to disseminate it in his own writings.

On 5 January 1547, Doré is once again recorded as having made an appearance at a meeting of the Faculty of Theology in Paris. This time, he joined the prior of S. Jacques in requesting the Faculty to refrain from placing a book by the former Master of the Order, Cardinal Cajetan, on the Index.[96] While the documentary evidence points to Doré having resided in Blois for the better part of the years between 1535 and 1547, despite his appointment as regent of studies at S. Jacques for a time and his later acceptance of the task of confessor to the Duke of Guise, he received a formal assignment in 1548 to S. Jacques where he was appointed by the Master of the Order to serve as lector.[97] Only two years later, he suffered the loss of his patron and close friend, Duke Claude, in whose honor he composed the *Oraison panegyrique* (1550), meant principally to console the widowed Antoinette de Bourbon. There, he makes reference to some very mysterious and sinister circumstances surrounding the duke's death:

---

[96] BR, p. 138, based on RCFT 2, fol. 149r°.
[97] AGOP, IV. 28. *Registrum Francisci Romei de Castiglione*, 16 June 1548, fol. 213v°.

> *Il est bien veritable & congneu, non seulement de medecins, qu'ilz l'ont attesté, mais aussi de tous qui l'ont veu, qui l'ont averé, que le corps est occis par poison...Les autres affirment ce mal naturellement estre venu par indigestion ou corruption de viande.*[98]

Whether the duke was actually poisoned or in fact died of purely natural causes, Doré seems to believe the former and interprets the vile deed as the result of envy on the part of Claude de Lorraine's rivals, though no names are mentioned. The suspicion is certainly plausible. Both Claude's son François and his grandson Henri, the second and third Dukes of Guise, would know violent deaths themselves. In any case, Doré remained faithful to the memory of his departed patron by continuing to take up *"le glaive spirituel de la parolle de Dieu"* against the errors of the Reformers with the appearance of his next work, the polemical *Anti-Calvin*, in 1551.

The close connections which had developed between Pierre Doré and the house of Guise over a period of six years prior to the duke's untimely death seem to have continued not only with the widowed duchess but also with the children, particularly with Charles, Cardinal de Lorraine and his brother Louis, soon to be named Cardinal de Guise in 1553. In fact, the former invited the theologian to accept a position as professor at the university of his episcopal city of Reims in 1551. The Master of the Order gave his assent to the proposal in June of that year.[99] How long Doré taught at Reims is difficult to ascertain. However, three of his books between 1554 and 1557 were published there by Nicolas Bacquenois. It is therefore not unreasonable to assume that he basically resided in Reims at least until then. During this time, however, he was also appointed by the General Chapter in Rome of 1553 to serve as a substitute lecturer of Sacred Scripture at S. Jacques.[100] How this appointment affected his position at Reims, if at all, remains a mystery. The only thing that can be said with certainty of this period of Doré's

---

[98] *Oraison*, fol. 24r°.
[99] AGOP, IV. 30. *Registrum Francisci Romei de Castiglione*, 3 June 1551, fol. 13v°.
[100] MOPH, 9, p. 357.

life is that whether he was teaching at the cardinal's university in Reims or at the Dominican studium in Paris, he nevertheless did not slacken the least bit in his writing, producing six works in the period between 1554 and 1557.

After 1557, however, Doré seems to have all of a sudden faded into the background, though Quétif and Échard mention him preaching Lenten homilies at Châlons-sur-Marne in that year. He perhaps continued to teach in Paris, but there is no documentary evidence of this. His writing, however, definitely came to an end. Although it would seem that the devotional writer found the energy to produce one final work over a decade later in 1569, the year of his death, we will see in the following chapter that *Le second livre des divins benefices* was actually written by Doré much earlier.

One unresolved question about this final period of Doré's life is whether or not he became prior of the Cistercian abbey of Val-des-Choux in the diocese of Langres in the late 1550s. André Duval, who of all the biographers has researched this question most closely, points out that although Doré's name is nowhere to be found on any of the existing lists of the priors at the abbey, a manuscript copy of a never-published work entitled *Mémoires nécrologiques, historiques et critiques pour servir à l'histoire du Collège général des Dominicains en l'Université de Paris* by a Dominican named Texte contains a notice on Doré affirming his priorship at the abbey.[101] The notice concerns an endowment which he left at S. Jacques for the annual celebration of a solemn Mass by the Faculty of Theology in honor of the Dominican saint, Peter Martyr:

> *Fondation de Monsieur Pierre Doré, Docteur, datée du 12 février 1563, pour célébrer à perpetuité, solennellement, la fête de saint Pierre, martyr, de l'Ordre des F.F. Prêcheurs, en présence des principaux docteurs de la Faculté de Paris. Cette fondation est inscrite sur une lame de cuivre, au-dessus de la table de la sacristie. L'an MV^{c}LXIII, Pierre Doré, Docteur en théologie **et Prieur de Notre Dame du Val du Choux, chef d'Ordre*** [emphasis mine], *fonda, lui vivant, en la Faculté de Théologie de Paris, une haute messe solennelle pour etre chanté dans l'Eglise de* [illegible] *à perpetuité, et ce par le commun accord et*

---

[101] Duval, *Doré*, p. 1642.

acceptation de toute ladite Faculté, et du consentement du prieur et couvent de cette dite maison...[102]

Given this small piece of evidence, it is entirely possible, as Duval suggests, that Doré was named to the position at Val-des-Choux by royal authority sometime after 1557 since the list of priors is incomplete precisely in the twenty-year period between 1556 and 1577. Why he, a Dominican friar, was chosen for this position and how much direction he actually would have exercised over the abbey or its thirty-plus dependent priories cannot be determined from the scant information at our disposal. Yet, his involvement at Val-des-Choux would certainly help to account for the seemingly abrupt end of his writing career in 1557.

The endowment mentioned by Texte in the *Mémoires nécrologiques, historiques et critiques* is further corroborated by the record of Doré's final appearance at a meeting of the Faculty on 4 November 1563. On this date, the Faculty accepted 408 *livres tournois* from their colleague for the annual memorial that he wished to be celebrated on the feast of Peter Martyr.[103] It is interesting that Pierre Doré seems to have identified strongly with this other Peter, an inquisitor and proto-martyr of the Order who was murdered by Lombard heretics in 1252. According to tradition, the saint, after receiving a hatchet blow to the head, dipped his finger in his blood and died while writing on the ground *Credo in Deum*. While Doré never expressed in his writings any desire to suffer martyrdom for the faith, the Peter Martyr-like zeal he demonstrated in refuting doctrinal error is unquestionable. The endowment he left contained explicit instructions that the celebration of the saint's feast should begin appropriately with "*un sermon, ou oraison latine De Defensione fidei, pour laquelle le dit St. Pierre a enduré le Martyre.*"[104]

---

[102] Manuscript, BNF—N Acq Fr 6537, fol. 279r°. Duval's article incorrectly identifies the manuscript number as 6538.
[103] BR, p. 138 based on RCFT 3, fol. 140r°.
[104] Manuscript, BNF—N Acq Fr 6537, fol. 279r°.

Is there something behind this apparent identification that Doré is making with the Dominican inquisitor and martyr of the thirteenth century? Perhaps what we see here is a man near the end of his life secretly hoping that his own life's work will have been a contemporary expression of the martyr's *Credo*, written not in blood but in the sweat and tears of someone who devoted all of his energies for the better part of thirty years to defending the teachings of the Church in the face of widespread heresy. There are many ways of being a martyr or witness to the faith. It is quite evident that Doré considered himself to be faithfully following in the footsteps of his patron in the Order even without ever having to endure physical suffering for the cause of Truth. His writings were his own way of imitating the glorious martyrdom of Peter of Verona. Doré went on to die a natural death at S. Jacques on 19 May 1569, the feast of the Ascension, at the approximate age of seventy-three.

The French Dominicans and the Reformation

Mention has already been made of the observant movement that was occurring within the Dominican Order prior to and concurrently with the Protestant reform movement. It was a time of renewed zeal and fervor, not only for observance of the rule, but also for the teaching of St. Thomas. This rediscovery of Aquinas was not limited to Paris where Crockaert literally founded a Thomistic school in the Jacobin studium. In fact it had begun a few years earlier with the friars at Cologne. The doctrine of Thomas was also propagated in Italy thanks to Cajetan and later in Spain thanks to Vitoria. Indeed, the Order on the whole seemed to be finally recovering numerically, spiritually and intellectually from the devastation which plague and the Great Western Schism in the Church had wrought in the fourteenth and early fifteenth centuries.

Yet, despite all these signs of revival, the response of Dominicans in general and the French Dominicans in particular to the Protestant Reformation was by and large tepid, if not simply non-existant. There were to be sure exemplary exceptions. As is to be expected, many friars served in the traditional role of inquisitor. Yet there was also a surprising number who became apostates and preachers of the Reform. Some died as martyrs for orthodoxy, others as martyrs for what they believed to be the true doctrine of the Gospel in its unadulterated form, free from "man-made traditions." Given this extreme diversity of reactions to the same event, it is important then to consider Pierre Doré against this very varied backdrop of responses to the Reformation among his own confrères. If it is already clear that he belongs to the group of those who opposed the ideas of the Reformation as heretical, it remains to be seen if there was anything distinctive about his approach in responding to the heresy. Does his work represent something original, or is it no different from what other like-minded friars were attempting to do?

From a corporate point of view, the Order's stance towards Lutheranism was unambiguous. The General Chapter of Valladolid in 1523, the first general chapter held after Luther's excommunication in 1521, set the tone for how friars throughout the Order should respond of the spread of *"pestifera et virulenta Martini Luteri dogmata."* It exhorted all those who were gifted in preaching or writing to put their gifts at the service of orthodoxy against the deadly teaching.[105] This same monition was repeated at the subsequent General Chapters of Rome in 1525 and 1530. The French friars, however, were relatively slow in executing the directives of the general chapters, if not in their preaching, at least in terms of their literary production. There is very little of a written response to the Reformation to speak of prior to the end of the 1530s. In fact, were it not for the work of Doré, the written opposition by French Dominicans would not have

---

[105] The complete text taken from MOPH, 9, pp. 186-187, is as follows: *Monemus omnes et singulos totius ordinis fratres ac praesertim qui litteris et praedicatione praecellent, et in domino hortamur, nec non si meritum obedientiae volunt, iniungimus illis, ut contra pestifera et virulenta Martini Luteri dogmata, quae paulatim serpentia in tantam perniciem eruperunt magnamque stragem in ecclesia ac ruina minantur, non solum orationibus, sed sanctis praedicationibus totis conatibus se opponant privatim ac publice in templis, domi, foris, apud populares, proceres et quoscumque principes orthodoxam fidem contra illius figmenta et haereses tueantur.*

begun appearing in force until a full decade later when the inquisitor of Toulouse, Esprit Rotier, began to take up the pen against the errors of Calvinism.

Was the slow response of the French friars to carry on a written warfare with the Reformers and their ideas typical of the other provinces and congregations where the unity of the Church was threatened, particularly in Germany and England? It would seem that the Dominicans in the Holy Roman Empire were a bit more pro-active in this regard than their French confrères. Mortier offers several examples including Johann Mensing, Conrad Köllin and Johann Dietenberger who early on wrote tracts, though all in Latin, refuting Lutheran doctrine.[106] As for the English friars who were faced not so much with combatting heresy in the 1520s as with having to deal with the schism of Henry VIII in 1534 when he declared himself to be head of the church in England, there was almost no response.[107] The province of England, in fact, was in many ways moribund and cut off from the rest of the Order even before Henry's break with Rome. No English friars, for example, were present at the General Chapters of 1523, 1525, 1530 or 1532.[108] Though numbering approximately 1,000 in 1534, according to Mortier, there is no evidence of a single English friar producing a written work in opposition to the king's reforms.[109] That is not to say that they all simply went along with the changes and pledged their fidelity to the king as head of the Church. On the contrary, a few like Richard Marshall, prior of Newcastle, strongly denounced the schism from the pulpit and then fled the country. The vast majority, unwilling to renounce allegiance to the papacy, did likewise and in

---

[106] See Mortier, *Histoire*, pp. 470-489. See also Nikolaus Paulus, *Die deutschen Dominikaner im kampfe gegen Luther, 1518-1563* (Freiburg im Breisgau: Herdersche Berlagshandlung, 1903).
[107] For further reading on the English Dominicans during the Reformation, see Francis Gasquet, *Henry VIII and the English Monasteries*, vol. 2 (London: John Hodges, 1889), pp. 238-276, and Bede Jarrett, *The English Dominicans* (London: Burns Oates and Washbourne, LTD, 1921), pp. 151-172. A more general discussion of the suppression of the friars under Henry VIII can be found in David Knowles, *The Religious Orders in England*, vol. 3 (Cambridge: University Press, 1959), pp. 360-366.
[108] Mortier, *Histoire*, p. 357.
[109] Ibid., p. 369.

so doing, "*évitèrent, en masse, le déshonneur de l'apostasie.*"[110] The reaction of the French Dominicans to the Reformation thus lies somewhere between the overall silence of the English friars faced with Henry VIII and the fairly rapid written opposition to Luther which appeared from the pens of German friars in the 1520s and -30s. But if the German Dominicans got involved in the theological fray much earlier than their French counterparts, they did not have anyone comparable to Pierre Doré who devoted his entire life's work to fighting heresy.

Based on the findings of Marie-Madeleine Fragonard, there were only four French Dominicans who wrote specifically in response to Lutheran errors prior to the beginning of Doré's career, that is between 1519 and 1537.[111] All of their works are in Latin and two were actually published only after their authors had died. The earliest example is an instruction justifying the doctrine on indulgences, *Questio utilissima modernis multum necessaria de relaxatione animarum a paenis purgatorii per indulgentias*, written by an Avignonese friar, Bernard de Croso. Of course, it was precisely the doctrine of indulgences that was Luther's first point of attack in his step-by-step alienation from the Roman church. De Croso's work, first published soon after his death in 1519, was re-edited in 1520 with an added notice that its teaching was specifically directed against the errors of the German, Martin Luther.[112] In 1523, the Saxon, Lambert Campester while living in Paris, produced two anti-Lutheran works, *Apologia in Martinum Lutherum, haereseos acephalorum ac sacrilegorum antesignanum* and *Heptacolon in summam scripturae sacrilegae Martini Lutheri in Apologia ejus contentam*. It was then almost a decade later before the next anti-Protestant works appeared. The *Tractatus catholicae eruditionis ad testimonium et legem recurrens* by the inquisitor Nicolas Morin was published posthumously in 1532 as a response to attacks against the ceremonies of the Church by certain heretics from Lyon. That same year appeared the *Destructorum haeresum* of the Tolosan

---

[110] Ibid., p. 364.
[111] See Fragonard, "Publications," Table 1. Forthcoming.
[112] See Robert Sauzet, *Les réguliers mendiants, Acteurs du changement religieux dans le royaume de France (1480-1560)* (Tours: Université de Tours, 1994), p. 78.

friar Arnaud Badet, who despite his office as inquisitor had the misfortune of being himself suspected of heresy because of the close associations he maintained with others of dubious allegiance.

An important question to be answered is to whom were these polemical treatises directed? Given the fact that only clerics and academicians knew Latin, it is clear that none of these works was accessible to the average literate lay person. Nor is it likely that they were written for the Reformers as a way of trying to convince them of their errors. What purpose then did they serve in the fight against heresy? In addition to being a kind of academic rebuttal of Luther's positions, they most probably were destined for preachers who would in turn communicate the orthodox teaching to the laity in their sermons. The idea of addressing the laity directly, of exposing for them the heretical doctrines and proposing the orthodox teaching in its place, was still very much of a taboo for Catholic theologians.

It would seem then that the French Dominicans did not take the strong exhortations of the General Chapters between 1523 and 1530 very seriously, at least in terms of a written response to heresy. Lack of documentation precludes any judgment being made on whether their preaching was in greater conformity with the desires of the chapters. However, while there is a veritable paucity of any overt refutations of Lutheran teachings by the French Dominicans, there is yet the possibility that they might have responded to heresy in a more disguised fashion, that is to say in the form of devotional or catechetical literature in which the essentials of the faith would be exposed for the common person. Such seems to be the case with *Le viat de salut*, a short catechism along the medieval model written by Guillaume Petit, doctor in theology, confessor to the king, and bishop, first of Troyes (1518) and later of Senlis (1527).[113] According to Francis Higman, the first edition of this little catechism most probably appeared as early as 1526.[114]

Unlike the polemical works in Latin discussed above whose stated purpose was to refute Lutheran errors, Petit's little catechism written in the vernacular is ostensibly nothing more than an exposition of the fundamentals of the faith which a person must know in order to be saved, thus its title "the way of salvation." It is primarily intended for the laity, *"pour leur enseignement & instruction, auquel pourront veoir & entendre ce qu'ilz doyvent croire."*[115] Yet, recognizing that the more learned might also profit from this printed work, Petit has taken pains *"de adjouster & mettre bonnes, saines, & solides doctrines pour les clerz."* Thus *Le viat de salut* is meant for both the simple faithful as well as for the theologically more sophisticated. The basic instruction in the faith is complemented at times by a deeper theological discourse. Admitting that some of the teaching might prove too difficult for the average layperson, Petit offers the following counsel:

> *Les simples donc prendront ce qu'ilz pourront mascher & entendre. Et le residu sans le despriser & contenner commettront au sainct esperit qui les pourra illuminer par sa grace, ou par gens clercz bien vivans, s'ilz veulent retourner a eulx pour apprendre. Les saiges pareillement supporteront l'aucteur qui principallement a ordonne ce livre pour instruire les ignorans & simple peuple.*[116]

From the above, it is clear that Petit is in favor of the "ignorant and simple people" coming to a deeper understanding of the faith. Whether or not his attitude is a reaction to the spread of heretical ideas is never made explicit.

---

[113] Petit's career and writings are briefly discussed by Guy Bedouelle, "Guillaume Petit, humaniste, théologien et politique," *Mémoire Dominicaine* 12 (1998/1), pp. 63-73; see also BR, pp. 367-373.

[114] See Francis Higman, "Premières réponses catholiques aux écrits de la Réforme en France, 1525-c.1540," in *Le Livre dans l'Europe de la Renaissance*, Actes du XXVIIIe colloque international d'études humanistes de Tours sous la direction de Pierre Aquilon et Henri-Jean Martin (Promodis: Editions du Cercle de la Librairie, 1988), p. 364 and also *Piety*, p. 341.

[115] Guillaume Petit, Preface to *Le viat de salut, ouquel est comprins l'exposition du simbole, des dix commandemens de la Loy, de la Paternostre & Ave Maria, Livre tressalutaire pour ung chascun chrestien* (Paris: Denis Janot, n.d.), n.p. [**Paris, BSG—D 8° 3335(5) Rés. Inv. 3707**].

[116] Ibid.

Nevertheless, the significance of Petit's work is that it represents the first attempt (if Higman's dating is correct) by a French Dominican to instruct the ordinary faithful in fundamental doctrine by means of the printed word.

However, account must be taken here of the fact that Petit is not simply a friar preacher but also a bishop. His position as chief shepherd and teacher of the faith in the diocese of Troyes gives an added dimension to his evident concern for the proper instruction of the flock, particularly one menaced by heresy. Guy Bedouelle points out that there is a noticeable change in Petit's attitude toward reform movements in the Church with the Faculty of Theology's condemnation of Luther on 15 April 1521. Prior to the condemnation, the royal confessor was known as a friend of the humanists and their protector at court. After 1521, however, his actions indicate a conscious decision to resist what has so clearly and officially been labeled as heresy even though he remains supportive of humanist values and goals. In 1526, for example, he proposed that the entire French hierarchy meet to discuss a common strategy for combatting the spread of Lutheran ideas in France.[117] It is in the context of Petit's growing resistance to reform that Bedouelle situates the bishop's two vernacular texts, *Le viat de salut* and *De la formation de l'homme*[118], remarking that, "*Ces textes, en fait, n'ont nullement pour but l'originalité de la pensée ou du style. Ils veulent plutôt répondre aux besoins des fidèles auxquels un évêque conscient de ses devoirs pastoraux se devait de répondre dans ce temps de 'préréforme catholique'*"[119] The episcopal dimension of Petit's desire to provide solid instruction to his flock is certainly at the heart of his literary production in French. In this regard, he most definitely stood out among his colleagues in the episcopate, for as we saw earlier, the vast majority of the French hierarchy at the time did not share the bishop of Troyes' alarm at the spread of Lutheranism, nor were they as conscientious in the fulfillment of their pastoral duties. Yet even if it is perhaps more as a bishop

---

[117] BR, p. 369.

[118] This work seems to have been published posthumously with the first edition appearing in 1538 (Paris: Olivier Maillard). See both Higman, *Piety*, p. 340 and BR, p. 371.

[119] Bedouelle, "Guillaume Petit," p. 68.

conscious of his pastoral responsibilities than as friar preacher that Guillaume Petit entered the field of combat against the Reformation, his Dominican origins and formation justify our consideration of his work as part of the Dominican response to the Reformation in France.

This, then, brings us back to the original point of the discussion. Is *Le viat de salut* a catechism pure and simple, or might it not also be a disguised refutation of Luther's reformed theology? It hardly seems polemical from an examination of its contents and structure. The three theological virtues serve as the organizing principle for a simple exposition of the Apostles' Creed (associated with the virtue of faith), the Our Father (associated with hope) and the Ten Commandments (associated with charity). Francis Higman, however, notices something very original in this seemingly unoriginal presentation. He is struck by the fact that Petit does not simply provide the vernacular text of these prayers, but he also gives a brief commentary for each article of the Creed, each petition of the Lord's prayer and each commandment of the Decalogue. Higman is convinced that the Dominican bishop is adopting this method of presentation as a response to an exposition of the very same texts based on the teachings of Farel and Luther which appeared under the title *Oraison de Jesuschrist* (1525).[120] He suggests that *Le viat* is quite probably meant to be an orthodox presentation of these basic Christian prayers in response to the *Oraison*, though Petit never once alludes to this himself in the text.

A closer look at the content of the catechism further corroborates the idea that Petit intends it to be more than a simple exposition of fundamental doctrine and that refutation of heresy is an underlying aim. In his discussion on the virtue of faith, for example, he insists that the faith which leads to salvation must be a living faith, "...*vive par bonnes oeuvres, en gardant les commandemens de Dieu, avoir les vertuz, faire oeuvres justes & dignes de loier, car la foy sans oeuvres est*

---

[120] Francis Higman, "Premières réponses," p. 364.

morte."[121] Is this merely a statement of the Church's traditional teaching on the necessary union of faith and works? Or is not more precisely meant to be a direct rebuttal of the Lutheran doctrine of justification by faith alone? Although neither Luther nor his doctrine of justification are mentioned here, it is difficult to imagine that Petit's insistence on the necessity of "living faith" for salvation has no connection at all with the position taken by the German Reformer. What we have here is a subtle, disguised form of refutation, one clothed in the trappings of catechetical instruction, but a refutation nonetheless. Thus, regardless of whether or not there is a formal connection between *Le viat de salut* and the *Oraison*, Petit's small catechism seems to be more than a basic instruction in the faith. As the above passage on faith and works indicates, *Le viat* is at the same time a covert response to at least certain doctrines of the Reformation. The mere fact of its being in the vernacular and being directly aimed at the ordinary lay person is another indication of Petit's intention to preserve the faithful from error by providing simple and solid instruction. Yet, it remains the sole attempt by a French Dominican prior to the beginning of Pierre Doré's career to provide an exposition or defense of orthodox doctrine which is aimed at the laity.

It seems, then, that the French Dominicans on the whole made little effort in the initial years of the Reformation to respond to the new heresy, at least in their writings. As it so happens, a surprisingly large portion of them were actually won over to the other side. Of the over one hundred Dominicans to be found in Robert Sauzet's compilation of mendicant religious who played a significant role in France during the period of 1480-1560, a solid third of them entered the ranks of the Reformed. Among the more famous of this group was Aimé Maigret. A disciple of Pieter Crockaert and contemporary of Francisco de Vitoria, Maigret was unquestionably one of the bright lights among the students at S. Jacques at the beginning of the sixteenth century. He produced a commentary on Aristotle's *De coelo et mundo* and the *De generatione et corruptione* in 1514 and 1519

---

[121] *Le viat*, n.p.

respectively. However, the promise he shone as a potential scholastic philosopher and theologian was never realized, for shortly after receiving his doctorate in 1520, he began to attract notice as a result of his less than orthodox preaching. His sermons at Lyon during Lent of 1524 and his sermon at Grenoble for the feast of St. Mark that same year led to serious accusations against him and to a formal investigation by the Faculty of Theology which took up several meetings in the early months of 1525. A few months before the Faculty began its deliberations, Maigret had his Grenoble sermon published in which he compared the vows of religious life and other penitential practices such as fasting and abstinence to a continuation of the Old Law whereby men were taught to seek salvation in themselves rather than by faith in God.[122] According to Fragonard, this publication gives him the distinction of actually being the first French Dominican to publish in the vernacular.[123] Both the Lyon sermons and the St. Mark sermon were censured by the Faculty and the unrepentant friar's name was soon to appear on the Faculty's lists of heretics.[124] Little is known of what happened to him after the censures, but he is believed to have taken refuge in Germany and to have died within a few years.

Many friars who, like Maigret, received condemnations for promoting heretical doctrine in their homilies, not only sought refuge in places such as Geneva or Strasbourg, where the new churches were well established, but continued then to minister as preachers of the Reform. Indeed, it seems that mendicant friars were among the most eager recipients and propagators of the new ideas.[125] Though perhaps the most famous Dominican to preach the Reform was the German, Martin Bucer, a good portion of his lesser-known French brethren also did much to further the aims of both Lutheranism and Calvinism, and that very often at the cost of their lives. However, unlike Bucer, who in

---

[122] This summary is taken from the entry on Maigret in BR, p. 293.
[123] See Marie-Madeleine Fragonard, "Guillaume Pepin," *Mémoire Dominicaine* 12 (1998/1), p. 49.
[124] His name appears on the lists of both the 10th and 15th of December, 1526 as well as that of the 16th of January, 1527. See BR, p. 295.
[125] See Higman, *Diffusion*, pp. 170 and 194.

addition to preaching sought to propagate the new teaching through the printed word as well, very few of the former French Dominicans seem to have been concerned with publication at all. In this respect, they resembled more their orthodox brethren who, as we have seen, were rather reticent to make use of the printing press in order to respond to the spread of Reformed theology.

But while the written response to heresy was rather weak, it must be acknowledged that the French Dominicans did not fail to fulfill their traditional function as watchdogs of the faith, particularly in the role of inquisitor. Guillaume Petit served as Inquisitor General of France long before the Lutheran outbreak, receiving the appointment from the General Chapter of 1507.[126] In the critical years following Luther's excommunication, the friars Valentin Lievin, Thomas Laurent, and Matthieu Ory all held the position of Inquisitor General in succession. Several other Dominicans served as regional inquisitors throughout the kingdom. Since the principal task of the inquisitor was normally to examine written propositions of those suspected of heresy, it is understandable that they would not have had much time to devote to a more pro-active defense of the faith by engaging in writing themselves. One of the notable exceptions to this general rule is Ory who produced a small treatise defending the use of images as well as a more extensive response to heretical doctrines in his *Alexipharmacum* (1544).[127] An even more prolific writer was the inquisitor of Toulouse, Esprit Rotier, who produced nine works between 1548 and 1563.[128] By and large, however, the Dominican inquisitors restricted themselves to rooting out heresy in the tribunal rather than addressing the erroneous teaching through the more public forum of publication.

From all that has preceded, one might get the impression that the French Dominicans in the early sixteenth century did not publish much at all, but this is

---

[126] MOPH, 9, p. 67.

[127] The full title is *F. Matthaei Ory dominicanae familiae theologi haeretice pravitatis per Gallias inquisitoris, summique pontificis a poenitentibus, ad haeresum redivivas affectiones Alexipharmacum.*

[128] See Sauzet, *Réguliers*, p. 214.

not the case. Farge's study of the Paris doctors of theology reveals some important statistics to the contrary. According to his findings, a quarter of the friars who were Paris graduates between 1500 and 1536 published at least one work, thus matching the 25% of secular masters in the same category.[129] The pre-eminence of the Dominicans in publishing activity is even more accentuated when they are compared to their fellow religious. In this contest, they account for 36% of all the religious masters who published at this time, more than double the Carmelites who are the next highest group at 17%.[130] Finally, the Dominican doctors wrote 71% of the titles published by all religious graduates in this same thirty-six year period—a total of ninety-seven titles by thirteen different authors.[131] A closer look behind these impressive statistics, however, reveals that the Dominican predominance is due in large part to the work of Pierre Doré. He alone accounts for a full third of the literary production by the Dominicans. What is more, if we take away the Spaniard Francisco de Vitoria's contribution of twelve titles to the total, our concern here being principally with the output of the French friars, then Doré's contribution becomes even more significant in relation to that of his confrères.

Aside from the few polemical works in Latin discussed earlier, the Dominican literary output in France prior to Doré's career is limited mainly to scholastic commentaries, for which Crockaert and Maigret are principally responsible, and the published sermons of Guillaume Pépin.[132] Pépin in fact was such a renowned preacher that it was commonly said at the time, "he does not know how to preach who does not know how to do it like Pépin."[133] According to Farge's statistics in the *Biographical Register*, the preacher's fourteen titles saw a total of eighty-eight printings, some well into the seventeenth century. While

---

[129] See Farge, "Dominicains," p. 26.
[130] See Table 24 in Farge, *Orthodoxy*, p. 105.
[131] Ibid.
[132] For a discussion of Pépin and his work, see Fragonard, "Pépin," pp. 49-62; see also BR, pp. 364-367 and Larissa Taylor, *Soldiers of Christ—Preaching in Late Medieval and Reformation France* (New York: Oxford University Press, 1992), pp. 37-51 and 210-217.
[133] "*Nescit praedicare qui nescit Pepinare.*" See DTC, p. 1185.

Pépin doubtless preached in French, his published sermons are all in Latin, indicating that they served more as models for clerics both in style and content rather than as devotional or instructional literature for the laity. The Reformation hardly figures in these sermons simply because, as Fragonard has pointed out, most of them were published prior to 1520 and thus before the outbreak of Lutheranism. Pépin's primary influence on the laity seems to have been in fostering Marian devotion, particularly the praying of the rosary, through his preaching.[134]

What emerges then from this brief overview of the French Dominicans in the early sixteenth century is that although their literary output significantly surpassed that of their fellow religious, only a tiny portion was devoted to refuting the new teaching of the Reformers, and, with the exception of Petit's *Le viat de salut*, none of it was meant for lay consumption. It is against this backdrop that the significance of Pierre Doré's literary career emerges. Not only is he largely responsible for the Dominican predominance in number of titles published as compared to other religious but he is also the first French Dominican to seriously respond to Reformation doctrine both through the printed word and in the vernacular. Perhaps using Petit's catechism as a model, he devotes much of his work to basic instruction in the faith, though his writings include much more advanced theology than what is found in *Le viat de salut*. But unlike Petit, Doré does not hesitate to engage in more open confrontation with the Reformers in his several polemical works. Although some of his confrères preceded him in terms of written polemics, Doré is the first to take his case directly to the laity by virtually abandoning the Latin language. It is he who ushers in an era among his fellow Dominicans of a more active defense of orthodoxy as that seen in the works of the inquisitor Rotier, the preaching and writings of Étienne Paris, auxiliary bishop of Rouen, and the fiery preaching of Pierre Divolé. For all intents and purposes, the writings of Pierre Doré represent the first serious

---

[134] Ibid.

response among the Dominicans in France to the exhortations of the general chapters in the 1520s and 1530s to combat the errors of the Reformation not only in preaching but also through the printed text.

Chapter 2
AN OVERVIEW OF DORÉ'S WORKS

It has already been pointed out that Pierre Doré stands out among his colleagues on the Faculty of Theology and also among his fellow Dominicans as a prolific writer whose work was specifically directed to educating the laity concerning the theological errors of the day and stirring up their hearts to a more fervent devotional life. The purpose here is to give an overview of Doré's writings that will provide the context for a closer examination in subsequent chapters of some of the key themes he returns to over and over again. First of all, just a brief look at his literary career reveals some impressive figures. In the thirty-two years between 1537 and his death in 1569 he produced at least thirty-five known works or an average of more than one per year! While that in itself is no small accomplishment, the total becomes even more impressive when one takes a closer look at the dates of publication. Here we see that Doré's most prolific years were actually in the decade between 1540 and 1550. Almost two-thirds of his works were written in that period alone, with the most intense activity occurring between 1544 and 1546. After 1557, however, Doré's pen seems to have run dry, though he lived on for another twelve years.[135] In reality then, his entire corpus was produced in a very intense twenty-year period.

---

[135] Although *Le second livre des divins benefices* was first published in 1569 (see Appendix 1) just prior to Doré's death, it was actually written much earlier as attested to by the *Extraict du privilege du Roy* printed at the beginning of the text wherein Henry II gives permission to have the

These statistics might certainly be much less impressive if it were shown that most of Doré's works were but brief tracts or devotional handbooks. While a few of the works do indeed match that description, the majority fall under a different category. Though the books themselves are usually small in size and format, a significant portion of them are quite thick between the covers. In fact many of them are several hundred pages long. The works of Doré are not for the most part short manuals, rather they are substantial treatments of a given subject. Clearly this was man who loved to write! But the sheer volume also indicates a sense of purpose motivating the author, a vocation if you will. A closer look now at the general character of Doré's work will help to throw more light on this sense of vocation that propelled him.

The Works and Subsequent Editions

Before examining the principal characteristics of Doré's writings, an accurate catalog of the works and their subsequent editions must first be established. In the historiography which already exists on Pierre Doré, only two works have attempted to provide as complete a listing as possible of the "Doréan" corpus and the editions which followed: the *Scriptores* of Quétif and Échard and much more recently Farge's *Biographical Register of Paris Doctors*.[136] It has already been noted that the enumeration of titles varies slightly in each work, with the Dominican bibliographers counting thirty-six separate titles while Farge counts only thirty-four. Another difference is that Farge, making use of various other bibliographical sources, lists a number of subsequent editions that are not found in the *Scriptores* listing. My own enumeration of Doré's works at thirty-

---

book published. The permission is dated 10 April 1551. Why it was not actually published until much later is unclear.
[136] Higman's *Piety and the People* should also be mentioned here as an important bibliographical source for Doré's writings. Unfortunately, the limited scope of the study, from 1511 to 1551, means that a number of Doré's works and editions are necessarily omitted from his list.

77

five volumes involves more than simply omitting a title from the Quétif-Échard bibliography and adding one to Farge's list. In a few instances, for example, I have listed as separate works titles that both Quétif-Échard and Farge count as a single work. Presumably their rationale in doing so was that the works in question were bound together. My own rationale for listing them separately is that although bound together, they nevertheless are different works with their own proper subject matter. In other cases, I have decided for various reasons to be explained shortly to omit certain titles from my count, most often because the works in question seem of too minor a significance. These titles are however still listed as an addendum of Appendix 1 for the sake of providing as complete a catalog as possible of Doré's literary activity. Finally, my research has brought to light both a previously unknown work and several previously unknown editions of other works. A more precise and detailed discussion of all the variations is thus in order here.

The first major difference to be noted in the listing I provide (see Appendix 1, p. 269) is the existence of a work prior to *Les voyes de paradis*, which until now was considered Doré's first work, the initial edition being that of the Lyonnaise publisher François Just in 1537. Our knowledge of this first edition of *Les voyes* is based primarily on the mention of it made by Quétif and Échard, as no extant copies are presently to be found. However, in Doré's next work, *Les allumettes du feu divin* (1538), a surprising piece of information jumps out from the text. Here, Doré calls to the reader's attention a small tract which he wrote several years earlier, "*Je pense que as veu mon compendieux & petit traicté que ay intitulé **La devise d'ung noble cueur, assis en Pierre de Vertu**, de long temps imprimé a Paris quand y faisois mon cours en theologie.*"[137] Curiously, not one of Doré's bibliographers ever mentions the existence of this little tract. Yet

---

[137] *Les allumettes du feu divin pour faire ardre les cueurs humains en l'amour de Dieu: Où sont declairez les principaux articles et mysteres de la passion de nostre Sauveur & Redempteur Jesus Christ* (Paris: n.p., 1538), fol. xxxi r°. **[Paris, BA—8° T 7367]**.

according to the Dominican's own testimony, it pre-dates what has always been considered his proto-work, *Les voyes de paradis*.

When exactly *La devise d'ung noble cueur* was first printed is difficult to determine, but from the indications given by Doré, it would seem to have been while he was apprentice-teaching as *biblicus* at S. Jacques, thus sometime between 1525 and 1528. Until recently, I believed that this brief mention in *Les allumettes* was the only proof we had of the existence of this earlier work.[138] The silence of the bibliographers, particularly Quétif and Échard, concerning this text seemed to me an indication that even in their day, no extant copies were to be found. However, I have since discovered that *La devise* is bound with the 1543 edition of *La caeleste pensée*. Consisting of only a few pages, it is a very brief explanation in verse of what Doré proposes as a heraldic emblem of the Christian life. Though not a book or a major work in the strict sense, the fact that it nevertheless appeared in print several years before any of his other writings has led me to include it at the head of the bibliographical listing. Furthermore, despite its brevity, it contains several of the major themes that appear in the subsequent works. The significance of *La devise d'ung noble cueur* as a summary and "herald" of Doré's later thought will be discussed later in Chapter 5.

Even with the addition of *La devise* to the bibliography, my enumeration of Doré's titles, it will be noted, still falls short of the thirty-six found in the *Scriptores*. Omitted are the following four titles that Quétif and Échard mention at the very end of their bibliography: 28. *Les soupirs de l'ame fidele*, 31. *L'esperance assuree*, 33. *L'oraison du profete David extraite du psalme* LXXXVI, and 34. *Oeuvres de penitence*.[139] No publication data is provided for these titles, except that the first two were published in Paris. Farge's list categorizes these very same titles as unpublished works.[140] The lack of accurate information coupled with the fact that no other bibliographers make any mention of them

---

[138] In my article, "Pierre Doré, écrivain spirituel et théologien des laïcs," *Memoire Dominicaine* 12 (1998/1): p. 40, I mistakenly claim that there are no extant copies of the work.
[139] QE, p. 205.
[140] See BR, p. 142.

gives the impression that these works were of minor significance and that probably no extant copies were to be found even in the eighteenth century if indeed they were ever published. Thus I have chosen not to include them with the principal works but have merely listed them as an addendum.

Another minor difference is that I list *La premiere partie des collations royales* and *La seconde partie des collations royales* as two separate works whereas Quétif and Échard list them as one only. My reason for doing so is that both were published separately in 1546 before being bound together in a single edition later during the same year. Also each work has its own dedication, albeit to members of the same family. The first part is dedicated to Duke Claude de Lorraine while the second part is dedicated to his wife, Antoinette de Bourbon. The fact of two different dedications and the separate publications both serve to justify a separate listing of the first and second parts of *Les collations royales*.

In terms of the differences between my list and Farge's, he too classifies the first and second parts of *Les collations royales* as one work rather than two. Also, I have omitted his inclusion of a poem of Doré (1544) found in a book of François de Sagan, *Le triumphe de grace et prerogative d'innocence originelle sur la conception et trespas de la Vierge esleu mere de Dieu*, simply because it is but a minor component in someone else's work.[141] Finally, Farge lists *La passion de Jesus selon les quatres evangelistes* as a separate work with a publication date of 1566, but it is in reality a type of appendix to the *Dyalogue instructoire des chrestiens*. Even were it published separately in 1566—and to my knowledge no extant copy of that particular edition has been found—it has been attached to the *Dyalogue* in all its different editions since 1538. Therefore, I chose not to include it as a separate title in my own catalog.

In addition to listing Doré's books in chronological order, Appendix 1 (p. 269) also gives the number of subsequent editions for each work along with information concerning translations. A more detailed presentation is provided in

---

[141] See Ibid., p. 141.

Appendix 2 (p. 271) where full publication data of the subsequent editions appears under each title. The reader, upon examination of Appendix 2, will notice that I have also listed the libraries where a given edition is located. Several editions, however, are simply followed by a reference to a bibliographical source. Such an entry means that an extant copy of this edition has yet to be found. Thus, the statistics on the number of editions given in Appendix 1 are based in part on the information provided by previous bibliographers of Doré. Although it would have been wonderful to find copies of all the missing editions, such research is a bit like looking for needles in a haystack, not to mention the fact that certain editions may have disappeared completely in the nearly five centuries since they were published.[142] Nevertheless, the statistics based on the copies that have been found coupled with the reliable information of different bibliographical sources allow us to draw some general conclusions concerning Pierre Doré's literary career.

First of all, the total number of subsequent editions is itself impressive— seventy-nine in all according to my count.[143] Of this number, fifty-four are within Doré's lifetime while the remaining fifteen are published after his death in 1569, even well into the seventeenth century. In fact, if Farge's information on this point is correct, the last edition, a Latin translation of *Les allumettes du feu divin*, seems to have been as late as 1691! This very late re-publication is an anomaly, however, and the real end of the editions comes about eighty years earlier, around 1610. Nevertheless, it is clear that Doré's popularity and relevance as an author extended beyond his lifetime. If his works did not go on to be recognized as classics, some of them at least continued to satisfy a certain demand in the reading public.

It perhaps comes as no surprise that the works which continued to be edited after Doré's death were not his polemical treatises, but rather his

---

[142] For example, both the libraries at Douai and Arras once possessed editions of Doré's works, but these were tragically destroyed as a result of the Allied bombings during the Second World War.

[143] Farge, *Orthodoxy*, p. 102 gives only fifty-two subsequent editions for Doré.

devotional writings. While the polemical *L'arche de l'alliance nouvelle* and the *Anti-Calvin* were both re-published once in Doré's lifetime, they do not figure among the books that continued to be sought out as France suffered through the fratricidal religious wars of the end of the century and finally arrived at the peace through toleration established by the Edict of Nantes in 1598. Rather it is Doré as spiritual writer who continued to be appreciated and sought out in the changed circumstances. If he is an important figure historically speaking for his anti-Protestant polemics, his more enduring legacy is as a spiritual theologian with *Les allumettes du feu divin, Les voyes de paradis, Le college de sapience, L'image de vertu,* and *La tourtrelle de viduité* being the principal works that continued to be edited after his death.

A closer look at the statistics to determine which were Doré's best-selling books reveals that by far the most popular were his earlier works. In fact, the first six all went through at least five editions, with *Les voyes de paradis* and *Les allumettes du feu divin* outstripping the others with a total of sixteen and fourteen editions respectively. Of these six best-sellers, all continued to be published after Doré's death except for the *Dyalogue instructoire* whose last edition came in 1545 and *La deploration de la vie humaine* whose last edition came in 1561. Although Doré went on to produce another twenty-seven works after the initial six, twelve of these were never re-published and another ten were edited only once. Yet, towards the very end of Doré's literary career, two works break this streak and can be considered the best-sellers of his later years. They are *Le livre de la victoire de toutes tribulations* with five editions and *La tourtrelle de viduité* with two. The statistics here, however, are a bit deceiving for the former is really a book of prayers translated from Latin into French by Doré and is not an original work. Nonetheless, the latter, a spiritual guide for widows, is original and resembles the early Doré in its devotional aspect. Again, the best-sellers all point to the fact that it is Doré as spiritual theologian who is most appreciated by the reading public and not Doré the polemicist.

That being said, a good number of the works that were never re-published or were edited only once are also of a devotional character. Is there any reason why they did not achieve the same popularity as the others? This is certainly a difficult question to answer for it is not as if we can conduct a poll of Doré's reading public and so discover why these writings did not prove as appealing as the others. Rather than speculate on this matter, the more important task for now is to focus on why a good portion of the Dominican theologian's work was in fact much in demand.

What then are the principal characteristics of the "Doréan" corpus that make it a significant contribution to the literary production of Reformation-era France? What can be said in general concerning the thirty-five major works published by Pierre Doré between the years 1537 and 1557? What kind of books are they? Whom did he have in mind when writing them, if anyone or any group in particular? To whom were they dedicated? What was the impetus for writing what he did? Is there any kind of plan uniting some or all of the works? What are some characteristics of Doré's style? What are some of the major recurring themes in his writings? These are some of the questions which this study will attempt to answer, first in a general way in this chapter, and then more specifically by taking a closer look at some of the major works in the chapters that follow.

Theological Instruction with an Appeal to the Heart

After characterizing Doré as a spiritual writer, it would seem to follow that I would describe his writings principally as works of piety or devotional works. Farge himself classifies twenty-five of his titles in precisely such terms.[144] But while such a broad category is fine for the sake of formulating statistics, as was

---

[144] See Farge, *Orthodoxy*, p. 102.

Farge's intent, it nevertheless fails to capture the more complex character of several of Doré's books which on one level are most certainly devotional in character and yet on another level are much more. At play in virtually all of his works is a desire not only to edify, inspire, and set aflame in the heart a personal devotion to Christ but also to instruct in the faith and nourish the intellect of the reader with solid theology, albeit on a fundamental level. There is an appeal to both heart and mind, to the emotional as well as the rational.

Despite the maxim that one should never judge a book by its cover, or even title, Doré's rather long and descriptive titles nevertheless serve to give the reader a very good idea of the content. The use of image and metaphor abounds. For example, Doré seeks to set on fire the hearts of the faithful with the matches of divine love in *Les allumettes du feu divin pour faire ardre les cueurs humains en l'amour de Dieu* (1538), to increase their thirst for God like the deer of Psalm 42 that longs for running streams in *Le cerf spirituel, exprimant le sainct desir de l'ame d'estre avec son Dieu* (1544), and to inspire them to virtue by looking to the Virgin Mary as model in *L'image de vertu demonstrant la perfection et saincte vie de la bienheuree vierge Marie, mere de Dieu* (1540). Other titles, while retaining the use of image and metaphor, reveal a more instructive character as for example *Les voyes de paradis que a enseignees nostre benoist Saulveur Jesus en son evangile* (1537), where Doré explains the Beatitudes, or *Le college de sapience, fondé en l'université de vertu, auquel cest rendue escolliere Magdelaine disciple et apostole de Jesus* (1539), where he invites the reader to learn discipleship in imitation of Mary Magdalene through a more intimate knowledge of Christ. But whether the emphasis of the title seems more devotional or more instructive, the content of the book almost always remains a balance of the two.

Still within the broader category of devotional works are a number of other titles which indicate a more practical concern, a sort of "how to" of the spiritual life. Here Doré's instruction covers the whole range from the spiritual life in general to more specific guidelines for a particular group. Examples of the former are the advice he gives on the proper way to pray for the gifts of the Holy Spirit in *La caeleste pensée de graces divines arrousée ou sont declairez les sept dons du sainct esprit & la maniere de les demander à Dieu* (1543) or a teaching on the contemplative life in *La passe-solitaire à tous amateurs de Dieu, & vie spirituelle, ou contemplative, donnée pour instruction* (1547). A good example of the latter is an instruction on the particular duties and obligations of Christian widowhood in *La tourtrelle de viduité enseignant les vefves comment elles doivent vivre en leur estat, & consolant en leurs adversitez, aussi les orphelins* (1557). Several works focus on how to lead a good Christian life and prepare for a good Christian death, for example *La deploration de la vie humaine, avec la disposition a dignement recevoir le S. Sacrement, & mourir en bon catholique* (1541), *Le livre des divins benefices, enseignant la maniere de les recongnoistre, avec l'information de bien vivre, et la consolation des affligez* (1544) and *La vie & la mort chrestienne, des epistres de S. Paul* (1556). Finally, some of the "how to" books deal with the proper preparation for the reception of the sacraments particularly the Eucharist in *La deploration de la vie humaine* and *La meditation devote du bon Chrestien sus le sainct sacrifice de la Messe* (1544), and the sacrament of penance in *La croix de penitence, enseignant la forme de soyconfesser* (1545).

If there is an instructive element to be found in all of Doré's devotional works, nevertheless the predominant characteristic remains the desire to stir up a more fervent love for Christ in the heart of the believer. However, other works do reveal more of a catechetical character. The goal in these books tends much more towards doctrinal instruction than moral formation. Nowhere does this aspect come across more clearly than in the *Dyalogue instructoire des chrestiens en la foy, esperance & amour en Dieu* (1538). Following the traditional format of a basic question-and-answer catechism, the *Dyalogue* nonetheless in many places offers instruction far beyond the fundamentals of the Catholic faith, taking on even the burning issues of the day—issues like the nature of faith, justification, grace and merit. These same issues are dealt with again in a much later work, *Dialogue de la justification chrestienne entre nostre saulveur Jesus & la samaritaine* (1554), this time not with theological definitions but with a biblical illustration of the encounter between Jesus and the Samaritan woman at the well as supporting the Catholic understanding of justification. The catechetical aspect remains, only the manner of presenting the doctrinal instruction has changed.

Finally, there are what can be called Doré's polemical treatises, works whose explicit purpose is to refute the doctrinal errors of the Reformers. As was pointed out in the Introduction, the goal here is not to engage the Reformers themselves in a theological debate, but rather to explain Catholic doctrine for the simple lay person, particularly those points which the Reformers have called into question, lest the unknowing believer fall prey to heresy. The *Dyalogue instructoire* is already a harbinger of this particular category. In fact, Doré proclaims in the opening paragraph that his *Dyalogue* is a response to a catechism written by the Bernese pastor Gaspard Megander in 1536, a French translation of which made an appearance in Lyon the following year. A more definitive step towards polemics is taken by Doré in 1543 with the publication of one of his few Latin works, *Paradoxa...ad profligandas haereses*, a listing of one hundred false propositions of heretics both ancient and contemporary and how they are refuted. The explicitly polemical treatises in French make their appearance just prior to 1550 and the titles leave no doubt as to their purpose: *L'arche de l'alliance nouvelle, et testament de nostre Saulveur Jesus Christ, contenant la manne de son precieux corps,* **contre tous sacramentaires heretiques** [emphasis mine] (1549), *Le nouveau testament d'amour de nostre pere Jesuchrist, signé de son sang. Autrement son dernier sermon, faict apres la cene, avec sa passion,* **ou sont confutées plusieurs heresies** [emphasis mine] (1550), and finally *Anti-Calvin, contenant deux defenses catholiques de la verité du sainct Sacrement et digne sacrifice de l'autel,* **contre certains faux escrits sortis de la boutique des**

sacramentaires calvinistes, heretiques [emphasis mine], *mis au vent et semez par certains lieux de ce roiaume, au scandale des fidelles et pusilles* (1551).

As Fragonard has noted in her study, there is a progression in Doré's polemics from a sort of global anti-Lutheranism to a more personalized attack against Calvin.[145] This is small wonder considering the fact that Calvin's *Institutes* made its appearance in French ten years earlier in 1541, although it seems that only a limited number of copies of this first edition were printed with dissemination occurring primarily in French-speaking areas of present-day Switzerland and not in France where censorship was already well in place.[146] Two more French editions appeared in 1545 and 1551 (both translations of previously revised Latin editions in 1543 and 1550). It would seem that censorship notwithstanding, enough copies of these editions were making their way into France so that their influence was being felt. Doré's *Anti-Calvin* is in fact a witness to the growing dissemination of Calvinist thought among the literate laity in the mid-sixteenth century.

We should note here that, with the exception of the *Paradoxa*, the more polemical works of the "Doréan" corpus make their appearance fairly late, well into the second half of Doré's writing career, which for all intents and purposes ends in 1557. However, this is not to say that a polemical spirit is absent from his earlier works. Indeed, it is there from the very beginning. In a letter to his readers which is found at the end of one of the 1538 editions of *Les voyes de paradis*, Doré makes his intentions quite clear:

> *Voyant que les chirurgiens & medicins espirituelz, cest assavoir les bons docteurs latins, ont donné la medecine contre la playe, ainsi quelle estoit venue, & ont escript en langaige latin livres salutaires contre l'heretique doctrine, dogmatizee par plusieurs faulx prophetes, eloquens et latins. Pareillement ma semblé bon & convenable, donner en francoys quelques bons livres, comme anthidore contre les pestiferes enseignemens qu'on peult prendre es meschans livres, qui en divers lieux se impriment en langue vulgaire, qui est chose trespernicieuse, & qui fort endommaige la*

---

[145] See Fragonard, "Publications." Forthcoming.
[146] See the Introduction by John T. McNeill to Calvin's *Institutes of the Christian Religion* (Philadelphia: Westminster Press, 1967), p. xxxvi.

Republique chrestienne: a quoy ne puis remedier (comme desireroye) sinon que en baillant le contrepoison, c'est a dire livre utile au simple peuple, lequel ne discorde a nostre foy, qu'il fault suivre, & non pas nostre esprit.[147]

Like the great Latin Fathers of former times who devoted their energies to propagating true doctrine in response to heresy, Doré sees his mission in a similar light. There is no ambiguity at all in his sentiments. His writings are meant to be an antidote against the poison of heresy and the plague of false teaching being disseminated through the printed word in the vernacular. But although the polemical element is present from the very beginning, the early works are not strictly speaking refutations in the same way as are the three that make their appearance around 1550. Aside from the occasional caustic references to the heretics, the early writings remain primarily devotional in character. Their explicit aim is to edify, not to refute. Yet at the same time, they can be said to form part of Doré's overall strategy of heresy-fighting in the sense that the best way to keep believers in the fold is to encourage their personal relationship with Christ as a truly Catholic ideal rather than allowing the Reformers to lay sole claim to this type of devotion. More will be said on this point in Chapter 5.

A few works that do not fit neatly into any of the categories mentioned above still need to be mentioned here. First of all, the first and second parts of *Les collations royales* were originally a set of Lenten conferences that Doré preached to his patrons, the duke and duchess of Guise, in the spring of 1546. It is one of the few examples we have, along with the homily Doré delivered in 1543 at the funeral of Admiral Philippe Chabot, of the Dominican's preaching. In *Les cantiques dechantees à l'entrée du Treschrestien Roy Henri second de ce nom, & de la royne de France en la ville de Paris, & le jour de la procession celebre, faicte par eulx en ladicte ville* (1548), we have a sampling of Doré's hymn-writing and poetic talents, or lack thereof. As the following verse on the

---

[147] *Les voyes de paradis que a enseignees nostre benoist Saulveur Jesus en son evangile, pour la reduction du povre pecheur*, (n.p., 1538). [**Amiens, BM—Rés. 143 A**].

Eucharist taken from a hymn entitled *Trene & elegie pour les heretiques sacramentaires qui sourdent en ce temps calamiteux* reveals, *Les cantiques* is less to be appreciated for its poetic quality than for the insights it provides into Doré's complete disdain for the Reformers who are characterized here as dogs and thieves:

> *Le sacrament si precieux*
> *De noz peres tant veneré*
> *Du corp de Jesus glorieux*
> *Las à ce jour n'est reveré*
> *Car les chiens*
> *Lutheriens*
> *Tous plains d'erreur*
> *Par grand mespris*
> *Larrons l'ont pris*
> *O grand horreur.*[148]

Finally, as we have already seen, the *Oraison panegyrique* (1550), a eulogy in honor of the deceased Duke of Guise, Claude de Lorraine, provides much insight into Doré's very close relationship with this important political family. Doré's admiration for his departed patron and friend is clear throughout as, for example, when he likens Claude's zeal for the faith to that of the Old Testament king, Josiah, who labored to restore observance of the Mosaic Law in ancient Judah. And as the prophet Jeremiah mourned the death of this faithful king of old, so now Doré laments the passing on of a new Josiah:

> *Jeremie sainctifié prophete, tu lamentas jadis la mort du bon roy Josias, grand solliciteur pour Dieu & de son honneur procureur...Pourquoy donc ne deploreray un second Josias, decedé, fervent zelateur de la loy divine, & la foy, & mes deplorations ne seront elles repliquées a jamais?*[149]

If the *Oraison*, overly effusive in its praise of the deceased duke and portraying him in the most heroic of terms, cannot be looked to as an objective portrait of

---

[148] *Les cantiques dechantees à l'entrée du Treschrestien Roy Henry second de ce nom* (Paris: Jean Ruelle, 1549), fol. Ciii v°-Ciiii r°. **[Washington, LC—PQ 1628.L24A67]**.

[149] *Oraison*, fol. 18r°-v°.

Claude de Lorraine, it nevertheless does provide important glimpses of Doré's own character and personality. It is one of the few places where the spiritual guide, ever-ready to reveal the truths of the faith to his readers, reveals something more of himself and of his emotional links to the Guise family. Further insight into the personal character of our friar can be gleaned from the dedications that accompany most of his works.

The Dedications

While there is no question that Doré wrote with a general reading public in mind, much of his work was nevertheless produced at the request of a specific person, almost always a noblewoman or nun. In fact, it is not at all an exaggeration to say that women played a very significant causal role in the coming-to-be of the "Doréan" corpus. Were it not for their requests for spiritual nourishment, Pierre Doré might never have become one of the most prolific authors of the period particularly in terms of his devotional works. Given his fiery zeal for the faith, he no doubt still would have made use of the printing press to combat the new ideas of the Reformers, but the language of choice for his polemical treatises would perhaps have been Latin rather than French. The *Paradoxa* might have been the standard for his other works rather than being the exception in a practically all-vernacular corpus. Unquestionably, it is women who determined the principal characteristics of Doré's works as being devotional and written in French.

A brief look at the dedications (see Appendix 4, p. 289) reveals some very interesting information concerning this female influence in Doré's literary production as well as in regard to his relationship with the upper classes of sixteenth-century French society. While not all of his works have a dedication, of the twenty-four that do, more than two-thirds are dedicated to women. Only five are dedicated to men and two have a general dedication to all Christians or to the

Catholic reader. More specifically, the few men and the women who are the recipients of these dedications are people of very high standing. Among the notable men are the kings, Francis I and his son Henry II, the cardinal archbishop of Bourges, François de Tournon, and, as to be expected, Doré's patron Claude de Lorraine. Noticeably absent are dedications to fellow religious or colleagues on the Faculty of Theology. The only male religious to receive a dedication is Pierre Lambert, one of Doré's confrères and a close friend from the Dominican priory at Blois. Among the women receiving dedications are several unnamed nuns as well as several more prominent women, both abbesses and countesses, who are named: Louise de Bourbon, abbess of Fontevraulx, Renée de Lorraine, daughter of Duke Claude and abbess of S. Pierre in Reims, Françoise de Bouchet, countess of Montfort, Catherine de Sarrebruche, countess of Roussy, princess Marguerite, daughter of Francis I and last but not least, Queen Catherine de Medici, wife of Henry II. Doré also dedicates one work to a blood sister named Marguerite—the only family member to receive mention. However, the unquestioned winner in the dedication category is none other than Antoinette de Bourbon, duchess of Guise and wife of Claude. She receives four dedications from Doré. An unnamed devout Parisian lady receives three while all the others receive only one each. Not only is it clear that the Guise family as a whole is very dear to Doré's heart with its different members garnering a total of seven dedications, but the matron seems to be especially beloved by the friar.

When we examine which books are dedicated to whom, the following general pattern emerges. The polemical works are almost exclusively dedicated to the men while the devotional works are almost exclusively dedicated to the women, with only one or two exceptions to the rule in each case. It is Queen Catherine de Medici who is the exception in the polemical category, receiving the dedication in *Le nouveau testament d'amour*. However, the fact that she is not just any woman but the queen makes her less of an exception here because the polemical treatises are in fact all dedicated to the monarchy or to those with important connections to the royal family such as the Cardinal de Tournon to whom Doré dedicates the *Paradoxa*. Since the polemical works are part of Doré's strategy for eradicating heresy in France, it is only natural that they be principally addressed to those who are in a position to complete the job by decree of law and/or use of military force. In fact, Doré does not hesitate to remind the Most Christian Kings of France of their duty to uphold the true faith and crush all manifestations of heresy, as when he writes to Henry II:

> *C'est certainement le moyen pour corroborer ton throne & sceptre amplifier, que de zeler l'honneur de Dieu, & la foy maintenir, mettre le coeur en la loy divine, & la faire en ton royaume estroictement observer & garder, en extirpant ou corrigeant blasphemateurs du nom de Dieu, & hereticques sacramentaires.*[150]

If working for the glory of God is not incentive enough for the kings to do their Christian duty, Doré does not fail to mention here the more temporal advantages of extension of power and prestige that a firm response to heresy will doubtless bring the crown.

This appeal to the royal power for resolution of the religious question is certainly not a strategy limited to the Catholic side. Calvin himself prefaces his *Institutes of the Christian Religion* with an open letter to Francis I asking him not to be swayed by the false accusations leveled against the Reformers by their adversaries, but rather to be open to the reasonableness of the Reformers' position and to see in them loyal subjects. The tone is more apologetic than belligerent, though he does not hesitate to offer biting criticism of the unreformed Church of Rome. Yet, he never makes an appeal in this preface for royal suppression of the corrupt religion in favor of the formal establishment of the Reformed church. The plea is for toleration only. Nevertheless, the principle of seeking the favor of the crown is the same for both the opponents and proponents of the Reformation.

As regards Doré's devotional works, the Dominican friar Pierre Lambert is the exceptional male to receive a dedication in this category. From the

---

[150] Dedication to Henry II, *L'arche*, fol. Avii r°.

dedication he receives in *La meditation devote du bon chrestien*, it is clear that he was a very close friend of the theologian, one to whom Doré sent a copy of each book upon its publication. As is typical between friends, Doré reveals certain sentiments to Lambert that are not found in the other dedications, principally a sense of great apprehension over the religious situation in their country. Writing in almost apocalyptic terms he confides to his friend "*...le brouillatz est si espez & si grand, au temps present des heresies qui sourdent, que si par la force du rayon du soleil de verité supernelle n'est vaincu, il me semble que je voy le declin du monde, & le jugement approcher.*"[151] Normally optimistic that Catholic truth will in the end prevail in these dark times, Doré here seems less sure of a happy outcome. This sense of impending judgment upon the people of France for abetting heresy comes across once again in another dedication to someone who is close to his heart, his only sister Marguerite, to whom is dedicated *La croix de penitence* (1545). In this dedication, Doré speaks of various natural disasters that had occurred in recent months including an earthquake, a solar eclipse, pestilence and famine. While allowing that these events could have been nothing more than the result of forces of nature, he nevertheless more readily believes and affirms to his sister that "*...de Dieu nous sont donnez pour nous engendrer terreur & espoventement de son jugement, qui nous induise à penitence.*"[152] What we see in these two dedications to his beloved sister and to a dear friend is a frank assessment by Doré of the perils involved with the spread of heresy, which in his view is drawing God's wrath upon the French nation, along with the need for both personal and national atonement for this abominable sin.

This acute sense of the precariousness of the situation helps to explain Doré's preoccupation with the nobility and those in a position of power. As he sees it, an aristocratic class that is well-formed, both intellectually and morally, is a key to winning the battle against heterodoxy. By first of all setting a good

---

[151] Dedication to Pierre Lambert, *La meditation devote du bon Chrestien sus le sainct sacrifice de la Messe* (Paris: René Avril, 1544), fol. Avi rº. **[Paris, BSG—D 8º 6197(1) Inv. 7892 bis FA]**.

[152] Dedication to Marguerite Doré, *La croix de penitence, enseignant la forme de soyconfesser* (Paris: Jean Ruelle, 1545), fol. A vº. **[New Haven, BRBL—Me45, D730, C87]**.

example of piety and moral living, and secondly by taking up the sword of justice in defense of the faith, the nobility are a potent weapon in the battle for the allegiance of the commoners to orthodoxy. For instance, in the closing lines of the dedication to princess Marguerite, daughter of Francis I, in *La caeleste pensée* (1543), Doré strongly encourages young people to follow the example of this royal model of virtue:

> *O si telle diligence & poursuyte de vertu estoit faicte des jeunes gens, ou si telle cure avoient les parens de leurs enfans pour les faire vertueux. Certainement vice n'auroit pas son regne comme il a, & vertu flouriroit en plusieurs plus que ne faict. Je desire pour fin la jeunesse francoyse venir veoir une flourissante & resplendissante en vertu marguerite au pres des lys tresodorans, & y cueillir la coeleste pensée, laquelle en vous (o tresillustre princesse) le bon dieu conserve sans fin en sa vigueur, avec immortalité de gloire. Amen.*[153]

In a play on the princess' name, which is French for "daisy," Doré here compares her to a flower of virtue blossoming near the sweet-smelling lilies of the French royal family. He builds up to this conclusion by presenting the princess as a young woman who, under the influence of the Holy Spirit, is taken up with the study of divine law and meditation on the Word of God. Her nobility of blood is complemented by her nobility of virtue, making her an ideal to be emulated.[154]

It should be mentioned here that Doré also holds in high esteem the role to be played by a mother in modeling the life of virtue for her children. He advises a certain widow of Blois to whom he dedicates *Le college de sapience* that she should frequent often the schools of good morals and bring along with her the entire family, especially the children.[155] As the most basic unit of society, the family is the place where faith and virtue are first learned and it is the mother who

---

[153] Dedication to Princess Marguerite, *La caeleste pensée de graces divines arrousée ou sont declairez les sept dons du sainct esprit & la maniere de les demander de Dieu* (Paris: Adam Saulnier, 1543), fol. av r°-av v°. **[Bordeaux, BM—T 7106]**.

[154] Ironically, this daughter of Francis I did not turn out to be the upholder of orthodoxy which Doré had made her out to be. See Romier, *Royaume*, pp. 34-35 for a discussion of Marguerite of Savoie's sympathies towards the Reformers during the reign of her brother, Henry II.

[155] "*frequente souvent les escolles de bonnes meurs, menes y toute ta famille, conduys y tes enfans.*" Dedication to a humble servant of Jesus, *Le college*, fol. Aiii v°.

plays the primary role in this formative education of young minds and consciences. It is in light of the central role of the Christian mother in transmitting the faith to a new generation that Doré's preoccupation with addressing the spiritual needs of women should be seen. Does it not make sense that an important way of redressing the errors of the Reformation would be to first educate those responsible for the intellectual and moral formation of the new generation? Yet, what is taught in the home must also be ultimately reinforced in the larger social grouping. This brings us back then to the fact that Doré's efforts to educate in the faith are also aimed at the aristocracy. For the Dominican, it is natural and fitting that the privileged of the upper classes assume the role played by parents or more particularly the mother at home in serving as models of faith and virtue for society at large.

But the nobility have much more than an exemplary or even didactic function to fulfill in the all-important battle for souls. Comparing them to the stork, which is reputed for killing snakes—one already has an idea of how the analogy will be used—Doré unequivocally states:

> ...la cicogne est ennemie des serpens, les meurtrist & occist du bec, & les devore & mange...Je desire ceste proprieté es riches & noblez mariez, qui ont puissance & credit pour destruire les Serpens envenimez de pestifere doctrine, qui las aujourd'huy en plusieurs contrees & pays, empoisonnent les ames de leurs erreurs.[156]

As the leaders of society, the nobility have tremendous resources at their disposal for rooting out the pestilence of the Reformation: wealth, soldiers and arms, as well as moral authority, all of which can be used to impose orthodoxy. It is little wonder then that Doré uses the dedications as a way of exerting influence over the ruling class and alerting them to their mission. His goal in the personal contacts he maintains with the rich and powerful as well as in the devotional books he writes for them is to enlist them in a spiritual battle against the ancient Serpent

---

[156] *La tourtrelle de viduité enseignant les vefves comment elles doivent vivre en leur estat, & consolant en leurs adversitez, aussi les orphelins* (Arras: Guillaume de la Rivière, 1605), p. 22. **[Cambridge, HOU—FC5 D7302 557tc]**.

who no longer tempts the faithful with a piece of forbidden fruit but with a supposedly purer version of the Christian faith.

Yet, as was pointed out at the beginning of this section, Doré's plan of attack against the Reformers did not derive solely from a set of preconceived ideas in his own mind. A significant number of his works were written at the request of devout noblewomen, both religious and lay, who sought from the doctor in theology nourishment for their souls. It was to "quench the ardent thirst and vehement desire" of the countess of Montfort, Françoise de Bouchet, who wished to know the path of virtue leading to heaven that he wrote *Les voyes de paradis*. An unnamed Parisian lady received in *Le livre des divins benefices* the consolation of the Scriptures which she so ardently sought. A more specific request for a commentary on Psalm 123 by "one of the prudent virgins," sister Charlotte de Genly of the Abbey of S. Pierre in Reims, was fulfilled with the publication of *La passe-solitaire à tous amateurs de Dieu*. These are but a few examples of how women were a major inspirational force behind the devotional works of Pierre Doré.

Not only did these aristocratic women help to determine the general character of the Dominican's works, but they also were one of the primary reasons for that work being written in French rather than in the Latin of the schools. As he dedicates his book on the Virgin Mary, *L'image de vertu*, to the Countess of Roussy, Catherine de Sarrebruche, Doré announces what will come to be a recurring theme, "*Je cuidoys bien avoir paravant mis fin a toute composition en langue Francoise & vulgaire: mais vaincu de charité Chrestienne, ay encor' fait ce present livre...*"[157] At several points in his career, Doré says that he is finished with producing works in French for the unsophiscated and will instead turn his attention to more scholarly writings in Latin for a "superior order of students." Such is his message in a letter entitled

---

[157] Dedication to Catherine de Sarrebruche, *L'image de vertu demonstrant la perfection et saincte vie de la bienheuree vierge Marie, mere de dieu, par les escritures, tant de l'ancien que du nouveau Testament* (Paris: Jean Ruelle, n.d.), fol. aaiii r°. **[Paris, BS—443 E-34]**.

"Submission de l'aucteur à la disposition de l'eglise" found at the end of *Le college de sapience*, his fourth work, which concludes, "*Et a tant faiz fin a toute composition en langue Francoyse. Cest assez long temps nourry de laict, l'enfance Chrestienne, il nous fault avec l'ayde de dieu preparer plus solide viande pour les plus grans.*"[158] Yet, it is but a short while later that, won over by Christian charity, he renounces his announced plan and writes once again in French for Dame Catherine.

It seems that his continued writing in the vernacular drew criticism from some of his colleagues on the Faculty of Theology, for we find Doré having to answer objections that such work is undignified for a theologian and doctor:

> *S'eslevera possible quelque autre contre moy, disant estre indigne a homme docteur Theologien, composer livres en langue vulgaire. A quoy je responds qu'entre la parolle dicte, ou escripte, y a peu de difference. Les docteurs preschent en Francoys au commun peuple, sans reprehension. Pourquoy ce qu'est presché, qui est sain, catholique & utile, ne leur sera il baillé, esposé & bien interpreté, à fin que la lettre presche quand n'en pourra plus la parolle? Qui est mon intention en cest oeuvre.*[159]

If theologians condescend to preach to the people in the vernacular, why not preach to the same people through the written word, a word which is in fact more lasting than the passing utterances of oral communication? However, Doré is certainly not advocating here that serious theological discussion be carried on in the vernacular. Latin remains the proper language of theological science. Yet he is clearly in favor of offering basic theological instruction in the language of the people, for this in his mind is really an extension of the priestly ministry of preaching the Gospel

Ultimately, what comes across in the dedications is a real sense of compassion for "the little ones" as Doré continues to renounce over and over again his own plans to concentrate on more scholarly endeavors in favor of the

---

[158] *Le college*, fol. Niii v°.
[159] *L'image*, fol. Av r°.

requests he receives for yet another devotional book in French. In explaining the inspiration behind his sixth book, *La deploration de la vie humaine*, the theologian describes himself as a merchant who had closed his shop in the hopes of retiring to a more quiet life of contemplation. Then along comes the abbess of Fontevraulx, Louise de Bourbon, begging that the shop be re-opened so that she might learn how to prepare herself for the worthy reception of Holy Communion. The merchant goes on:

> *De ce labeur me voulant excuser, par autant que mon huys avois desia fermé, & m'estois enclos au secret de mon estude, reposant sur la lecture des sainctz docteurs Latins, n'as cessé, ainsi que sage vierge, ayant ta lampe de charité ardente en la main, frapper souvent à ma porte, en escriant à mon oreille: Desnirez vous le pain aux petis?*[160]

Like the nagging widow of the Gospel (cf. Luke 18:1-8) who wins a favorable hearing from the judge wearied of her complaints, the countess prevails over the theologian desirous of quiet contemplation to renounce his retirement out of pity for the little ones. Although the nun's request does take Doré away from much cherished study, contemplation, and composition of works in Latin, he is clearly moved by the plea on behalf of the theologically unsophisticated who are hungering for the bread of true doctrine. If he is initially reluctant to continue writing in the vernacular, the oft-repeated requests of certain important women convince him of the absolute necessity of providing devotional literature in the language of the people and of thereby fighting the Reformers with their own weapons.

---

[160] Dedication to Louise de Bourbon, *La deploration de la vie humaine, avec la disposition à dignement recevoir le S. Sacrement, & mourir en bon catholique* (Paris: Nicolas Barbou, 1541), fol. Aii r°-v°. **[Paris, BSG—D 8° 6428(2) Rés. Inv. 8142]**.

Doré's Sources and Pedagogical Methods

So far we have seen that the majority of Doré's works, while basically devotional in character, at the same time fit into a much broader program of theological instruction for the ordinary faithful in response to the new teaching of the Reformers being propagated both in the pulpit and on the printed page. Some of his works are more explicitly polemical; others are of a more catechetical nature. A brief examination of the dedications has also shown the important role played by certain religious and laywomen of noble birth in inspiring a good portion of Doré's writing. But if they helped to determine the predominantly devotional character of his work with their requests for spiritual nourishment, it was he himself who perceived the pressing need for a more effective written response to Reformation theology. His idea was simple: concentrate on forming the ruling class, instruct them in the truths of the faith, encourage them to live a virtuous life that others might emulate, and call them to arms in defense of orthodoxy. For better or worse, this was Doré's program for restoring unity of faith to a religiously divided France.

It remains to be seen how the Paris theologian sought to express his message in his extensive writings. Is there a discernable pedagogical method that comes through in the different works? What are the principal sources on which he relies? How does his intellectual formation influence the particular approach he uses in his own instruction? A general overview of the "Doréan" corpus would not be complete without a brief examination now of his methods and sources.

In regard to sources, the most striking aspect any reader of Doré encounters is the absolute primacy given to Scripture throughout his work. As will be discussed shortly at greater length, Doré is anxious to prove the Reformers wrong in their claim that much of the medieval church's belief and practice represents a radical departure from the scriptural witness. The goal is to expose this claim as lacking any solid foundation by demonstrating that all of the

Church's doctrines, in particular the points of controversy with the Reformers, are in fact firmly grounded in the revealed Word of God. That is not to say that Doré ignores what the Church considers to be the other fount of divine revelation, sacred Tradition. Magisterial pronouncements of both councils and popes do make an occasional appearance, especially in the later works. However, it must be said that Tradition in this sense plays a very minor role in Doré's program of instruction for the simple reason that it does little to refute the Reformers' position on *sola scriptura*.

If councils and popes get somewhat short shrift in the "Doréan" corpus, references to and citations from the Fathers of the Church do abound. In fact, Doré manifests a thorough acquaintance with the patristic sources, both Greek and Latin. Of course, the Reformers themselves were well-versed in the Fathers, particularly the teaching of the *doctor gratiae* St. Augustine whom they often quoted in support of their positions. Small wonder, then, that the Fathers also hold a prominent place in Doré's writings. His intention is to reclaim these great doctors of the faith and their teaching for the Roman Church.

As revered an authority as the patristic sources are in the Dominican's work, they nevertheless take second place to the teaching of the foremost scholastic theologian of the Middle Ages, Thomas Aquinas. Doré not only often makes references to his elder brother in the Order, he even at times gives a summary of Thomistic thought on a given point without all the trappings of a scholastic argument. In other words, he tries to adapt Aquinas' teaching in a way that ordinary people might more easily grasp it. His reliance on Thomas is particularly evident in his attempt to present the Catholic understanding of justification. More will be said on this point in Chapter 3. What is clear is that Doré's formation at S. Jacques in the midst of the Thomistic revival that occurred there in the early sixteenth century bore fruit in his own work years later.

Although it would be fair to say that Doré is of one mind and heart with his elder brother Thomas in terms of theological perspective, he is not strictly speaking a scholastic theologian, at least not in the way he presents theology. There is no trace of the scholastic method in his work. In addition, there is evidence that he was familiar with or even influenced by the intellectual movements of his own time, particularly the humanist movement. Throughout his works, one encounters an appreciation for several humanistic values; allusions to ancient Greek and Roman literature, an interest in the sources of Christian doctrine, a belief in the importance of translating the Scriptures into the vernacular for the benefit of the faithful. While he did not hide his disdain for certain aspects of humanism and certain humanists like Erasmus, he nevertheless demonstrates a respect for at least some of the movement's objectives in his literary production.

In terms of Doré's pedagogical style, the most significant characteristic is his copious use of images and metaphors to illustrate his points. Indeed, he shows himself a master in this regard. While at times the metaphors border on the eccentric or the analogies are stretched almost to the breaking point, most often they prove both engaging and highly instructive. No doubt it is this masterful use of images and metaphors that made Doré a best-selling author in his time. He also shows himself to be a master polemicist, painting the Reformers in the vilest of terms. This, too, is an important aspect of his pedagogy for, in his mind, the differences between truth and error must be clearly delineated. In presenting the position of his opponents, Doré is little concerned with accuracy or citations. Rather he is content simply to present to his readers the clichés of Reformed theology. Pedagogically, his goal is not to get involved in subtle theological distinctions on the different points of controversy, distinctions which in any case would be lost on the theologically uninitiated. The goal is to portray the error in its simplest terms without regard for complete accuracy and to focus instead on a proper explanation of the orthodox position.

Each of the above points concerning Doré's sources and pedagogical method will now be discussed in greater detail.

--*The Primacy of Scripture*

One of the battle cries of the Reformation, *sola scriptura* is the foundation upon which the edifice of Reformed theology is built.[161] Early on, it was invoked as the basis for the rejection of several doctrines and practices that had developed in the Church over the centuries. Beginning with Luther's attack on indulgences on that fateful October day in 1517, any doctrine or practice for which there was little or no scriptural basis was called into question and eventually repudiated as a man-made accretion sullying the pure religion founded by Christ. *Sola scriptura* thus became the basis for the Reformers' rejection of purgatory, the papacy, the ministerial priesthood, five of the seven sacraments, prayers to saints and the veneration of relics, to name but a few. At the very root of the principle, of course, was the much more fundamental rejection of Tradition as the other means by which divine revelation is conveyed in every age until the end of time. What was called into question was the age-old understanding that the Scriptures in and of themselves are not the sole repository of revealed truth, that much of the apostolic teaching had not been committed to written form but had been handed on orally and preserved through the centuries through apostolic succession. For the Reformers, Tradition was not a source of revelation but rather the source of all the errors that had crept into the Church and had made it, in the sixteenth century, unrecognizable from the original church founded by Christ.

Given the fundamental role that the principle of *sola scriptura* plays in the determination of Protestant theology, it comes as somewhat of a surprise to see that Doré never directly addresses their rejection of Tradition. While quick to refute their arguments against other basic doctrines and practices, he never really

---

[161] Florent Gaboriau in *L'écriture seule?* (Paris: Fac-éditions, 1997), p. 73 points out that the phrase "*sola scriptura*" is actually not to be found anywhere in Luther's writings. Nevertheless, there are passages of his works that express the principle, if not the phrase as such.

speaks out in defense of the unity of Scripture and Tradition. This is in marked contrast to the approach later taken by the Council of Trent which, at the very outset, addresses the issue in no uncertain terms affirming of the revelation given by Christ:

> ...that this truth and rule are contained in written books and in unwritten traditions which were received by the apostles from the mouth of Christ himself, or else have come down to us, handed on as it were from the apostles themselves at the inspiration of the holy Spirit. Following the example of the orthodox fathers, the council accepts and venerates with a like feeling of piety and reverence all the books of both the old and the new Testament...as well as the traditions concerning both faith and conduct, as either directly spoken by Christ or dictated by the holy Spirit, which have been preserved in unbroken sequence in the catholic church.[162]

Such a resounding affirmation of the unity of Scripture and Tradition is noticeably absent in the Dominican theologian's otherwise ardent defense of the faith. What we see instead is Doré taking up the challenge of *sola scriptura* by seeking to give the Reformers exactly what they have demanded, scriptural proof for the doctrines that they have called into question.

Doré finds a metaphor for the challenge and his solution to it in the "tribute money" episode recounted in Matthew 17:24-27. There, Peter is asked by the collectors of the Temple tax whether or not Jesus fulfills his duty in this regard. Christ uses the opportunity to make the point that it is foreigners who normally pay taxes while sons are exempt. Nevertheless, to avoid scandal, he then tells Peter that he will find a coin worth twice the tax in the mouth of the first fish he pulls out from the sea and that he is to give it to the collectors for both of them. For Doré, the Reformers are like the tax collectors of this Gospel pericope, demanding a payment from the Lord which he is not required to give them. The metaphor is completed with Doré portraying himself as Peter who nevertheless

---

[162] Session 4, 8 April 1546. Translation taken from Norman P. Tanner, *Decrees of the Ecumenical Councils*, vol. 2 (Washington: Georgetown University Press, 1990), p. 663.

gives the tax collectors the tribute money at Christ's command. As he explains to his confrère and friend, Pierre Lambert:

> *Ce que Jesus Christ commanda à Sainct Pierre, il me semble que à moy aussi la dict, en ce temps que heretiques demandent à nostre seigneur le didrachme qui n'est point tenu de bailler...Il ma esté advys que je ouy la voix de nostre seigneur qui m'a dict, va à la grande mer de l'escripture saincte, & des sainctes traditions & ordonnances ecclesiastiques, & jette ton hameçon pour pescher le poisson & trouver le statere de verité catholique & response de la foy à ce que soit satisfaict à ceux qui exigent le tribut.*[163]

The payment demanded by the sixteenth-century "tax collectors" (read here the heretics) is nothing other than the scriptural proof they require for accepting a doctrine as valid. Confronted with their insistence on this point, Doré recognizes the importance of throwing his net into the great sea of the Scriptures in order to fish out the proof that will confound them on their own grounds. It should be noted that in this citation he also affirms the validity of *"les sainctes traditions & ordonnances ecclesiastiques"* as sources of Catholic truth. However, his primary objective seems to be to "pay the tax" by proving that the fundamental truths which the Reformers have called into question may be demonstrated directly from the Scriptures themselves.

It is this spirit that in fact animates the *Dyalogue instructoire*, Doré's catechism. The dialogue between his two chosen interlocuters, the centurion Cornelius of the Acts of the Apostles, chapter 10, and St. Peter, is often very lively with the centurion in several instances urging the apostle to explain a point further. Indeed, one of his favorite questions to St. Peter is "Where is this teaching found in the Scriptures?" Through Cornelius, the disciple who is unafraid of challenging the master, Doré's intense desire to answer the Reformers on their own terms is unveiled, a desire to provide his readers with the scriptural basis for the seven sacraments, for the idea of temporal punishment due to sin, for

---
[163] Dedication to Pierre Lambert, *La meditation*, fol. Aiiii v°.

prayers on behalf of the dead and for a host of other doctrines rejected by the Reformers as "unscriptural."

We see the same principle at work in Doré's treatise on the Virgin Mary, *L'image de vertu*. In the prologue, he explains that while *vitae Christi* abound in the devotional literature of the time, he has never before come across a life of the Blessed Virgin. Given the Dominican Order's traditional devotion to Our Lady, he feels a duty now as a son of St. Dominic to remedy the situation by himself composing a *vita Mariae*. But what will be his sources for such a project? He desperately wants the Scriptures to be his principal source, yet this poses a dilemma which he describes in the prologue to the work, "*Et pour fonder mes propos en l'escripture Saincte, à fin de plus les auctoriser, me suis au commencement estonné grandement, que ne trouvois point livre en la saincte bible, qui parlast de toute la vie de nostre Dame.*"[164] The first part of his remark is both astonishing and revelatory. He wishes to base his life of the Virgin on the Scriptures so that it will thus be more authoritative! A little further on, he makes the remark that given the "calamitous times," he will refrain from including pious stories or accounts of miracles in his work and instead construct it solely on the foundation of solid doctrine. Once again we have a confirmation of his conviction that the only way to do battle with the Protestants is to fight fire with fire, or more precisely scriptural citations with scriptural citations. Yet, the dilemma remains of where to find a basis in the Scriptures for a life of Mary given the fact that the Gospels are highly discreet in her regard. Tradition, fortunately, provides Doré with a solution, for as he points out, several Fathers of the Church have seen the bride in the Song of Songs as an image of Mary. Thus, his *vita Mariae* in which he wishes to portray the virtues of the Mother of God is based on an allegorical interpretation of the Song of Songs. It should be noted here that in much of his exegesis, not only in *L'image de vertu* but also throughout his work, he relies heavily on the allegorical sense of Scripture.

---

[164] Prologue to *L'image de vertu* (Paris: Nicolas Bonfons, 1588), fol. Aiii r°. **[Paris, BNF—Inv. D 32767]**.

But does he succeed in his project of providing scriptural proof for all the doctrines rejected by the Reformers? Is his exegesis convincing? At times, yes. For example, his response to Cornelius' question on the origin of the sacraments consists by and large of those scriptural texts traditionally interpreted as pointing to the divine institution of each sacrament. Trent will later cite many of the same passages in its own decrees on the sacraments. However, in his discussion of the sacrament of confirmation, Doré claims that its institution can be seen in Jesus' blessing of the little children (cf. Mt. 19:13-15). We see here an example of Doré reading into a scriptural text something that is not there, of taking a passage out of context and imbuing it with a meaning that is completely alien to its original sense. At times, his highly allegorical interpretation of Scripture leaves something to be desired.

This is precisely the criticism leveled against Doré by the Calvinist polemicist Daniel Chamier. His *La confusion des disputes papistes* (1600) is meant to be a response to those whom he considers to be the major Catholic apologists of the sixteenth century, including Bellarmine, Eck, and Cochlaeus. The fact that Doré is among the thirty-nine "papist" theologians on Chamier's list of opponents is an indication of his significance in the Catholic reform movement of the sixteenth century. The Genevan apologist makes two references to Doré in this work and both times it is to critique his exegesis as completely absurd. In the first instance, he writes, "*Daurat* [Doré] *en ses vraiment Paradoxes, pour maintenir l'adoration de la croix, allegue de l'onziesme aux Hebrieux, que Jacob adora le bout de sa verge: & toutesfois l'Apostre avoit escrit, qu'il adora sur le bout de sa verge.*"[165] Chamier is referring here to the fifth paradox of Doré's *Paradoxa...ad profligandas haereses* (1543) where the Dominican attempts to provide scriptural proof for the Church's tradition of venerating the cross on Good Friday. He could not have found a better example to demonstrate the at times bizarre character of Doré's exegesis, in this case of Hebrews 11:21. The verse

---

[165] Daniel Chamier, *La confusion des disputes papistes* (Genève: François Lepreux, 1600), p. 14. [Paris, BNF—D^2 4245].

describes how prior to his death, Jacob blessed the sons of Joseph, "bowing in worship over the head of his staff" (RSV). Not only does this verse have no connection whatsoever to the cross of Christ, but Doré, misquoting it, has Jacob adoring his staff! And this is supposed to be scriptural proof of the validity of the Church's practice of venerating the cross! Chamier can well mock Doré's use of Scripture here and his exegesis.

What is evident in this example is that Doré's overriding desire to find proof in the Scriptures for everything that the Reformers challenge leads him to make some very dubious connections or interpretations in several instances. The allegories are occasionally stretched beyond the point of having any real meaning or significance. Yet, there are other times when Doré's exegesis is quite insightful and a powerful response to the Protestant position. Examples of his successful use of Scripture passages in defending Catholic doctrine will be brought out in the subsequent chapters on the major issues of the Reformation debate. However, it must be said in conclusion that Doré's valiant attempt to "pay the tax" on all the points of controversy is ultimately an unattainable goal, for there are some doctrines and practices which cannot be proved from Scripture alone apart from Tradition. A clearer presentation of the meaning and importance of Tradition might have served the Dominican better in his objective of answering the doctrinal challenge of the Reformers rather than simply trying to fight them on their own terms.

If Doré's exegesis at times leaves something to be desired, he is nevertheless to be commended for the fact that his work is so thoroughly grounded in Scripture. In fact, he regards the Word of God as true spiritual nourishment that must be made accessible to the laity. To this end, whenever he quotes a scriptural verse from the Latin Vulgate, he always provides a translation in French for the "simple" folk throughout his writings. While not exactly encouraging vernacular translations of the Bible in its entirety, Doré clearly wants the passages and verses he incorporates into his works to be understood by his readers so that they might find in these citations the consolation and nourishment they seek from the Word of God.

If he is anxious to provide the laity with what he often refers to as "the bread of Scripture," the Dominican nevertheless is not of the same opinion as the Reformers that the ordinary faithful should simply read the sacred texts in the vernacular on their own. Commenting on 1 Corinthians 14:27-28 where St. Paul counsels those who have the gift of tongues to remain silent if there is no one present in the assembly to interpret, Doré makes the point that simply being able to read the words of the Scriptures is not enough. Such a reading is both unedifying and dangerous if there is no one present who can help to interpret the meaning of the text:

> *C'est icy le point, la ou je me fonde: Si le peuple n'est point edifié qui est ignorant & non scavant, par ce que seullement y veoit la lettre de la Bible en francoys, ou aultre langue, ou en faict la lecture, pourquoy la fault il luy bailler? C'est autant que parler selon le don des langues sans interpreteur, ce que defend S. Paul, a raison que il n y a point de edification, mais plus tost en plusieurs occasion de ruyne.*[166]

In order to truly profit from the Word of God, then, the laity requires the services of a knowledgeable guide, someone who is instructed in sacred science, in other words the theologian. Thus Doré counsels the widow for whom he writes *Le college de sapience*, "*Si autrement veulx entrer au profondz des mysteres de l'escripture, prens ung patron de navire, qui te saiche conduire en ceste mer.*"[167] To this end, the Parisian Master portrays himself at one moment as a new Philip the deacon who explains the meaning of Scripture to the Ethiopian officer (*Le college de sapience*) or another time as a new Moses who descends from the mountain of contemplation in order to explain to the people the tablets of the New Covenant, that is the Beatitudes (*Les voyes de paradis*). Hence, while Doré is very much in favor of making the Word of God more accessible to the laity by

---

[166] *Le college*, fol. lxiii v°.
[167] Ibid, fol. lxiii r°.

presenting it in the vernacular, he does not go so far as to promote the idea of giving them the bare text without commentary. To leave them adrift in the vast sea of the Scriptures without having anyone at the helm to guide their reading is, in his mind, to condemn them to shipwreck in the faith.

Perhaps the following exhortation from the prologue to *Le livre des divins benefices* best summarizes Doré's approach and objective in making the Scriptures available to the laity:

> *Venez doncques petis & grands, apprendre à dire voz graces & divines louanges, en disant le Psalme ensuyvant, que j'ay de Latin en Francoys traduict, & exposé pour vostre enseignement & profit, tant pour l'entendement, que pour la volunté. L'entendement aura erudition & instruction: & la volunté sera excitee à devotion & ferveur de soy espandre es divines louanges, lesquelles dechanter en ce monde, est commencer ung paradis...*[168]

First of all, he explains here that there is a two-fold aspect to his work: a translation of the Scripture passage from Latin into French and then an exposition of its meaning for the benefit of his readers. As he indicates, the translations are his own and are not drawn from already existing French translations.[169] The benefit he hopes that readers will reap from his commentary is also two-fold. His purpose is to provide instruction which will not only satisfy the mind's desire to know the truth but also excite the will to a greater love for God, a love which in this case finds expression through praise of the divine goodness for all his blessings. It is not a question then of merely providing the faithful with scriptural texts and leaving them to arrive at whatever interpretation which might come to their minds. For Doré, scriptural texts in the vernacular must always be exposed by a theologian in such a way that the faithful will understand the significance of

---

[168] Prologue to *Le livre des divins benefices, enseignant la maniere de les recongnoistre, avec l'information de bien vivre, et la consolation des affligez selon qu'il est comprins au psalme 33 de David, qui se commence, Benedicam dominum* (Paris: Jean Ruelle, 1544), fol. Av v°. **[Paris, BNF—Inv. D 86037]**.

[169] For example, the humanist Lefèvre d'Etaples had completed a French translation of the New Testament in 1523 followed by a translation of the Old Testament five years later.

the words they now can read in their own language, and in understanding be moved to embrace the truth with their hearts and wills as well as their minds.

--*The Fathers and Aquinas*

As mentioned previously, although Scripture occupies the central place in Doré's writings, the Fathers of the Church are by no means neglected. The Parisian Master demonstrates a solid acquaintance with the large repertoire of patristic thought in his citations. The clear favorite is Augustine, but also cited with relative frequency are Jerome, Ambrose, Gregory the Great, John Chrysostom and Cyril of Alexandria. It is almost impossible to determine, however, which writings in particular he is drawing from, for he only rarely gives a reference. He is content simply to leave his readers with "Augustine says" or "Chrysostom says." He also makes a fair amount of references to the more "modern" doctors of the Church, such as Anselm, Bernard and Albert the Great. Of this group, it is Bernard, the mystical abbot of Clairvaux, who is most often quoted, particularly his commentary on the Song of Songs and his Marian thought of which Doré makes ample use in *L'image de vertu*, his own work on the life of the Virgin. Although the Dominican is intent on providing a scriptural basis for this theological exposition, he does not hesitate to incorporate the wealth of wisdom offered him in fifteen hundred years of meditation on the Scriptures by the great teachers of the faith. Thus he explains:

> *J'ay aussi cité les docteurs approuvez de l'Eglise, comme tesmoings irreprochables & irrefragables, non pas que je vueille mesler les parolles de l'homme avec celle de Dieu...mais pourtant que lesdictz anciens docteurs catholiques ont eu l'esprit de Dieu, afin que par eulx congnoissons quel est le vray sens de l'escripture.*[170]

---

[170] Dedication to Henry II, *L'arche*, fol. E r°-v°.

True, he admits, the words of the Fathers cannot compare in dignity with the Word of God. Nevertheless, as he observes, these men have been acknowlegded to have been imbued with the Spirit of God and thus serve as trustworthy guides who offer the correct way of interpreting and reading the Scriptures.

As much as Doré reverences the authority of the Fathers, there is another authority whose name appears more frequently in the Dominican's writings. It is Aquinas, the great scholastic theologian, who is the most important of Doré's sources after the Scriptures themselves. As broad as is his knowledge of the patristic heritage, so does he manifest a wide-ranging familiarity with the writings of his elder brother. More often than not, he even provides the reader with at least the name of the work from which a particular citation is drawn though rarely is the reference more precise than that. Most commonly found in the "Doréan" corpus are citations from Aquinas' *Summa Theologiae*, and to a lesser extent from the *Commentary on the Books of the Sentences* as well as various other works, particularly the scriptural commentaries. In evidence is the solid grounding that Doré received in Thomistic thought during his theological formation at S. Jacques. To be sure, he is not a commentator of Thomas like his contemporary Francisco de Vitoria nor can he be said to be providing a systematic exposition of Thomistic theology for the reading public. What he does in several places, however, is to give a brief summary of Aquinas' thought on a given point of doctrine that he is exposing for his readers. It is certain that these fragments drawn from Thomas' writings represent the first time that the theologically unsophisticated laywomen and laymen of France are exposed to at least a small portion of the medieval doctor's thought.

A good example of how Doré incorporates the teaching of Aquinas in his writings is seen in this extract from *Le college de sapience*. The fourteenth chapter opens with an explanation of the first article of the first question of the *Summa Theologiae* where Thomas discusses the necessity of *sacra doctrina* or of the truth revealed by God. Doré offers the following summary of the article:

> *Sainct Thomas deduict en sa premiere partie de sa somme de Theologie, question premiere & article premier que il a esté necessaire pour le salut des humains, estre une doctrine selon divine revelation, que nous disons Theologie, c'est a dire science de dieu, ou sermon de dieu. Et sa raison est, car l'homme est ordonné a dieu, comme a sa derniere & supernaturelle fin, laquelle surpasse la comprehension de tout esperit humain. Or fault il, la fin estre congneue de ceulx qui leurs operations en elle doibvent ordonner. Il sensuit doncques que il a esté necessaire pour le salut de l'homme, avoir congnoissance par revelation de dieu & de ses faictz, laquelle est nommée Theologie vraye sapience, comme il dict par le prophete.*[171]

What we have here is a very accurate rendition of the substance of Aquinas' response to the question without all of the formal aspects which are characteristic of the scholastic argument, for example the objections raised prior to the solution, the *sed contra* and the concluding responses to the objections. It is an exposition of Thomas' teaching minus all the unnecessary complications of the scholastic form in which the uninitiated would surely lose their way. This summary of the first article of the *Summa* also illustrates the theological character that permeates Doré's works. Although the stated aim of *Le college de sapience* is to instruct and inspire readers in the practice of virtue, it is clear that Doré also has in mind their intellectual formation by introducing them to serious theological thought.

More frequently, Doré merely cites Thomas in the same way that he cites the Fathers, to explain or support a point he is making. For example, in his discussion of the difference between the first three Beatitudes and the five that follow, he simply quotes the explanation given by Aquinas in his commentary on St. Matthew saying, "*Les trois dessusdictes beatitudes sont baillees pour retirer l'homme de mal, mais ceste cy qui est la quatriesme avecques les aultres sont baillees pour adresser l'homme a bien faire.*"[172] Such citations, while certainly of less significance than Doré's occasional summaries of Aquinas' thought as illustrated above, are nonetheless indications of a desire on his part to introduce the ordinary laity to the thought and teachings of the great doctor. While it is

---
[171] *Le college*, fol. lxxix r°-v°.
[172] *Les voyes*, fol. Cv v°.

perhaps too much to say that he set out to popularize Thomism in France, there is no doubt that his writings represent an attempt to make some of Aquinas' insights accessible in French and in summary form to a theologically uneducated public.

--Traces of Humanism

From what has preceded, it is already evident that Doré was sympathetic to certain humanistic values if not quite an avowed humanist himself, for the idea that the Scriptures should be translated from the Latin to the vernacular in order that they might be accessible to the faithful was one of the hallmarks of the religious humanist movement of the northern Renaissance. Yet, unlike his confrère Guillaume Petit, who as confessor to the king used his influence at court to protect and promote humanists such as Erasmus, there is no evidence that Doré had any close connections with the humanist circle in France. What is more, he manifests a definite disdain for the humanist tendency to be highly critical of the institutional church and its manifest abuses. Of Erasmus' biting critique of the Church in the *Moriae Encomium* he states unequivocally:

> On fait brusler les livres pernicieux...car comme dit Sainct Paul, les mauvais colloques corrompent les bonnes moeurs, ce qu'est bien verifié des colloques d'Erasme, plains de lubricité, & d'irrision de gens Eccelesiastiques, & des estats de Religion, pourquoy justement ont esté defendus de lire aux enfans en nostre université.[173]

In his eyes, Erasmus' sarcastic swipes at ecclesiastical abuses were just as destructive of the true faith as the doctrinal errors of the heretics. Although Doré certainly acknowledged the abuses in the Church of his day, he did not adopt the critical and satirical stance towards the Church that often characterized the humanists. Neither did he share the humanists' disdain for scholastic theology nor their critical attitude towards Scripture (critical in the sense of a taking a

---

[173] Prologue to *L'image*, fol. Av v°.

scientific/philological approach to Scripture study). Yet, there is nevertheless evidence in his works of a humanistic training and even an appreciation for certain aspects of the movement.

The essence of religious humanism was perhaps the desire to recover the pure and simple doctrine of the faith as expressed in the Scriptures. But in order to truly return to the source, to have a direct contact with the Word of God, one had to be able to read the Scriptures in the original Hebrew or Greek, free of the imprecision and error of a translation. The humanists' love of ancient languages was thus put at the service of a new appreciation for the original scriptural texts in the course of which Jerome's fourth-century Latin translation known as the Vulgate, the standard text of the Church, was found to be seriously deficient and full of errors. It was in view of correcting the Vulgate and providing a more faithful translation of the New Testament that Erasmus produced his *Novum Instrumentum* in 1516.[174] The *Instrumentum* consisted of the biblical text in the original Greek alongside Eramus' new Latin translation accompanied by notes in which he explained variations between his translation and that of the Vulgate.[175] While Doré most certainly did not share the highly philological approach to Scripture taken by Erasmus or the other humanists, he does seem to have appreciated their emphasis on the need to be able to read the Scriptures in the original language.

Evidence of Doré's support for the study of the classical languages is found in a passage from *Le college de sapience* where he is praising the Faculty of Theology as the most noble of all of Paris' university faculties. What is most interesting here, however, is that he goes on to encourage King Francis I to establish a school of classical languages for the greater "adornment" of the city:

> *Je prie la bonté de Dieu souveraine, donner la force & vertu au trespuissant Roy Francoys nous eriger en icelle ville pour consomer*

---

[174] Subsequent editions of the translation would be titled the *Novum Testamentum* rather than *Instrumentum*.
[175] The 1527 edition actually contained the Vulgate text along with the original Greek and Erasmus' new Latin translation.

> *l'aornement dicelle ung college de troy Langues, ainsi qu'il a bonne voulenté. On veoit desia en Paris flourir ces troys langues. Dieu par sa grace veille tout estre a sa gloire & honneur, et ampliation de la saincte foy catholique. Par ce moyen reluyront troys fleurs de lys dor, en troys langues Latine, Grecque et hebraique.*[176]

It is evident that Doré is firmly convinced of the importance of the classical languages for the study of theology when he implies that the establishment of the college for languages will contribute to the expansion of the Catholic faith. He also seems to speak as one who has himself benefited from study of the ancient languages. There are a few instances in his works where he attempts to explain a Greek word to his readers and one instance of a Hebrew word in *La passe solitaire*. While not a proponent of the humanist approach to Scripture, he nevertheless does seem to share the humanist appreciation for the utility of classical languages as a tool for the theologian in better understanding the sense of the sacred text.

It is most likely that Doré based the translations of Scripture found in his works on the Church-approved Vulgate version rather than on Erasmus' *Novum Testamentum*, which was rather controversial in its day.[177] Nevertheless, he was familiar with the Erasmian translation and in two instances used it to support his position against that of the Reformers. The point in question in the following example is that of the ministerial priesthood and Doré is attempting to show that St. Paul himself refers to this distinctive priesthood in his first letter to Timothy:

> *De ceste prestrise nouvelle escript sainct Paul à son disciple Thimothee.*
> **'Noli negligere gratia quae in te est, quae data est tibi per prophetiam,**

---

[176] *Le college*, fol. lxxiii v°-lxxiiii r°. Doré, writing the above in 1539, seems to have something else in mind here than the *Collège des Lecteurs royaux* which Francis I established in 1530 as a center of humanistic studies.

[177] For example, an English student at Louvain, Edward Lee, strongly criticized Erasmus' translation in his *Annotationes in Annotationes noui testamenti Desiderii Erasmi* asserting that his changes from the Vulgate had the effect of calling into question several fundamental doctrines of the faith. For a study of the debate between Lee and Erasmus see Robert Coogan, *Erasmus, Lee and the Correction of the Vulgate: The Shaking of the Foundations* (Geneva: Droz, 1992). See also Erika Rummel, *Erasmus and his Catholic Critics*, 2 vols. (Nieuwkoop: De Graaf, 1989) for a broader study of the controversy surrounding Erasmus' *Novum Testamentum*.

> *cum impositione manuum presbyterium.'* Ou (selon la translation d'Erasme) on list: *'**Authoritate sacerdotium.**'* Ne metz point en non chaloir le don qui est en toy, lequel t'est donné par prophetie, avec l'imposition des mains, ou l'autorité de prestrise.[178]

The verse that Doré cites here from 1 Timothy 4 is taken from the Vulgate. But lest the Reformers try to dispute St. Paul's evident reference to the priesthood by claiming it is one of the many errors of the Vulgate, Doré points out that even Erasmus' Latin translation supports the traditional interpretation. A few lines later, he invokes Erasmus once again, this time showing how in one of his annotations he affirms that the idea of "minister" also includes the idea of one who sacrifices.[179] This particular citation and its significance will be taken up in greater detail in Chapter 4. Leaving aside for now Doré's defense of the ministerial priesthood as such, the point to be made here is his willingness to make use of Erasmus' work in his exposition despite the fact that, as we have seen, he has no great love for the humanist's views on the Church. It is one more example of both Doré's familiarity with humanist scholarship and his appreciation for some of its achievements.

Another hallmark of humanism was a renewed appreciation for the Graeco-Roman culture of classical antiquity. From Plato and Homer to Cicero and Virgil, classical philosophy and literature were the backbone of a humanist education. Throughout his works, Doré demonstrates both the familiarity with and appreciation for the classics that characterized the humanists. He claims, for example, that his *Livre des divins benefices* is actually modeled on a work by Seneca in which the Roman philosopher provides instruction on how to give and receive a benefaction.[180] However, whereas Seneca is concerned with gifts exchanged between human beings, Doré is concerned with the proper response of human beings to "divine" benefits received from on high. Yet another example of

---

[178] *L'arche*, fol. 148v°.
[179] Ibid., fol. 149v°.
[180] Though Doré does not mention the work by name, he is referring to Seneca's *De Beneficiis*.

the Dominican's appreciation for classical literature is seen in his sermon at the funeral of Admiral Philippe Chabot in 1543 where he makes an allusion to Thucydides' history of the Peloponnesian War and compares his present eulogy of the deceased admiral to the funeral oration delivered by the great Athenian statesman Pericles in honor of the valiant deeds of those who have lost their lives in the war. Here again, however, Doré distinguishes the pagan model from its Christian successor:

> *Par ainsi avec ethniques & payens, nous convenons en un faict, mais non pas en intention...Ils louent l'homme pour à luy seul ascriber gloire, mais nous le louons, pour donner principalement gloire à Dieu, qui tant de dons & graces a departy à celuy dont voulons parler, feu messire Philippes Chabot...*[181]

While the Dominican theologian imitates Pericles in praising the great deeds of the dead warrior, his intention is far more elevated and ordered not to the glorification of a mere human being, but of God, who alone is the source of the warrior's virtues.

The connections with classical literature continue in *L'arche de l'alliance*, Doré's treatise on the Eucharist, which he begins with an invocation of divine assistance for his task of explaining this most elevated mystery of the faith, much in the same way as the ancient poets Homer and Virgil called upon the Muses for inspiration:

> *Si...les Poetes & Orateurs Graecz qui ont escript, pour entreprendre composer livres fabuleux, font invocation à quelque Muse, ainsi que faict Homere au commencement de ses Iliades. Lequel a ensuivy le poete Latin en ses Eneides. Et mon institution est à present de parler & escripre d'un des plus haulx & arduz mysteres de nostre foy, à scavoir du sacrement des sacremens, & secretz des secretz, ne doibz certes (comme aussi ne puis) tel ouvrage attenter, & si grande province & charge eslire ou accepter, sans t'appeller en mon ayde, o divine & infinie sapience, estant de ma propre insuffisance congnoissant.*[182]

---

[181] "Sermon funebre, faict es exeques de feu messire Philippes Chabot grand Admiral de France" in *La deploration de la vie humaine* (Paris: Jean Ruelle, 1554), fol. 181r°. [**Paris, BNF—Rés. D 32764**].
[182] *L'arche*, fol. I r°-v°.

The preceding three examples all give evidence of the breadth of Doré's familiarity with the classical literature of ancient Greece and Rome. While he clearly appreciates the beauty and wisdom which the ancients achieved and does not hesitate to imitate some of their stylistic techniques, he is not the kind of humanist who sees the classics as an end unto themselves. The examples indicate that the reference point for Doré is always the greatness of God and not the greatness of man. Thus, he is a humanist insofar as he appreciates the achievements of the ancient world, but he also insists that classical values are perfected only in a Christian context.

--*The Extensive Use of Metaphors and Images*

Any good teacher knows that examples and metaphors are an important element of pedagogy. Without them, instruction remains dry, abstract and often difficult to grasp. It is in this ability to paint an image, to draw a helpful analogy for his readers that Doré demonstrates he is a gifted teacher. While his writings contain very little by way of original thought, they are rich in metaphors, examples, allegories and analogies through which he gives evidence of a real originality in presentation. Undoubtedly, his masterful and appealing use of metaphor to make his point was one of the major factors behind his popularity as a writer. While on occasion the metaphors appear a bit exaggerated and even bizarre, particularly to modern sensibilities, by and large they achieve their intended effect in instructing the reader in an engaging way.

As mentioned earlier in this chapter, Doré's penchant for using images is already evident in the titles of his works. Very often, the images are drawn directly from Scripture, particularly the psalms. The title of *Le cerf spirituel*, for example, utilizes an image borrowed from Psalm 42. Already in the psalm itself, the deer that longs for running streams is likened to the soul that thirsts for God.

But in his commentary, Doré takes the metaphor as given and then develops it much further in order to teach a lesson on temptation. If the deer represents those who are spiritually-minded, then the carnal are likened to an ass or mule according to Doré. Just as the mule is used as a beast of burden in the service of a human master, so the carnal are in fact slaves of the devil. The just, however, run free like the deer, enjoying the liberty of the children of God. Yet Satan, like the hunter who delights in savory venison, preys upon the spiritual deer hoping to feast on the capture of a good Catholic. And how does the spiritual deer react when he hears the horns of temptation sounded by the hunter? Doré continues:

> *A ceste occasion comme le cerf est craintif, quant escoute le cornet du veneur, pareillement sont gens spirituelz craintifz, & à tout son de tentation, sont en crainte d'estre prins par peché, & sont sur leurs gardes, vont legerement comme cerfz, & s'enfuyent es haultes montaignes de contemplation, & refuge à dieu & par ce moyen eschappent la main du veneur ennemy de nostre salut.*[183]

The fear of falling prey to the wiles of the evil one leads the spiritual deer to seek refuge on the mountain summits of contemplation. Thus the original metaphor of the deer as the soul which thirsts for God is maintained, yet Doré has masterfully developed it in such a way as to teach an important lesson on the freedom that is ours in grace and how to avoid falling prey to the devil who seeks to deprive us of this liberty through the lure of temptation. It is an allegory that encourages the reader to avoid sin by ascending the heights of contemplative prayer.

Scripture is not the only source from which Doré draws his images and metaphors. Many of them are in fact rooted in the world of his experience, that is to say in the academic world and in courtly life. The best example of the former is found in *Le college de sapience* where Mary Magdalene is schooled in discipleship at the "university of virtue." Among the many metaphors in this work drawn from university life, one of the more fascinating is when Doré describes Christ's formation of the apostles in terms of a Master in Theology

---

[183] *Le cerf*, fol. 6r°.

forming students who progress through the various university grades. The apostles finally achieve the rank of "doctor in theology" when they are infused with the grace of the Holy Spirit at Pentecost. But what is the point of this rather amusing metaphor? Doré proceeds to make an important connection between these apostolic "doctors of theology" and their successors who are not only the bishops but also "...*les docteurs de la foy, lesquelz du glayve de la parolle de dieu, deffendent et deffendront* [l'église], *comme fortz et vaillains chevaliers du Roy des Roys.*"[184] In Doré's mind, the "doctors of the faith" who make up the Parisian Faculty of Theology carry on the apostolic mission of proclaiming and defending the true faith, and thus enjoy a certain share in the episcopal ministry. What first appears, then, as an anachronistic metaphor of the apostles as theology students at the university is used by Doré to make a more serious point concerning the Faculty of Theology's role in maintaining orthodoxy in the French Church.

In *L'arche de l'alliance*, we find an example of an analogy drawn from Doré's other world, his close associations with the aristocracy and the royal court. Like the university, the court serves as an important source for metaphors throughout his works. The utility of images drawn from court life in illustrating the kind of relationship one should have with God is not difficult to perceive. What better way to discuss the respect and devotion owed to God than to compare it to the loyalty which subjects owe to their king? Thus the king of France often serves as an image in Doré's works for the King of Kings. In the following example, Doré is emphasizing the importance of a proper preparation for reception of the Holy Eucharist through which God himself comes to dwell in the communicant. It is as if a French subject were told to expect an imminent visit from his king:

> *Certainement si nous avons à recepvoir un roy temporel, comme nostre treschrestien roy de France, sans faire aucuns preparatifz à bien le recepvoir, & ne aorner aucunement le logis, ains plus fort, si le mettions en un lieu, ord salle, & pestifere, ne serions nous pas contempteurs de la royalle dignité, & par ce faict coulpables de crime de lese majesté: &*

---

[184] *Le college*, fol. xiiii v°.

120

> *dignes par ce moyen pour nostre negligence, & comtempnement grand, estre asprement punis? Il n'y a doubte que ouy.*[185]

The point is well made. To receive the king of France into one's home without giving him the proper respect that is his due would constitute a serious offense for which the miserable subject would be punished. How much more, then, should the communicant assure that his spiritual house is in order and that he is free from grave sin before receiving the king of the universe in the humble abode of his heart. To partake of the body of the Lord unworthily is to eat it to one's condemnation. Once again, Doré uses an analogy quite adeptly to bring home an important point.

Yet, as with his exegesis, so his use of metaphor and allegory is not always a success, at least when read from a contemporary perspective. In one of his more original (some might say bizarre) works, *Anatomie et mystique description de membres & parties de nostre saulveur Jesuschrist* (1546), Doré attempts to provide one of his spiritual daughters with material for meditation, in this case a detailed description of the different parts of Christ's body, each of which has a mystical significance. As odd and as distasteful as his proposition might seem to us, it nevertheless demonstrates that Doré is quite up-to-date with the new scientific practice of his time of dissecting corpses in order to better understand the anatomy of the human body. The purpose of his anatomical study of Christ is of course more elevated. Each meditation is meant to serve as a way of imprinting Christ's image within the devout reader: in her eyes, her mouth, her heart, her soul, her entire being. And so Doré discusses the mystical meaning of each part of Christ's anatomy, beginning with the head.

Not all of the analogies found in this anatomical study are distasteful. In fact, many are quite fitting. For example, the Dominican compares the hair that adorns the head of Christ to the virtues which should adorn the soul, "*...car comme les cheveux sont l'aornement du chef, ainsi les vertus de l'ame sont*

---

[185] *L'arche*, fol. 81r°.

l'aornement d'icelle."[186] It is when he attributes maternal imagery to the Savior and speaks of the "breasts of Christ" as feeding us that he seems to go beyond the bounds of propriety. *"Chose inaudite en nature,"* he writes, *"qu'ung homme ait du laict es mammelles, pour alaicter ses enfans, cela appartient aux meres: mais grace triumphe par dessus nature."*[187] The whole point of this bizarre metaphor is to say that the two breasts of Christ represent his feeding us with his body and his blood. Another possible interpretation Doré admits is that the two breasts represent the Old and New Testaments through which we are fed with the milk of doctrine.

While no one would take exception to the point that Christ feeds us with both the Eucharist and with the revealed Word, the image of breast-feeding used to convey the point seems inappropriate for relating such a marvelous truth. Christ after all was not only fully human but also fully male! Yet, there does exist a whole tradition of both medieval and patristic development of precisely such mother-imagery in reference to Christ. In a fairly recent study on the topic, Caroline Walker Bynum points out that "the nursing Christ" as an image of the Eucharist is found as early as the second century in the writings of Clement of Alexandria and that medieval theologians such as Bernard of Clairvaux and Guerric of Igny also make extensive use of the allegory.[188] German Dominican mystic nuns of the fourteenth century, Margaret Ebner and Adelheid Langmann, recount mystical experiences in which they imitate the example of the beloved disciple John by "leaning on the breast of Christ" and "drinking the milk of grace and wisdom" to be found there.[189] Clearly, then, Doré's own use of the breast-feeding analogy is not so bizarre when considered within this context of medieval

---

[186] *Anatomie, et mystique description de membres & parties de nostre saulveur Jesuschrist* (Paris: Jean de Brouilly, 1546), fol. 120v°. [**Aix-en-Provence, BMJ—C. 8976**].
[187] Ibid., fol. 151v°.
[188] See Caroline Walker Bynum, *Jesus as Mother—Studies in the Spirituality of the High Middle Ages* (Berkeley: University of California Press, 1984), pp. 110-135.
[189] See Leonard Hindsley, *Margaret Ebner* (New York: Paulist Press, 1993), p. 125 and also Leonard Hindsley, *The Mystics of Engelthal—Writings from a Medieval Monastery* (New York: St. Martin's Press, 1998), p. 177.

allegory. It is safe to say that his contemporaries would most probably not have been as bothered by the image as are we moderns.

The few examples presented here have attempted to give some sense of both Doré's proficiency as well as his eccentricity in the use of metaphor and analogy. There are times when the image is more amusing than edifying, times when the analogy seems too far-fetched to be truly effective or instructive. Nonetheless, more often than not, Doré demonstrates a masterful use of such techniques in both conveying the lesson at hand and inspiring his readers to greater devotion.

--*The Art of Polemics*

In his refutation of Protestant theological positions, Doré never once cites a source for the particular "heretical poison" he is refuting. Nor does he ever make any real distinctions between the positions of the different Reformed churches. Luther, Zwingli, Calvin—all are lumped together as if they thought with one mind and heart. One of the more glaring examples of Doré's failure to take into account the real differences existing between the Reformers themselves is in *L'arche de l'alliance* where he presents the Protestant position on the Eucharist as a denial pure and simple of the real presence. However, this is far too facile and inaccurate a portrayal of what Luther, for example, believed concerning the Eucharist. A more detailed discussion of the different positions taken by the Reformers, specifically Luther and Calvin, on the Eucharist will be given in Chapter 4. The point for now is that Doré is not concerned to fairly represent the distinctions existing in Reformation theology. His fight is against a global Protestantism. Lutherans and Calvinists are equally heretics as far as he is concerned and there is no need to treat them as separate groups with differing beliefs.

There is no doubt as to Doré's approach. It is one of a holy war against a powerful enemy and all the Reformers are painted in the blackest of terms. At stake in the conflict is the eternal salvation of souls and the unity of the body of Christ. Given these high stakes, the most serious punishment must be meted out to those who have put themselves at enmity with the traditional faith. Repeatedly, Doré advocates the complete suppression and eradication of heretics along with their books:

> *Et a bon droict telz livres dangereux, & plains de corruption, ce doibvent brusler avecques leur aucteurs. Car si les faulx monnoyeurs, on mect boullyr, pourquoy non ceulx qui dogmatizent, & font ung faulx coing de la Foy, laquelle est ordonnée a subvenir a la vie spirituelle plus necessaire que la corporelle?*[190]

If those who counterfeit money are severely punished for their crime of fraud and cheating others of what is their due, how much more should the heretics suffer the ultimate punishment for their crime of passing off error for truth and thereby cheating the undiscerning believer out of eternal life.

Doré finds scriptural justification for his radical position in John 15:1-10, the discourse on the vine and the branches. There, Christ says that anyone who does not remain in him is like a branch that withers and is eventually thrown into the fire. For the Dominican, this image corresponds exactly to the heretics of his day who have cut themselves off from Christ and his Church and like withered branches are good only to be pruned and burned. He explains:

> *Et fault icy observer avec Cyrille, que à ces branches inutiles l'humeur de la vigne est ostée, c'est à sçavoir l'Esprit du Seigneur, devant que soient mises au feu: ne plus ne moins que nous voyons en ceulx qui sont eslevez es honneurs, dignitez, & offices de ce siecle, quand ilz ont commis quelque grand cas, comme crime de lése majesté, devant que d'estre puniz de justice, par decapitation ou autrement, on les depose premierement de leur office, & la robbe, ou marque & enseigne de leur magistrat leur est ostée. Fait ainsi Dieu, devant qu'envoyer l'ame infructueuse au feu, luy oster la dignité d'adoption des enfans par le sainct Esprit, lequel elle perd, estant branche couppée de la vigne. Cecy*

---

[190] *Le college*, fol. xv r°.

> *convient à tous pecheurs, & specialement aux heretiques, divisez de l'eglise, & preciz du corps mystique, pourquoy ilz n'ont point le sainct Esprit, dont les convient mettre au feu, comme inutile serment de la vigne, & non seulement sont inutiles, mais dommageables & pernicieux aux autres bonnes branches de la vigne, qui sont les bons fideles.*[191]

Although he believes the heretics will certainly burn in the eternal fire of God's punishment for their treason against his Church, Doré makes it clear here that they should also be put to the flames even in this life because they threaten to infect and corrupt the good branches which remain. They are a menace to society at large and should be punished as such. Furthermore, they deserve such treatment because in cutting themselves off from the body of Christ, they have in effect renounced their adoptive sonship in Christ and are thereby deprived of the gift of the Holy Spirit. As far as Doré is concerned, they have brought judgment upon themselves. It is only fitting then that they suffer the full consequences of their denial of the faith.

Given our friar's complete disdain for the Reformers, it should come as no surprise that he has little concern to accurately portray their positions nor does he bother to provide citations for the positions he refutes. In polemics, one is usually content with painting the opponent's position only in the most general of terms, lest finer distinctions serve to dilute the black and white argument into a far less definite gray. There is never any gray to be found in Doré's writings. The difference between truth and error is made plainly visible for all to see. His very general presentation of Reformation doctrine coupled with the complete absence of citations might lead to the impression that Doré did not actually read the opponents he was refuting. It seems as if the source for his knowledge of Protestant positions is nothing more than clichés or hearsay, that he himself did not have firsthand knowledge of their theology.[192] However, while the

---

[191] *Le Nouveau Testament d'amour de nostre pere Jesuchrist, signé de son sang. Autrement son dernier sermon, faict apres la cene, avec sa passion, ou sont confutées plusieurs heresies* (Paris: Jean Ruelle, 1557), fol. 148v°. [**Neuchâtel, BPU—NP ZQ 889**].

[192] This point is made by Fragonard, "Stratégie," p. 182.

impression is justified, there is nevertheless evidence that Doré was very well aware of exactly what his opponents were saying and that his rather general and imprecise portrayal of the Reformers' doctrines was therefore quite conscious and deliberate.

In the first place, Doré himself alludes to having both seen and read certain heretical works. For example, there is Megander's catechism to which the *Dyalogue instructoire* purports to be a response, even though as Higman points out, there is actually very little correspondence between the two texts.[193] Doré also recounts in another work how during his first year in the service of Claude de Lorraine, he caught one of the duke's guests on Easter day with "a pernicious little book, full of Lutheran flour." He writes, *"Je prins le livre, & l'ayant leu & veu le poison de dedans, le bruslay."*[194] While the title of the book remains a mystery to us, it was doubtless one of Luther's tracts. Finally, in 1550, Doré writes of "correcting" and "washing" the errors out of an anonymous text shown him by a printer entitled *Le miroir de patience*, which is then re-published with his own *La piscine de patience*. Higman has pointed out that *Le miroir de patience* is actually "...an unknown and archaic translation of Luther's *Tessaradecas Consolatoria.*"[195] However, Doré was most probably completely unaware of that fact since he does not use his usual invectives against Luther in describing the text. In any case, these three examples demonstrate that his criticism of Reformation doctrine was not founded merely on hearsay. He clearly knew first-hand through his reading exactly what the Reformers were saying.

Besides his open admission of having read Megander's catechism as well as the "pernicious little Lutheran book" of the duke's houseguest, there is hidden textual evidence that Doré was also quite familiar with and even admiring of some of John Calvin's writings. In fact, *L'arche de l'alliance* contains indisputable proof that Doré had read a good portion of Calvin very closely.

---

[193] Higman, *Réfutation*, p. 58.
[194] *Oraison*, fol. 57r°.
[195] Higman, *Piety*, pp. 188-189.

126

Approximately three-quarters of the first chapter of *L'arche* entitled "*De la difference des deux alliances que Dieu a faict avec l'homme*" is not merely a paraphrase of Calvin but is copied practically word for word from Book II, Chapter VII of Calvin's *Institutes*[196] on how the purpose of the Old Covenant was to foster the hope of salvation until Christ should come.[197] This "direct quotation" is never cited as being extracted from the *Institutes* but appears as an integral part of Doré's own text. And that is not all! Doré also incorporates several paragraphs, once again copied almost word for word, of Calvin's *Petit traicté de la Saincte Cène*, first published in Geneva in 1541 by Michel du Bois, in his *L'arche de l'alliance*. What follows are two examples of the "lifted" passages, with Calvin's text on the left and Doré's on the right[198]:

Davantage, si la raison de communiquer à Jesus-Christ est que nous ayons part et portion en toutes les grâces qu'il nous a acquises par sa mort, il n'est pas seulement question que nous soyons participants de son Esprit, mais il nous faut aussi participer à son humanité, en laquelle il a rendu toute obéissance à Dieu son Père pour satisfaire à nos dettes, combien à proprement parler que l'un ne se puisse faire sans l'autre. Car quand il se donne à nous, c'est afin que nous le possedions entièrement. p. 131.	*Davantage, si la raison de communiquer à Jesus Christ, est afin que nous ayons part & portion en toutes les graces qu'il nous a acquises par sa mort, il n'est pas seulement question que nous soyons participans de son esprit, mais il nous fault aussi participer à son humanité, en laquelle il a rendu toute l'obeissance à dieu son pere, pour satisfaire à noz debtes.* fol. 54r°.
La troisième utilité gît en ce que nous y avons une véhémente exhortation à vivre saintement et surtout à garder charité et dilection fraternelle entre nous. Car puisque là nous sommes faits membres de Jésus-Christ, étant incorporés en lui et unis avec lui comme à notre chef, c'est bien raison que, premièrement, nous soyons faits conformes à sa pureté et innocence, et spécialement que nous ayons	*D'abondant avons par cecy une vehemente exhortation à vivre sainctement, & sur tout à garder charité & dilection fraternelle entre nous: car puis que là nous sommes faictz membres de Jesuschrist, estans incorporez en luy, & uniz avec luy comme à nostre chef, c'est bien raison que premierement nous soyons faictz conformes à sa pureté & specialement que nous ayons*

---

[196] The first French edition appears in 1541, thus eight years prior to Doré's *L'arche de l'alliance*.
[197] I am deeply indebted to Francis Higman for this discovery. It is he who first noticed it and who graciously alerted me to be on the lookout for further instances of Doré lifting material from Calvin.
[198] Text of Calvin taken from Irena Backus and Claire Chimelli, eds., *La Vraie Piété: Divers traités de Jean Calvin et Confession de foi de Guillaume Farel* (Geneva: Labor et Fides, 1986), pp. 121-151. Text of Doré is first edition of *L'arche de l'alliance* (Paris: Benoît Prevost, 1549). **[Paris, BNF—Inv. D 21877]**.

ensemble telle charité et concorde, comme doivent avoir les membres d'un même corps, **combien que pour entendre droitement cette utilité, il ne faut pas estimer que notre Seigneur seulement nous avertisse, incite et enflambe nos coeurs par le signe extérieur. Car le principal est qu'il besogne en nous intérieurement par son Saint-Esprit, afin de donner efficace à son ordonnance qu'il a destinée à cela comme instrument par lequel il veut faire son oeuvre en nous.** *Par quoi, en tant que la vertu du Saint-Esprit est conjointe avec les sacrements quand on les reçoit dûment, nous avons à espérer un bon moyen et aide pour nous faire croître et profiter en sainteté de vie, et singulièrement en charité.* p. 134.	*ensemble telle charité & concorde, comme doibvent avoir les membres d'un mesme corps.* *Aussi, en tant que la vertu du S. esprit est conioncte avec les sacremens, quand on les recoipt deuement nous avons à esperer un bon moyen & ayde, pour nous faire croistre & profiter en saincteté de vie, & singulierement en charité, dilection fraternelle.* fol. 65r°.

The second example shows how Doré at times omits a segment of the text he is copying. These appropriated texts prove that he indeed read his opponents, particularly Calvin, and that his refutation of their positions was based on first-hand knowledge and not merely on the clichés being bantered about in the heat of controversy.

What are we to make then not only of this apparent plagiarism but also of the fact that Doré copies whole paragraphs from his most hated enemy, one to whom he consecrates an entire work as a direct refutation? First of all, the idea of copyright or of personal ownership of one's published thought was unknown in the sixteenth century. Thus what to us appears as a flagrant case of plagiarism was actually a rather common and accepted practice. That Doré copied from another what he thought was good and useful for his own purposes is not astonishing, for most authors of the time did the very same thing. What is truly hard to believe is that the person from whom he borrowed was someone he considered to be a heretic and son of Satan. It shows that despite all the rhetoric and polemics against the Reformers found in his work, Doré in fact respected Calvin as a thinker and theologian, if only secretly. Read in the context of Doré's *L'arche de l'alliance*, the passages incorporated from Calvin sound completely orthodox. One would never guess that they are actually the words of the foremost of the Reformers. Given Doré's unflagging allegiance to orthodoxy, it goes without saying that what he copies from Calvin has met with his approval in terms of its conformity with the true faith. The fact that he does not give Calvin credit for his occasional orthodoxy confirms our friar's concern to keep the tenor of the debate polemical, for the gravity of the Genevan Reformer's errors outweighs any modicum of truth to be found in the rest of his work.

It is clear then that Doré's presentation of Protestant doctrine, often stereotypical and never including references to actual texts, is deliberately so for the sake of polemics, for the evidence that he was familiar with their writings is indisputable. His purpose is not to find common ground or to enter into dialogue with the Reformers, but rather to do battle with them in the belief that the salvation of souls is at stake. Although he has obviously found some grain of truth, indeed perhaps even several grains, in Calvin's writings, to openly admit that would have been tantamount to taking the force out of his own argument that the poisonous doctrine of the Reformers was a serious threat to society.

Another point which must be made is that we cannot conclude that Doré's borrowing from Calvin indicates a lack of originality or an inferior intellect. The passages that the Dominican "borrows" from his Genevan counterpart are skillfully woven into the fabric of his own particular points as well as into the larger structure of the book itself which is specifically his creation and corresponds neither to the *Institutes* nor to the *Petit traicté de la Saincte Cène*. It is actually a credit to Doré that, when reading the passages in question, there is no noticeable rupture in thought pattern or change in style. The copied texts flow very naturally both with what precedes and what follows. There is never the sense that this is no longer Doré speaking but someone else. Those who in the past have harshly criticized Doré's convoluted literary style as compared to the elegance of Calvin's prose would be forced to think twice about this assessment given the practical indistinguishability of their styles in *L'arche de l'alliance*. Setting aside our modern sensibility to plagiarism, Doré demonstrates in these instances of "borrowing" an ability to take an idea that someone else has expressed clearly and effectively and work it into a new context without any sense of it being out of place there. It is not so much, then, the idea itself that is lifted from Calvin, but the manner of expressing it, for the skillful way it fits into Doré's structure indicates that he could have easily expressed the same thought in his own words had he wanted to do so.

To be sure, our friar would certainly be horrified that his secret is now out, that his defense of orthodoxy contains some "Calvinist flour." It is unfortunate that his unyielding opposition to the Reformation did not permit him to openly acknowledge the elements of truth he discovered in the Genevan Reformer's thought and subsequently utilized. However, we must keep in mind that Pierre Doré considered himself to be at war and in war there can be no compromise with the enemy. It was to ensure the victory of orthodoxy that he engaged in the art of polemics, an art of clear distinctions between the good and the bad, the right and the wrong. Yet, while this polemical thrust led him at times to intentionally misrepresent the "Lutheran" or "Calvinist" position on a given issue, it must nevertheless be affirmed that his principal objections to Reformed theology were based on an accurate knowledge of what his opponents taught. One may thus find fault with Doré for his polemical spirit, but one cannot accuse him of entering the theological fray against the Reformers with nothing more than misconceptions of their positions based on hearsay, for he knew exactly where they stood.

Chapter 3
JUSTIFICATION, GRACE, MERIT AND FREE WILL

The preceding chapters have served as an introduction to Pierre Doré and his voluminous work within the context of Reformation-era France. We have seen that the Dominican theologian was motivated in his career by a sense of vocation to provide the laity with devotional and theological literature in French as a way of responding to the vernacular works of the Reformers that, in his view, were the vehicle for disseminating the poison of heresy. His particular approach and method in providing the antidote of Catholic truth for his readers has been examined in a broad overview. Now it is time to take a closer look at what he wrote and to draw out the principal elements of his thought. What are the recurring themes of his works? What are his preoccupations, the issues he chooses to focus on? How exactly does he go about refuting the erroneous doctrines of Luther and Calvin and presenting the orthodox position?

Given that practically all of Doré's work is in some sense a response to Reformed theology even if the majority of his books are not explicitly polemical, it seems appropriate to arrange the material of the second part of this study according to the great issues which were at the heart of the Reformation debate. Thus the present chapter will examine his discussion of the highly controversial issue of justification by faith with the related questions of grace, merit and free will. The succeeding chapter will take up the question of the Eucharist, a no less controversial point for both Reformers and defenders of orthodoxy alike. Here we will see how, for Doré, the issues of the real presence and of the effects of the sacrament are at the fore of the debate on the Eucharist. Finally, we will explore how our friar's promotion of the virtuous life in his devotional works really forms the heart of his attack on Reformation theology. Though the primary aim of these works, generally speaking, is to urge the reader to a more affective union with Christ, the life of virtue which this union makes possible nevertheless represents a challenge to the Protestant view of grace and nature. It is in this sense that the devotional writings in fact play a central role in Doré's anti-Protestant program.

It should be stated from the outset that the reader will not find here a detailed presentation of the positions of either of Doré's principal opponents, Luther and Calvin, on the points at issue. The purpose of these chapters is principally to expose the Dominican's handling of the issues in question. The Reformers' positions will be treated only insofar as they help to throw light on Doré's response as well as to demonstrate that the Dominican did not always fairly represent what his opponents were saying. But apart from that, minute and detailed presentations will be omitted as beyond the scope of this present work. Thus the reader should not expect an extensive analysis or evaluative judgment of the various doctrinal positions. What is of primary interest here is the content of Doré's theological exposition as well as the way in which he presents it for his "theologically unsophisticated" reading public.

Sola Fide: Refuting the Cornerstone of the Reformation

In the well-known passage on the virtue of charity in his first letter to the Corinthians, St. Paul writes of the three theological virtues, "So faith, hope, love abide, these three; but the greatest of these is love."[199] Playing off of this verse a

---

[199] 1 Corinthians 13:13, RSV.

bit, it can be said that for the sixteenth-century Reformers there are three fundamental doctrines from which everything else in Christianity flows: *sola scriptura, sola gratia,* and *sola fide*—and the greatest of these is *sola fide*. These are the bedrock doctrines, if you will, of Reformed theology. *Sola scriptura,* the idea that the Scriptures alone are the basis for what is believed, and Doré's reaction to it have already been discussed in detail in Chapter 2. The doctrine of *sola gratia* proclaims not only the primacy of grace in man's redemption, a primacy which is in fact affirmed in the constant tradition of the Church, but goes further by asserting that it is grace **alone** which saves and that man in no way cooperates in his redemption. This doctrine flows from the more fundamental principle of *sola fide,* the notion that we are justified by faith alone rather than by faith and good works as was traditionally taught in the Church. Although the origins of *sola fide* lie in the very personal and intense struggle of Martin Luther to satisfy without success the demands of a righteous God, it has since become the veritable cornerstone of the Protestant edifice. In fact, it can be said that the Reformation stands or falls on this fundamental principle.[200] Just as love is the greatest of the virtues, *sola fide* can be said to be the greatest of the three fundamental doctrines of Reformed theology, greater even than *sola scriptura* because the Scriptures themselves are interpreted and judged in its light.[201]

The basis for the doctrine of justification by faith is found principally in Paul's letters to the Romans and to the Galatians where the apostle argues against certain judaizers in the Christian community that it is not observance of the Mosaic Law that makes a person righteous but rather faith in Jesus Christ. For

---

[200] In introducing his discussion of justification in Chapter XI of Book III of the *Institutes*, Calvin writes "we must so discuss [justification by faith] as to bear in mind that this is the main hinge on which religion turns...for unless you first of all grasp what your relationship to God is, and the nature of his judgment concerning you, you have neither a foundation on which to establish your salvation nor one on which to build piety toward God." McNeill, 1, p. 726. For the citation in French, see Benoît, 3, pp. 204-205.

[201] Gaboriau, *L'écriture,* p. 76 points out that Luther places *sola fide* "*au dessus de tout, pour juger de tout, y compris de l'Ecriture.*" This leads the German Reformer to establish a sort of hierarchy among the New Testament books, for example exalting the letters of Paul while dismissing the letter of James because the latter seems to contradict the salutary doctrine of justification enunciated by Paul.

Luther, an Augustinian of the strict observance who was at the same time racked by a scrupulous conscience which constantly condemned him for not being able to fulfill the demands of righteousness, the full meaning of Paul's message in the letter to the Romans struck him one day, proving to be both an answer to his personal dilemma and the beginning of his rejection of the traditional understanding that we are made righteous by both faith **and** good works proceeding from love.[202] But nowhere in his letters does Paul ever state that we are justified by faith **alone**. Nevertheless, in 1522, when translating the New Testament into German, Luther took it upon himself to add the word to the apostle's statement in Romans 3:28, "For we hold that a man is justified by faith **alone** apart from works of the law," claiming that this insertion more accurately conveyed Paul's intended meaning.[203] Yet, despite this manipulation of the biblical text to suit his own purpose, Luther's insistence that we are justified by faith alone and not by works struck a responsive chord that was wholeheartedly embraced and transmitted by the Reformers who followed him.[204] In a Church where indulgences, whether earned by performing a prescribed work of penance or purchased to benefit the construction of the new St. Peter's basilica in Rome, seemed to convey to the popular mind the idea that we can work, or even worse, buy our way into heaven, the doctrine of *sola fide* seemed to be a retrieval of authentic biblical teaching which restored the emphasis on the passion and death of Christ as the unique source of our salvation.

While it is impossible here to provide a detailed exposition of the various nuances which different Reformers gave to the doctrine of justification, a brief discussion of the general understanding is nonetheless necessary in order to better

---

[202] This experience is generally dated by most scholars as occurring at some point in 1515. See Alister McGrath, *Reformation Thought* (Oxford: Blackwell, 1996), p. 97.

[203] See Jaroslav Pelikan, *Reformation of Church and Dogma (1300-1700)* (Chicago: University of Chicago Press, 1984), p. 252.

[204] Calvin himself defends Luther's addition of the word "alone" to the Pauline idea of justification by faith in the *Institutes*, III. XI. 19.

appreciate Doré's response to the teaching.[205] Using Calvin's precise and succinct definition as the norm, it is understood that "justified by faith is he who, excluded from the righteousness of works, grasps the righteousness of Christ through faith, and clothed in it, appears in God's sight not as a sinner but as a righteous man."[206] What is important to understand is that faith, for the Reformers, is not a kind of "work" that we do in order to become righteous. Otherwise, they could well be accused of logical inconsistency in condemning the works-righteousness they perceived in Catholic theology and simply substituting it with this "work" of faith. Faith, then, is rather the way in which we receive the righteousness of Christ so that our sinfulness is covered over and we become acceptable to God. In other words, we are completely passive in the act of justification which is solely God's work on our behalf. Thus, justification is "the acceptance with which God receives us into his favor as righteous men and...consists in the remission of sins and the imputation of Christ's righteousness."[207] "Acceptance" and "imputation" are key terms here, for they underscore the fact that justification is not, in the Protestant view, to be equated with transformation in grace or regeneration. Ultimately, the justified remain sinners, but they are "accepted" by the divine favor and made pleasing to God by being clothed in the righteousness of Christ.

Given the centrality of justification by faith to the theological framework of the Reformers, it comes as no surprise that defenders of orthodoxy in the sixteenth century focused much of their energies on refuting this doctrine as being neither scriptural nor as having any basis in Tradition, particularly in the writings of Augustine whom the Reformers saw as their champion on this issue. One of the most potent weapons in their scriptural arsenal was the letter of James where the author unequivocally states that there is a necessary relationship between the faith that justifies and good works. "What does it profit, my brethren, if a man

---

[205] For a discussion of the differences in substance and emphasis concerning the doctrine of justification by faith among the Reformers, see McGrath, *Reformation*, pp. 109-112.
[206] *Institutes*, III. XI. 2. McNeill, 1, pp. 726-727. See Benoît, 3, p. 205.
[207] Ibid.

says he has faith but has not works? Can his faith save him?...Faith by itself, if it has no works is dead."[208] Defenders of orthodoxy cited this passage over and over again as the proof-text *par excellence* of the erroneous position of the Reformers on justification. It is no wonder that Luther had little love for the letter of James and tended to dismiss it in light of the greater authority of Paul. Calvin, who more honestly admitted that the same Spirit who taught through Paul also taught through James, explained away the difficulty by claiming that James used both "faith" and "justification" in a different sense from Paul.[209]

This is not the place, however, to provide a comprehensive review of the sixteenth-century Catholic response to the Protestant view of justification nor of the way in which the Reformers countered the objections raised by their detractors. Of interest in this study is how Pierre Doré chose to handle the issue in his own defense of orthodoxy. Judging from the titles of his works, only one seems to deal explicitly with the issue of justification, the relatively late work, *Dialogue de la justification chrestienne* (1554). But the conclusion one might draw from this evidence that the Dominican theologian does not seem to have been as preoccupied with the question of justification as his contemporaries could not be further from the truth. Although the titles do not necessarily reveal the fact, this question receives a significant amount of attention throughout the "Doréan" corpus along with the related issues of the nature of grace, the relationship of grace and human free will, and the idea of how we can be said to merit eternal life.

Echoing Paul's affirmation in 1 Corinthians 13 that the virtue of charity is greater than faith, Doré's refutation of *sola fide* proceeds from and constantly returns to the idea that the faith which saves must be a living faith, or one which is "formed by charity," to borrow the classical expression of scholastic theology. Like a *leitmotif*, this phrase appears over and over again throughout his works. At the heart of his counterattack is a desire to show that the Catholic understanding

---

[208] James 2:14, 17, RSV.
[209] See *Institutes*, III. XVII. 11

of justification and related issues is firmly grounded in Pauline theology. Thus, the proof-text from the letter of James does not figure very strongly in Doré's works. In fact, the specific verse on faith and works is cited but a few times. The impression given is that Doré is anxious to show that James is not the only solid scriptural basis for the Catholic position, although he never states this explicitly. Nevertheless, by the very fact that he grounds his exposition of the orthodox doctrine on justification in varied passages from throughout the New Testament, it is clear that his intention is to prove that the Reformers can claim neither St. Paul nor the Gospels in support of their doctrine of *sola fide*.

Since not a single work of Doré contains a comprehensive treatment of justification and related issues, the *Dialogue de la justification chrestienne* included, it has seemed best to me to present his discussion of these issues according to the principal scriptural passages which he uses to illustrate the Catholic position. The most important of these is the passage mentioned above on the theological virtue of love drawn from 1 Corinthians 13 which the Dominican uses to affirm the unity of the virtues and to make the point that faith cannot stand by itself. The Beatitudes from Chapter 5 of Matthew's Gospel serve as the basis for a discussion of the notion of merit in the Christian life. Finally, the dialogue between Christ and the Samaritan woman in the Gospel of John, Chapter 4 is used to illustrate the process of justification which includes a free-will response on the part of the person who is justified. To be sure, a variety of other Scripture passages also come into play in Doré's exposition. Some of these will be highlighted in the course of the presentation under the appropriate section. However, the three major passages I have singled out as the organizing principal of this chapter illustrate most clearly I think his desire to prove that there is no scriptural foundation whatsoever for the Reformers' teaching on justification by faith **alone**.

"...And the Greatest of these is Love": The Necessity of Formed or Living Faith

"What must I do to be saved?" When all is said and done, this basic question is what the debate on justification is all about. A correct answer is of vital importance to the believer because the stakes are either beatitude or damnation for all eternity. It is not without reason then that the very first topic of discussion in Doré's catechism, the *Dyalogue instructoire* (1538), is precisely this question of how it is possible for us to obtain eternal life. The quality of the dialogue between the centurion Cornelius and the master teacher St. Peter on this point merits an ample citation:

> *COR. De puys que suis venu a usaige de raison et recongnois que ne me suis pas faict et formé moymesmes, je demande: veu qu'en ce monde ne me voy pas en estat de felicité que me commande celluy qui ma faict pour estre saulvé.*
>
> *SP. Il veult trois choses: c'est assavoir foy, esperance et amour en luy.*
>
> *COR. Scauroit on aultrement me donner a entendre que c'est de la foy.*
>
> *SP. Ouy, en disant que foy est ung don de dieu par lequel on croit a la verité premiere certainement et sans evidence: revelée en l'escripture et a l'eglise.*
>
> *COR. Ou est il escript que je doibz avoir la foy.*
>
> *SP. Sainct Paul en ladicte epistre [Heb.] chap. vi dict que sans la foy il est impossible de plaire a Dieu.*
>
> *COR. Ceste foy descripte est elle suffisante pour me saulver?*
>
> *SP. Ouy, si elle est vifve: ayant avec foy bonnes oeuvres faictes en grace, aultrement elle est morte et ne saulve point: car telle foy ont les dyables, ainsi que escript S. Jacques et n'en sont pas meilleurs.*[210]

---

[210] *Dyalogue instructoire des chrestiens en la foy, esperance, & amour en Dieu* (Paris: Jean Real, 1538), fol. Aiii v°-Aiiii r°. [**Paris, BNF—m8989**]. The revised edition (Paris: Jean de Brouilly, 1545), [**Washington, LC—BV4833, D6**], contains the following insertion: "*Ouy, si elle est vifve & unie avec confidence de dieu, ayant avec foy bonnes oeuvres...*" It would seem that Doré has taken account here of the Protestant insistence that the faith which saves must also include a confidence in God's promises. On this point, Calvin remarks, "...there is a far different feeling of full assurance that in the Scriptures is always attributed to faith. It is this which puts beyond doubt God's goodness clearly manifested for us [Col. 2:2; I Thess. 1:5; cf. Heb. 6:11 and 10:22]...For this reason, the apostle derives confidence from faith..." *Institutes*, III. II. 15. McNeill, 1, p. 561. See Benoît, 3, p. 33.

Nowhere does Doré explicitly make mention of the passage from 1 Corinthians 13 in the above citation. Yet this passage is clearly the foundation for the answer given to Cornelius' first question that in order to be saved three things are necessary, the theological virtues of faith, hope and love in God. And as we see just a few lines later, after St. Peter gives his pupil the classical Thomistic definition of faith as a gift from God by which we adhere to him as First Truth, the inquisitive Cornelius cuts right to the heart of the issue by asking if faith as so defined is sufficient to be saved. "Yes," responds St. Peter, but with a very important qualification. Doré here almost seems to agree with the Reformers' assertion that faith alone suffices for salvation, though it should be pointed out that his definition of faith given above differs significantly from the way in which the Reformers understood it.[211] Yet, he goes on to emphasize that the faith which leads to salvation must be a living faith. In other words, true faith must be properly understood as being completed by hope and charity. Only a faith which expresses itself in good works has the power to save. We see at the end of the citation one of the few occasions where the Dominican makes allusion to the passage from the letter of James on the necessity of good works in the Christian life. But the real foundation of his argument, as illustrated by the very title of the catechism, *Dyalogue instructoire des chrestiens en la foy, esperance, & amour en Dieu*, is the insistence on the unity of the virtues and their perfection through love as expressed by St. Paul in 1 Corinthians 13.

The point is even more fully developed and clearly presented in *Le college de sapience* (1539), the work which immediately follows the *Dyalogue*. This time, Doré offers several images to help concretize the theological discussion for his readers and makes an explicit reference to the passage in 1 Corinthians. He opens the discussion by first of all explaining that although St. Paul at times in his letters simply says that we are justified by faith without mentioning the other

---

[211] Calvin, for example, formally defined faith as "...a firm and certain knowledge of God's benevolence toward us, founded upon the truth of the freely given promise in Christ, both revealed to our minds and sealed upon our hearts through the Holy Spirit." *Institutes*, III. II. 7. McNeill, 1, p. 551. See Benoît, 3, p. 23.

virtues, his statements are not to be interpreted as thereby asserting the sufficiency of faith, as if hope and charity were not also necessary for our salvation:

> *Quand doncques on dict & on lict en l'escripture que la foy saulve, justifie, & beatifie, on ne ouste pas pour cela a esperance, & charité et oeuvres bonnes, salvation, justification, & beatification. Car esperance & charité sont argumens de foy entiere & vive, par lesquelles vertus est congneue estre vifve & non morte.*[212]

In a similar fashion to that seen in the *Dyalogue instructoire*, Doré argues that the virtues of hope and charity as evidenced in the practice of good works point to a faith that is alive and not moribund. It is a living faith only, one completed by hope and love, which justifies and saves. Once again, the essential point is that the theological virtues are so interconnected that they must always be considered in relation to one another:

> *Il y a telle coherence pour l'estat present entre ces troys vertus, que l'une sans l'autre n'est parfaicte, la similitude a ce convenable, on peult prendre en ung arbre, ou sont rameaulx ou branches, le tronc, & la racyne: Car tout ainsi que n'est pas arbre qui n'a racyne, mais seullement tronc et boys mort, ne aussi sans branches ou rameaulx n'est pas arbre, mais seullement ung tronc. Pareillement la racyne est charité, le tronc la foy, & les branches haultes eslevées esperance, & n'est point une vertu sans l'aultre en sa pleine consummation.*[213]

We have a very good example here of Doré the teacher explaining his point through the use of an image, in this case, the three principal parts of a tree to illustrate the unity of the three theological virtues. A tree can no more exist without roots than faith can exist without being rooted in love. Although he does not advert to the fact, Doré draws his point in this section from the *Summa Theologiae*, 1a2ae, q. 65, a. 4, where Aquinas discusses whether faith and hope can ever exist apart from charity. Briefly, the scholastic master determines that while they can exist without the greatest of the virtues, they are not virtues properly so-called if charity is not present, or as Doré puts it, "*l'une sans l'autre*

---

[212] *Le college*, fol. cxi r°.
[213] Ibid., fol. cxi r°-cxi v°.

n'est parfaicte." In other words, for faith to lead to salvation, it must be formed by charity. As for the image of the tree with charity as the root to illustrate the relationship between the virtues, perhaps this too is an inspiration from St. Thomas who writes in the following article, "Charity is the **root** [emphasis mine] of faith and hope in so far as it gives them the perfection of virtue."[214] But lest we lose sight of the original point of the discussion in *Le college de sapience*, Doré proceeds immediately to bring this discussion on the unity of the theological virtues back to the issue of justification by faith:

> *Autant que il y a de difference entre une charogne & corps mort & l'homme vivant, entre ung noir charbon & le charbon ardant & allumé, entre une chandele estaincte & celle qui est allumée, autant y a il de discrepance entre foy vive, conjoincte a esperance & charité, & celle qui est morte, sans les deulx dictes vertus theologalles ses compaignes: La chandelle laquelle ne art point, est aussi bien chandelle que celle qui est allumée, le charbon est aussi charbon, comme celuy qui est embrasé, et le corps mort s'il avoit l'esperit en soy, seroit aussi bien dict homme, comme ung aultre. En ceste facon foy sans esperance & charité est foy appellée, comme celle qui est vive, Theologiens appellent informe, laquelle est es chrestiens estant en peché. Mais ceste foy ne saulve point, ne justifie point, ne beatifie point, comme celle qui art de charité, & reluist de esperance: Pourtant escript l'apostre en la premiere epistre aux chorinthes, xiii. Et quant j'auray toute foy, tant que je transmue les montaignes, et que je n'aye point charité, je ne suis rien.*[215]

Although the distinction in the above discourse between formed and unformed faith is unquestionably scholastic, the theology it expresses is ultimately Pauline. In bringing out this distinction, Doré is introducing his readers to a rather sophisticated theological discourse not found in any of Paul's letters. Yet, he goes on to show that the difference between the two types of faith is nothing more than an elaboration of the apostle's insistence in the first letter to the Corinthians that apart from love, none of the virtues, not even faith have any real meaning. Faith finds its fulfillment in love, and only when it is accompanied by hope and

---

[214] *Summa*, Ia2ae, q. 65, a.5, arg. 2. See Blackfriars, vol. 23, p. 195.
[215] *Le college*, fol. cxi v°-cxii r°.

love does it have the power to justify. The Dominican theologian's point is that this is a scriptural truth, not a fanciful invention of medieval theologians.

The examples that Doré uses in the citation above to illustrate the difference between formed and unformed faith of a lighted candle as opposed to a candle without flame or of a living person as opposed to a corpse are certainly helpful metaphors for understanding the impotence of faith without charity. But he is not content merely to provide metaphors of the living faith which justifies. Throughout his works, he also points to concrete examples in the Scriptures of people who were justified precisely because their faith was perfected by love. Of the biblical figures whom the Dominican invokes, perhaps none is more controversial than Abraham, who "believed the Lord; and he reckoned it to him as righteousness."[216] After all, the example of Abraham is the centerpiece of St. Paul's argument in the letter to the Romans that we are justified by faith and not by works of the Law.[217] By extension, then, the patriarch is also the exemplar for the *sola fide* of the sixteenth-century Reformers. But just as Doré refuses to let his opponents claim St. Paul as their own, so too does he attempt to reclaim Abraham for the Catholic cause as an example of one who is justified by a living faith:

> *Par tout cecy nous devons recueillir, contre tous Lutheriens, que la foy ne suffist pour estre justifiez, ou estre amys de Dieu, ains est requise charité qui nous fait garder ses commandemens. Regardons cecy en Abraham nostre grand pere, de qui est escript qu'il a eu foy, & luy a esté reputé à justice, & a esté appellé l'amy de Dieu. Mais comment a il esté amy de Dieu en croyant? L'escripture le manifeste, quand Dieu luy dit, Sors de ta terre & de ta parenté & viens en la terre que je te monstreray: ce qu'il feist pour l'amour de Dieu, qui fut plus grand qu'à sa terre, n'à ses parens, ce que monstra plus apertement quand voulut immoler son filz: ainsi nous convient il faire, pour estre vrays amys de Dieu, car avec la foy est requise charité...*[218]

---

[216] Genesis 15:6, RSV.
[217] See Romans 4.
[218] *Le Nouveau Testament*, fol. 180r°-v°.

In invoking Abraham, Doré of course has to address the issue of what Scripture says about him being accounted just by God as a result of his faith. His point is that, implicit in the patriarch's faith was the love which impelled him to act in accordance with God's will. It is in leaving his ancestral home, in translating his faith into an act of love, that Abraham proved pleasing to the Lord. His later willingness to sacrifice his only son Isaac would be an even greater act of faith formed by charity. For Doré, it is clear then that love perfects Abraham's faith by impelling him to action in response to the call to friendship with God. His argument is reasonable, but it still seems to be at odds with what St. Paul writes in Romans, "For if Abraham was justified by works, he has something to boast about, but not before God. For what does the scripture say? 'Abraham believed God, and it was reckoned to him as righteousness.'"[219] Unfortunately, Doré fails to point out that the context of the apostle's reference to Abraham here is a well-developed argument against the idea that salvation can be obtained through observance of the Mosaic Law. Had the Dominican provided a clear explanation to his readers of the tensions in the early Church between Jewish converts and Gentile converts which necessitated Paul's insistence that we are justified by faith in Christ apart from the Law, his reclamation of both St. Paul and Abraham from the Protestant camp would have been even more solidly grounded.

Yet another biblical figure whom Doré points out as an example of the Catholic understanding of justification is the good thief from Luke's account of the crucifixion. The context in which he is invoked is actually a discussion on the vice of despair in *Les allumettes du feu divin* (1538) where Doré proposes the repentant criminal as a sign that even the greatest sinners can expect to obtain the mercy of God if they turn back to him with a contrite heart full of hope. It is the thief's confident hope expressed in that beautiful statement, "Jesus, remember me when you come into your kingdom," which obtains an outpouring of mercy from Christ who returns the answer, "Truly, I say to you, today you will be with me in

---

[219] Romans 4:2-3, RSV.

Paradise."[220] The Dominican goes on to explain that the thief's entry into eternal life is not only a result of divine mercy but also of divine justice on account of the condemned man's "good works" in the exercise of the virtues of faith, hope and charity:

> *Et fault noter que en la salvation de ce larron n'y a pas eu seullement misericorde, mais aussi justice, a raison de ses bonnes oeuvres, car tout premierement il a eu ferme esperance en Dieu, comme avons declairé. Item vraye foy, par laquelle a confessé la puissance divine & majesté royalle & eternelle...Item a la vertu de charité, reprenant son compaignon qui persistoit blasphemant dieu, & usant de correction fraternelle dict: Et ne crains tu point dieu?*[221]

Curiously absent in this commentary on the thief's virtues, especially his faith, is the catch phrase "faith formed by charity" and this for two reasons. First of all, *Les allumettes du feu divin* precedes both the *Dyalogue instructoire* and *Le college de sapience*, the works where Doré introduces the theological concept to his readers. Secondly, the primary point of the example here is to exhort sinners to confidence in God's mercy rather than to refute the Reformation doctrine of *sola fide*. Nevertheless, Doré's insistence that the good thief obtained mercy for his sins through an exercise of hope in his request to be remembered by Christ, faith in his acknowledgment of Christ's innocence and divine kingship, and charity in his rebuking the other thief for blasphemy, does serve as a veiled refutation of the doctrine of justification by faith alone, even if that is not his primary intention here.

Abraham and the good thief are by no means the only scriptural models that Doré points to as exemplifying a living faith. Among others highlighted are Mary Magdalene and the Samaritan woman whom Jesus encounters at the well. But our friar is also anxious to identify more contemporary examples of living faith for his readers and not merely historical figures from the biblical past. Here it is his patron and friend, the Duke of Guise, who serves as the exemplar. In his

---

[220] See Luke 23:42-43, RSV.
[221] *Les allumettes*, fol. xc r°-v°.

eulogy upon the Duke's demise, the confessor praises the virtuous deeds of his gentle master, not merely for the sake of honoring the deceased but also to teach a valuable lesson in theology. Never one to let a teachable moment pass by, he speaks of the duke's faith as having cleansed him of his sins and then goes on to say of this faith:

> *Il est requis d'avoir une foy laquelle (ainsi qu'escript sainct Paul)* [Gal. 5] *soit par charité operante. C'est le poinct ou je veulx descendre, en monstrant que sa foy, de charité a esté formée & vivifiée: N'est ce pas charité entiere que d'aymer pour l'amour de Dieu ses ennemys? voyre jusques a celuy qui luy a baillé, ou fait bailler le venin dont est mort? Or vous avez ouy cy dessus, comment il a protesté luy pardonner, & ne hayr personne vivant: Sa charité l'a fait en la vie, & la mort, estre grand aulmosnier envers les paouvres. Il a esté maintefois avec vous (madame) visiter les prisonniers es chartres, & prisons obscures, & en a delivré plusieurs en payant leurs debtes.*[222]

The opponents of the house of Guise might not necessarily recognize the man Doré is describing here as a paragon of charity and magnanimity. Whether or not Claude de Lorraine was as virtuous as his confessor paints him out to be, however, is beside the point. What matters is how Doré makes use of the duke as an illustration of someone whose faith was formed and vivified by charity. Little did the duke realize that even in death, he would be brought into battle against the heretics whom he had combatted in life! Another interesting point is Doré's citing here of Galatians 5:6 where St. Paul writes, "For in Christ Jesus neither circumcision nor uncircumcision is of any avail, but **faith working through love**" (RSV), demonstrating once again that *sola fide* is not an authentically Pauline doctrine. From the good patriarch Abraham, to the good thief, to the good Duke of Guise, Doré constantly returns to the idea that the faith which saves and justifies must be accompanied by hope and love, otherwise it is useless.

The fifteenth chapter of John's Gospel provides the Dominican with a perfect image for what happens to those who may have faith but have not love. In

---

[222] *Oraison*, fol. 62r°-v°.

the discourse on the vine and the branches, Doré says that the branches that are part of the vine represent all those who are incorporated into Christ by faith. Yet, not all the branches of the vine are the same. Some are fruitful, others are not. For Doré, it is clear that the branches which bear fruit represent the faithful whose faith is formed by charity:

> *Entendons que nostre conglutination & union avec Jesus Christ, est voluntaire, & se parfait par foy & charité. La foy est en nostre entendement, & nous donne vraye congnoissance de Dieu: mais charité nous fait garder ses commandemens. Qui m'aymera (dit il) gardera mes commandemens. Ceulx donc qui sont conjoincts avec Jesus Christ seulement par la foy, ou seule confession de bouche, & non par le lien de charité, sont branchez, mais sans fruict. Et qu'en fera le vigneron? Il les couppera de sa serpe, & les jettera hors de la vigne: dont il est evident que non seulement sont couppez & rejettez de Jesus Christ ceulx qui font mal, & portent mauvais fruict, mais aussi qui ne font point de bien, & ne portent bon fruict.*[223]

The first sentence of this citation makes reference to our "voluntary" union with Christ the vine, the implication being that there is an exercise of free will involved in determining whether we bear fruit or not. A branch's barrenness is not due to any deficiency in the vine, but rather to a deficiency in itself and one which is willed, that is an unwillingness to be bound to the vine in love. The notion of free will and its place in the debate on justification will be more fully discussed in the following sections of this chapter. For now, it serves to justify the pruning by the vinedresser of the barren branches, which because of their freely chosen fruitlessness are cut off from the vine and thrown into the fire.

Doré does carry the metaphor too far when he goes on to apply it to the Reformers in a very literal way, insisting that because they have cut themselves off from Christ by embracing false doctrine, they should be burned as useless branches. As already mentioned in Chapter 2, since they have forfeited the life-giving grace of the Holy Spirit, "*les convient mettre au feu, comme inutile serment de la vigne, & non seulement sont inutiles, mais dommageables &*

---

[223] *Le Nouveau testament*, fol. 138r°-v°.

pernicieux aux autres bonnes branches de la vigne, qui sont les bons fideles."[224] Unfortunately, Doré is not speaking metaphorically here, but very literally advocating a thorough pruning of heretical elements from the Church and society, precisely because they threaten the well-being of the healthy branches by drawing them into doctrinal error. But in his desire to keep heresy from spreading, Doré seems to overlook an important detail of the scriptural passage he invokes as offering license to burn heretics, for it is the Father and he alone who cleans the vine of useless branches (cf. John 15:2). However, the primary use of this passage to once again bring out the distinction between living faith and unformed faith remains a valid one. Although Doré invokes a wide variety of Scripture passages and biblical figures in sounding the theme that we are not justified by faith alone, each one is fundamentally an illustration or elaboration of the Pauline theme in 1 Corinthians 13 that the greatest of the virtues is not faith, but love.

"Blessed are you...": A Discussion of Merit and Free Will

In the *Institutes*, Calvin decries the introduction of both the term and the notion of "merit" into theological discourse saying, "...I wish that Christian writers had always exercised such restraint as not to take it into their heads needlessly to use terms foreign to Scripture that would produce great offense and very little fruit."[225] Although the term itself is indeed not to be found in Scripture, Doré attempts to prove that the notion of merit is in no way foreign to the Gospel. It is in the Sermon on the Mount of Matthew's Gospel (chapters 5-7), particularly the initial section on the Beatitudes, that the Dominican theologian finds solid scriptural evidence for the notion of merit in the Christian life along with the implication that we somehow freely cooperate in our salvation. At issue is the understanding that salvation is both a gratuitous gift from God, one which

---

[224] Ibid., fol. 148v°.
[225] *Institutes*, III. XV. 2. McNeill, 1, p. 789. See Benoît, 3, p. 266.

no human being could ever hope to merit, while at the same time being something for which we must strive by living a virtuous life. How can this be? In what sense is it possible to say that we must merit the eternal life that Christ has won for us by his death? Closely related to the idea of merit is that of grace. For the Reformers, the doctrine of *sola fide* represented a retrieval of an orthodox understanding of the role of grace in the Christian life that had been obscured by the medieval Church's emphasis on merit, works, satisfaction and penance, to the point of being completely distorted. It was a question in their mind of countering a contemporary Pelagianism once again with the Augustinian doctrine of grace. The problem thus faced by Doré was to show that true Catholic doctrine lay between the two extremes of the old Pelagian heresy on the one hand, basically the idea that man can achieve salvation by his own efforts and that grace is nothing more than a helpful aid, and the new "heresy" of *sola gratia* espoused by Reformed theology on the other.

In the dedication of his first major work and best-seller, Doré explains to Françoise de Bouchet, countess of Montfort, *"Pour estancher l'ardente soef & vehemens desir, qu'en vous recongnois, ma tresillustre Dame, a scavoir les droictes voyes qui menent a la beatitude celeste...ay escript ce petit traicté, nommé Les voyes de Paradis."*[226] Like the young man of the Gospel who asks Jesus, "What must I do to inherit everlasting life?" (See Mt. 19:16), the countess de Montfort seeks counsel from her spiritual guide concerning the sure path that leads to paradise. In *Les voyes de paradis*, the Dominican responds to the request by offering a brief commentary on Matthew 5:1-12 in which he presents the Beatitudes as eight resting places on the road to eternal happiness. This is not to say, however, that there are eight different destinations. He explains:

> *La similitude a ce propos convenable est du viateur qui loge en divers logis & hostelleries quand il va par pays. Et toutesfois ne tend qu'a ung lieu qui est sa propre terre. Ainsi sont divers logis de vertueuses*

---

[226] Dedication to Françoise de Bouchet, *Les voyes*, fol. Ai v°.

> *operations, par lesquelles nous tendons a ung pays celeste & une gloire eternelle qui est a veoir dieu.*[227]

Each beatitude represents a different virtue such as poverty of spirit, purity of heart, mercy towards others, etc., in the exercise of which the disciple of Christ tends toward the final end promised us of eternal beatitude, much as a traveler continually tends towards his final destination at each stop along the way. Doré goes on to point out to his spiritual daughter that beginning with the second beatitude, "Blessed are the meek...," all the beatitudes offer a reward in return for a virtuous act, in this case "they shall inherit the earth."[228] Thus, in the very construction of each beatitude from the mouth of Christ, the idea of merit through the exercise of virtue is built in, for a reward is not something freely given but must first be earned in some way:

> *...en ceste beatitude & en toutes les autres il y a toujours le merite qui precede & puis sensuyt le sallaire: le merite est d'estre doulx & aymable, la retribution est d'avoir possession de la terre. Ainsi peult on facilement veoir es autres beatitudes, pour donner a entendre que par vertu on vient a gloire, & par merite on gaigne paradis.*[229]

Doré's insight here is not original. It is an idea that goes back to the Fathers and is also taken up by Aquinas in the *prima secundae* of the *Summa*, q. 69, a. 2. In fact, much of Doré's exposition on the Beatitudes in *Les voyes de paradis* is solidly grounded in Aquinas' own discussion in the four articles of question 69. Although he does not provide direct quotations or references when the phrase "as St. Thomas says" appears, he nevertheless accurately paraphrases and summarizes the medieval theologian's teaching for his readers.

While the last sentence of the above citation with its reference to "winning paradise" by one's merits is akin to throwing oil into the fire of the debate on *sola fide* and *sola gratia*, it must be remembered that *Les voyes de paradis* is not

---

[227] *Les voyes*, fol. Bvii v°.
[228] Contemporary versions list this as the third beatitude, but Doré is following the Vulgate.
[229] *Les voyes*, fol. Biii v°.

primarily a polemical work intended as a rebuttal of a specific point or points in Reformed theology. Rather, it belongs more to the category of Doré's devotional works in which he is primarily concerned to provide basic theological instruction for his readers and to stir up the flames of devotion within their hearts. Nevertheless, his exposition of the Beatitudes here with the particular focus on the notions of virtue and merit certainly represents a challenge to his opponents who completely reject any sense in which a believer can be said to merit eternal life, despite the fact that this is the most evident meaning of Christ's words, "Blessed are you when men revile you and persecute you and utter all kinds of evil against you falsely on my account. Rejoice and be glad, **for your reward is great in heaven**."[230]

It is in his commentary on the fourth beatitude, "Blessed are those who hunger and thirst for righteousness," that Doré takes up the problem of how sinful human beings can perform virtuous acts which are meritorious of eternal life. Speaking of just acts which one might perform, he readily admits that *"en ce monde nostre justice ne peult estre totallement parfaicte, car comme escript sainct Jehan en sa premiere canonique au premier chapitre, si nous disons qu'il n'y a point peche en nous, nous sommes seduictz & verité n'est pas en nous."*[231] Yet, while acknowledging that our acts of virtue always remain imperfect in this life, he clearly denounces the notion put forth by Luther in particular that our acts can never be pleasing in the sight of the Lord because even when a person is gratuitously justified by God, he remains always a sinner. This is the idea that the believer is *simul justus et peccator*, a phrase coined by Luther in his commentary on the Letter to the Romans. According to his understanding, God merely imputes justification to those who put faith in his promises, but this grace does not actually change us interiorly. We remain sinners whose every act is displeasing to God. The force of his position comes through as he comments on Romans 4, verse 7:

---

[230] Matthew 5:11-12, RSV.
[231] *Les voyes*, fol. Cvi v°.

> For even the good works which are done while the tinder of sin and sensuality are fighting against them are not of such intensity and purity as the Law requires, since they are not done with all of our strength, but only with the spiritual powers which struggle against the powers of the flesh. Thus we sin even when we do good, unless God through Christ covers this imperfection and does not impute it to us. Thus it becomes a venial sin through the mercy of God, who does not impute it for the sake of faith and the plea in behalf of this imperfection for the sake of Christ. Therefore, he who thinks that he ought to be regarded as righteous because of his works is very foolish, since if they were offered as a sacrifice to the judgment of God, they still would be found to be sins. [232]

It is not merely a question then of our good works always being imperfect. According to Luther, they are always sins in the sight of God, which is why we need to be covered in the justice of Christ so that the sin will not be imputed.[233] For Doré, however, the truth expressed in 1 John 1:8, "If we say we have no sin, we deceive ourselves," does not lead to the conclusions drawn by Luther in his explanation of what it means to be *simul justus et peccator*:

> *Mais cecy* [1 John 1:8] *fault sainement entendre & se garder de lutheriser ou desvier de la foy, selon laquelle nous tenons que oeuvres justes nous pouvons icy faire esquelles n'y a aucune offence comme en aymant dieu ainsi que il a commandé, & en detestant peché & de plusieurs aultres sainctes operations...*[234]

Unfortunately, apart from merely affirming, in opposition to Luther, that we are capable of virtuous though imperfect acts in this life which merit the reward of eternal life, Doré never really explains how or why this is true in *Les voyes de paradis*. The full explanation only comes a year later in a section of the *Dyalogue instructoire*.

---

[232] *Luther's Works*, ed. Hilton Oswald, vol. 25, *Lectures on Romans—Glosses and Scholia* (Saint Louis: Concordia Publishing House, 1972), p. 276. For the citation in the original Latin, see Weimar, 56, p. 289.

[233] Calvin expresses the same thought in the *Institutes*, III. XIV. 8 when he writes, "We therefore hold to be beyond doubt what ought to be a mere commonplace even to one indifferently versed in the Scriptures, that in men not yet truly sanctified works manifesting even the highest splendor are so far away from righteousness before the Lord that they are reckoned sins." McNeill, 1, p. 775. See Benoît, 3, pp. 252-253.

[234] *Les voyes*, fol. Cvi v°.

The discussion on merit in the *Dyalogue* is one of Doré's true achievements. It is among the clearest, most straightforward and precise theological expositions in his entire corpus. All the questions left unanswered by the presentation in *Les voyes de paradis* concerning how we can be said to perform virtuous acts meritorious of eternal life are in the present work voiced by the ever-curious Cornelius and ably resolved by the ever-unflappable St. Peter. What follows is a generous excerpt demonstrating the quality of Doré's treatment of the difficult issues of merit and grace:

> *COR. Qu'esse que merite?*
>
> *SP. C'est l'oeuvre bonne de l'homme faicte en grace, par laquelle il dessert & gaigne qu'on luy rende salaire, & retribution eternelle: jouxte la promesse & convention de Dieu faicte avec nous.*
>
> *COR. Est il possible ainsi meriter envers Dieu? Nous ne le pouvons obliger a nous: car tout bien est il pas don de Dieu?*
>
> *SP. On ne peult pas meriter avoir ceste premiere grace de Dieu par laquelle on vient a estre justifié: car grace est le principe de merite, & qui ne la point comment meriteroit il? Mais qui a la grace de dieu, par bonnes oeuvres merite avoir Paradis. Et toutesfoys en meritant nous ne faisons pas Dieu obligé a nous: mais il s'est obligé a soy mesmes: car il luy a pleu de sa bonté nous promettre son royaulme, en gardant ses commandemens comme il dit en l'evangile,* **Si vis ad vitam ingredi, serva mandata (mat. xix).** *Si tu veulx entrer en la vie, garde les commandmentz.*
>
> *COR. Ce qui vient de grace et de liberalité, comment peult il estre avec merite qui est joinct avec justice?*
>
> *SP. Il n'y a point de repugnance, car ainsi plaist a Dieu de sa grace d'accepter nostre oeuvre pour merite. Nostre seigneur a merité paradis, et toutesfoys nous l'avons par la grace de Dieu...*
>
> *COR. Y a il quelque dignité en noz oeuvres pour avoir ung si grand bien qu'est paradis?*
>
> *SP. Non pas si nous les considerons hors de grace, & entant qu'elles procedent de nous: mais quand par divine grace sommes aulcunement deifiez, noz oeuvres qui viennent du Sainct Esperit habitant en nous sont dignes de gloire avec ce que la paction de dieu et son decret, y est qui aux ouvriers en sa vigne qui est nostre mere saincte eglise, jouxte sa*

> *convention donnera le denier de retribution eternelle: comme il a dict en la parabolle evangelique en sainct Mathieu vingtiesme chappitre.*[235]

As with the exposition on the Beatitudes, so this present discussion on merit is largely drawn from St. Thomas, question 114 of the *prima secundae*. Yet, it is Aquinas presented in a readable form which even an uninitiated layperson could easily understand. What is especially important in the above exposition is the emphasis on the primacy of grace, an emphasis that was not so apparent in *Les voyes de paradis*. Doré makes it very clear here that apart from grace it is impossible to merit eternal life. It is the saving death of Christ and that alone which merits the gift of paradise for us. On this point, there is complete accord with the Reformers. The divergence comes with the affirmation that those who are in the state of grace and under the inspiration of the Holy Spirit perform good works which themselves are meritorious of eternal life. It is not a question of God "owing" us the reward, as Doré explains, for God is never indebted to us in justice and everything he gives us is his free gift. Rather it has pleased him to promise the kingdom to those who through his grace keep the commandments and do works of charity. The primacy of grace is thus preserved as well as is the affirmation that we have a role to play in our salvation.

And yet, there seems to be a contradiction in saying that we merit eternal life through good works done in grace if Christ's death has already merited the gift for us. Is Christ's death then not sufficient in and of itself? The notion of merit at worst seems to dilute the efficacy of his passion and at best is completely superfluous in the scheme of salvation. Not to worry, however. Cornelius has noticed the apparent contradiction and put the question to St. Peter who responds:

> *Le merite de Jesuschrist est suffisant comme cause universelle du salut humain: mais il fault qu'il soit appliqué par les sacramentz & foy formée de charité, qui n'est sans oeuvres meritoires: desquelles le merite de Jesuschrist est cause, comme il dict en l'evangile de sainct Jehan, 15 chappitre, Je suis la vigne, & vous estes les sepz: Ainsi que le sep ne*

---

[235] *Dyalogue instructoire*, fol. I v°-lii v°.

> *peult produire le raisin s'il n'est planté en la vigne, aussi ne pouvez vous fructifier si vous ne demourez en moy. Par la vertu de foy vive sommes plantez en Jesuschrist qui est la vigne, & par ce moyen produisons fruict meritoire de la vie eternelle, & digne d'icelle...*[236]

For Doré, there is no contradiction in affirming the necessity of meritorious works in addition to Christ's redemptive passion, for all merit proceeds from Christ. The passage on the vine and the branches from John 15 illustrates the point well. By virtue of being grafted onto Christ by "*foy formée de charité*," his merits are not only applied to us but bear the fruit of good works meriting eternal life.

To assert that good works contribute to salvation is in no way a form of Pelagianism as far as Doré is concerned, for grace must always precede the virtuous act which leads to eternal life. In two subsequent writings, *La caeleste pensée de graces divines* (1543) and *La premiere partie des collations royales* (1546), Doré explicitly denounces the Pelagian confidence in man's ability to avoid sin and live virtuously apart from grace. For example, in his Lenten conferences for the Duke and Duchess of Guise, he offers the following commentary on verse 16 of Psalm 24 (Vulgate version),[237] which he translates as "*Mes yeulx sont continullement vers le Seigneur, car il tirera mes piedz hors de la retz*:"

> *Aulcuns sont qui pour leur garder de tomber en la fosse de peché ne regardent qu'a leurs piedz, c'est a scavoir, qui cuydent avec Pelagien l'heretique, par leur propre diligence, cheminer droict, sans clocher jamais, & broncher, ou chanceller en peché, par la vertu de leur franc arbitre seullement, & sans la grace, ou ayde supernelle: mais bien au contraire, dict le Psalmiste, que si Dieu ne garde la ville en vain faict le guet, celuy qui la garde sans moy, c'est a dire, sans mon ayde (dit Jesus Christ) vous ne pouvez rien faire.*[238]

Doré's anti-Pelagian stance here is unambiguous. We cannot look to our own feet, that is our own faculty of will, to extricate ourselves from the net of sin,

---
[236] Ibid., fol. lii v°.
[237] According to the present system of enumeration, the verse in question is actually verse 15, not 16.
[238] *La premiere partie des collations*, pp. 176-177.

rather our eyes must be fixed on the Lord from whom alone comes our help. Yet with God's grace, we can accomplish things that before were impossible to us. What distinguishes Doré's presentation of grace and merit from the Protestant stance is the allowance that the primacy of grace does not of necessity exclude the notion that we can freely will to perform works meritorious of eternal life. Rather, grace moves the will and empowers us to live the Beatitudes and thus inherit the rewards promised to the meek, the pure, those who hunger for justice and those who are persecuted for the name of Christ.

The Woman at the Well: A Living Image of How Justification Takes Place

In the preface to the *Dialogue de la justification chrestienne* (1554), Doré informs his readers that he will do more than simply present what they should believe concerning the manner in which we are justified, he will illustrate it "...*peincte au vif en une pauvre Samaritaine justifiée par nostre justificateur Jesus en ce petit dialogue.*"[239] The image is drawn from Chapter 4 of John's Gospel where Jesus, en route to Galilee from Judea and wearied from the journey, stops to rest at a well in the Samaritan town of Sychar. There he encounters a woman who has come to draw water and asks her for a drink. For Doré, the entire encounter serves as a beautiful illustration of the process of justification since the woman, as the Gospel recounts, is an adulteress and yet by the end of the account is transformed into a disciple. In a masterful way, the Dominican shows how each moment in the dialogue between Christ and this woman corresponds to the essential truths which the Church has always taught concerning both the primacy of grace and our free cooperation with that grace in order to be justified. To be sure, these are truths which Doré has affirmed in his previous works, as this chapter has shown. But what sets the *Dialogue* apart is that it is really a

---

[239] Preface to *Dialogue de la justification chrestienne entre nostre saulveur Jesus & la Samaritaine* (Paris: Jean Ruelle, 1554), fol. Aii v°. [**Paris, BA—8° T 6959**].

compendium of his teaching on the matter in which he presents in a very clear and concise manner the Catholic understanding of the process of justification complete with a very appropriate illustration from Scripture. Although it is one of Doré's shortest works, consisting of a mere 56 folios, it is in my judgment also one of his finest. That being said, it is difficult to understand why this work did not turn out to be a best-seller. In fact, it was not even re-published once in a subsequent edition. Perhaps the rather restricted subject matter made for only a limited appeal among Doré's devotees. In terms of the work's theological content, however, it remains a gold mine for better understanding our friar's project of responding to Reformed theology by demonstrating the scriptural basis of the orthodox position on the points of debate.

Before discussing the content of this little masterpiece, it should be pointed out that Doré cites several times the Council of Trent's decree on justification which was promulgated at the end of the sixth session on 13 January 1547, seven years before the *Dialogue*'s publication. These citations, translated by Doré into French, are perhaps the first time that the French reading public is exposed to at least the major elements of the council's teaching on the subject.[240] Thus, the *Dialogue* can be considered a means by which Trent's determinations on the question of justification were popularly disseminated in France, a felicitous consequence if not the primary motive for which Doré included the citations. It should be noted, however, that the *Dialogue* is not simply a summary presentation by Doré of the conciliar teaching. It is rather a compendium of his own exposition of the orthodox understanding of justification which appeared in his previous works, long before the council itself took up the matter. The conciliar statements are cited by way of demonstrating that he is in complete accord with the teaching of the magisterium.

---

[240] For a discussion on the diffusion of Tridentine conciliar texts in France, see Alain Tallon, *La France et le concile de Trente (1518-1563)* (Rome: Ecole Française de Rome, 1997), pp. 533-547. According to Tallon (p. 538), the Genevan Reformer Calvin holds the distinction of being the first to provide a French translation of the Tridentine decrees in 1547, obviously not with the idea of making the decrees better known but rather of pointing out the errors to be found there.

What Doré is most anxious to prove in this new exposition is that the primacy of grace and the role of human free will are both essential components of the process of justification. Neither one excludes the other, though grace necessarily precedes our cooperative action. The Dominican theologian points out that the primacy of grace in justification is clearly shown in the episode of the Samaritan woman at the well in the fact that Jesus is the one who arrives first at the scene and also the one who initiates dialogue with the adulteress, "*...pour demonstrer qu'en la justification du pecheur c'est luy qui premierement parle a nostre cueur, & met bonnes affections en nous.*"[241] Apart from grace, we are incapable of any movement towards God. It is he who must initiate dialogue with the soul through his gift of grace. On this point, Doré and his Protestant opponents are in complete agreement.

The sinner's absolute need for grace extends to the preparation which itself is necessary to receive the grace of justification, namely a turning towards God and a turning away from sin. The will is powerless to make this choice on its own. Even this initial turning towards the ultimate good is impossible to us unless God himself first moves us. Here Doré makes reference to Aquinas' discussion of the issue in the *Summa Theologiae* where the essential point is that man can in no way prepare himself for grace except by a gratuitous assistance from God which moves him from within.[242] He goes on to explain that this divine assistance comes from outside us, through the preaching of the Word, the good example of others, or even the experience of trials and sufferings, all of which may serve to turn us to God, but that we must also be moved from deep within our hearts. Thus the conversation which Jesus initiates with the Samaritan woman is primarily for Doré an image of how God prepares the soul for justification by a movement of his grace.

---

[241] *Dialogue de la justification*, fol. 15r°.
[242] Though he does not provide a citation, the article to which he refers is from the Ia2ae, q. 109, a. 6.

Yet, the fact that God must first move us in order that we may turn to him does not mean, as the Reformers would assert, that we remain passive in our justification. Continuing his exposition of Christ's dialogue with the woman at the well, Doré points out that the Lord opens the conversation with a request, "Give me a drink." He goes on to remark that Christ's real thirst here is not so much for water as it is a burning desire to justify the adulteress, to give her the living water of grace, for a few verses later, Jesus says to her, "If you knew the gift of God, and who it is that is saying to you, 'Give me a drink,' you would have asked him, and he would have given you living water."[243] The Dominican comments that "...*voulant donner de l'eaue de grace a la Samaritaine il demande d'elle avoir de l'eaue. Il veult la justifier, mais il exige d'elle un cueur contrict resolut en eaue de larmes de penitence.*"[244] For Doré, the request Jesus makes of the woman is a perfect illustration of how the sinner must respond to the initial movement of grace within by turning towards God and away from sin in order to be justified. In other words, the will must freely cooperate with grace in preparing for the gift of justification by true contrition and penance for past sins. It is precisely here that Reformed theology departs from the traditional understanding, according to Doré who explains to his readers:

> *O que plusieurs sont ignorans de ce don* [of justification]. *Dessus tous l'ignorent heretiques modernes qui l'attribuent a la seule foy, de sorte que selon eulx autre chose n'est requise qui doive cooperer pour obtenir la grace de justification, & qu'en nulle maniere n'est necessaire d'estre preparé & disposé par le mouvement de sa volunté. Ce que le sacré concile Tridentin a determiné estre anatheme.*[245]

As mentioned earlier in this chapter, the Reformers insisted that justification was God's work alone in us, that we passively receive his gracious favor towards us by laying hold of his promises through faith. There is no sense in which a desire

---

[243] John 4:10, RSV.
[244] *Dialogue de la justification*, fol. 16r°.
[245] Ibid., fol. 20v°. The anathema from the Council of Trent to which Doré makes reference here is Canon 9 of the sixth session.

for justification and contrition for sin must precede the favor bestowed by God. Rather, repentance is something that flows from justification in their view. Even to speak in terms of a freely-willed and necessary cooperation with grace is to allow man a power that is beyond him in the Protestant view. That is why Doré's interpretation of Christ's request for a drink of water from the Samaritan is crucial to his discussion of justification, for it represents the necessity of a voluntary active response on our part to God's initiative.

In order to better illustrate his point, Doré goes on to compare justification to a kind of spiritual marriage between God and the soul. Just as the marriage between man and woman requires a mutual consent that is freely given one to the other, so must there be a free response on the part of the soul to God's desire to justify it. *"Dieu le veult,"* he reasons, *"il convient aussi l'ame le vueille & y consente."*[246] The consent of the will that is required for justification, Doré explains, involves a two-fold movement, compunction for sin coupled with a desire for grace. This is not to say, however, that the will acts apart from grace. The theologian is quick to affirm, *"Il fault en la justification du pecheur, que le franc arbitre touché de Dieu soit esmeu à detester peché, desirer grace, & demander pardon."*[247] It is a question here of the will cooperating with the grace God gives to turn away from sin and desire the gift of justification.

The dialogue of John's Gospel once again provides Doré with an image for how God moves the human will to freely desire the grace he wishes to give. As Christ continues to speak to the woman about the living water, he elicits within her a growing desire to obtain this water so that finally she responds, "Sir, give me this water, that I may not thirst, nor come here to draw."[248] Her heart has been moved by the words of the Lord, but her response is free and reveals her desire for the water of grace that will justify her. To support his point on the necessity of our free-will response, Doré cites not only the Council of Trent, but

---

[246] Ibid., fol. 27v°.
[247] Ibid., fol. 27r°.
[248] John 4:15, RSV.

even more importantly a phrase from the *doctor gratiae* himself, St. Augustine, "*celuy qui nous a creé sans nous ne nous justifie pas sans nous.*"[249] We see the Dominican bringing to bear here the witness of both Scripture and Tradition against the Protestant insistence that the human will plays no role in justification. The citation from Augustine is particularly damning because the Reformers so often looked to the bishop of Hippo as the champion of their cause. Yet, even he who upheld the absolute primacy and necessity of grace against the teaching of Pelagius nevertheless affirmed that justification does not occur "without us," that is without our free-will cooperation.

Finally, the woman at the well demonstrates the consequences of being justified. Having been moved by grace to desire the living water which Christ wishes to give her and having admitted that she has no husband, for in fact she has had five and the man she has now is not her husband (see John 4:16-18), she is now ready for the grace of justification which Doré describes as receiving from Christ the remission of sins and the infusion of the theological virtues of faith, hope and charity. What he is describing is not merely a "covering" over of her sinfulness nor her "appearing" as righteous before God while remaining in reality a sinner, but a real transformation in the interior of her being. The evidence of her transformation lies in the fact that she becomes a veritable apostle, an instrument through whom her townsfolk come to believe in Jesus as the Messiah. As the Gospel attests, "many Samaritans from that city believed in him because of the woman's testimony."[250] Doré interprets her newfound desire to evangelize as a sign that she has been filled with the living water which satisfies all thirst:

> *Voyons qu'il est bien veritable ce que nostre seigneur avoit dict de son eaue, que celuy qui en boit n'aura plus de soif. L'experience on voit en ceste femme qui en a beu & n'a plus de soif, car laisse sa cruche pleine*

---

[249] *Dialogue de la justification*, fol. 27v°. Although Doré does not provide a reference for his readers, the citation is from Sermon 169. XI. 13, "*Qui ergo fecit te sine te, non te justificat sine te.*" See PL, 38, p. 923.
[250] John 4:39, RSV.

161

> *d'eaue sans en boire & s'en va: elle va evangelizer Jesus Christ, pourtant delaisse toute charge qui la pourroit retarder de son office.*[251]

Having been given to drink from the fountain of justifying grace, the adulteress is transformed from sinner into an apostle who performs the good work of evangelization. The fact that she is no longer interested in the water from the well, leaving her jug there in her haste to proclaim the good news, is an image of the interior transformation that has occurred as a result of the water of grace she has received. For Doré, the former "whore" as he calls her, is also a reassurance to poor sinners that no one is ever so steeped in sin as to be beyond hope of salvation. If Christ experienced the thirst to justify this woman, *"n'est-ce pas appertement prouvé qu'il ne rejecte personne, & qu'il n'a point esgard aux qualitez des personnes, & que tout homme qui par vraie foy vient a luy se recognoissant pecheur, & se soubmettans a sa misericorde, ne sera point refusé? Certainement ouy."*[252] The "dialogue of justification" in Chapter 4 of John's Gospel, then, not only illustrates the process by which sinners are justified, but is also an appeal to sinners to follow the Samaritan's example in desiring the living water which Christ ardently desires to give them.

As important and as well-done as the *Dialogue de la justification chrestienne* is, it nevertheless is incomplete in that it does not really take up the issue of merit which is so important for a proper understanding of the Catholic position on justification. Of course, the Gospel episode of the woman at the well does not lend itself to such a discussion. As an illustration of the process by which we are justified, the dialogue between Jesus and the Samaritan woman serves Doré's purposes well. However, demonstrating that we must freely respond to the grace of justification is only a partial response to the *sola fide* of the Reformers. In light of our cooperation with grace, it is also necessary to explain how we can be said to merit eternal life through our good works.

---

[251] *Dialogue de la justification*, fol. 55r°.
[252] Ibid., fol. 53v°.

Fortunately, Doré took up this point in his much earlier catechism, the *Dyalogue instructoire* (1538). Thus, although the *Dialogue de la justification chrestienne* can be considered a compendium of Doré's teaching on justification, it cannot stand completely on its own as his definitive response to *sola fide* but must be complemented by what preceded it in the other works previously mentioned.

Conclusion

From the above presentation, it is strikingly apparent that Pierre Doré faithfully followed his principle of "throwing his net in the sea of the Scriptures" in order to find the fish with the tribute money in its mouth, a metaphor for searching out and exposing the scriptural foundation of Catholic doctrine in response to the Reformers. His reassertion of the traditional teaching that we are justified not by faith alone but by both faith and good works consists almost exclusively of examples drawn from the Scriptures which serve to illustrate the essential theological points that bear on the issue. From Abraham, to the good thief, to the woman at the well, the point is made that these figures were justified by a living faith, one formed by charity and that each voluntarily cooperated with the graces being accorded them. In addition to pointing out these examples, Doré also devotes a good portion of his exposition on justification to reclaiming St. Paul from the Protestant camp. Here it is Paul's teaching on charity in 1 Corinthians that serves as the linch-pin of his argument. Neither are the Gospels neglected, particularly the Beatitudes which provide Doré with a springboard for discussing the idea of merit in the Christian life.

For all this attention given to Scripture, the Dominican as we have seen also relies heavily on the insights and teaching of his elder brother Aquinas on the questions of justification, grace and merit. In fact, readers of Doré are exposed to some rather complex theological distinctions, distinctions for example between formed and unformed faith, though explained in such a way through the use of metaphor as to be more easily grasped by the uninitiated. It is clear that our friar is not content to nourish his readers with pious platitudes. Drawing from his scholastic intellectual formation at S. Jacques, he introduces them to a Thomistic understanding of grace and merit. True, he does not always advert to the fact that he is feeding them with insights from the great scholastic theologian, the discussion on merit in the *Dyalogue instructoire* being a case in point. Not once in that exposition does he actually cite St. Thomas. Nevertheless, as has been shown, the substance of the exposition is taken directly from the *Summa*. Solidly grounded in Scripture and clarified by the penetrating thought of Aquinas, Doré's presentation of the orthodox view of the justification of believers is designed both to prove that it is the Reformers themselves who have departed from the true meaning of the revealed Word and to provide the faithful with a theological antidote to the heresy of *sola fide*.

Chapter 4
THE EUCHARIST:
TRANSUBSTANTIATION AND "DEIFICATION"

When the Council of Trent was reconvened by Pope Julius III in 1551 after a four-year hiatus, it picked up the discussion on Reformed theology where it had left off and resumed its unfinished work on the sacraments. The Council Fathers had earlier reaffirmed the traditional teaching of the sacraments as being seven in number at the seventh session in March 1547. At the top of the agenda now in what was to be the second period of the council (1551-1552) was a response to the Reformers' positions on the Eucharist. While all but the most radical of Reformed churches continued to consider the memorial of the Last Supper as a sacrament, they universally denied the Catholic assertion of a substantial change occurring in the consecrated elements, otherwise known as the doctrine of transubstantiation. It comes as no surprise then that at the heart of Trent's decree on the Eucharist was a strong reassertion of this doctrine, a reaffirmation of the real and substantial change which takes place in the consecrated bread and wine so that the sacrament is a true communion with the body and blood, soul and divinity of Christ.[253]

---

[253] The Council's teaching is succinctly expressed in this sentence from the decree, "But since Christ our redeemer said that it was truly his own body which he was offering under the form of bread, therefore there has always been complete conviction in the church of God—and so this holy council now declares it once again—that, by the consecration of the bread and wine, there takes place the change of the whole substance of the bread into the substance of the body of Christ our

The decree and canons concerning the Eucharist were approved on 11 October 1551 at the thirteenth session. That very year, Doré produced one of the most explicitly polemical of his works on the very same subject matter, his *Anti-Calvin, contenant deux defenses catholiques de la verité du sainct Sacrement*. In the prologue, Doré explains that this work is a response to two small anonymously written tracts against the holy sacrifice of the Mass that he came upon while preaching in Dijon. Although the author chose not to reveal himself, the book is manifestly in Doré's mind a product of *"l'officine & boutique des forcenez, seduits, seducteurs Calvinistes."*[254] The appearance of the *Anti-Calvin*, however, did not mark Doré's first real treatment of orthodox teaching on the Eucharist. Nor was his defense of the "most holy sacrament of the altar" in any way dependent upon or related to the official response of Trent on the subject. It in fact pre-dated and in many ways anticipated the Council's treatment.

Two years prior to Trent's decrees on the Eucharist, the Dominican theologian produced a substantial treatise of 233 folios in defense of the sacrament entitled, *L'arche de l'alliance nouvelle* (1549). It should be carefully noted that of the three polemical works Doré produced between 1549 and 1551, both *L'arche* and the *Anti-Calvin* have the Eucharist as their principal subject matter. This fact speaks volumes! There is no clearer indication that for Doré, the Reformers' attacks on the real presence of Christ in the Eucharist posed the greatest threat both to the Church and to the good of the individual believer. He saw these attacks as no less than the work of Satan, who having wounded humanity from the very beginning by sin, now sought through his heretical ministers to deprive poor sinners of the means of healing for their sins provided by Christ in his body and blood:

Lord, and of the whole substance of the wine into the substance of his blood." See Tanner, *Decrees*, 2, p. 695.

[254] Prologue to *Anti-Calvin, contenant deux defenses catholiques de la verité du sainct Sacrement et digne sacrifice de l'autel* (Paris: Sébastien Nivelle, 1568), fol. Aii v°. **[Geneva, BPU—Bc 3515]**

> *L'ennemy d'humain salut cauteleux, sachant que la ou il blessoit l'homme par peché, par la viande & breuvage salutaire du corps precieux de Jesus & son sang, estoit guary du tout, s'esforce par hereticques ses ministres tollir la medecine, à ce que l'homme demeure languissant à la mort.*[255]

Doré, it should be noted, was not alone in demonizing his opponents on this score. Calvin likewise attributed what he considered the Roman Church's errors concerning the Eucharist to the work of the devil who, "*selon sa manière accoutumée s'est efforcé dès le commencement de contaminer [le saint sacrement] d'erreurs et de superstitions pour en corrompre et détruire le fruit.*"[256] The polemics and demonization seen here on both sides demonstrates that a correct understanding of the Eucharist was deemed to be of vital importance for the life of the believer by Reformers and defenders of orthodoxy alike.

As already mentioned, the core issue in the controversy surrounding the Eucharist was that of transubstantiation, of whether or not the elements of bread and wine undergo a substantial change to become the body and blood of Christ while retaining the appearance or, in philosophical terms, the accidental qualities of bread and wine. However, closely related to the Reformers' denial of transubstantiation was their rejection of several other practices and doctrines of the Roman church to which they took exception, notably the adoration of the consecrated host, the idea of the Mass as a sacrifice which has the power to take away sins, and the belief in a ministerial priesthood instituted by Christ for the offering of this sacrifice.[257] While Doré's most complete response to the Reformers' positions on all these points is to be found in his *L'arche de l'alliance*, it is by no means the only place where he exposes Catholic doctrine on the Eucharist for the laity.

---

[255] Dedication to Henry II, *L'arche*, fol. Avi r°.
[256] From Calvin's *Petit traicté de la Saincte Cène* which first appeared in 1541. See Backus, *Vraie Piété*, p. 140.
[257] These are precisely the principal criticisms of the "papist" teaching on the Eucharist found in Calvin's *Petit traicté de la Saincte Cène*. See Ibid., p. 124.

For example, in an earlier and much smaller work, *La meditation devote du bon chrestien* (1544), he seeks to explain "the ceremonies performed at the sacrifice of the altar." His intent here is to provide the laity with a brief explanation of the different parts of the Mass and their origin, "*...pour exciter tous chrestiens à ouyr devotement la messe, ayans reverence aux sainctes ceremonies dicelles, desquelles lutheriens & meschans gens heretiques, & schismatiques se mocquent.*"[258] But if his stated purpose is to defend the Mass from the mocking assaults of the heretics, there is perhaps a yet deeper reason why Doré feels a need to provide this liturgical aid for the faithful. One of the principal criticisms leveled by the Reformers against the Roman liturgy of the time, and a justified one at that, was that it was rendered completely unintelligible by priests mumbling away in Latin, thereby reducing the faithful to being spectators of some quasi-magical ritual rather than being understanding participants in a divine mystery. Could it be then that Doré's *La meditation devote du bon chrestien* was an attempt to correct this abuse by carefully explaining the different parts of the Mass to the laity? Although he never explicitly admits this, it was most probably a hidden motive.

Still earlier, the Dominican theologian consecrated a major segment of *La deploration de la vie humaine* (1541) to a discussion on how one should properly dispose oneself to receive Holy Communion. The book is divided into three major sections; the first being a series of meditations on the vanity of earthly life, the second a presentation on the Eucharist itself, and the third a discussion on how to prepare for a good Christian death. There is a definite cogency to this structure, for the middle section serves to link the other two. In a passing world full of misery and trial, the Eucharist is both sustenance for the journey as well as the pledge of future beatitude, thus serving as an incentive to the Christian to prepare well for the eternal life to come. While a theological element is clearly present in these earlier works on the Eucharist and the sacrifice of the Mass,

---

[258] Dedication to Pierre Lambert, *La meditation*, fol. Aiii v°.

nevertheless the emphasis is more on stirring up devotion in the heart of the believer than on the kind of doctrinal instruction found in *L'arche de l'alliance*. Doré's intent in both *La meditation devote* and *La deploration de la vie humaine* is primarily to incite the reader to a greater sense of awe, wonder and love before the mystery of the God truly present in the consecrated bread and wine of the Eucharist.

In addition to the four works already mentioned, the *Dyalogue instructoire* (1538) also contains an important section on the Eucharist, as is to be expected of a catechism. Here we see in summary form the principal elements of what Doré will expand upon in his later writings: a reaffirmation and explanation of the doctrine of transubstantiation, a listing of conditions for a worthy reception of the sacrament, and a discussion of the sacrament's principal effects. This brings to five the number of Doré's works which contain significant expositions of Eucharistic doctrine, a relatively small percentage of the thirty-five writings in the "Doréan" corpus. Yet, this is a somewhat deceptive statistic because Doré actually discusses the Eucharist in some way in almost every one of his works. His reverence for the sacrament is unquestionable, as is his desire that it be acknowledged for what it truly is, the body and blood of Christ. In this desire, he sees himself as a faithful imitator of Aquinas whose own Eucharistic devotion is evidenced in the office he composed for the feast of Corpus Christi:

> ...car apres que S. Thomas d'Acquin, docteur angelique, & religieux de nostre ordre, a composé l'office du S. Sacrement qui est dechanté en l'Eglise, il m'est advis qu'il me touche aucunement de plus pres, defendre l'honneur d'iceluy, & l'amplier pour toutes voyes possibles...[259]

And so it is in the footsteps of his saintly brother Thomas that Doré carries on his present battle against the errors of the Reformers concerning the Eucharist.

In one of his more poignant metaphors, he likens Christ's gift to the Church of the Eucharist to the human tradition of leaving a ring or other love

---

[259] Dedication to Henry II, *L'arche*, fol. Eiiii r°-v°.

token to a beloved friend as a way of being remembered by that friend. He continues:

> Doncques nostre seigneur, aymant sa noble espouse l'esglise tresardamment, pour laquelle c'est exposé a tous tourmentz endurer, jusques a la mort, & tout son sang espandre, ne luy a point failli, a luy laisser son corps precieux et sang, en recordation de sa passion et souvenance de luy, que toutesfois on ne voit point de l'oeil corporel, car est caché soubz les especes sacramentelles: A la verité, ce eust esté ung paouvre don, pour ung si grand seigneur, indigne d'ung tel prince & bon amy, donner tant seullement ung morceau de pain pour memoire de luy...[260]

For Doré, the Protestant insistence that the bread of the sacrament remains bread and the wine remains wine effectively makes a mockery of the gift of love which Christ left as a memorial to his beloved spouse the night before his passion and death. It is an insult to the divine majesty to claim that the bread is merely a "sign" of Christ's body and blood and not the actual substance. It is against this backdrop then that his efforts to educate the minds of his readers concerning the Eucharist and enflame their hearts to a greater devotion for the sacrament must be seen.

Transubstantiation Resoundingly Affirmed

A metaphysical term, the word "transubstantiation" was a relatively new addition to the deposit of faith in Doré's time, having been asserted for the first time in an official way by the Fourth Lateran Council but three centuries earlier in 1215. It comes as no surprise then that the sixteenth-century Reformers, using their criterion of *sola scriptura*, unhesitatingly rejected the doctrine as a human invention of the medieval Church. As Calvin put it, *"Ce mensonge, premièrement, n'a nul fondement de l'Ecriture et n'a aucun témoinage de l'Eglise*

---

[260] *Le college*, fol. lix r°.

ancienne et, qui plus est, ne peut nullement convenir ni subsister avec la Parole de Dieu."[261] For his part, Doré was also quite reticent in using the term. In fact, the word "transubstantiation" never once appears in his writings until the relatively late work, *L'arche de l'alliance* (1549). But if he avoided the use of the term itself for a good part of his literary career, he most certainly did not shrink from expressing and asserting the essence of the doctrine itself throughout his works, even among the earliest.

In the following discussion extracted from the relatively early *Dyalogue instructoire* (1538), the disciple Cornelius asks the master St. Peter, "*Ne recoit on que pain et vin en ce sacrement?*" Doré here, as often in the *Dyalogue*, has the centurion taking on the role of devil's advocate, in this case voicing the Protestant position that no substantial change takes place in the consecrated elements. Of course, it must be admitted that Cornelius' statement is a rather crass caricature of what both Luther and Calvin taught concerning the Eucharist, for both held that the body and blood of Christ were truly received in the sacrament though the elements themselves remained unchanged. Yet, their differing theories of the real presence are of little interest to Doré. It is clear that as far as he is concerned, once transubstantiation is denied, there can be no true reception of Christ in the Eucharist. Rather, the sacrament is reduced to a physical ingestion of mere bread and wine.

Responding then to Cornelius' question, St. Peter (ie. Doré) goes on to answer with assurance, "*Apres la consecration faicte, il ne demeure substance de pain ne de vin, mais est contenu tout Jesuschrist soubz les accidens & especes.*"[262] What we have here in one of Doré's earliest works is the classical expression of the doctrine of transubstantiation without any mention of the term itself. When the word finally appears in *L'arche de l'alliance* eleven years later, it is accompanied by the following apologetic:

---

[261] From the *Petit traicté*. See Backus, *Vraie Piété*, p. 142.
[262] *Dyalogue instructoire*, fol. Hiii v°.

> *Ce vocable de transsubstantiation, combien qu'il soit prins de ladicte decretalle,* [a reference to the decrees of the Fourth Lateran Council], *& qu'on soit nay depuis trois cens ans: afin que cela nous donnions à l'adversaire. Toutesfois icelle transsubstantiation ou mutation est chose, qui nous a esté baillée en l'Eglise, & enseignée il y a plus de mille & cinq cens ans. Il ne fault disputer du vocable, quand la verité est patente.*[263]

While ceding to his opponents the relative novelty of the term, Doré argues here that it nevertheless expresses something very ancient, what has been believed and taught about the Eucharist from the origins of the Christian community. This would explain his reticence to actually mention "transubstantiation" in his writings, for his objective is not to defend the term as such but rather to reaffirm the underlying truth it seeks to express. If the Reformers can rightly object to the lack of scriptural foundation for the word "transubstantiation," Doré wants to prove that the reality of a substantial change is nevertheless unquestionably grounded in the Word of God.

It goes without saying that the key scriptural text in the debate over transubstantiation is the account of the Last Supper where Christ institutes the Eucharist as the memorial of his passion and death. The synoptic gospel writers provide a unified witness to the fact that the night before he suffered, Christ took bread, blessed it, and proclaimed, "This is my body." For Doré, this verse is the indisputable scriptural proof that the bread of the sacrament is in fact no longer bread, but the real body of Christ. He is incredulous at the inability of the Reformers, who pride themselves on a strict adherence to Scripture, to accept something that is so plainly obvious, saying:

> *Nous suyvons les pures parolles de Jesus Christ sans rien adjouster, ne gloser. O pauvres gens, ces parolles,* **Hoc est corpus meum,** *sont comme esclair, tonnere contre vous. Qu'opposera à l'encontre l'esprit estonné de telle vive voix du Seigneur? Vous vous ventez estre evangeliques, & suyvre la parolle de Dieu, crians:* **Verbum domini, verbum domini,** *& que ne la gardez-vous donc? Quand est ce qu'avez leu, ou en quel*

---

[263] *L'arche*, fol. 115r°.

> *endroit & passage, que Jesus ayt dict: Voyla le signe memoratif de mon corps, ou seulement la figure?*[264]

The tone is mocking—"you are the ones who boast of being evangelical, of clinging to nothing but Scripture—yet we are the ones who accept the pure words of Jesus Christ, without adding anything or glossing them over." Despite the tone, however, his point is a valid one. The inherent weakness of the Reformers' denial of transubstantiation lies in the fact that their position necessitates an interpretation of what Christ actually meant when he said, "This is my body," rather than simply accepting his words at face value. The cherished principle of *sola scriptura* in this case places the burden of proof on those who would deny that the Eucharist is the real body and blood of the Lord rather than on those who hold that a substantial change in fact occurs.

It should be mentioned here that Luther himself, while denying transubstantiation, could not in conscience deny the evident meaning of Christ's words in the institution narrative. He alone among the major Reformers continued to believe in a real, actual presence of Christ in the consecrated elements.[265] What he could not accept was the idea of the substance of the bread being completely annihilated and replaced by the substance of Christ's body. Such a philosophical invention was in his mind completely opposed to the Eucharistic reality described in the Gospel. Thus he chose to explain the real presence in terms of the body of Christ being present "in" or "with" the bread of the Eucharist, a theory which later came to be known as consubstantiation.

For Doré, however, the Lutheran attempt to maintain the real presence with the theory of consubstantiation still falls short of corresponding to the literal

---

[264] Ibid., fol. 119r⁰-120v⁰.
[265] In his *Babylonian Captivity of the Church*, Luther writes, "For my part, if I cannot fathom how the bread is the body of Christ, yet I will take my reason captive to the obedience of Christ [II Cor. 10:5], and *clinging simply to his words* [emphasis mine], firmly believe not only that the body of Christ is in the bread, but that the bread is the body of Christ." See Helmut Lehmann, ed., *Luther's Works*, vol. 36 (Philadelphia: Fortress Press, 1959), p. 34. For the same citation in the original Latin, see Weimar, 6, p. 511.

sense of Christ's words. Though he mentions neither Luther's name nor the word "consubstantiation" in the following rebuttal, he is in fact responding directly to the German Reformer's theory when he writes, "*Nostre seigneur ne dict pas:* **Hic est corpus meum**. *Icy est mon corps, mais il dict:* **Hoc est**, *c'est un pronom qui demonstre la substance.*"[266] Doré's point here is very subtle. The demonstrative pronoun "*hoc*" is a neuter nominative and thus refers to the body (*corpus*) also a neuter nominative. In order for Luther's explanation of the real presence to be valid, the sentence would have to read "*Hic est*" where the masculine pronoun "*hic*" would then refer to the masculine noun "*panis*" or bread. Or in other words, "this (bread) is my body."[267] But it is not a question of the body of Christ being present along with or in the bread. Doré's point is that the "*hoc est*" indicates a transformation of the bread into the substance of the body of Christ. Perhaps the debate here seems rather academic, a dispute over grammatical technicalities. Whether one holds for transubstantiation or consubstantiation seems inconsequential really, for the latter theory serves to uphold the idea of the "real presence" which is the principal issue. Yet, there is more at stake than simply upholding the real presence, for the theory of consubstantiation still falls short of corresponding to the evident meaning of the words of institution as recorded in the Gospels, words which, as Doré has explained, point to a definite transformation in the bread which becomes the body of Christ. The question ultimately is, which notion more adequately and completely corresponds to the words of Christ?

Another key scriptural passage in Doré's argumentation for the Catholic understanding of the Eucharist is Chapter 6 of John's Gospel, the famous Bread of Life Discourse. His commentary on different verses of this chapter occupies the better part of two chapters in *L'arche de l'alliance nouvelle*. Interestingly, Luther completely discounted this Johannine discourse as having any reference to the

---

[266] *L'arche*, fol. 53v°.
[267] On this very point, Luther argues in *The Babylonian Captivity* that because Hebrew has no neuter gender, "this" refers to the bread and not to the body. See *Luther's Works*, 36, p. 34. See Weimar, 6, p. 511.

175

sacrament, insisting that "...it does not refer to the sacrament in a single syllable."[268] Pointing out the fact that the sacrament had not yet been instituted at the time of the discourse, the German Reformer goes on to argue in his *Babylonian Captivity* (1520) that Christ was speaking here not of a sacramental eating, but rather a spiritual eating, one consisting of faith in the Incarnate Word. This is clearly brought out in his mind when Christ says near the end of the discourse in verse 63, "My words are spirit and life."

Without referring explicitly to Luther on this point, Doré nevertheless attempts to show that John 6 does indeed contain clear references to the Eucharist. He argues that in the entire discourse, Christ actually speaks of three different breads: the first is the manna which was given to the Jews in the desert, the second bread is the revelation of himself as the Divine Word, and third bread is his flesh hidden under the veil of the sacrament. The argument develops in this way:

> *Si quelqu'un pense diligemment à l'ordre de toutes ses parolles de nostre seigneur, & prent garde de pres à la difference des temps, desquelz use nostre Seigneur, congnoistra & voirra plainement que le tiers pain dont il parle, est celuy de l'Eucharistie: car en parlant du premier pain, il use du verbe praeterit,* **Dedit***, Moyse a donné. En parlant du second pain, il use du verbe present,***Dat***, Mon pere vous donne le pain du ciel. Mais en parlant du tiers pain, qui est sacramentel, il use du verbe futur,* **Dabo***, Je vous donneray. Ou fault bien entendre que deux fois il a usé de ce verbe. Ainsi que on list au vray texte correspodant au Graec,* **Panis quem ego dabo, caro mea est, quam ego dabo pro mundi vita***...Promettoit donc nostre Seigneur donner le pain sacramentel, qui est sa chair, pour viande à manger: & non seulement pour nourriture la donneroit, mais aussi la donneroit & exposeroit à la mort.*[269]

Doré here points out the distinction that Jesus makes between the bread that Moses **gave** to the Israelites, the bread that the Father **gives** in the revelation of the Son, and the bread that he himself **will give**, which is his flesh for the life of the world. This use by Jesus of the future tense answers Luther's objection that

---

[268] Ibid. p. 19. See Weimar, 6, p. 502.
[269] *L'arche*, fol. 101r°-v°.

because the sacrament was not yet instituted, Christ could not be making reference to it in his discourse. For Doré, it is clear that Jesus is here alluding to the institution of the Eucharist where he will give as food the very same flesh that he will offer on the cross in sacrifice for our sins.

Doré finds further support for the doctrine of transubstantiation in the letters of St. Paul. In his mind, one of the clearest indications that the early Christian community revered the Eucharist as the true body and blood of the Lord is seen in Paul's first letter to the Corinthians where the apostle recounts the tradition he received concerning the institution of the Eucharist. The key is 1 Corinthians 11:27-28: "Whoever, therefore, eats the bread or drinks the cup of the Lord in an unworthy manner will be guilty of profaning the body and blood of the Lord. Let a man examine himself, and so eat of the bread and drink of the cup" (RSV). Doré comments:

> *L'apostre dict que se fault disposer & esprouver, pour le recepvoir dignement. Qui est signe evident, que apres la consecration faicte, il y a aultre chose que pain & vin. Car a telle viande, n'est requise probation de soyesmesmes & ne disposition interieure ou preparation, si non que la prendre avec benediction de dieu.*[270]

It should be noted that this admonition to examine one's conscience before receiving the Eucharist, while it definitely denotes the belief that the consecrated bread is more than ordinary food, does not therefore necessarily uphold the doctrine of transubstantiation itself, at least not in the eyes of the Reformers who even while denying transubstantiation accepted the Pauline idea expressed here that one could partake of the Eucharist to one's condemnation if it was eaten unworthily. Calvin, for example, is quite in harmony with Paul when he writes:

> *...car quiconque approche de ce saint sacrement avec mépris ou nonchalance, ne se souciant pas beaucoup de suivre où le Seigneur l'appelle, il en abuse perversement...Ce n'est pas donc sans cause que saint Paul dénonce une si griève condamnation sur tous ceux qui le prendront indignement. Car s'il n'y a rien au ciel ni en la terre de plus*

---

[270] *Le college*, fol. lviii r°.

grand prix et dignité que le corps et le sang du Seigneur, ce n'est pas petite faute de le prendre inconsidérément et sans être bien préparé.[271]

Clearly, Calvin gives evidence here of a deep reverence for the Eucharist, even making reference to receiving the "body and blood of the Lord." It must be admitted that in his Eucharistic theology, he maintains the notion of a "real presence" and communion with the body of Christ, though he denies both the Roman and Lutheran explanations of the presence. The particularities of his position will be discussed at greater length in the following section of this chapter. But for now, it is evident that both the defenders of orthodoxy and the Reformers could agree on the necessity of receiving the Eucharist worthily while remaining in disagreement as to the nature of Christ's presence in the consecrated species.

A much more interesting and original use of Pauline theology by Doré to support the Church's understanding of the Eucharist involves a novel way of applying the apostle's teaching on the marriage bond. The key texts he mentions here are 1 Corinthians 7:4 where the apostle says, "For the wife does not rule over her own body, but the husband does; likewise the husband does not rule over his own body, but the wife does" (RSV), and Ephesians 5 where he describes marriage as an image of the union which exists between Christ and the Church. Doré points out that as the loving bridegroom of the Church, Christ "...*en vray don & nom de mariage luy a baillé, non un signet & verge d'argent, mais son propre corps.*"[272] Just as a husband gives authority over his body to his wife as part of the exchange of love, so Christ has given authority over his true body in the Eucharist to the Church. The implication Doré draws from the mystery of Christ's union with the Church is that such a union must involve a true gift of himself and not merely a sign of his presence.

Moving beyond the witness of the Gospels and St. Paul, Doré's quest for scriptural proof of the doctrine of transubstantiation is by no means limited to the

---

[271] From the *Petit traicté*. See Backus, *Vraie Piété*, p. 134.
[272] *Le Nouveau Testament*, fol. 186v°.

New Testament. He points out how the Eucharistic miracle of the transformation of the bread's substance into the body of Christ is in fact prefigured in certain passages of the Old Testament as well. Two of his examples will be discussed here: the deception of Isaac by his son Jacob (Genesis 27) and the miracle of the prophet Elijah in the presence of the prophets of Baal (1 Kings 18). In both instances, Doré provides a highly allegorical interpretation of the biblical text, interesting for its originality yet ultimately unconvincing as solid scriptural evidence for the truth concerning the Eucharist which he seeks to defend.

Doré first of all sees an analogy for the hidden presence of Christ in the Eucharist in the young Jacob who, at his mother Rebecca's urging, disguises himself as his older brother Esau in order to receive the paternal blessing that belongs to the firstborn male. The deception involves covering his arms with animal skins to imitate the hairy arms of his brother and wearing his brother's robes with their particular fragrance. Although the elderly father Isaac, blind and approaching death, has his suspicions concerning the son who kneels before him, he is ultimately convinced by the ruse and imparts his blessing on Jacob, thinking that he is Esau. For Doré, this is a metaphor for how our senses are deceived in the Eucharist. Underneath the appearance of bread lies the true body of Christ. Just as the Esau kneeling before Isaac is really Jacob, so the sacramental bread is substantially a different reality than what it appears to be. Doré writes:

> *Quand donc le prestre doibt consacrer & benistre le pain, c'est à dire Isaac benistre Jacob, Esau s'en part de la maison, car s'en va la substance du pain, & ne demeure au logis que le vray Jacob, qui est nostre seigneur au sacrement, tant seulement demeure Esau en similitude & sa semblance, c'est à dire ses robbes avec leur odeur, & les peaux pelues. Aussi la consecration faicte, ne demeurent que les accidens, ou similitude du pain, c'est à scavoir l'odeur, la couleur, saveur, durté, ou solidité & sont deceuz noz sens, là est deceue la veue troublé d'Isaac...*[273]

---

[273] *L'arche*, fol. 74v°.

As a way of explaining what occurs in transubstantiation, the analogy here in fact is very appropriate. Doré provides his lay readers with a concrete image for understanding the philosophical concepts of substance and accident as they are employed in defining the transformation that occurs in the sacramental bread. Less convincing, however, is his claim that this scriptural passage is actually a prefigurement of the Eucharist. The obvious Old Testament prefigurement of the Eucharist is the Passover meal celebrated by the Hebrews upon their liberation from slavery in Egypt. By ignoring this more obvious parallel in favor of recourse to a passage whose Eucharistic allusions are tenuous at best, Doré falls short in his attempt to demonstrate that the doctrine of transubstantiation is already prefigured under the Old Covenant.

The same problem occurs in an example given in *La deploration de la vie humaine* (1541), taken from the first book of Kings. Here Doré invokes the incident where the prophet Elijah challenges the prophets of Baal to a trial by fire in order to determine which god is the true God. The contest involves preparing a sacrificial bull without setting it to fire. It is either Baal or the God of Israel who must prove himself by sending fire to consume the sacrifice. After a day of supplication and incantations, the prophets of Baal fail to rouse their god to the task. It is then that Elijah calls on the living God to manifest himself before all the people, at which point the Lord sends down fire from heaven to consume the sacrifice. Once again, Doré sees here a figure of the Eucharist, explaining that at the altar of sacrifice, the priest like Elijah invokes the power of the Lord over the bread and wine. The living God in response sends fire from heaven (an image of the Holy Spirit) at which point "...*est devoree l'hostie, en ceste sorte que ce n'est plus pain, ce que estoit par avant, mais le vray corps de nostre seigneur.*"[274] Once again, we have an example here of a highly allegorical interpretation of a scriptural passage which ultimately detracts from more than it supports Doré's defense of the Eucharist for the passage in question is interpreted completely out

---

[274] *La deploration*, fol. 26r°.

of context. What is clear is the Dominican's absolute attachment to the doctrine of transubstantiation, for the whole purpose of the tortured analogy is to affirm the complete consummation of the substance of bread which occurs at the moment of consecration so that it becomes the real body of Christ. Nonetheless, from an exegetical standpoint, Doré's quest to find scriptural proof of transubstantiation in the Old Testament seems to depend too much on forced allegories rather than on clear and indisputable prefigurements.

Yet, returning for a moment to the Jacob analogy, the Dominican does bring out an interesting parallel which cuts to the heart of the debate surrounding the real presence of Christ in the Eucharist. He points out that Isaac was completely deceived by Jacob in all of his senses but one, that of hearing. The blind father recognized the voice of Jacob, though the hairy arms he felt and the odor of the robes he smelled were those of his first-born Esau. In the end, he was deceived because he did not put faith in what he heard. For Doré, the parallel with the Eucharist is clear. He says that we too are deceived in all of our senses by the bread, which retains the appearance, odor, and taste of ordinary bread. Only our ears receive a different testimony when they hear the words "This is my body." It is a question then of believing the Word of God that is heard rather than what the other senses mistakenly perceive.

Doré sees a fittingness in the fact that the baptized are called to make an act of faith in the real presence through the Word they hear proclaimed at the consecration. Recalling the account of the temptation in Genesis, he points out that it was through listening to the false promises of Satan that our first parents were deceived. Succumbing to the serpent's trickery and taking delight in the forbidden fruit that was presented to them, they discovered the death that lay hidden therein. For this reason:

> ...estoit fort convenable que la foy des catholiques saulvez de mort commençast par l'ouye, c'est à sçavoir en escoutant la parolle du saulveur, suadant menger d'une viande ayant la vraye vie en soy cachée,

ou noz sens exterieurs n'ont leurs plaisirs vains, ains sont deceuz, fors l'ouye...[275]

It is a persuasive argument. As a way of making reparation for the infidelity of Adam and Eve who were deceived in hearing, the faithful are now asked by the Lord to believe in his word, that the food now offered them, though outwardly having the appearance of bread, is really his flesh for the life of the world. This parallel as well as the Isaac parallel both serve to bring the Reformation debate over the Eucharist down to it most basic level. In other words, does one simply accept the testimony of Scripture at face value and believe the words, "This is my body"? Or does one begin to interpret what Christ really meant when he made this statement on the night before he died because one cannot accept the idea of the bread being something other than bread? Doré's position is clear—the Reformers should learn from the mistake of Isaac who failed to believe what he heard as well as Adam and Eve who allowed themselves to be deceived by giving ear to Satan rather than the Lord.

Although our friar seeks to base his proof for the real presence on the solid foundation of Scripture, he does not hesitate to offer his readers other evidence based on ordinary experience. In *Le college de sapience*, for example, we see him pointing to the consolation and peace often experienced upon reception of the consecrated elements as proof that what is received in the Eucharist must be more than ordinary bread. If communion results in such holy sentiments as increased fervor, interior joy, renewed strength to confront the trials of life, a yearning for the goods of eternal life, then there must be a supernatural source for these graces. Doré asks, "*Seroit ce ung pain materiel, qui auroit telle vertu & efficace?*" then immediately responds, "*Non pour vray: mais c'est la vertu qui part de Jesus. Si a l'avoir touché a la frange de sa robbe, une femme a esté guarie, ce n'est de merveilles, si quand on le recoipt tout dedans soy au sacrement de l'autel, on sent*

---

[275] *L'arche*, fol. 74r°.

en soy l'efficace de la presence de Jesus christ."[276] Just as the healing power sensibly experienced by the woman with the hemorrhage (cf. Mt. 9:20-22) came from her physical contact with Christ, it is to be expected that the faithful who receive the body of Christ in the Eucharist will also experience the healing and transforming power of his presence. We will see in the final section of this chapter how Doré develops this idea of communion with the body of Christ to speak of our healing, our transformation in grace, even our deification. But here his principal point is to offer yet further evidence of the reality of transubstantiation by asking his readers to ponder the source of the sensible consolations which they may have experienced in Holy Communion.

The danger with this kind of proof based on personal experience is that it is highly subjective. It could very well be that some people have never or perhaps only rarely had any sensible experience of Christ's presence after receiving communion. Based solely on their experience, then, such people would be hard pressed to defend the idea that the Eucharistic bread is really the body of Christ. Obviously, the reality of the Eucharistic presence of Christ cannot be made dependent on whether or not the recipient feels any different after receiving it. Doré sees full well the limits of placing too much emphasis on the sensible effects resulting from communion as a sign that the bread is truly the body of Christ. Ultimately, such consolations are but a confirmation of what is believed and not a basis for that belief. It is for this reason that Doré returns over and over again to the necessity of faith in the real presence, regardless of what the senses perceive or the consolations that may be interiorly experienced. The real foundation for this faith can only be the word spoken by Christ. As he explains the words of consecration in *La meditation devote*, Doré insists, "*Il faut sortir hor de l'experience naturelle, & venir au champ de l'escripture, & croyre fermement aux parolles de Jesus Christ, il luy fault faire cest honneur que tout ce qu'il dict est*

---

[276] *Le college*, fol. lix v°.

veritable: Car il ne peult mentir."[277] It is the truthfulness of God which, for Doré, is the ultimate reason for accepting the doctrine of transubstantiation. Although it is a mystery beyond our comprehension that what looks and tastes like ordinary bread is the body of Christ, we are called to accept the mystery above all because Christ himself said, "This is my body."

The Problem of Local Presence

We come now to a metaphysical problem that arises from the assertion of the real presence of Christ in the sacrament. If one accepts the teaching that the bread and wine of the Eucharist are truly the body and blood of Christ, not merely in figure but in substance, then one must somehow explain how the body of Christ can both be present at the right hand of the Father in heaven and at the same time be present in many different places whenever and wherever the Eucharist is celebrated. For Calvin, such an explanation was not possible, thus bringing him to reject the Roman doctrine of transubstantiation as well as the Lutheran teaching of consubstantiation on the grounds that both led to absurd claims which in his mind either served to detract from the heavenly glory of Christ or failed to respect his true humanity. Thus, he argues in the final book of the *Institutes*:

> But we must establish such a presence of Christ in the Supper as may neither fasten him to the element of bread, nor enclose him in bread, nor circumscribe him in any way (all which things, it is clear, detract from his heavenly glory)...Let us never (I say) allow these two limitations to be taken away from us: (1) Let nothing be withdrawn from Christ's heavenly glory—as happens when he is brought under the corruptible elements of this world, or bound to any earthly creatures. (2) Let nothing inappropriate to human nature be ascribed to his body, as happens when it is said either to be infinite or to be put in a number of places at once.[278]

---

[277] *La meditation*, fol. Ciii r°.
[278] *Institutes*, IV. XVII. 19. McNeill, 2, pp. 1381-1382. See Benoît, 4, pp. 396-397.

What is interesting to note in the argument here is that even while Calvin objects to substantialist views of the Eucharist as being incompatible with the fact of Christ's ascension to the right hand of the Father, he is at pains nevertheless to maintain belief in "a presence of Christ in the Supper" without subscribing to notions of a substantial change taking place. What exactly, then, does he mean by "presence" if he rejects any notion of a substantial presence of the body and blood of Christ in the Eucharist? He means basically a spiritual presence, one that insures a true communion of the believer with the body and blood of Christ without positing that the Risen Lord must somehow actually be present in the bread or that the bread be transformed into his body. To deny a real communion with Christ, according to Calvin, would be to deny the evident meaning of his words at the Last Supper as well as to rob the sacrament of all value. Yet, this real communion is not brought about by the actual transformation of the Eucharistic elements. Rather it is the mysterious working of the Spirit that effects the union of believers with Christ as they partake of the sacramental bread and wine in faith. Of this mystery, Calvin concludes, "Now, if anyone should ask me how this takes place, I shall not be ashamed to confess that it is a secret too lofty for either my mind to comprehend or my words to declare. And, to speak more plainly, I rather experience than understand it."[279] The absurdities of saying that Christ is somehow enclosed in the bread (consubstantiation) or that the true body of Christ is not only in heaven but in every tabernacle on earth containing the consecrated species (transubstantiation) thus make a mockery of the mystery of the Eucharist which for Calvin can only be a spiritual communication with the body of Christ.

For the most part, Doré also prefers to defer to the mystery rather than to get involved in a philosophical explanation of the substantial presence, which he otherwise so ardently defends in his writings as we have seen. At one point in *L'arche de l'alliance*, he addresses the problem raised by Calvin as to how the

---

[279] Ibid., IV. XVII. 32. McNeill, 2, p. 1403. See Benoît, 4, p. 420.

glorified Christ seated at the right hand of the Father can at the same time be present in the consecrated host with this very simple assertion:

> *A cecy je donne brefve responce, que soubz invisible forme, il est au sacrement, qui a porté le nom d'Emmanuel, c'est à dire Dieu avec nous, non pour trente & trois ans, ains tousjours jusqu'a la fin du siecle, selon sa promesse.* **Ecce ego vobiscum sum, usque ad consummationem seculi** (Mat. 28).[280]

There is no attempt whatsoever here to explain the manner of Christ's Eucharistic presence. For Doré, this sacramental presence of the Lord Jesus is quite simply both a continuation of the mystery of the Incarnation as well as a fulfillment of the promise which Jesus made to the disciples at the end of Matthew's Gospel that he would be with them always until the end of time. As the Dominican theologian so plainly puts it, Jesus did not bear the name Emmanuel, God-with-us, merely during the brief period of his earthly life. Indeed, he is Emmanuel until the end of time by continuing to be truly present to his people, though in an invisible manner, in the sacrament of the Eucharist.

It is interesting to note at this point that whereas Calvin's attack on transubstantiation focuses rather extensively on the problem of local presence, Doré is almost silent on the issue.[281] Perhaps he considers the issue a bit esoteric for his readers and thus hesitates to give it much attention, for he addresses the problem but once, and that indirectly, in his *L'arche de l'alliance*. It should be mentioned that in accord with the teaching of Aquinas, Doré is as opposed to the idea of a local presence of Christ in the Eucharist as is the Genevan Reformer. To accept the doctrine of transubstantiation is thus not to be equated with believing that the consecrated bread of the Eucharist is the glorified body of Christ in the strict physical sense. Aquinas treats the problem in question 76 of the *tertia pars*, article 5, determining that Christ's body can in no way be said to be locally

---

[280] *L'arche*, fol. 116v°-117r°.
[281] In Chapter XVII of the *Institutes*, on "The Sacred Supper of Christ," the problem of local presence is discussed in some way or other in sections 10, 12, 16-19, 26-32. In marked contrast, Doré's treatment in *L'arche de l'alliance* covers but three folios, from 39r°-41r°.

present in the sacrament. Kilian McDonnell offers this commentary on the Thomist position:

> If St. Thomas would have to choose between two possibilities, presence in a naked sign or local presence in the strict physical sense, then he would be forced to say that Christ is present only in the naked sign because local presence is absolutely excluded. The body of Christ is true body and this body is in heaven. Exclusion of any kind of local presence is a central concern for both Calvin and Thomas. But there are not, for Thomas, two possibilities but three, the third possibility being presence *in sacramento*: *non solum in significatione vel figura, sed etiam in rei veritate*. *Veritas* is often a substitute for *substantia*. The mode in which Christ is present *in rei veritate* is the sacramental mode.[282]

Given the relative agreement that exists between the Thomist position on local presence and Calvin's own rejection of the notion, we can begin to understand at least one reason why the issue receives so little attention in Doré's polemics by comparison with the extensive treatment given it in the *Institutes*. Nevertheless, insofar as Calvin's objection to local presence leads in turn to a denial of the substantial presence of Christ in the Eucharist, Doré does sense the need to offer his readers a limited explanation for how Christ is present in the sacrament, if not locally so. He does this precisely by stressing the sacramental mode of Christ's presence in line with St. Thomas.

In Chapter 6 of *L'arche de l'alliance*, Doré provides a three-fold explanation for how the body of Christ can be in several locations simultaneously and yet remain undivided. For Calvin, this was precisely one of the absurdities consequent in the doctrine of transubstantiation and a violation of the second of his established limitations for explanations concerning "the presence of Christ in the Supper."[283] If the Eucharist is the substance of Christ's body and blood, as the Roman Church claims, then that body cannot be said to be in a number of different locations at once and still be a veritable human body. This would in

---

[282] Kilian McDonnell, *John Calvin, the Church, and the Eucharist* (Princeton: Princeton University Press, 1967), p. 304.
[283] See citation[278], p. 183.

effect result in a rejection of the true humanity of Christ and therein lies one of the many problems with the notion of transubstantiation in Calvin's mind. Although Doré does not advert to the fact that he is responding directly to the Genevan Reformer on this point, that in fact is what he attempts in the relatively brief treatment of the issue in Chapter 6 of *L'arche de l'alliance*.

The chapter, entitled *De l'admirable manne, contenue en l'arche du testament*, sets out to examine the principal differences between the manna which God originally provided for the Israelites in the desert and the new manna of the Eucharist. It is in this context of demonstrating the vast superiority of the new manna over its Old Testament figure that Doré takes up the problem of how it is possible for the body of Christ to exist simultaneously in different locations:

> *Encore y a il chose plus admirable en la manne des Chrestiens, qui ne fut onques en celle des Juifz, c'est à scavoir, qu'un mesme corps de Jesus Christ est ensemble en divers lieux en plusieurs autelz, & hosties, ou portions d'icelle, quand elle est divisée.*[284]

He goes on to admit that this presence of the one, undivided body of Christ in the Eucharist in various places and on various altars is indeed a marvelous wonder which is difficult to understand. Nonetheless, he proposes to offer his readers three explanations for how this miracle is possible.

First of all, he cites the authority of Scripture, in this case a verse from the prophet Malachi, 1:11, "For from the rising of the sun to its setting my name is great among the nations, and in every place incense is offered to my name, and a pure offering…"(RSV). Doré explains that "the pure offering" spoken of by Malachi which is made "in every place" is in fact a foreshadowing of the sacrificial offering of the New Law.[285] This notion of the sacrificial nature of the Eucharist will be dealt with more extensively in the next section of this chapter. What is important to grasp for now is that Doré is using this verse as a kind of

---

[284] *L'arche*, fol. 39r°.
[285] Calvin sees in this oft-quoted text in support of the sacrifice of the Mass a prophecy rather of the spiritual worship that will be offered to God by believers throughout the earth. See *Institutes*, IV. XVIII. 4.

proof-text for the doctrine that the body of Christ is offered and received in its entirety without suffering division whenever and wherever the Eucharist is celebrated. While his application of this verse to the Eucharistic sacrifice is certainly valid within the Christian tradition, it is difficult to see how it really serves his point here concerning the reality of Christ's presence in the sacrament.

Next, the Dominican theologian claims to offer an argument from reason based on the implications of the hypostatic union, the union of both a divine and human nature in the person of Christ. He writes:

> ...le filz de l'homme participe la puissance du filz de Dieu pour l'unité d'une personne, qui est divine en deux natures, & pourtant que le filz de Dieu est essentiellement en toutes choses, ainsi a donné au filz de l'homme, qui est une personne avec luy, que son corps soit sacramentellement en divers lieux.[286]

Because the human nature of Christ has the divine person as its proper subject, it therefore shares in the extraordinary powers of the divine nature. Thus it is possible for the true body of Christ to be actually present in the Eucharistic species throughout the world. Doré is here introducing an important distinction, the idea of a "sacramental" presence of Christ's body in the Eucharist as opposed to a "local" presence, which we have already seen must be excluded from an orthodox understanding of the sacrament. This distinction is further clarified with his citation of a magisterial pronouncement of Innocent III[287] (as is typical with Doré, no reference is offered for this citation), in which the medieval pope states:

> La haultesse du celeste & divin conseil, a proposé que tout ainsi que trois personnes font en unité d'essence, c'est à sçavoir, le pere, le filz, & le S. esprit: Pareillement fussent trois substances en unité de personne, c'est à sçavoir la divinité de Jesus Christ, le corps, & l'ame, comme donc nostre saulveur Jesus Christ selon nature divine, fust es choses crées en trois manieres: c'est à sçavoir en toutes choses par essence, par grace es seulz justes, & en l'homme qu'il a prins par union ypostatique: **a voulu pareillement qu'iceluy selon sa nature humaine,**

---

[286] L'arche, fol. 39v°.
[287] Innocent was pope from 1198-1216.

fust existant en trois sortes, au ciel localement, au verbe personellement, en l'autel sacramentellement [emphasis mine].[288]

In further distinguishing here the three types of presence possible to the human nature of the Son of God, that is "local" presence of the body of Christ in heaven, a personal union with the Divine Word, and a "sacramental" presence in the Eucharist, Doré is in effect attempting to answer Calvin's objections to the doctrine of transubstantiation by affirming that the real presence of the body of Christ in the sacrament is of a completely different mode than the natural order. Unfortunately, he goes no further than to simply state the fact of the sacramental order according to which Christ is present in the Eucharist without really trying to explain it to his readers.

One wonders, in any case, if these readers would really have grasped the subtleties of the above theological distinctions. Yet, as he so often does throughout his writings, Doré comes to the rescue with a metaphor to help make his point. This time, the metaphor is not his own, however, but is drawn from the *Summa*, IIIa, q. 76, a. 3. The Eucharist, he explains, is like the face of man reflected in a mirror. If the mirror is broken into pieces, each piece continues to reflect the whole and undivided face of the man. The same is true of the Eucharist, "*Si donc la forme du pain est en plusieurs parties divisée, en toutes sera à Dieu unie, c'est à sçavoir le vray corps de Jesus Christ.*"[289] Though the one bread is divided into many parts, nevertheless the substance of Christ's body, itself undivided, is to be found in each part. The point ultimately is that Calvin's objections to transubstantiation on the basis of certain logical impossibilities are without foundation, for the fact of the hypostatic union allows for the human nature of Christ to have several modes of presence. To affirm, then, that Christ is substantially present in the Eucharist neither detracts from the glory he enjoys at

---

[288] *L'arche*, fol. 39v°.
[289] Ibid., fol. 40r°.

the right hand of the Father nor does it offend against the doctrine of his true humanity.

It must be admitted that Doré's presentation on this topic leaves much to be desired. It is cursory and fails to measure up to Calvin's well-thought-out argumentation against transubstantiation based on the problem of local presence. Clearly, Doré did not consider this particular aspect of the debate surrounding the Eucharist to be of great significance. Of far greater concern to the Dominican theologian was the attack of the Reformers on the notion of the Eucharist as a sacrificial offering with the consequent rejection of the ministerial priesthood as specifically instituted by Christ to perpetuate this sacrifice in time. In denying both priesthood and sacrifice, the Reformers were in his mind stripping the Eucharist of all power and meaning.

A Defense of the Ministerial Priesthood and the Eucharist as Sacrifice

Ever caustic towards his erring opponents, Doré criticizes their denial of the ministerial priesthood and the sacrificial nature of the Eucharist in Chapter 21 of *L'arche de l'alliance* by asserting, "*Voyons icy clairement contre les Lutheriens mauldictz, que prestrise ou sacrificature en la nouvelle loy, n'est pas chose inventée des hommes, ains est de l'ordonnance de dieu, & tradition de Apostres.*"[290] Though the Lutherans alone are mentioned by name in this invective, it could most certainly have been applied to all the Reformers who without exception condemned the Roman Mass and the priests who were its ministers. Abstracting from the highly polemical tone of the statement, we get a glimpse here of how Doré intends to proceed in answering the challenge of Protestant theology as regards the ministerial priesthood. The core of his defense will be to demonstrate that the priesthood is both a divinely-willed institution, one

---

[290] Ibid., fol. 148v°.

prefigured under the Old Covenant but radically transformed by Christ in the new dispensation, and is an institution maintained by apostolic tradition in obedience to the will of Christ.

What makes Doré's approach on this point rather intriguing is that the brunt of the Reformers' energies were directed instead to dismantling the whole notion of Eucharist as sacrifice, in their eyes a form of works-righteousness which smacked of Pelagianism and was completely incompatible with the principle of justification by faith alone. For them, it was the perverse introduction of "the sacrifice of the Mass" which had brought about a corresponding perversion of the true sense of the ministerial office, so that the Eucharist was no longer a communal act of thanksgiving led by a presbyter but the private act of a priest offering sacrifice. As Kilian McDonnell points out, the Mass as experienced by the Reformers prior to their break from Rome was highly clericalized in character:

> ...it was the priest who offered and it was the priest who, with the exception of once a year, received the fruits of the sacrifice, communion. And Calvin wondered what all these ceremonies, usually carried out by a solitary priest, had to do with the worship of the people of God...It was in a very real sense the priest's mass.[291]

Given the state of the Eucharistic liturgy in the sixteenth century, it is understandable that the Reformers would have been so anxious to assault and dismantle the whole notion of sacrifice. Take away the sacrifice and there no longer would be a *raison d'être* for a priestly caste which reserved the duty of sacrifice and its fruits to itself. The Eucharist would be liberated from the shackles of clericalism.

Doré responds to this challenge not so much by defending at length the sacrificial nature of the Eucharist, though he does certainly re-affirm it, as by focusing instead on the historical institution of the ministerial priesthood, a priesthood distinct from that in which all the baptized participate. If he can demonstrate that Christ instituted a priesthood and not merely an office for

---

[291] McDonnell, *Calvin*, pp. 280-281.

maintaining order in the community, it follows that the Eucharist must in fact be a sacrifice, for it is of the essence of priesthood to offer sacrifice in expiation for sin. At the very outset of his *L'arche de l'alliance*, Doré brings out the vital connection between priesthood and the act of sacrifice in a "Protestation de l'Auteur" which follows the dedication. He explains to his readers why he will make use of the term *sacrificateur* in the work even though the Reformers have given the word a perjorative sense in their own writings:

> ...ne voulant en rien communiquer aux heretiques, ne mesmes en aucuns motz ou termes dont ilz usent, esquelz y a quelque venin caché, mesme soubz les syllables. Que si j'use de ce terme & mot, sacrificateur, pour celuy qui faict sacrifice, c'est pour plus grande expression de ce nom prestre, par lequel nous ne debuons entendre seulement l'ancien, mais selon l'intelligence & acception commune de l'Eglise qui le prend pour ministre ecclesiastique, qui offre à dieu sacrifice à l'autel, qui pour ce est nommé sacrificateur prestre.[292]

Because the priest is necessarily one who offers sacrifice, Doré's objective is to confirm that the Eucharist is indeed a sacrifice offered to the Father by proving that Christ himself instituted the new priesthood that would make this offering.

Both Luther and Calvin, and with them the entire Reformed tradition, denounce in no uncertain terms the way in which the Lord's Supper has suffered corruption through the centuries with the introduction of sacrificial terminology into the rites of the Mass, particularly in the canons and collects. In accordance with the principle of *sola scriptura*, Luther calls attention to the fact that the language of sacrifice in the celebration of the Supper has no basis in the Gospels and thus he advises, "...in this rite let the priest bear in mind that the gospel is to be set above all canons and collects devised by men, and that the gospel does not sanction the idea that the mass is a sacrifice."[293] As he interprets the gospel accounts of the Supper, the Eucharist is primarily a promise of forgiveness of sins. This forgiveness is gained by the believer when the sacrament is received in

---

[292] Doré, *L'arche*, "Protestation de l'Autheur," fol. Iii v°.
[293] *Luther's Works*, 36, p. 54. (from *The Babylonian Captivity*). See Weimar, 6, p. 525.

faith, not through the offering of sacrifice by a priest which is a work. To refer to the Supper as "sacrifice" in fact involves a contradiction, for a sacrament is a gift to be received and not a work to be accomplished. This point is made in *The Babylonian Captivity of the Church* (1520):

> They all imagine that they are offering up Christ himself to God the Father as an all-sufficient sacrifice, and performing a good work for all those whom they intend to benefit, for they put their trust in the work which the mass accomplishes, and they do not ascribe this work to prayer. In this way the error has gradually grown, until they have come to ascribe to the sacrament what belongs to the prayers, and to offer to God what should be received as a benefit.[294]

The German Reformer is here distinguishing between the offering of prayers for others, a kind of sacrifice, and the celebration of the Supper which involves receiving the promises of Christ in faith. If the Eucharist is something received from God, then it cannot at the same time be a sacrifice or a sin offering to God. Even aside from this apparent logical contradiction, the account of the Last Supper contains no references to Christ offering himself as a sacrifice to the Father. What he offers his disciples is his body and blood for the remission of sins. Thus the Roman church's adherence to the notion of Eucharist as sacrifice is for Luther one of the ways in which it keeps the real meaning of the sacrament captive, hence the title of his work, *The Babylonian Captivity of the Church*.

Having disavowed the sacrifice of the Mass, Luther logically proceeds to a denial of a priesthood which is distinct from the common priesthood of believers. For him, in fact, the essence of priestly ministry in the Church is not the celebration of the Eucharist but the preaching of the Good News of salvation. With his customarily dogmatic tone, he declares that "whoever does not preach the Word, though he was called by the church to do this very thing, is no priest at all, and that the sacrament of ordination can be nothing else than a certain rite by which the church chooses its preachers."[295] Granted that the proclamation of the

---

[294] Ibid., p. 50. See Weimar, 6, p. 522.
[295] Ibid., p. 113. See Weimar, 6, p. 564.

Gospel is an important charge of the priestly office, one which was being neglected by a good portion of the bishops and clergy in the early sixteenth century, Luther nevertheless goes to the opposite extreme by virtually equating ministry with preaching to the detriment of any sacramental function. Moreover, he goes on to argue that since all the faithful by virtue of their baptism are incorporated into the royal priesthood mentioned in 1 Peter 2:9, the authority to preach is then one that belongs in common to the baptized. As he explains, "...we are all equally priests, that is to say, we have the same power in respect to the Word and the sacraments. However, no one may make use of this power except by the consent of the community or by the call of a superior."[296] The sacrament of ordination which sets apart certain of the baptized and confers on them a new character is thus a fiction in his eyes, a human invention. It is a fiction perpetuated by the idea that the essence of the priesthood is to offer the sacrifice of the Mass rather than to preach the Gospel. By assaulting the sacrificial nature of the Eucharist, Luther has cleared the way for his condemnation of the ministerial priesthood as distinct from the common priesthood of believers.

In his own rejection of the Roman Mass, Calvin echoes Luther's thinking when he writes, "There is as much difference between this sacrifice and the sacrament of the Supper as there is between giving and receiving."[297] For him also, the sacrament as instituted by Christ is rather a gift to be received with thanksgiving and faith, not a work of atonement or satisfaction to God for sin. That satisfaction for sin was made once and for all by Christ on Calvary. The notion of Eucharist as sacrifice is therefore abhorrent to Calvin precisely because it "suppresses and buries the cross and Passion of Christ."[298] Implied in the Roman church's understanding of the Mass, as the Genevan Reformer sees it, is the conclusion that Christ's sacrifice on the cross was in fact ineffective. Basing

---

[296] Ibid., p. 116. See Weimar, 6, p. 566.
[297] Calvin, *Institutes*, IV. XVIII. 7. McNeill, 2, p. 1435. See Benoît, 4, p. 455.
[298] Ibid., IV. XVIII. 3. McNeill, 2, p. 1431. See Benoît, 4, p. 450.

himself principally on the Letter to the Hebrews, he argues that both the sacrifice of Christ on the cross and his priesthood are unique. The former cannot be repeated, the latter cannot be shared with or passed on to others. The ministerial priesthood is thus an affront to the eternal priesthood of Christ:

> First, indeed, this ought to be taken as an actual fact (which we have asserted in discussing the papal Mass) that all who call themselves priests to offer a sacrifice of expiation do wrong to Christ. Christ was appointed and consecrated priest according to the order of Melchizedek by the Father with an oath [Ps. 110:4; Heb. 5:6], without end, without successor [Heb. 7:3]. He once for all offered a sacrifice of eternal expiation and reconciliation; now, having also entered the sanctuary of heaven, he intercedes for us.[299]

While Calvin and Luther attack the sacrificial nature of the Eucharist from different perspectives, they concur in the conclusion implicit in this denial that the authentic celebration of the Lord's Supper does not require a separate and distinct order of priests. It is this conclusion which Doré sees as demanding a counter-attack.

The defense of the priesthood, as our theologian presents it in Chapter 21 of *L'arche de l'alliance*, begins by dividing salvation history into three general periods: the time preceding the Law, the age of the Mosaic Law, and finally the era of the New Covenant. Each of these ages, the Dominican asserts, is marked by a type of priesthood that offers sacrifice to almighty God. Prior to the Mosaic Law, the Scriptures bring out several examples of faithful men who offered sacrifice to the Lord: Abel who offered the choice portion from his flock and Abraham who was willing to sacrifice his only son Isaac to the Lord are but two of several figures mentioned in this section by Doré. Yet perhaps the most fitting example, the one who prefigures Christ most closely, is Melchizedek. Not only is

---

[299] Ibid., IV. XIX. 28. McNeill, 2, p. 1476. See Benoît, 4, p. 496.

he king of Salem, he is also a priestly figure for he offers bread and wine, a foreshadowing of the Eucharist, and blesses Abraham.[300]

With the advent of the Mosaic Law comes the establishment of an institutionalized priesthood, one that is hereditary. Aaron, brother of Moses and a Levite, is chosen by God as the high priest of this first covenant. Thus it is the tribe of Levi that is singled out from among the descendants of Abraham to offer the sacrifice prescribed by the Law in atonement for sin. Curiously, this is all Doré has to say concerning the levitical priesthood, a strikingly brief presentation when compared to the several pages he devotes to the priesthood of the era before the Law. Finally, of course, comes the New Law and with it the institution of a new priesthood, that of Christ. Up to this point, Doré has said nothing controversial, except perhaps his interpretation of Melchizedek's offering as a prefiguration of the Eucharist. He has basically given his readers an adapted presentation of the development of the priesthood as found in Hebrews 7. Neither Luther nor Calvin would find much to challenge in this historical overview.

Where the Reformers and the Dominican part ways, however, is in their understanding of the new and eternal priesthood of Christ. For the Reformers, as already mentioned, Christ is the sole priest of the New Covenant. Claiming the authority of Hebrews 7 for their position, they assert that there is no longer a need for other priests in the new dispensation because Christ lives forever.[301] While acknowledging that the levitical priesthood has been definitively surpassed by Christ, Doré goes on to argue that this does not necessarily mean that other priests are thereby abolished in the New Covenant:

---

[300] Concerning this particular interpretation of Melchizedek's offering, one that was common among the Catholic apologists of the sixteenth century, Calvin retorts that "Melchizedek gave bread and wine to Abraham and his companions, to refresh them, wearied by their journey and battle. What has this to do with sacrifice?" *Institutes*, IV. XVIII. 2. McNeill, 2, p. 1431. See Benoît, 4, p. 450.
[301] Hebrews 7:23 states, "The former priests were many in number, because they were prevented by death from continuing in office; but he holds his priesthood permanently, because he continues for ever" (RSV).

> *Finablement en la nouvelle loy, est cessée la vieille prestrise, & une nouvelle instituée par Jesus Christ, qui est le souverain prestre & sacrificateur, selon l'ordre de Melchisedech, & les autres sont ses ministres, qu'il a ordonnées: car tout ainsi que la loy ancienne, est transferée en la nouvelle plus parfaicte, la vieille prestrise est pareillement tranferée en une autre plus excellente & digne beaucoup...*[302]

The argument here is quite simple and logical. In the same way that Christ did not abolish the law but fulfilled it, so does he not abolish the former priesthood but instead fulfills and transforms it in such a way that it surpasses the old while at the same time continuing to be perpetuated with the incorporation of others as members. Although Christ is without question the sovereign priest of the New Covenant, he has nevertheless willed that others would share in his one priesthood.

At this point, Doré takes up the objection raised by the Reformers based on the assertion of the Letter to the Hebrews: if Christ's priesthood is eternal then what need is there for others to take his place in the priestly office? First of all, he rhetorically asks what the priesthood of the Old Covenant prefigured if not that of the New Covenant? Again the emphasis is on the idea of continuity and fulfillment, that Christ does not necessarily abolish the institutions of the past, he transforms them. Of course, the Reformers here would respond that the levites indeed foreshadowed the new priesthood. That new priesthood, however, is an office held by Christ alone. He is the sole priest of the New Covenant. In response, Doré goes on to offer an interesting if not completely compelling argument for the reasonableness of other men being given a participation in the one, eternal priesthood of Christ. He reasons thus:

> *Jesus, pour vray, est nostre grand pontife, & prestre selon l'ordre de Melchisedech, qui ensemble est roy de Chrestiens, comme aussi Melchisedech estoit roy, & toutefois ce roy qui a detruict les royaumes & empires, selon que l'a descript Daniel. Il y a vrais rois treschrestiens & catholiques soubz luy, aussi estant le grand prestre & pontife il a*

---
[302] *L'arche*, fol. 148r°-v°.

> *ministres soubz luy, par lesquelz sa prestrise est exercée, & non autre. Je dis d'avantage que Jesus est le seul prestre, qui s'est offert à son pere, qui ensemble est le prestre ou sacrificateur, le sacrifice & hostie, qui a appaisé le pere, & nul est ou sera tel en ce renc. Mais le prestre a de sa livrée en sa loy nouvelle, qui faict le mesme sacrifice qu'il a faict, selon son commandement, quand il a dit:* **Hoc facite in meam commemorationem.**[303]

Doré cleverly attempts in this passage to catch his opponents in a logical contradiction, for if they allow that Christian kings derive their authority in the temporal realm from Christ, the unique and eternal king, why then do they not allow that Christ would also confer on others a share in his priestly authority? If Christian monarchs share in the kingship of Christ, it would seem to follow that members of the clergy likewise share in his priesthood. To make this allowance is in no way to detract from the unique role of Christ as both priest and sacrifice. Doré very carefully explains the teaching of the Church on this point. Jesus is indeed the sole priest who has offered himself to the Father in atonement for sin, and no one else is his equal in this. Nevertheless, his unique sacrifice continues to be made present in the Eucharistic celebration from generation to generation by those men who have been chosen to share in his eternal priesthood.

Of course, the heart of the matter is whether or not there is any Scriptural basis for the ministerial priesthood as it exists in the Church. In other words, is the ministerial priesthood really of divine origin? In the last sentence of the above citation, Doré offers his readers the traditional proof-text for the sacrament of holy orders, "Do this in memory of me." As he explains, Christ commands the apostles at the Last Supper to continue to offer the same sacrifice which he himself offers, that of his body and blood. This question concerning the divine institution of holy orders was one answered much earlier by Doré in his catechism, *Dyalogue instructoire* (1538). In this work, it will be recalled, Cornelius the inquisitive centurion challenges St. Peter to offer a scriptural

---

[303] Ibid., fol. 149r°-v°.

foundation for each of the seven sacraments. As regards the ministerial priesthood, St. Peter has this to say to his pupil:

> Du dernier sacrement qui est Ordre, son institution est entendue par ce que dict nostre seigneur en sainct Matthieu, xxvi chappitre: Faictes ce en ma commemoration. Et en sainct Jehan, xx: Recepvez le sainct esperit, desquelz vous remettrez les pechez ilz son remitz et pardonnez. Car ces deux appartiennent a l'ordre sacerdotale, c'est ascavoir puissance au regard du vray corps de nostre seigneur qui se monstre en la consecration dicelluy, et puissance sur le corps mistique dicelluy, comme en l'absolution des pecheurs penitens.[304]

In this reply, Doré couples the Last Supper command with the text from John 20:22 concerning the authority to forgive sins as solid scriptural proof for the share which Christ willed his apostles to have in his priestly authority. That the apostles themselves understood their commissioning as collaborators in Christ's priestly office to be in fact the establishment of a new priesthood is clear from the provision they made for the priestly office to continue beyond them. Doré points to both Timothy and Titus as not only having received the priestly office from Paul but as being charged with ordaining others in turn. Basing himself on Titus 1:5, he remarks:

> ...car Tite avoit par la disposition de sainct Paul obtenu la supereminence de prestrise. Le mesme Apostre advise l'Evesque qu'il ne soit pas hastif de mettre la main sur autruy pour l'ordonner prestre, ou diacre, afin qu'il ne communique point à son peché, qu'il fera mal adminstrant les sacremens, quand insuffisant & non idoine seroit ordonné.[305]

In this particular verse, Paul gives his disciple Titus instructions on the kind of men he should appoint for ministry in the Christian community. What Doré is trying to demonstrate here is that apostolic tradition merely continued what Christ himself established, an order of priests whose principal role in the Christian community, as he pointed out in an earlier work, was to offer the Eucharistic

---

[304] *Dyalogue instructoire*, fol. Fviii v°.
[305] *L'arche*, fol. 148v°-149r°.

sacrifice and to dispense forgiveness of sins in the name of Christ through the sacrament of penance.

The Reformers, of course, do not dispute the institution of a ministerial office in the Christian community, for the Scriptures abound with evidence on this point. It is the understanding of that ministerial office as "priesthood" to which they object. The Scriptures, after all, never mention the word "priest." Timothy and Titus are referred to as "bishop" or overseer. Those whom they appoint as subordinates are called "presbyters" or elders. Neither term necessarily connotes any notion of priestly office as Doré has described it, nor do they necessarily preclude the notion. Thus, he must offer an explanation for why the presbyters are *de facto* priests if not in name. He begins by raising the objection proferred by the Reformers and then proposing a reason for why the apostles were reluctant to employ the term "priest" for the ministers of the New Covenant:

> *Si encores replique contre ceste verité la mensonge d'heresie qui luy contrarie, par ce qu'au nouveau testament on ne list point que ce nom de prestre ou sacrificateur soit donné aux ministres ecclesiastiques, mais bien sont anciens ou ministres. En rien n'esmouvera le Chrestien ceste objection, s'il regarde & diligemment considere à la raison pourquoy ce a esté faict: car je diz que grande cautelle & prudence en cela observe l'escripture, ou es Apostres qui usoient de telz noms: car de leur temps estoit encores le temple ou on sacrifioit, & là estoient les prestres, ou sacrificateurs: pourquoy à ce que ne fist confusion en parolles, pour monstrer la difference de la vieille prestrise, & la nouvelle, usoient de nouvelles appellations...Mais ou le temple a esté ruiné, & les prestres, alors ont esté appellez ministres ecclesiastiques, prestres, ou sacrificateurs.*[306]

As Doré explains it, the apostles early on were understandably prudent in choosing to refer to the ministers of the Christian community as elders rather than as priests, otherwise there might have been confusion with regards to the priesthood and sacrifices of the Old Covenant which continued to be exercised among the Jews. However, once the Temple was destroyed and cultic sacrifice was no longer an element of Judaism, the initial reticence of the Christian

---

[306] Ibid., fol. 149v°.

community gave way to an open recognition of the presbyters as priests of the New Covenant.

Yet this preoccupation with terminology is quite beside the point as far as Doré is concerned, for he argues that no matter what the ministers of the early Church were called, they nevertheless exercised a priestly function from the beginning:

> *D'abondant que fault il se soucier du nom de l'office, quand l'office de prestrise estoit? Regardans ce qui est escript aux Actes des Apostres trezieme, Et sans aucune contradiction apparoistra cest office avoir esté exercé en l'Eglise, ou le texte a ainsi. Il y avoit en l'Eglise, qui estoit en Antiochie, aucuns prophetes & Docteurs, & Barnabas, & Simon qui estoit appellé Niger, & Lucius Cyrenien, & Manahen...& Saul, & eulx* **ministrans** *ou* **sacrifians** [emphasis mine] *au Seigneur, & jeusnans, leur dist le S. Esprit: Separez moy Barnabas & Saul pour l'oeuvre, auquel je les ay appellez. Quand ilz eurent jeusné, & prié, ilz mirent les mains sur eulx, & les laisserent aller: ou fault noter, que là ou en nostre lettre il y a au Latin, ministrantibus, les autres lisent, sacrificantibus. Erasme ne l'a pas oublié en ses annotations de la diction graecque* λειτουργεωτων, *qui est le propre de ceulx qui ministrent es choses sacrées, ou sacrifient. Il est donc constant, & indubitable, que prestrise & sacrificature est en la nouvelle loy, & si sont ministres de Dieu appellez, ou pasteurs, ou anciens, ou prestres, ou aussi evesques.*[307]

Although Doré did not have much use for Erasmus and his scholarship in general, we see here that he was indeed familiar with the *Annotationes* of the humanist and used it when it suited his purpose. In this case, Doré informs his readers of an alternate reading of Acts 13:2, where "*ministrantibus*" might also be translated as "*sacrificantibus*," based on the etymology of the original Greek "λειτουργεωτων" which involves the notion of making a sacred offering. This alternate reading is acknowledged by no less an authority than Erasmus himself. Ultimately, the point which Doré wishes to impress on his readers is that regardless of what the early leaders of the Church may have been called, they exercised the priestly office of Christ himself by offering the sacrifice of his body and blood.

---

[307] Ibid., fol. 149v⁰-150r⁰.

It must be admitted that Doré's presentation of the sacrificial nature of the Eucharist is quite undeveloped by comparison with both Luther and Calvin's reasoned arguments against the idea. In fact he never really addresses their objections directly. Nowhere does he discuss the problem raised by Luther of how the Eucharist can be an offering made to God when it is a gift to be received in faith. Nor does he answer Calvin's assertion that the sacrifice of the Mass in effect robs the passion of Christ of its meaning and power. In this instance, Doré merely reaffirms with no further elaboration the Church's teaching that the Mass is a continuation of that one, perfect sacrifice offered by Christ on Calvary. It should be further noted that this affirmation occurs within a discussion on the validity of the ministerial priesthood. Doré, it seems, does not see the sacrificial nature of the Mass as the issue of central importance in his heresy-fighting program. Even in *La meditation devote du bon Chrestien sus le sainct sacrifice de la Messe* (1544), where ostensibly the subject would be treated, there is in fact little commentary offered as to what it means for the Mass to be a sacrifice. As mentioned earlier in this chapter, Doré's concern in this work is primarily to explain the rites of the Mass so that the laity might more piously participate in it. Though he repeatedly refers to the sacrifice offered during the Mass, he in fact devotes very little time and space to either defending or fully explaining it.

Of clearly far greater concern to the Dominican theologian is the necessity to defend the priesthood which has been charged by Christ to perpetuate the Eucharist in time. Why does he concentrate so much on affirming the legitimacy of the ministerial priesthood? Although he never says so explicitly, the reason probably has to do with his sense that without the priesthood, there is in fact no Eucharist, no real presence of Christ in the elements of bread and wine. At the moment when the sacrament was instituted, it was the Twelve alone who were present and who were commissioned by Christ to "do this in remembrance of me,"—a fact which Doré does not fail to mention in his presentation. Tradition has seen here a divinely-willed act, the origin of the new priesthood exercised in and through Christ. To reject this priesthood, then, is in reality to render the Eucharist an empty symbol, for only those who share in the one priesthood of Christ have the power and authority to transform the material elements of bread and wine into the gift of Christ's body and blood. Given this consequence, it is no wonder that Doré saw the debate concerning the sacrificial nature of the Mass to be of secondary importance. The Reformers' challenge to the ministerial priesthood was of much greater significance because it called into question the very existence of the Eucharist itself.

Despite Doré's insistence that the Eucharist is the central act of the priesthood, he nevertheless affirms that the priest must also be about the business of preaching the Gospel, for the Word of God is in itself manna for the soul. Whether he is taking Luther's critique of the pre-Tridentine clergy to heart or whether he is speaking from his experience as a friar of the Order of Preachers, Doré acknowledges the necessity of good preaching to prepare souls for the proper reception of the food from heaven. The story of Elijah fleeing from the wrath of Jezebel (see 1 Kings 19:1-8) provides him with the allegory for the point he is attempting to make. He interprets the angel sent to comfort and feed the weary Elijah during his journey as a figure of the priest who awakens the pilgrim with the Word of God and then strengthens the believer with the bread of the Eucharist:

> *Bien se repose & dort a son ayse le chrestien…l'ange de dieu par lequel est entendu le prebstre, apporte le pain & l'eaue pour son viatique, qui luy donne ung doulx resveil par le son de la parolle de dieu, & evangile qui presche…A cest ange, c'est à dire le prebstre, le messagier de dieu envers le peuple, convient & non a aultre consacrer le vray corpus domini, & le bailler & distribuer aux aultres…Cest ange, c'est à dire le prebstre, resveille l'homme, comme dit est, par le bruyt de la parolle de dieu qui presche a noz oreilles, laquelle parolle est aussi la pitance, manne, & nourriture de l'ame.*[308]

---

[308] *La deploration*, fol. 47r°-48r°.

What is evident in this allegory is that Doré's defense of the priesthood is in no way an *apologia* for the actual state of the clergy in his time. The angel who awakens Elijah is a reminder to the clergy of their duty to bring the faithful the comforting sound of the Gospel message, a duty which a good portion at the time were neglecting. It is also interesting to note how Doré likens the proclamation of the Word to a manna that nourishes, an emphasis rarely seen among Catholic writers who tended to focus exclusively on the Eucharist as the food of the soul. Doré seems to strike a good balance here between word and sacrament as a twofold spiritual nourishment. But if he acknowledges the place of preaching as a priestly duty, he does not fail to affirm in this allegory that the ultimate reason why the priesthood exists is the celebration of the Eucharist, for the priest alone and no one else has the authority to consecrate the elements so that they become the true body and blood of Christ for the satisfaction of the weary and hungering faithful.

Unfortunately, Doré's attempt in *L'arche de l'alliance* to demonstrate the priesthood as a divinely-willed institution falls somewhat short of the mark. The problem lies in his desire to answer the Reformers on their own terms, *sola scriptura*. While the New Testament certainly offers some evidence of the institution of the priesthood, for example the Lord's command to his apostles at the Last Supper, the proof is not self-evident and can be reduced to a question of interpretation. Luther, as pointed out, did not subscribe to the traditional understanding of this passage. Thus, Doré's citation of certain key texts in support of the ministerial priesthood is open to criticism in part because he fails to underscore the validity of Tradition as a basis for interpreting the Scriptures. Here more than elsewhere, the weakness of answering Reformation theology solely with the Scriptures themselves comes through, for unless the role of Tradition as a conduit for belief and practice is affirmed, it is impossible to build a solid case for the divine institution of the priesthood merely by citing passages from the New Testament. It is the way the Church has interpreted these texts from earliest times which gives force to the argument.

Practical Counsels: Preparing to Receive the Eucharist

In addition to the specifically doctrinal issues addressed by Doré in his treatment of the Eucharist, there is also a more practical concern which is very much in evidence, particularly in the early, more devotional works where we see a strong emphasis on how a person should prepare himself to properly receive the sacrament. Thus we move in this study from Doré the instructor in theology who defends the doctrine of transubstantiation to Doré the director of souls who also draws out the practical implications of the doctrine. The principal point of this counsel is to aid his readers in satisfying the Pauline directive found in 1 Corinthians 11:28 on the necessity of examining one's conscience before partaking of the body of the Lord. We have already seen how our friar cites this particular verse as scriptural proof of transubstantiation, for why else would the apostle urge such an examination of conscience if the bread and wine of the Eucharist were but ordinary food. But polemics aside, Doré is also concerned to explain how the Pauline directive might properly be observed by those who are already convinced that the sacrament is indeed the true body and blood of Christ.

Mention has been made in Chapter 2 of how Doré uses the analogy of preparing one's home to receive an important guest such as the king of France to illustrate the even greater necessity to prepare the home of one's soul to receive the Lord of Lords in the Eucharist. A more biblical image he employs to make the same point is the figure of John the Baptist. Just as the precursor prepared the way of the Lord by disposing the people to receive him, "...*pareillement l'advenement d'icelluy en nous par sacramentelle manducation, doibt proceder quelque disposition pour nettoyer les voyes de nostre conscience devant la face du seigneur.*"[309] It is in order to assure that those who approach the sacrament will do so with the appropriate dispositions that Doré offers some very explicit counsels to his readers on the subject.

That the Dominican takes this matter seriously is manifested in the fact that a list of twelve conditions for receiving the Eucharist worthily appears in no less than three different works: *Les allumettes du feu divin* (1538), *Dyalogue instructoire des chrestiens* (1538), and *La deploration de la vie humaine* (1541). Although there are minor variations each time, the lists are substantially identical. As is his custom, Doré also has recourse to images to illustrate his points. In *Les allumettes*, it is the laying of Christ's body in the sepulchre which serves as the metaphor for the conditions necessary for him to repose sacramentally in our hearts. For example, the myrrh used for the burial symbolizes the mortification of the senses which should precede a worthy reception of the body of the Lord. The white burial shroud represents the purity of body and soul required, etc.[310] Later, in *La deploration*, Doré draws a parallel between the ritual preparations for eating the paschal lamb of the Exodus and the preparations required for partaking of the flesh of the new paschal lamb. This time, it is the bitter herbs which symbolize the need for compunction, mortification and penance while the stipulation of eating the Passover meal with belts tightened stands for the purity and chastity required for participating in the new Passover.[311] Thus in each work, the conditions for worthy reception of the Eucharist are basically the same. It is only the metaphor that changes.

Before proceeding on to some of the other conditions which Doré enumerates in his list, it should be noted that the above-mentioned conditions of purity and contrition for past sin seem to receive greater attention and emphasis than most of the others. In both *Les allumettes* and *Dyalogue instructoire*, purity and mortification are placed at the head of the list and even though they appear

---

[309] Ibid., fol. 27v°.
[310] *Les allumettes*, fol. liii r°.
[311] *La deploration*, fol. 33r°.

further down in the list given in *La deploration*, they still receive more detailed commentary there than most of the other conditions. Given that the sacrament is an encounter, indeed a communion with God himself, it goes without saying that the Dominican theologian would emphasize the importance of true contrition for one's sins and a certain purity of heart as well as a detachment from things of the world in order that the communicant might truly be a fitting dwelling place for the Lord. As regards purity, Doré makes it a point here to highlight the chastity required, even of married couples, before receiving communion. He does not indicate for how long a period a couple should abstain from the marital act before approaching the sacrament, nor does he seem to insist upon this discipline as an absolute rule. Rather, basing himself on the counsel offered by St. Paul in 1 Corinthians 7:5 that a man and wife should not deprive each other of the marital act except by mutual consent for a time in order to be free for prayer, he argues in the *Dyalogue instructoire* that preparing to receive one's Creator is all the more reason to temporarily abstain from sexual relations. The idea here is that if one wishes to experience spiritual delights, he must first of all renounce the pleasures of the flesh, even those that are legitimate. It should be noted that there is nothing at all extraordinary in these counsels offered by Doré to his readers to help them prepare for worthy reception of the Eucharist. The emphasis on contrition and purity as the principal elements of a good preparation is traditional. Where Doré's originality comes through is principally in the metaphors he uses to describe the conditions.

Other requirements which appear in the Dominican's list include a devout meditation on the events of the passion as well as the importance of fervently desiring this communion with the Lord. But perhaps the most important element of all among Doré's twelve conditions is his insistence on the necessity of a plenitude of faith in the sacrament, "*en croyant fermement soubz les especes sacramentelles estre le vray corps de Jesus.*"[312] It is a given, of course, that one's

---

[312] *Les allumettes*, fol. liii v°.

reception of the sacrament should presuppose a belief in Christ's real presence in the consecrated species. However, the question arises, does lack of faith in the sacrament therefore mean that bread alone is received by the communicant? For Calvin, the answer to this question would be "yes." Unbelievers who approach the sacrament receive the sign alone; their lack of faith prevents them from actually communing with the body of Christ through the power of the Spirit. He asserts that although the body is offered to all, it is not received by all, but only by those who have faith.[313] While Doré also insists on the necessity of faith for a proper reception of the Eucharist, he is in no way upholding the Genevan Reformer's position here, for the sacrament in his understanding is objectively speaking the body and blood of Christ regardless of whether the recipient believes it or not. Nevertheless, such a faithless reception of the body of Christ in no way profits the recipient. Thus Doré, following Aquinas[314], distinguishes between two types of eating of the Eucharist:

> *La premiere est espirituelle par la foy. La seconde est sacramentelle laquelle ne peult prouffiter sans, la premiere, comme a Judas ne prouffita recepvoir sacramentellement nostre seigneur, mais il nuist grandement. La disposition donc requises pour la manducation sacramentelle, est avoir la premiere manducation espirituelle par la foy vifve...*[315]

Lack of faith on the part of the communicant does not alter the fact that the body of Christ is truly received in a sacramental eating. However, only a spiritual eating, that is one to which the recipient brings a living faith, renders the sacramental eating fruitful and efficacious. To partake of the Eucharist without faith, without a spirit of contrition, in impurity and with a cold heart, is to eat it to one's condemnation, as was the case with Judas, the betrayer. For Doré, the Eucharist is a marvelous gift, one which the faithful should not fear approaching.

---

[313] See *Institutes*, IV. XVII. 33.
[314] See IIIa, q. 80, a. 1. Aquinas himself is echoing here a distinction made by Augustine in his *Tractates on the Gospel of John*, 26.11.2.
[315] *La deploration*, fol. 50r°-50v°.

Yet, at the same time, they can only profit from this gift of grace if they are first properly disposed in mind, heart and body. It is to this end that the Dominican offers sound, practical advice on the conditions for receiving the sacrament which, while not explicitly connected to his polemical concerns in the Reformation debate, nevertheless serves to reinforce the *leitmotif* of his teaching on transubstantiation.

An Encouragement to Frequent Communion

The emphasis placed by Doré on conditions for a worthy reception of the Eucharist leads to the assumption that he was in favor of a regular frequentation of the sacrament provided that the stated conditions had been fulfilled. But we might wonder what exactly would constitute a "regular frequentation" for the Dominican? This question of Doré's position on frequent communion is an important one because the encouragement of the laity to receive the body of Christ more frequently was one of the hallmarks of the Catholic reform movement in the sixteenth and seventeenth centuries. The Council of Trent set the tone which would later be taken up by spiritual writers such as Francis de Sales on the importance of frequent reception of the Eucharist. In Chapter 8 of the decrees from the thirteenth session of the Council we read:

> ...the holy council with true paternal affection enjoins, exhorts, begs and entreats *through the tender mercy of God* [Lk. 1:78] that each and all who are marked by the name of Christian ...should believe and reverence these sacred mysteries of his body and blood with such constancy and firmness of faith, such dedication of mind, such devotion and worship, that they may be able to receive frequently that life-supporting bread, and that it may be for them truly the life of the soul and the unending health of the mind...[316]

---

[316] Tanner, *Decrees*, 2, p. 697.

The encouragement to more frequent communion seen here stands in marked contrast to the practice of the medieval church where the norm for the laity was to receive communion but once a year at Eastertide.[317] For the most part, communion was reserved to the priest while the laity were relegated to adoring the consecrated elements at the elevation, a kind of communion through the eyes. This distortion of the purpose of the Eucharist was rightly pointed out by the Protestant Reformers who also objected to the practice of denying the cup to the laity when they did receive communion.

Whereas Doré affirms the doctrine of transubstantiation from the very outset of his literary production, he undergoes a noticeable change in position on the issue of how frequently communion should be received. Early on in *Les allumettes du feu divin* (1538), for example, he explains how the fire of charity is lighted in the souls of Christians "*quand recoivent leur createur, ou a pasques ou au lict de la mort.*"[318] Here we have a testimony to what was the normal practice of the time. Reception of communion was an infrequent occurrence, usually limited to the yearly celebration of Easter and the hour of one's death. The Dominican neither defends nor condemns the practice in this passing remark but quite simply gives witness to what is the norm.

It is not until six years later that we see Doré offering a defense of the norm, a defense of infrequent communion, in light no doubt of Protestant attacks on the Church's practice. In his brief work on the Mass, *La meditation devote*, he begins the section on the moment of communion by explaining that in the early church the priest, after communicating himself, would normally distribute communion to the rest of the faithful because "*la ferveur & devotion du peuple estoit plus grande, & aussi qu'il n'y avoit pas si grand nombre de chrestiens.*"[319]

---

[317] The Fourth Lateran Council (1215) enjoined the obligation of receiving the sacrament *ad minus in pascha* or at least at Easter. While never meant to serve as a limit, this precept established a minimum requirement which in practice the faithful satisfied as an obligation without often exceeding.

[318] *Les allumettes*, fol. xiii v°.

[319] *La meditation*, fol. Dii r°.

In other words, he is attempting to argue that communion is no longer frequently received for practical reasons—too many people—and because somehow the faithful of his day are not as worthy of the sacrament because of their lack of fervor. But then he goes on to offer a rather strange and unconvincing analogy for why the laity are really not missing anything by being deprived of frequent communion with the body of the Lord:

> *Quand le pain materiel est mangé, combien qu'il entre seullement par la bouche, si esse qu'elle seule n'en est pas nourrie, mais aussi tous les aultres membres du corps. Pareillement quand le prebstre, seul communie & recoipt le vray corps de Jesus Christ à la messe & son vrai sang, ce n'est pas seullement à luy qu'il proffite, mais aussi ayde il aux aultres membres, & bons fidelles qui l'adorent, & le mangent par foy vive & le recoipvent spirituellement, ce que represente la distribution du pain baillé à tous, & cela sert de entretenir la paix entre les membres, qui sont tous alimentés d'une mesme viande...*[320]

Given his strong belief in the real presence of Christ in the Eucharist and the many graces which the sacrament affords, his position here is rather incongruous. While it is true that nourishment received by mouth and stomach as it is digested produces beneficial effects for the entire body, to claim that the faithful are likewise nourished in grace even though the priest alone receives the body and blood of Christ is unconvincing, to say the least. The analogy is a failed attempt by Doré to support what is a distortion of the real purpose of the Eucharist, which is meant to be food for the entire body of the faithful and not merely the clergy. What we see here is an example of Doré defending an abuse, but why? In the heat of controversy, the initial reaction is sometimes to defend one's position simply because it is being challenged without regard for whether the position itself is justified. This seems to be the case here, where the zealous Doré employs specious arguments to uphold a practice which is clearly unjustified simply because it has come under attack by the enemy.

---

[320] Ibid., fol. Dii r°-Dii v°.

Yet, Doré undergoes a noticeable conversion of heart on the question of frequent communion, one that is evident in his later works, beginning with *L'arche de l'alliance* in 1549. Thus, his change of attitude precedes the Council of Trent's pronouncements on the matter and was not influenced by the Council's determinations. Ironically, however, the passage of *L'arche* where Doré most strongly encourages more frequent reception of the Eucharist by the laity is not his own. It is, in fact, one of the several passages he "borrows" from John Calvin, of course without citing his source![321] The quotation in question is lifted practically word for word from the Genevan Reformer's *Petit traicté de la Saincte Cène*:

> *Si on m'interrogue qui est le temps d'en user* [the sacrament], *on ne peult pas bien limiter à tous pour certain: car il y a aucunefois des empeschemens particuliers, qui font que l'homme faict bien s'en abstenir. Et d'avantage nous n'avons point de commandement expres pour contraindre tous Chrestiens à en user chacun jour, si est ce que si nous regardons bien à la fin à laquelle le Seigneur nous meine, nous congnoistrons qu'il seroit bon (comme je le conseille) que l'usage fust plus frequent que beaucoup ne l'ont.*[322]

The key sentence here is the affirmation that in view of the end to which the Lord calls us, that is eternal life, the faithful should make more frequent use of the special aid provided in the sacrament of the Eucharist to attain the goal. That the words here are really Calvin's does not necessarily mean that Doré was therefore influenced by the Reformer's thought in his apparent change of heart concerning more frequent reception of communion, particularly since he believed Calvin's denial of transubstantiation effectively stripped the sacrament of any real meaning. It is more likely that Doré had come to realize the incongruity of his own strong belief in the transforming power of the Eucharist while at the same time defending a practice or custom which limited access to the sacrament, for

---

[321] Calvin's desire was that the Eucharist be celebrated once a month in the reformed churches. However the Genevan council allowed for only four celebrations per year. See Higman, *Diffusion*, p. 117.
[322] *L'arche*, fol. 96r°. Cf. also Backus, *Vraie Piété*, p. 138.

just prior to the above citation, he affirms that *"ce sacrement est un remede que dieu nous a donné pour subvenir à nostre foiblesse, fortifier nostre foy, augmenter nostre charité, nous advancer en toute saincteté de vie, d'autant plus en debuons nous user."*[323] What he discovered on the matter in Calvin's *Petit traicté* was simply a well-expressed formulation of something he himself had come to believe which he then proceeded to incorporate in his own work.

Doré's new mindset concerning frequent communion continues to make itself evident in his successive works. In *Le nouveau testament d'amour* of 1550, he addresses in particular the concerns of scrupulous souls who refrain from partaking of the sacrament out of an exaggerated sense of unworthiness. *"Entendez donc ames craintifves,"* he writes, *"qui desirez bien souvent recevoir le sainct sacrement, mais n'osez de paour d'estre trouvees indignes. Il ne fault pas pour la seule estimation d'indignité, se soustraire de la saincte communion."*[324] He goes on to assure the scrupulous that a spirit of contrition and sacramental confession completely wipe out sin, making them fit to receive the all-holy One. As for the sense of unworthiness which may continue to trouble them even after receiving absolution, he insists that no one is ever really "worthy" to eat the body of the Lord. As long as one is free from grave sin, one should not let a sense of unworthiness keep him from receiving communion. The tone is not only assuring but it is evidence of a real movement on Doré's part from being a defender of an abuse to being an active agent for change in the Church's practice concerning reception of the Eucharist.

As part of his new-found attitude, Doré encourages frequent communion not only as a remedy for past sins, but also as a preventative medicine or a kind of inoculation which strengthens the communicant for the battle against temptation. He chastises those who would put off receiving communion, warning that too long of an abstinence from this heavenly food leaves a person much more susceptible to a fall from grace:

---

[323] Ibid.
[324] *Le Nouveau testament*, fol. 191r°.

> *Si aujourd'huy tu delaisses pour quelque apprehension, trouble ou tentation, à recevoir, possible que demain reviendra plus fort, & par ainsi pourras estre longuement empesché de recevoir ton Sauveur, de plus en plus estre rendu inepte, refroidy, pesant & indevot.*[325]

Doré's reasoning is compelling. To abstain from communion because one is experiencing temptations or some kind of fear is in effect to give the enemy the upper hand and to practically assure his victory whereas to receive the living God in the Eucharist gives the beleaguered person an invincible strength in combatting evil influences. Once again, Doré's promotion of frequent communion is based on his belief in the salutary effects of the sacrament not only for the healing of sinners, but also for their strengthening in the face of temptation.

Finally, the Dominican promotes the Eucharist as a communion with love itself. Those consecrated to a life of virginity or those who have lost their spouse are particularly exhorted to frequent the holy sacrament where they will be nourished on divine love. In one of his final works, a guide to the spiritual life for widows, Doré offers the following counsel to the "turtledoves" who have lost their husbands:

> *Car la vraye Tourtre se laisse affamer au corps, ou y endurer faim, pour estre saoullée & remplie de viande spirituelle au dedans. Et pour mieux s'engresser, frequente souvent la table de nostre Seigneur, en recevant le precieux corps d'iceluy, en la Saincte Hostie & Sacrement d'Eucharistie. O viande amoureuse! O Sacrement d'amour & de dilection! Qui le frequente ne vit que d'amour.*[326]

Whereas a bodily fast and discipline of the appetites are good for the soul, such discipline does not apply in matters of spiritual food. On the contrary, the faithful should feast often on the precious body of Christ offered in the Eucharist. Although Doré's advice here is addressed specifically to widows, there is no doubt that he would favor its extension to all the faithful.

---

[325] Ibid., fol. 194v°.
[326] *La tourtrelle*, fol. 54v°-55r°.

Thus, our friar makes a complete about-face on the question of frequent communion. While in the heat of battle with the Reformers he at first defends what had been the normal practice since the Middle Ages of only a yearly or infrequent reception, he eventually realizes that for the light of Catholic truth on the Eucharist to shine forth, the laity must be encouraged to actually experience the graces of the sacrament in receiving it on a more regular basis. It is inconsistent on the one hand to defend the real presence of Christ in the consecrated bread and wine and on the other to deny the faithful access to communion with the Eucharistic Lord. If the sacrament is something more than a memorial of the Last Supper, if it is the true body and blood of Christ, that is all the more reason to counter Reformation theology by promoting a more frequent use of this summit of all gifts.

Deification: The Principal Effect of the Eucharist

The preceding sections of this chapter have brought out several aspects of Doré's presentation of the Catholic understanding of Eucharist. First of all, a good portion of it is meant to be a response to the principal issues called into question by the Protestant Reformers, most especially the doctrine of transubstantiation. Secondly, much of it anticipates and is perfectly consonant with the subsequent teaching of the Council of Trent on the sacrament. But there is an important difference between the Council's own teaching on the Eucharist and Doré's extensive treatment of it in various works. Whereas the conciliar decrees concentrate almost exclusively on refuting the doctrinal positions adopted by the Reformers, Doré's defense of the sacrament goes beyond this more restricted concern to include a broader discussion of the manifold benefits which the Eucharist affords the communicant. Perhaps the centerpiece of this discussion is a strong and repeated affirmation of the sacrament's principal effect; our deification by this real contact with the author of grace. Here a more mystical side of Doré comes to the fore as he encourages the faithful to see in the sacrament Christ himself calling them to intimate union with him, a union through which our human nature is brought to perfection in virtue even in this life.

Mention was made in the previous section that Doré over the years came to encourage frequent communion as a medicine for healing the wounds of past sins and as a kind of inoculation for resisting the allurement of future temptations. Yet even these salutary effects, marvelous as they are, are of relatively minor significance when compared to the incredible union between God and man which is the sacrament's principal end. Indeed, this union is so intimate and real that we can be said to be deified as a result. The idea of our deification or divinization through grace is certainly not original to Pierre Doré. It is a notion with a very long tradition, one that is prominent in the writings of the Fathers, particularly though by no means exclusively those of the East. Yet such a profound exaltation of sinful man, while firmly grounded in the Christian tradition, is unthinkable in the mindset of Reformed theology because the notion of deification is closely related to the idea that justifying grace actually transforms the interior of our being, perfecting nature, to use the language of Aquinas. While the Reformers do speak of regeneration or rebirth in Christ which involves the restoration in us of the image of God "that had been disfigured and all but obliterated through Adam's transgression,"[327] or while they also admit our adoptive sonship in Christ, they never go so far as to say that through grace, we become like God. Although judged righteous in Christ by a gracious God, the believer is always, to once again borrow Luther's phrase, *simul justus et peccator* in the Reformers' view.

However, for Pierre Doré, a proper understanding of the Eucharist and its effects demands a rejection of this notion that we are simultaneously righteous and sinners. In virtue of being a communion with Christ's own life, the Eucharist is not only the pledge of the future glory that will be ours in heaven but is the effective means by which we are deified even now. Nor is there anything

---

[327] Calvin, *Institutes*, III. III. 9. McNeill, 1, p. 601. See Benoît, 3, p. 73.

scandalous in the idea that human beings are transformed and perfected in this way, for such is God's love for us that he desires to be one with us and share with us all that is his. Doré offers this comment on the institution of the Eucharist at the Last Supper:

> *Et apres graces dictes,* [Jesus] *par charité departit le pain consacré, & le donna à ses Apostres. Charité de soy est unitive, & de deux ne faict qu'un. Par ceste charité qu'avoit Jesus à nous il a prins noz maulx de peine, & nous a donné ses biens. Ce qui est à luy est à moy, par ce, qui est à moy est à luy.*[328]

Just as in marriage, man and woman become one flesh, so through reception of the Eucharist the believer is made one with Christ in a union of love. This union is God's gift springing from the divine charity which takes our sins in exchange for his perfections, for in love all is shared. Thus God's graciousness is not limited to merely reckoning us as righteous while leaving us in our sins. Doré makes it clear that God's graciousness as manifested in the gift of the Eucharist is ordered to our actually being made righteous by being given a real share in Christ's perfections.

For the Dominican theologian, the Eucharist represents the restoration of everything that humanity had lost as a result of the fall in the Garden of Eden. He explains that through the gift of his true body and blood in the sacrament, Christ grants humanity that which Satan had falsely promised to Adam and Eve in proposing that they eat of the forbidden fruit. This fruit from the tree of the knowledge of good and evil, the Deceptor had claimed, would make them like gods. Desirous of divine status, the two fell for the ruse and thereby ruptured the intimate relationship they had to that point enjoyed with their Creator. But God in his providence has now provided his children with the true nourishment which actually fulfills this deep human desire for immortality. What humanity had sought to obtain through sin, on its own terms and apart from God, is now graciously bestowed on us as a gift. Doré makes this precise point both in

---

[328] *L'arche*, fol. 53r°.

L'arche de l'alliance[329] and earlier in *La caeleste pensée* (1543). In this particular work, he provides the reader with a program of meditations for each day of the week. Thursday is to be devoted especially to meditation on the gift of the Holy Spirit and the gift of the Eucharist, both of which are given us by God for our growth in holiness. It is here that Doré links the Eucharist with the idea that it represents the fulfillment of the deification that Adam and Eve longed for and sought to grasp apart from grace by yielding to the temptation of the serpent:

> *Icy doibt penser le chrestien, pourquoy dieu nous a faict ce grand bien & benefice, & l'utilité d'iceluy, certes sa esté par tresimmense charité qu'il a eu à nous...voulant par ce moyen unir le chief avec les membres, c'est a dire nous unir & joindre à luy, car **par ceste refection nous transmue en luy & faict comme dieux, ce que faulsement avoit repromis le serpent, par la comestion du fruict prohibé** [emphasis mine]. O providence infinie, & sapience de dieu treshaulte, par le moyen par lequel le diable a voulu nous faire mourir, par le mesme moyen a dieu ordonné nous donner vie, le diable a voulu par ung mourceau nous empoisonner & faire mourir, & dieu a voulu par la viande aporter vie et sancté perpetuelle.*[330]

Just as death came to mankind through a morsel of forbidden fruit, so now God in his providence restores the gift of life to us through another refection, that of the Eucharist. Moreover, this gift of life is in actuality God's own life so that in receiving the body of Christ "we might be perfect as our heavenly Father is perfect."[331] True virtue and righteousness are possible for us precisely because Christ lives in us through the Eucharist.

The Dominican insists that the fruit of Christ's saving death communicated to us through Holy Communion not only restores to us the promise of eternal life, it also restores the bond of intimacy with God which had been shattered by the original sin of our first parents. But this new bond of intimacy is far different from the old, for the Eucharist effects such a union between the believer and Christ that the believer is actually transformed into him to become

---

[329] See fol. 107v°-108r°.
[330] *La caeleste pensée*, fol. 62v°-63r°.
[331] See Matthew 5:48, RSV.

219

god-like. Borrowing an idea already present in the Fathers, notably St. Augustine, he notes that *"quand le corps de nostre seigneur est dignement prins par les fidelles au Sainct sacrement, il ne convertissent pas ceste viande en eulx, ainsi que il font toute autre mais au contraire l'homme est mué & converty espirituellement en dieu."*[332] It is important to note here the emphasis placed on the "worthy" reception of the Eucharist, which brings about the intended fruit of deification. As mentioned earlier, the effect of the sacrament does depend upon our receiving it in faith as well as with a certain purity of heart and heartfelt contrition for past sins. Union and deification are God's work in us, but we must be properly disposed to his transformative action. And as usual, Doré has an apt image for this deification of man which occurs through communion with the body and blood of the Lord, the image of a consuming fire which converts what it consumes into itself:

> *Nostre Dieu, dict l'escripture, est comme feu qui consume: Or le feu, de sa force & condition, il convertist tout en sa nature, tout ce qu'on luy applicque, pareillement quand nous recepvons dignement ce sainct sacrement, qui est comme le feu qui consume l'or, il nous allume & embrase du tout, & nous convertist en luy: & par ainsi l'homme deifié peult dire avec S. Paul aux Galatiens,* **Vivo ego, iam non ego, vivit vero in me Christus** *(Galat. 2). Je viz, & non pas moy, mais Jesus Christ en moy.*[333]

The Lord, welcomed and received in Holy Communion, is indeed the consuming fire who does not so much destroy as refine, purify and transform everything he touches so that the one so consumed can truly say that Christ is living in him. It should be mentioned that the citation of Galatians 2:20 here is taken out of context and actually has nothing to do with the Eucharist. Paul is speaking in this

---

[332] *La deploration*, fol. 134v°. Doré here is echoing the following passage from Augustine's *Confessions*, VII, 10, "I realized that I was far away from you. It was as though I were in a land where all is different from your own and I heard your voice calling from on high, saying '**I am the food of full-grown men. Grow and you shall feed on me. But you shall not change me into your own substance, as you do with the food of your body. Instead you shall be changed into me**' [emphasis mine]. See *Confessions*, trans. R. S. Pine-Coffin (New York: Penguin Books, 1980), p. 147.
[333] *L'arche*, fol. 27v°.

verse about how, justified by faith, he has died to the law and has been crucified with the Lord so that Christ is now living in him. Nevertheless, even though Doré takes it out of context, he is not using the verse as a proof-text for his point that through the Eucharist we are divinized. Rather he sees it simply as an appropriate expression of the intimate union that is in fact effected between the believer and Christ in the sacrament.

A word needs to be said here about how our friar distinguishes the effects of the Eucharist from those of the other sacraments. When Cornelius asks St. Peter in the *Dyalogue instructoire* to explain the meaning of "sacrament," the master provides a very succinct definition: *"c'est ung signe de chose sacree, sanctifiant l'homme."*[334] But while all the sacraments convey grace which sanctifies human beings, the Eucharist nonetheless surpasses all the others in two ways, according to Doré, who explains later in *L'arche de l'alliance*:

> *Premierement il a couronne d'excellence sur tous autres sacremens mesmes de la loy nouvelle, pour autant qu'en iceulx on reçoipt quelque portion de grace: mais icy est receu celuy qui est l'autheur de grace, la plenitude & fontaine de toutes graces: pourtant appelle on ce sacrement Eucharistie. La seconde préeminence de ce venerable sacrement, procedante de la premiere, est que les autres dignifient l'homme par grace: mais cestuy deifie, & est donné...pour deification de l'homme.*[335]

The Dominican here unhesitatingly affirms the surpassing richness of the Eucharist over the other sacraments precisely because it is Christ himself who is received—not simply a portion of grace, as he puts it, but the author, the source of all graces. And once again, the point is made that this summit of the sacramental life is specifically ordered to our perfection and deification through intimate union with the Godhead. Although Luther and Calvin sincerely cherished the gift of the Eucharist and its benefits for believers, nowhere did they recommend it in such exalted terms.

---

[334] *Dyalogue instructoire*, fol. Fv r°.
[335] *L'arche*, fol. 27v°.

If, as Doré has explained, the Eucharist fulfills a deeply felt human desire to rise above the weaknesses of the human condition, ultimately it fulfills God's desire to be one with his creatures. The theologian asserts, "*Ceste fiance donc de se ingerer à la table dominique, ne provient tant de noz merites, que de ineffable bonté du Seigneur qui le veult.*"[336] It is the divine desire for intimacy with us that led to the institution of the sacrament on the eve of the Passion. Unworthy though humanity is to have been so favored, the Eucharist confronts us with the unfathomable mystery of God's love which grants us something we could never merit. It is a mystery which, as Doré points out, should arouse in us both a profound reverence for the sacrament as well as a burning desire to receive it:

> *O combien desire le seigneur que le recepvions en nous, qui crye a si haulte & patente voix, & qui par tant de voyes nous y incite: Certainement il monstre que ses delices, comme dict l'escriture, sont estre avec les filz des hommes. Plus outre, fault considerer ce qui peult de nostre partie nous allecher, a venir en devotion au S. sacrement: Et je diz, que c'est pour racheter noz negligences & nos omissions qui sont grandes, car par ce sacrement toutes choses sont restaurees. Nostre maladie & langueur est ostee par ceste medicine: Nous sommes purgez de noz concupiscences & pechez par ceste hostie de placation, nous sommes consolés es tribulations & pressures, par ceste manne consolative...Nous avons infusion de grace & augmentation de vertu, car c'est la fontaine & qui est celuy qui considerant tant de moyens allectifz n'est enflambé d'ardeur de venir a ce sacrement, pour le recepvoir?*[337]

With all the graces of forgiveness, healing, strengthening and growth in virtue, and ultimately our deification which the sacrament affords, those who fail to approach it with ardent desire are in fact denying themselves of a most priceless treasure. And what of those who, in Doré's eyes, go so far as to despise the sacrament as the substantial presence of Christ and deny its principal end which is the deification of man? These heretics are like the unfaithful Jews portrayed in the Bread of Life discourse who fell away from Jesus because they could not accept his teaching:

---

[336] *Le Nouveau Testament*, fol. 191v°.
[337] *La deploration*, fol. 54v°-55r°.

> *Juifz & Capernaites, & leurs successeurs heretiques modernes ne recoipvent point ceste parolle de Jesus, tenant dict bien Cyrille [Cyrillus in Joan.] de la conditions des folz, qui ont ceste coustume de detracter & mesdire de la haulte & excellente doctrine, ou science, qu'ilz n'entendent point, blasphement, dict l'Apostre, ce qu'ilz ignorent.*[338]

For Doré, the Reformers' rejection of the traditional understanding of the Eucharist and its profoundly transforming effects ultimately amounts to a rejection of the divine charity which instituted the sacrament in order that we might be united in love with the Godhead. To reject the Eucharist is to reject Christ and thus the heretics have brought God's judgment down upon themselves. As with the Jews who found Jesus' teaching concerning the Bread of Life too difficult to accept, they too can no longer be considered true disciples.

Conclusion

And so we have come full circle in this examination of Doré's teaching on the Eucharist. The effects of the sacrament depend upon the fact that the Eucharist is really and truly the body and blood of Christ. Otherwise, there is no power in it to deify, there is no power of healing and forgiveness of sin, there is no strengthening in the face of temptation. Both Luther and Calvin of course admitted this point, which explains why they so forcefully held to the idea of a real presence in the sacrament despite their vociferous objections to the doctrine of transubstantiation. Indeed, it is precisely because of Calvin's belief in a real presence that Doré could borrow the Genevan Reformer's own words on frequent communion and the importance of actually communicating with Christ's body and blood. The difference is that for Doré, there can be no real communication with the body of Christ without transubstantiation. Throughout his own discussion of the Eucharist, Doré makes it clear that the Reformers' rejection of

---

[338] *L'arche*, fol. 98r°-v°.

this doctrine has in effect robbed the sacrament of all real meaning. Their attacks on the Mass and the priesthood instituted by Christ have reduced the Eucharist to an empty and impotent symbol. Insist as they might that they continue to commune with the body and blood of the Lord, they are in fact receiving mere bread and wine, for having rejected the constant belief of the Church as well as the priesthood which alone has the power to confect the Eucharist they have in fact spurned the gift itself which Christ left to his disciples.

Clearly, for Doré, the consequences of the Reformers' errors concerning the Eucharist are much graver than their heretical position on *sola fide*, which is why he devotes more time and space to the sacrament in his works than to any other topic. His counterattack, however, is carried out not only on the heady level of doctrine. On the contrary, it also reaches out to the heart with a mystical element to his instruction which seeks to entice the reader to discover in the Eucharist a personal encounter with divine love. The communicant brings to this encounter his sins and weaknesses and in return receives all that is needed for justification, salvation, and holiness of life. Thus Doré encourages his readers to pray the following in preparation for Holy Communion:

> *Mon saulveur je viens a vous a celle fin que soys saulvé. O mon medecin je viens a vous, a celle fin que soys guary...O ma redemption & justification, je viens a vous, a celle fin qu'elle soit justifiée...Je viens tout froyct me approchant du feu, a celle fin que soit eschaufée mon ame en amour & dilection.*[339]

This prayer sums up well our friar's reverence for the sacrament and its powerful benefits. The Eucharist, as the summit of all the sacraments, is the means by which the grace of salvation is preeminently communicated to the faithful. For Pierre Doré, then, this sacrament must be loved and defended at all costs, not only as a doctrine necessary for salvation, but as the real presence of the Savior himself hidden under the accidents of bread and wine, the Savior who alone justifies and sanctifies.

---

[339] *La deploration*, fol. 102v°-103r°.

Chapter 5
THE VIRTUOUS LIFE AND MARY ITS IMAGE

Our examination of Pierre Doré's writings in the second portion of this study has focused thus far on his attempts to answer two of the principal challenges posed to Catholic theology by the Reformers: the notion that the believer is justified by faith alone and the denial of the doctrine of transubstantiation. It is clear that for the Dominican theologian these are the fundamental issues of the Reformation debate which have the most profound consequences for the well-being of the Christian faith. Yet, despite the significant amount of space he devotes in his literary production to exposing the orthodox position on these issues, it would be a mistake to think that his life's work is really nothing more than a kind of point-by-point rebuttal of the principal tenets of Reformation theology. While it is true that he consciously sets out to provide his readers with a doctrinal antidote to the poisonous venom of heresy being propagated in the vernacular by Luther *et al*, he does so within the context of a broad-based education and formation in the faith. Francis Higman, in discussing Doré's *Dyalogue instructoire des chrestiens en la foy, esperance, & amour en Dieu* (1538), makes the point:

> *La signification principale, enfin, de cet exposé de Pierre Doré ne réside pas dans sa qualité de catéchisme en soi. Dans le contexte de la réforme, avec son insistance sur la foi du croyant, et donc sur l'enseignement du peuple, Doré offre le premier exposé sérieux et*

détaillé de la doctrine de l'église catholique en langue française, qui essaye de répondre sur le même plan aux publications de la réforme.[340]

What Higman says here of the *Dyalogue instructoire* can in fact be applied more broadly to the "Doréan" corpus in general. The Dominican's writings, taken as a whole, offer readers a thoroughgoing instruction in the "teachings of the Church," the deposit of the faith in all its richness and not simply in isolated truths. While the *Dyalogue instructoire* as a catechism provides such instruction in a more systematic and complete way, the other works can also be seen as fitting into this larger scheme of promoting the believer's intellectual and moral formation in the faith. Thus, Doré's goal is not restricted to simply preserving the faithful from specific errors, a kind of defensive or reactionary posture over and against the Reformation. On the contrary, he also takes the offensive, realizing that the best way to keep the laity within the fold is to offer an orthodox alternative to the Protestant insistence on the necessity of an informed faith as leading to a deeper personal relationship with Christ.

It is precisely within this optic that the devotional works which comprise the better part of Pierre Doré's literary activity can be better understood. Neither explicitly polemical nor controversial, these works of piety are quite simply ordered toward stirring up the minds and hearts of the faithful to a more affective union with Christ and to a life of virtue as the full expression of that loving union. This goal is perhaps best summed up in Doré's best-selling *Les allumettes du feu divin pour faire ardre les cueurs humains en l'amour de Dieu* (1538) where he explains in the dedication:

> *Et tout incontinent comme de volonté de la haut inspiree sans dilayer ay mis mon estude à chercher nouvelles bottes d'allumettes (ainsi que congnoistras par ce present livre que je te dedie), lesquelles trouvées par l'ayde de Dieu, en importunant les forces de mon esprit, t'ay allumé un feu, qui n'est autre que Divin, ayant le brasier si treschaut, que si ton coeur n'est plus froid que marbre, en t'approchant des tisons ardens*

---

[340] Higman, "La réfutation," p. 65.

d'iceluy, seras d'amour celeste esprise: en laquelle, je supplie le bon Dieu nous entretenir & garder sans fin.[341]

Our friar's concern here and throughout his devotional works is far more mystical than polemical. Love or charity is the predominant theme as he seeks to ignite the fire of the love of God in the hearts of his readers and to teach them how to keep that fire burning and undimmed. We have seen how Doré's presentation of the Eucharist emphasized the notion of Holy Communion as an encounter of love with the God who desires intimacy with us and that this encounter effects a very real change in us. A similar note is sounded in the devotional works where the burning theological issues of the day give way to a more pressing preoccupation: to inspire the faithful to a more personal relationship with Christ in a union of love which blossoms in a life of virtue.

Are the devotional writings, then, part of a different enterprise, one completely unrelated to Doré's anti-Protestant crusade? I would submit that the answer to this question is most definitely "no." Although, as discussed earlier in Chapter 2, the Dominican spiritual director produced many of his devotional works at the behest of prominent French noblewomen, both religious and lay, who were seeking personal guidance in order to grow in the spiritual life, there is a sense in which Doré's response to these women encompasses far more than their personal concerns and forms part of a greater project. That project is to take the wind out of the Reformers' sails by reclaiming the emphasis on a personal relationship with Christ as a truly Catholic ideal. An objection might be raised here that works of piety for the laity, which encouraged such a relationship, were not uncommon either prior to the Reformation or as it unfolded. Is there anything really distinctive then about Doré's contributions in this particular genre of religious literature?

---

[341] Dedication to a devout religious sister at the royal monastery of Poissy, *Les allumettes*, pp. 4-5. **[Paris, BS—443 E-38]**.

The distinctive character of the Dominican's devotional works lies in the higher level of theological discourse to be seen there through which he attempts to instruct the reader as well as edify. Examples of this decidedly intellectual quality will be forthcoming. Furthermore, the devotional works issue a challenge, albeit one that is more implicit than explicit, to Reformed theology with its dim view of human acts as always being tainted in some way by sin. By underscoring over and over again that the Christian life is ultimately a call to perfection in charity and that this perfection is at the same time a gift of God's grace as well as our life's work, Doré is reaffirming the notion that grace actually perfects and transforms human nature provided that we cooperate with it. Thus transformed, we are enabled to perform truly virtuous acts which are pleasing in God's eyes and which are meritorious of eternal life. The devotional writings, then, ultimately serve to reinforce the arguments which Doré develops more explicitly in his polemical works against the foundation stones of Reformed theology: *sola fide* and *sola gratia*. Far from representing a different enterprise, they in fact play a very central role in the Dominican's attempts to arrest the progress of the Reformation among the ordinary faithful.

The "Rock of Virtue": A Keynote and Herald of the "Doréan" Project

Our friar's promotion of an affective union with Christ which in turn blossoms into a life of virtue is not a theme that gradually emerged over the course of his literary career. On the contrary, it originated with his very first work, *La devise d'ung coeur assis en Pierre de vertu*, written sometime between 1525 and 1528 when he was apprentice-teaching as *biblicus* at S. Jacques. It is hard to imagine that the young theologian had any conception at the time that this would mark the beginning of a very long and fruitful apostolate to the laity. Yet, this proto-composition of a mere 4 folios can be seen as heralding some of the central recurring themes of his subsequent literary production. The work is very simply a brief explanation in verse of the core elements of the Christian life, accompanied by the diagram reproduced below:

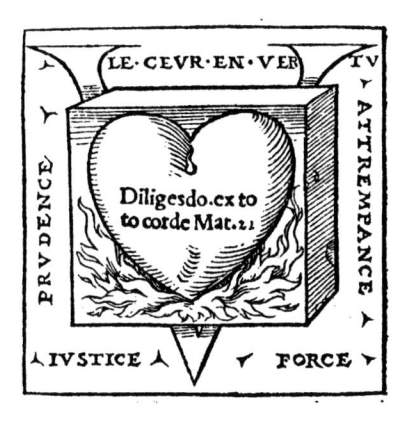

The Christian is here represented by the heart which is set in the stone of virtue, who is Christ. The four sides of the square stone represent the four cardinal virtues of prudence, justice, fortitude and temperance. The fire engulfing the heart is the fire of divine love with which the soul desirous of eternal life must burn. Originating from the stone itself, this love comes from Christ who sets the heart afire. Doré also speaks of water gushing from the heart (seen here as a drop). Although difficult to discern from the illustration, this drop is purifying water representing a contrite spirit which cleanses from all sin. Finally, while again difficult to discern from the image, the heart is described as clothed in golden cloth representing the virtue of charity without which the soul cannot be admitted to the wedding feast of the heavenly banquet. Having thus explained the symbolism of the heart in the stone of virtue as depicted in the diagram, Doré concludes with this exhortation:

> *Hommes mortelz, qui hault intronisez*
> *Voulez estre mis en la gloire,*
> *Ce devys vous conseille que lysez,*

> *En laissant esbat transitoire,*
> *Saulves vous qui craignez le tonnere*
> *En vous mussant dedans la pierre*
> *De vertu, dont ne laisses la voye,*
> *Et aures de Paradis la Joye.*[342]

The principal point is that in order to gain heaven, the Christian must be firmly grounded in Christ and his virtues, set aflame with his own love, purified by his grace through contrition and finally clothed in the golden robe of the virtue of charity which expresses itself in good works toward others.

There is nothing overtly polemical to be found in this brief exposé, save a passing comment that the Church, founded on the rock of Christ "*...durera tant que le firmament,/Car ne porront Heretiques pervers,/L'édifice renverser à l'envers.*"[343] Yet, this proto-work of Doré, while essentially a pious exhortation, sounds a theme that is both consonant as well as strikingly dissonant from the thought of the Reformers. To be firmly grounded in Christ, the rock of salvation and virtue, is unquestionably a shared conception of the essence of the Christian life. However, *La devise* speaks of this grounding as being more the result of love than of faith (though Doré does not neglect to mention the importance of faith), and it also asserts the real possibility as well as the necessity of cultivating all the virtues with God's grace in order to be saved. In so doing it poses a discreet challenge, one which our friar will continue to develop in various ways, both to the Reformers' exclusive emphasis on the role of faith in salvation as well as their portrayal of justification and salvation as a much more passive process rather than one which involves our necessary participation.

For Doré, our ability to live a virtuous life by being firmly grounded in Christ, the "rock of virtue," represents a restoration of God's original plan for humanity. The first chapter of *Le college de sapience* (1539), a more developed exposition on the virtuous life, opens with a description of the state of original

---

[342] *La devise d'ung coeur assis en Pierre de vertu*, bound with *La caeleste pensee de graces divines* (Paris: Adam Saulnier, 1543), fol. Zii v°. **[Bordeaux, BM—T 7106]**.
[343] Ibid., fol. Z r°.

justice, or the state of mankind before original sin. In this primordial state, which Doré compares to being enrolled in a "college of wisdom," man was in perfect harmony with God and himself since:

> ...en ce beau college regentoient toutes nobles vertus, aiant leur domicile en l'homme & l'addressant en toutes bonnes meurs. Verité l'apprint a parler, Justice a cheminer droict, Paix l'entretenoit & paisiblement le gouvernoit, Foy et Prudence tenoient la premiere reigle des escolles, & endoctrinoient ou esclarcissoient l'esperit, Charité et Esperance comme en seconde reigle informoient la voulenté, Force adressoit la partie inferieure, que on dict l'irascible, Attrempance en la derniere reigle regentoit sus la partie concupiscible, tellement que par l'université des vertus, a esté rendu l'homme plus scientifique et plain de sapience...[344]

As Doré explains here, the period before the fall of Adam and Eve was one in which the virtues reigned in human nature. Untainted by sin, the human intellect was graced with true wisdom and the will was always ordered toward the good. A yet more precise definition of the state of original justice is provided just a year later in *L'image de vertu* (1540) where Doré describes the grace given to Adam and Eve as one of right-ordering to God and right-ordering of the passions:

> Mais qu'est ce que justice originelle, dont l'homme est privé par le peché originel?...Je responds que c'est un don de Dieu donné à Adam en son origine ou naissance, pource est il appellé don originel, grace, ou justice originelle, par lequel don raison immediatement estoit subjecte à Dieu, volonté à raison, sensualité à la volonté & raison, & les animaux & bestes brutes subjectes à l'homme...Ce don ne pourroit estre sans grace, par laquelle l'homme conformant son vouloir à celuy de Dieu estoit justifié & meritoit la vie eternelle Et faut entendre ce que dit Anseaume apres S. Aug. que nostre premiere pere Adam avoit receu de Dieu ceste justice originelle, pour luy & toute sa posterité.[345]

We have here a good example of the rather high level of theological discourse that characterizes our friar's works of piety, complete with references to Anselm and Augustine. Unfortunately, as is his custom (one might even say bad habit), no citation is provided for his reference to their teaching on this matter.

---

[344] *Le college*, fol. 5r°.
[345] *L'image*, fol. 11v°-12r°.

Nevertheless, his point here is that God created humanity in his image and likeness, complete with all the virtues. Graced with the natural powers of intellect and will, the first man and woman possessed the added grace of a mind perfectly subjected to God and appetites perfectly ordered under the direction of right reason and the will. What is more, these gifts were not to be theirs alone but were meant to be shared in by all their posterity. In other words, the life of virtue is not something alien to human nature; rather it is the way in which human beings were created to live.

The fall from original justice, however, introduced the present state in which humanity finds itself, one of both alienation from God and an interior alienation within oneself between what the mind knows to be good and what the will so often in fact chooses to do. St. Paul describes this alienation best when he writes, "For I do not do the good I want, but the evil I do not want is what I do," (Romans 7:19, RSV). It is in order to bring this alienation to an end and to restore the divine image in us that Christ came to reconcile us with the Father by his death. This restoration having been effected in us through the grace of baptism, we are now empowered to overcome the weakness and disorder resulting from original sin and to once again live virtuously, though certainly the life of virtue is not without struggle. Nonetheless, Doré emphasizes that in the midst of the struggle, we have an exemplar to gaze upon as a reminder of the virtuous life we are now capable of achieving through grace. That exemplar is the Virgin Mary, whom he addresses as "the image of virtue." As will be seen, it is not an exaggeration to say that the Mother of God in fact is at the very center of the Dominican theologian's teaching on the virtuous life.

Mary, the Mirror of Virtue

Until now, nothing has been said in this study about the place of the Virgin Mary in the Reformation debate. Indeed, controversy surrounding the Mother of God was quite muted, a rather surprising fact considering that the devotion to Our Lady, which came to full flowering in the medieval church, was as strong as ever in the early 1500s. Lucien Febvre remarks that, far from being a time when religion was losing its influence over the masses, the beginning of the sixteenth century was a time of intense popular piety and devotion centered around two poles, the suffering Christ and the Virgin Mary. He writes that around this cult of the Virgin, "...*des pratiques s'organisaient et tendaient à la glorification de celle qui, de plus en plus apparaissait comme le canal des grâces faites aux hommes par son divin fils.*"[346]

Probably the most significant factor in the spread of Marian devotion in the late Middle Ages was the popularization of the rosary, principally though not exclusively through the preaching of the Breton Dominican Alan de Rupe at the end of the fifteenth century. Promoted as the "layperson's psalter" or as a technique for meditating on the principal moments of the lives of Christ and Mary, the rosary was also seen as a way of obtaining both spiritual and temporal blessings through the Virgin's intercession.[347] The ever-growing importance of the Virgin Mary in popular religion was not, however, merely a phenomenon of the masses. Theologians and popes also made significant contributions in this regard. In 1498, the Faculty of Theology in Paris gave its support to the still highly-contested doctrine of the Immaculate Conception with a formal definition.[348] Earlier, in 1477, the Franciscan pope Sixtus IV had approved the yearly celebration of the feast on 8 December. Without doubt, the figure of Mary

---

[346] Febvre, "Les origines," p. 30.
[347] For more on the history of the rosary and its relation to Marian piety in the Middle Ages, see Anne Winston-Allen, *Stories of the Rose—The Making of the Rosary in the Middle Ages* (University Park, PA: Pennsylvania State University Press, 1997).
[348] Farge, *Orthodoxy*, p. 163.

loomed large in the religious consciousness of the Church immediately prior to the Reformation.

Yet in contrast to the incontestable and central importance of the Virgin in the devotional life of the period, her place in the controversies between Reformers and orthodox theologians is relatively insignificant, and by comparison with the other burning theological issues of the day practically non-existent. Mary is mentioned in but a few passing remarks in Calvin's *Institutes*, for example. The only controversial statement among them is that praying to Mary, as with praying to any of the saints, involves elements of superstition and is an offense to God.[349] Perhaps the relative silence observed by Calvin and others concerning the Virgin was itself a rebuff to the centrality of Mary in the devotion of the period. Nonetheless, it is rather striking that the Reformers spent so little ink trying to refute the increasing attribution of what in their mind would constitute a quasi-divine status to the Virgin Mary.

Given the Reformers' seeming lack of interest in Marian issues, the fact that Pierre Doré consecrates his fifth major work to providing a life of the Virgin, and one solidly based in Scripture as was pointed out in Chapter 2, seems a disproportionate response. This is even more true when one considers that *L'image de vertu* (1540) is in fact the Dominican's longest work.[350] Aside from Doré's preoccupation to provide a solid scriptural basis for his portrait of Mary, the book is otherwise little marked by controversy or polemics, at least as regards the Reformers. In fact, the polemics here are directed instead to fellow theologians who refuse to accept the doctrine of the Immaculate Conception. What is more, Doré's ardent support of the doctrine puts him at odds with the majority of his fellow Dominicans of the period, who, following St. Thomas, affirm Mary's sanctification in her mother's womb but not her preservation from the stain of original sin. In response, Doré goes to great pains to show that

---

[349] See *Institutes*, III. XX. 22.
[350] The different editions of the work range in size from 333 folios to 508 folios, depending on the format and size of the characters.

Aquinas originally held for the Immaculate Conception but then changed his mind on the matter. How he does this and why will be discussed shortly in greater detail. The point for now is that *L'image de vertu* at first glance seems to have little connection with Doré's anti-Protestant strategy. Yet, despite the absence of any explicitly polemical agenda directed against the Reformers, Doré's *vita Mariae* forms the centerpiece of his teaching on the virtuous life and as such, it offers a powerful argument for the transforming power of grace in our lives as exemplified in the life of the Virgin.

From its title, it is evident that the principal accent throughout the work is on the Virgin Mary as exemplar or model, though Doré does not neglect also to point out her role as mother, as most powerful of intercessors after Christ, and as fountain of graces. Yet for the Dominican, she is first of all a model, not so much of discipleship as of the virtuous life since in her all the virtues are to be found in their perfection. Alluding to the tradition that St. Luke was the first to have produced an image or a physical representation of Mary, Doré goes on to affirm that her life is really a masterwork of the artistry of the Holy Spirit:

> *On dit sainct Luc avoir painct nostre Dame, & faict la pourtraicture de son corps. Le Sainct Esprit a faict la paincture de l'ame, Image de toute vertu, accomplie par tout, car d'un tel ouvrier, si excellent & parfaict, faut bien dire que l'ouvrage soit magnifique.*[351]

It is Doré's aim in *L'image* both to sing the praises of the divine artist who formed Mary and to demonstrate her perfection of life, "*...qui tant est exemplaire & attractive à bien.*"[352] Although his admiration of the Mother of God at times borders on the excessive, as when in the Prologue he describes her as "the eighth wonder of the world," the guiding principle always remains to present her as a model of virtue which the faithful will be drawn to imitate precisely because she is what we in our sinfulness yearn to be: all-beautiful.

---

[351] Prologue to *L'image*, n.p.
[352] Ibid.

Drawing on a traditional comparison found in the writings of the Fathers of Mary's beauty to that of the moon, he likens the attractive power of the Virgin to that of moonlight which gently brightens the dark night:

> Belle comme la lune, laquelle luist en la nuict, ainsi est claire nostre dame au milieu de la nuict de tous humains conceuz en obscurité de peché, mais ceste clarté n'est pas venue d'elle, ains est de Dieu, qui l'a de peché preservée, ainsi comme la lune a sa clarté du Soleil.[353]

One might think that to speak of Mary in such elevated terms as spotless and as possessing the pure light of the virtues in their plenitude would discourage poor sinners in attempting to imitate such an impossible ideal rather than attracting them to the virtuous life. Yet Doré holds up her beauty as a sign of hope, like the gentle moonlight which brings comfort to those still journeying through the dark night of sin. It is a light to which sinners are attracted, not repulsed. However, the point is clearly made here that Mary's light, her goodness, does not come from within her but rather is a reflection of the divine light in the same way that the moon is not a source of light in itself but merely reflects the brightness of the sun. Thus it is not a question of elevating her to divine status on a par with the Trinity, but rather of showing how she perfectly reflects the divine image in which all human beings were created.

In Defense of the Immaculate Conception

This leads us into a discussion concerning the unquestionable enthusiasm which Doré manifests for the doctrine of the Immaculate Conception, a doctrine which he reiterates at several points and to which he devotes a substantial defense in *L'image de vertu*. For the Dominican theologian, to speak of the divine image in Mary is to speak of an image never tarnished nor defiled, and therefore never in

---

[353] *L'image*, fol. 23v°.

need of being restored. In Mary, humanity is given an image of that original justice possessed by Adam and Eve prior to the fall. She is the perfect example of what God meant humanity to be as his image and likeness. It should be mentioned here that the tradition of the Church from earliest times had always held for Mary's sinlessness in view of her vocation to be *Theotokos* or God-bearer. But whether or not this sinlessness extended to her being preserved from the stain of original sin at the moment of her conception was still a point of theological debate in the sixteenth century, though by this time the doctrine of the Immaculate Conception was firmly established if not yet formally defined. The Council of Basel in 1439 had stopped just short of formal definition, declaring the teaching that the Mother of God through a singular grace had never actually been subject to original sin, to be in accord with the Catholic faith, with right reason and with Sacred Scripture. It went on to prohibit anyone to teach or preach the contrary and stated that the doctrine should be embraced by all the faithful.[354]

Despite the clarity of the council's teaching on the matter and its prohibition of teaching otherwise, the doctrine's standing remained dubious because of the fact that the council was considered schismatic. From its convocation in 1431, the Council of Basel had been continually at odds with Pope Eugenius IV over its decidedly conciliarist stance. Schism came in 1437 when the council fathers demanded the pope to appear before it to answer charges of simony and heresy for disdaining its decrees. Eugenius retaliated by condemning the council and decreeing its transfer to Ferrara in Italy. While the vast majority of fathers continued to meet in Basel in defiance of the papal bull, Eugenius was

---

[354] "*Nos vero diligenter inspectis auctoritatibus & rationibus, quae iam a pluribus annis in publicis relationibus ex parte utriusque doctrinae coram hac sancta Synodo allegatae sunt, aliisque etiam plurimus super hac re visis, & matura consideratione pensatis,* **doctrinam illam differentem gloriosam virginem Dei genitricem Mariam, praeveniente & operante divini numinis gratia singulari, numquam actualiter subjacuisse originali peccato; sed immunem semper fuisse ab omni originali & actuali cupla, sanctamque & immaculatam; tanquam piam & consonam cultui Ecclesiastico, Fidei catholicae, rectae rationi, & sacrae scripturae, ab omnibus catholicis approbandam fore, tenendam & amplectendam, diffinimus & declaramus, nullique de cetero licitum esse in contrarium praedicare seu docere** [emphasis mine]." The full text can be found in J.D. Mansi, *Sacrorum conciliorum nova et amplissima collectio*, vol. 29 (Paris: H. Welter, 1904), p. 183.

to gain the upper hand with his council in Ferrara, transferred once again to Florence in 1439.[355] Meanwhile, despite its growing unpopularity, the Council of Basel went on to proclaim the superiority of a general council over the pope as a truth of the faith and declared Eugenius deposed on 25 June 1439. The *defacto* schism that had existed since 1437 was now official. The decree on the Immaculate Conception, then, a product of the thirty-sixth session of the council on 15 October 1439, was issued by a council in full schism and for that reason was never accorded official recognition. The council's prohibitions against preaching or teaching anything contrary to the doctrine thus had no force.

But if the Council of Basel failed to end debate on the Immaculate Conception, the doctrine nevertheless gained momentum at the end of the fifteenth century from both the papacy and the Faculty of Theology in Paris, as mentioned earlier. And as far as Pierre Doré was concerned, the question was in fact closed. Thus he could unhesitatingly proclaim in *L'image de vertu*:

> *Adam & Eve ont esté en speciosité grande, formez de Dieu, mais semblablement par orgueil, ont esté diformés comme vieux diables. Et finablement toute creature, hors l'humble Marie, que Jesus a faicte à sa semblance, **sans tache ne macule, ne d'originel, ne de veniel, ne mortel*** [emphasis mine].[356]

In defense of his assertion here that all human beings were tainted by original sin save "the humble Mary whom Jesus formed in his likeness," he cites not only the Faculty of Theology's decision of 1498 to have all doctors and licensed masters swear on oath to defend the doctrine, but he also cites the Council of Basel's definition of 1439.[357] While it is certain that Doré is trying to give all possible proof to his readers that the doctrine of the Immaculate Conception is built on solid theological reasoning, his mention here of *"le **sacré** Concile assemblé à*

---

[355] For further details, see Paul Ourliac, "Le schisme et les conciles (1378-1449)" in *Histoire du christianisme des origines à nos jours*, vol. 6, ed. Michel Mollat du Jourdin and André Vauchez (Paris: Desclée-Fayard, 1990), pp. 121-131.
[356] *L'image*, fol. 4v°.
[357] See Ibid., fol. 17r°-v°.

239

Basle" also gives evidence of his conciliarist sympathies and gallican spirit, a spirit which pervaded the Faculty of Theology and the French church in general at this time. In fact, it should be noted as an aside that in his voluminous defense of orthodox doctrine, he barely ever says a word in defense of papal authority, despite the fact that this was one of the principal doctrinal targets of the Reformers.[358] However, to return to the point at hand, it is not Doré's apparent sympathy for conciliarism or his gallican stance in regards to the authority of the apostolic see that is of principal concern here, but rather his enthusiasm for the doctrine of the Immaculate Conception, an enthusiasm not generally shared by his fellow Dominicans of the period. The reason for his enthusiasm will be discussed shortly. However, it is first important to examine exactly how he defends his departure on this issue from the generally accepted position held by the vast majority of his confrères.

Dominican reticence towards this doctrine is perhaps difficult to understand given the Order's tradition of filial devotion to the Virgin Mary with the nightly singing of the *Salve Regina* from the earliest days of its existence and the promotion of the rosary devotion beginning in the late fifteenth century. Yet, it is Aquinas who imparted to his brothers in the Order a sense of misgiving on this issue, arguing in the *Summa*, IIIa, q. 27, a. 2 that it is not fitting that Christ should not be the savior of all human beings. Had the Virgin Mary never contracted original sin, she would have had no need for redemption. Therefore, she could not have been sanctified at the moment of her conception, but only at some point afterwards.[359]

---

[358] The major exception to Doré's general silence on the issue of papal authority is a brief response found in the *Dyalogue instructoire* to the question of whether the pope can err in matters of faith. Here Doré insists that the pope "...*ne peult errer en determination de la foy & dispositions des bonnes meurs: car dieu la promis [Luc xxii]*..." fol. Fiii v°-Fiiii r°. The promise to which Doré is referring here is Christ's announcement to Peter, "Simon, behold, Satan demanded to have you, that he might sift you like wheat, but I have prayed for you that your faith may not fail; and when you have turned again, strengthen your brethren" (Luke 22:31-32, RSV).
[359] In the response to the second objection of q. 27, art. 2, Thomas writes, "If the soul of the blessed Virgin had never contracted the stain of original sin it would have diminished the dignity of Christ in his capacity as saviour of all. But after Christ, who as universal saviour did not need

It must be admitted that Dominican opposition to the doctrine through the centuries up to its formal definition by Pope Pius IX in 1854 was often more related to rallying behind Aquinas and defending his position at all costs than to having a real theological objection to the doctrine itself, particularly by the sixteenth century when the magisterium of the Church had taken a clear stance on the issue. However, in the century and a half since the proclamation of the dogma, a number of articles by Dominican theologians have attempted to show that St. Thomas would not have opposed the doctrine in the way in which it was finally expressed,[360] for the definition of 1854 carefully safeguards Christ's redemptive role as extending to all of humanity when it declares the Immaculate Conception as Mary's preservation from original sin *in view of the merits of Christ Jesus Savior of the human race* [emphasis mine].[361] Yet, long before this modern attempt to rehabilitate Aquinas in regards to the Immaculate Conception, Pierre Doré himself went to great pains to show that St. Thomas in his early works maintained Mary's preservation from original sin and only later changed his mind with the writing of the *Summa*. Though he never explicitly states his purpose in doing so, he is undoubtedly trying to demonstrate that the traditional Dominican opposition to the doctrine out of devotion to Aquinas is unfounded.

---

salvation, the purity of the blessed Virgin was greatest of all. Now Christ in no way contracted original sin but was holy in his conception, as Luke says, *And so the child will be holy and will be called the Son of God*. But the blessed Virgin did indeed contract original sin but was cleared from it before her birth." See Blackfriars, 51, p. 13. It also should be noted here that St. Bernard of Clairvaux, the greatest of Marian devotees during the Middle Ages, opposed the doctrine of the Immaculate Conception for the same reason. See Pelikan, *Christian Tradition*, 4, p. 46.

[360] See for example, Thomas Mullaney, "Mary Immaculate in the Writings of St. Thomas," in *The Thomist*, XVII 4 (1954): pp. 433-68, who argues that "...as St. Thomas understood and meant that proposition [that Mary was conceived in original sin], it is in no way opposed to the truth defined by Pius IX. In St. Thomas' view, as in that of his contemporaries generally (following the ancient naturalists), *conception* preceded the infusion of a human soul by a very considerable time. During all that time there was as yet no apt subject for divine grace, for the fetus, prior to its animation by a human soul, was considered to be of infra-intellectual nature, consequently incapable of grace. As we shall see, this is an argument used by St. Thomas to show that Our Lady could not possibly have been sanctified before the infusion of her soul..." p. 439.

[361] "*Declaramus, pronuntiamus et definimus, doctrinam, quae tenet, beatissimam Virginem Mariam in primo instanti suae conceptionis fuisse singulari omnipotentis Dei gratia et privilegio, intuitu meritorum Christi Jesu Salvatoris humani generis, ab omni originalis culpae labe praeservatam immunem, esse a Deo revelatam atque idcirco ab omnibus fidelibus firmiter constanterque credendam.*" Denz., c. 2803, p. 776.

The first few chapters of *L'image de vertu* contain the most concentrated presentation of Thomistic doctrine in the entire "Doréan" corpus. While by no means a detailed nor comprehensive presentation, Doré nevertheless gives his readers succinct paraphrases of various determinations of St. Thomas concerning the Virgin Mary. The first is drawn from the *Summa*, Ia, q. 25, a. 6 where Aquinas discusses whether or not God could have made some things more perfectly. Doré sums up the Master's solution for his readers, particularly the response to the fourth objection, in this way:

> ...qu'il y a trois choses si parfaictes, que meilleures ne peuvent estre. La premiere est l'humanité de Jesus, en ce qu'elle est unie a Dieu lequel est un bien souverain, qui ne peut estre meilleur. La seconde est la beatitude eternelle, par ce qu'elle gist en vision & fruition de Dieu, qui est bien infiny: & ainsi qu'il ne peut estre meilleur Dieu, aussi plus grande gloire & felicité, que d'estre heureux en Dieu. La tierce, est la benoiste vierge Marie, par une mesme raison, car elle est mere de Dieu, dont elle a quelque dignité presque infinie de ce bien infiny, qui est Dieu.[362]

Right away, it is clear in this paraphrase that Aquinas has a great esteem for and appreciation of the dignity of Mary, going so far as to say in this article that it approaches the infinite dignity of God himself, precisely because her dignity has its source in him. His opposition to the Immaculate Conception has nothing to do with a lack of respect for Mary's privileged status as Mother of God. While he determines in the article that God can always make something he has created better, not in terms of its nature but in terms of its qualities, he cannot have made the humanity of Christ more perfect than it was, nor could heaven be a more perfect good, nor could the virgin Mother of God have been more perfect, for these three goods are intimately related to the divine goodness which itself is perfect. Doré's intention to present the Virgin Mary as a model of perfection and virtue is well-served by this Thomistic determination. However, this is not the only end which the article serves. It also lays the groundwork for Doré's

---

[362] *L'image*, fol. 6v°-7r°.

discussion in the following chapter of *L'image* on Thomas' authentic position concerning the Immaculate Conception.

Before proceeding to give citations from Aquinas in support of Mary's preservation from all sin, including original sin, Doré first turns to the Song of Songs for a scriptural attestation to the fact. The key verses in his view are where the Beloved of the poem exclaims, "There are sixty queens and eighty concubines, and maidens without number. **My dove, my perfect one, is only one** [emphasis mine]."[363] Tradition had long made the connection between the one and only perfect dove with the Virgin Mary as the highly favored daughter of the Most High. However, Doré interprets the perfection of the dove as a reference not only to Mary's sinlessness during her earthly life but to her preservation from original sin as well. Although Christ the Beloved has many queens, concubines and maidens (speaking metaphorically of course), each one having a certain beauty and perfection in grace, his perfect dove (Mary) has the singular privilege of never having been tainted by sin whatsoever:

> *Par le singulier don que Dieu a fait a la glorieuse vierge Marie, qui est de l'avoir seule en toutes autres pures creatures, preservée de peché originel, on peut arguer l'amour qu'a eu Dieu à elle, de luy avoir donné ce que ne donna jamais à pure creature, depuis la ruine de l'homme. C'est une qui est sans tache en sa conception, belle comme une image.*[364]

One might certainly take issue with Doré's extension of the metaphor of the perfect dove to encompass a reference to the Immaculate Conception. But if the Song of Songs 6:8-9 is deficient as a proof-text of the doctrine, it nevertheless does support the idea of the Virgin Mary's singular beauty among all creatures, a beauty which might well include not only the perfection of all the virtues, but also a freedom from that sin which tarnishes all the descendants of Adam.

All of this serves as a prelude to Doré's subsequent citing of two key texts from Aquinas that seem to unquestionably support the doctrine of the Immaculate

---

[363] Song of Songs 6:8-9, RSV.
[364] Ibid., fol. 10r°.

243

Conception. The examples, taken from Aquinas' commentary on the 'Hail Mary' and his commentary on the *First Book of the Sentences* of Peter Lombard, both of which were written prior to the *tertia pars* of the *Summa*, are put forward as proof that St. Thomas originally supported the doctrine before adopting a contrary position. While Doré offers his readers no explanation for the scholastic theologian's apparent change of mind on the issue as evidenced in the IIIa, q. 27, a. 2 discussed above, he does excuse the great theologian on the grounds that the doctrine was not as yet formally defined by the Church—an excuse which no longer applies in Doré's mind to his fellow Dominicans who continue to maintain Thomas' position in spite of the definition of the Council of Basel. While the reprimand to his confrères remains implicit, it is nevertheless made more forceful by the texts which Doré cites as evidence of Aquinas' true position on the matter:

> *Mais tres-heureuse est nostre Dame, sanctifiee par grace si abondante, que jamais ne contracta peché originel. Ainsi l'a escrit sainct Thomas d'Aquin en son opuscule de l'exposition de la salutation Angelique, & au premier livre des sentences, là où il dit ainsi. Une purité est plus grande, quand est plus esloignee de son contraire, qui est impurité & macule, & pource peut on trouver une purité cree plus grande? En sçauroit on pourpenser es choses crées de Dieu, quand de nulle infection de peché est inquinée?* ***Et telle a esté la purité de la bienheureuse Vierge, laquelle a esté sans peché originel, veniel & mortel*** [emphasis mine]*: toutesfois ceste purité est moindre que celle de nostre sauveur Jesus, vray Dieu & homme, entant que de soy pouvoit contracter peché sans la grace de Dieu, dont a esté remplie, mais Jesus Christ n'a peu offenser. Voyla qu'a determiné sainct Thomas en ses sentences, combien qu'apres il ayt dit avec les autres opinion contraire. Mais pour lors n'estoit diffiny par l'Eglise, comme il est aujourd'huy, que nostre Dame en sa conception est immaculee. L'ennemy n'a peu imprimer son image de peché en elle, car le sainct Esprit l'a prevenue en benediction de grace, & paincte de ses couleurs vives.*[365]

Unfortunately, Doré provides no direct quotation or reference for the first example he cites from St. Thomas' exposition on the 'Hail Mary,' *In salutationem angelicam scilicet AVE MARIA*, in support of his argument that Aquinas actually upheld Mary's Immaculate Conception. However, the text in question would

---
[365] Ibid., fol. 11v°-r°.

seem to be the following statement which Thomas makes in commenting on the phrase, *Dominus tecum*, "the Lord is with you": *"Ipsa enim purissima fuit & quantum ad puritatem: quia ipsa Virgo, **nec originale** [emphasis mine], nec mortale, nec veniale peccatum incurrit."* The statement indeed appears to be unequivocal, a forthright affirmation from the Angelic Doctor that the Virgin Mary never incurred original sin. Yet it is the subject of much controversy for several reasons. First of all, there is a serious and well-founded objection that the words, *nec originale*, are in fact an interpolation.[366] Doubtless, Doré would in all probability not have been aware of the suspicion concerning the inauthenticity of the words. Nevertheless, he cannot be completely absolved on the basis of ignorance since the statement remains controversial for reasons that he could not have failed to notice.

At two points prior to the disputed sentence, Aquinas makes statements that clearly contradict any notion of Mary's never having contracted original sin. As he comments on the angel's greeting of Mary as "full of grace," he clearly affirms that although the virgin of Nazareth possessed the plenitude of grace and therefore avoided all sin more perfectly than anyone else after Christ, *"...peccatum enim aut est originale, **& de isto fuit mundata in utero**; aut morale, aut veniale, & de istis libera fuit."*[367] In fairness to Doré, it is possible to see a certain ambiguity in the statement here that concerning original sin, Mary was made clean in the womb. Was this cleansing a sort of preserving grace at the moment of her conception, as our friar would want to assert, or is Aquinas upholding a cleansing of original sin after her conception? However, all doubt as

---

[366] In a book review of J. F. Rossi, *Quid senserit S. Thomas Aquinas de Immaculata Virginis conceptione* (Piacenza: Collegio Alberoni, 1955), J. Robilliard and P. de Contenson, *RSPT* 39 (1955): 464-465 relate Rossi's examination of 49 manuscripts of the *In salutationem angelicam* with the following results: 35 include the words *nec originale*, 7 contain minor variations, 4 completely omit the words, and 3 substitute the phrase *"ab originali in utero matris sanctificata fuit nec peccatum mortale nec veniale incurrit."* For this reason, T. Mullaney, "Mary Immaculate," p. 437, n. 13 refuses to draw any conclusions concerning Aquinas' position based on a phrase whose authenticity is in doubt.

[367] *Divi Thomae Aquinatis Doctoris Angelici Ordinis Praedicatorum Opera*, vol. 8 (Venice: 1775), p. 37.

to Thomas' position is cast aside a few lines later when he writes, "*Sed Christus excellit Beatam Virginem in hoc quod sine originali conceptus, & natus est. Beata autem Virgo in originali est concepta, sed non nata.*"[368] Here we have a clear statement that the Blessed Virgin was conceived in original sin and sanctified in her mother's womb at some point prior to her birth. Thus the phrase, *nec originale*, which Doré regards as conclusive, even if it is authentically from Thomas' hand, in no way constitutes definitive proof that he upheld the doctrine of the Immaculate Conception in his exposition on the Hail Mary. On the contrary, it poses serious problems of interpretation. In his determination to prove that Aquinas was really a proponent of the Immaculate Conception, Doré seems to have built his argument, at least thus far, on a wisp of straw, never even alluding to the preceding statements of the exposition which clearly contradict the idea.

However, the second passage which the Dominican theologian cites as proof of his point, from Thomas' commentary on the *Sentences* of Peter Lombard,[369] is much more solid. This time, he gives a very accurate paraphrasing of what Aquinas writes there concerning the purity of the Mother of God, "*laquelle a esté **sans peché originel, veniel & mortel**.*" Here, there is no dispute whatsoever as to the authenticity of the phrase *et talis fuit puritas beatae Virginis, quae a peccato originali et actuali immunis fuit.*[370] It would seem that Aquinas upholds the Immaculate Conception in this instance in no uncertain terms, thus giving substance to Doré's point that the great scholastic in fact did change his mind on the issue, for the commentary on the *Sentences* was written long before

---

[368] Ibid., p. 38.
[369] See citation [365], p. 243.
[370] I Sent., d. 44, q. 1, art. 3, ad. 3. See *Scriptum Super Libro Sententiarum*, ed. P. Mandonnet (Paris: P. Lethielleux, 1929), p. 1023. The full passage which Doré paraphrases is as follows: "*Ad tertium dicendum, quod puritas intenditur per recessum a contrario: et ideo potest aliquid creatum inveniri quo nihil purius esse potest in rebus creatis, si nulla contagione peccati inquinatum sit; et talis fuit puritas beatae Virginis, quae a peccato originali et actuali immunis fuit, tamen sub Deo, inquantum erat in ea potentia ad peccandum.*

the *tertia pars* of the *Summa*.[371] This is not the place to pursue a discussion on the reasons for St. Thomas' change of mind, nor how his later teaching might be reconciled with what he states in the *Scriptum super libros Sententiarum*. The point is that Pierre Doré, in his defense of the doctrine of the Immaculate Conception, shows that a good Thomist need not be automatically opposed to the teaching, for Thomas himself at one point upheld it. But if the more proximate motive of this exposition seems to be to convince his fellow Dominicans of the folly of their continued opposition to the doctrine, all in the name of being faithful to Thomas, the ulterior motive of insisting on the doctrine is to affirm that Mary's complete triumph over sin, even original sin, is like a ray of moonlight enlightening the dark night of our earthly pilgrimage and a sign of the virtuous life which the grace of Christ makes possible for each one of us. In the overall scheme of things, the Immaculate Conception is one of the foundation stones of Doré's response to the Reformers' assertion that real virtue which makes us pleasing to God is impossible for sinful human beings. In her sinlessness and life of virtue, Mary glorified and delighted the Most High. Although she alone received the grace of never contracting sin, her Immaculate Conception is a pledge to us of our own eventual transformation for a life of perfection.

Mary's Triumph and Ours

Thus far, we have seen how Doré attempts to demonstrate for his readers the foundation for the doctrine of Mary's preservation from original sin in the Song of Songs, in the teaching of Aquinas and with the definition of the Council of Basel in 1439. But since his stated goal in writing *L'image de vertu* is "*pour fonder mes propos en l'escripture Saincte, a fin de plus les auctoriser*," as was pointed out in Chapter 2, it is important to see a few examples of what he has

---

[371] In their response to J. Rossi's *Quid senserit*, Robilliard and De Contenson (n. [366] above) argue that the phrase in question is not as conclusive as it appears. See RSPT 39 (1955): 465.

managed to "dig up in the field of Scripture" concerning Mary's graced life. Drawing on the ancient patristic comparison of Mary as the new Eve, an extension of the Christ-Adam parallel found in the letters of Paul, Doré writes that in the work of redemption it was fitting that Christ should have a helper similar to him in plenitude of grace. Applying the account of the creation of woman in Genesis 2:18-25 to Mary's creation in grace, he comments:

> *Il n'est pas bon que l'homme Jesus soit seul, faisons luy un adjutoire semblable à luy (dit Dieu) c'est à sçavoir une creature en plentitude de grace, & perfection de justice originelle, comme une image ayant similitude avec luy, combien que non pas esgalle, car il est Dieu, pere & autheur de nostre salut, & chef en plus haut lieu que les membres en dignité, soit nostre dame ou autre creature.*[372]

Just as woman is the "suitable partner" for man, "bone of his bones and flesh of his flesh," so the Virgin Mary is the one human being in whom the image of God is perfectly realized. She is graced with that original justice which was lost for all of humanity through the sin of Adam and Eve. This is why Doré holds her up as the image of virtue, for by looking at her, sinful human beings see what they are meant to be as sons and daughters of God. It should be noted, however, that the Dominican is always very careful to affirm that although Mary's dignity and perfection of life is similar to that of the God-man, it is nevertheless a lesser dignity. He is the author and source of grace; she is but the lowly recipient of divine favor. There is no sense in which she is in any way equal to God, a type of demi-goddess. She is fully human, yet perfectly human and therefore a model of that to which we are called.

At the same time, Doré does not hesitate to assert that the Virgin Mary's role is not simply one of modeling but also of an active participation in God's victory over sin in the world. He speaks of *her* triumph over Satan, likening her to the Israelite heroine, Judith, who delivered her people from the power of the Assyrian army by decapitating its general, Holofernes. Although the Book of

---

[372] *L'image*, fol. 3v°.

Judith was considered to be apocryphal by the Reformers, Doré nevertheless points to the story as yet another scriptural witness to the Virgin Mary and her powerful assistance on our behalf:

> *Ceste courageuse dame Judith, a figuré nostre Dame, c'est une des Hebreux, dont elle est venue laquelle a trenché la teste à Holofernes, ennemy du peuple de Dieu, car par divine grace & vertu, la teste du serpent qu'il mettoit au monde par peché originel, a esté coupée, de sorte qu'il n'a eu lieu en nostre Dame, dont il a receu confusion, & le tient abbatu souz ses pieds, elle triomphe par dessus, par l'aide de Dieu, victorieuse dessus l'ennemy, qui sus elle jamais n'a peu avoir domination ne puissance.*[373]

What is most interesting to note here is Doré's insistence that Mary's triumph over Satan, although due solely to God's grace, is nevertheless *her* victory. "***Elle triomphe par dessus***," he states. Thanks to the grace she received of being preserved from contracting original sin, the head of sin, like that of Holofernes, has been severed at its origin. To be sure, this is God's doing, but the victory takes place in the depths of Mary's being and thus can be said to be *hers* as well so that the new Eve triumphs in the primal confrontation with evil where the first Eve failed. The victory is complete because not for one moment, from her conception to her earthly passing, did the enemy ever have any power or domination over her. Since the very purity of her being so confounds Satan and humiliates him, she is put forth by Doré in a special way as the *"reparatrice de l'honneur des femmes."*[374]

But if the Virgin Mary through her sinless life restores honor to womanhood, she also gives hope to all sinners, men and women alike, that the graces of Christ's victory over sin and death may indeed transform and perfect them as well. Thus, Doré encourages his readers to contemplate Mary, not only for the purpose of imitating her, but also to be so attracted by her beauty as to want to renounce sin and embrace the virtuous life:

---

[373] Ibid., fol. 5v°-6r°.
[374] Ibid., fol. 30r°.

> *O pecheur tout souillé de peché, indigent de la grace & misericorde de Dieu, sans laquelle ne peut estre sauvé, approche toy, & te mets devant cest image, contemple sa beauté, & voy qu'aupres d'elle, tu comparois comme ord & salle des ta conception, devant celle qui est toute pure & munde en son immaculée conception, ainsi salle comme tu es, ne pourras entrer en Paradis, car nulle chose coinquinée y pourra entrer...Donc nettoie tes macules, prie la benoiste dame, que par son moyen soyent effacées.*[375]

Like a mirror, Mary perfectly reflects the divine image to those who contemplate her and in so doing, allows them to see how still unlike that image they are in their sins and impurity. However, this true vision of oneself is not a cause for despair, as Doré sees it, but rather an incentive to desire change, to desire the beauty of the virtues which adorn the Virgin's life and so gain paradise. Lest the Dominican theologian be accused of Pelagianism here, he makes it clear in the first line of this citation that no one is saved apart from the grace and mercy of God. Yet, as Chapter 3 on the doctrine of justification pointed out, Doré upholds the traditional teaching over and over again, the present example included, that salvation is a matter of our cooperation with grace as well. The final sentence of the above citation, where he exhorts the sinner to "wash his stains" is to be understood not as if one has the ability to cleanse oneself from sin, but as a reference to the contrition and penitence which are the fruits of grace. He also encourages the sinner to "pray the blessed lady" for he sees Mary as powerful intercessor in one's personal struggle with sin.

This encouragement to turn to the Virgin as intercessor is more than just a pious exhortation from a preacher to his flock. In fact Doré himself sets the example for his readers by ending every chapter with a prayer of supplication both honoring Mary and asking her to obtain a particular grace. The following prayer found at the end of the second chapter provides a good sense of what the rest are like:

---

[375] Ibid., fol. 9v°-10r°.

> *O bien heuree vierge, faites je vous supplie decouler en moy de ceste plenitude de grace, de laquelle ne me vois sanctifié, mais de plusieurs pechez contaminé. C'est à vous a qui on doit avoir recours pour trouver Jesus nostre sanctification. Helas dame, si vous plaist pour moy interceder, qu'une goutte d'eau de sanctification qui est l'eau beniste de grace, vienne sus moy, vostre plenitude n'en fera point amoindre, ne celle de vostre fils, car tousjours est fluante comme clere eau de fontaine...O Dame moy ayant honte des ordes & sales taches de mon ame, je viens à vous toute belle & munde, à fin que par vostre moyen mon ame soit reblanchie & lavée par Jesus qui est nostre justice, & sanctification, grace & salvation. Amen.*[376]

There are several important items to be noted here. First of all, Mary is invoked as one who has the power to obtain grace for poor sinners through her power of intercession. Her ability in this domain is seen as a natural consequence of her privileged status of being "full of grace." In fact, Doré, in the tradition of Bernard of Clairvaux, does not hesitate to draw the full implication of her plenitude of grace by asking for a share in it—*"faites je vous supplie decouler en moy de ceste plenitude de grace."* At the same time, there is never the sense that Mary is herself the source of grace or salvation. Following closely in the footsteps of Aquinas in this regard, Doré is always careful to relate the Virgin's role to that of Christ her son. Through Mary's intercession, the sinner "finds Jesus our sanctification," for Christ is at the source of her own sanctification. The closing sentence of the prayer encapsulates what for Doré is the essence of Marian devotion, principally that the sinner in contemplating Mary both sees his impurity and is drawn by her beauty to desire his own cleansing for which he seeks her intercession and a share in her grace. However, the grace of forgiveness and sanctification, while coming through Mary, is not hers but solely that of "Jesus, who is our justice and sanctification, grace and salvation." As this prayer demonstrates, Doré's is a balanced Mariology and one that is always in reference to the saving role of Christ.

---

[376] Ibid., fol. 17v°-18r°.

This point is reinforced in *Le Nouveau Testament d'amour* (1550) where Doré unequivocally states that *"...Jesus Christ est seul absolut & entier exemplaire de parfection de vie, qui par son esprit fait que ayons force en nous selon son exemple, former & bien instituer nostre vie, singulierement en amour, nous est baillé comme image d'amour & d'obeissance, qui a tant aymé le Pere que luy a obey jusque à la mort de la croix."*[377] There is no contradiction between what the Dominican rightly affirms here and what he wrote earlier concerning Mary, for although *L'image de vertu* proposes the Mother of God as an exemplar of perfect virtue, her perfection and dignity is always qualified as being of a lesser degree than that of her Son because it does not come from within her. It is for this reason that she is referred to as the "image of virtue," for she is not goodness in itself, but rather the perfect reflection of the divine goodness. Thus, Christ as the man-God is the only "absolute and complete exemplar of perfection of life," and he alone is the source of grace which enables us to follow his example of obedient love. Yet, Doré can still point to Mary as the most perfect example after Christ of a life completely conformed to grace and thus one that is worthy of contemplation and imitation. To say that Christ is the absolute and complete exemplar does not exclude the possibility of there being a similar though lesser exemplar, the "suitable partner" to return to Doré's use of the story of the creation of woman as an analogy for Mary's relationship to Christ. As the new Eve, she represents what the grace of the new Adam can accomplish in those who freely cooperate with it.

The Struggle to Live Virtuously: Fanning the Flames of Divine Love

From what has preceded, it might seem as if Doré has an overly optimistic view concerning human ability to embrace a life of virtue and to grow in perfection with God's grace. It seems, for him, to be merely a question of

---

[377] *Le Nouveau Testament*, fol. 159v°.

contemplating the exemplars, Christ and the Virgin Mary, and allowing oneself to be so drawn by their dignity that one immediately abandons the pleasures of the flesh and forever embarks on the road of virtue, proceeding from victory to victory thanks to the divine assistance, which is never lacking. Yet, such a view runs counter to the daily human experience of the often intense struggle involved in overcoming vice and temptation in order to live a virtuous life. Doré, however, is not unaware of the tensions that remain between the flesh and the spirit in those who have been freed from original sin in the waters of baptism and he often addresses the issue in various works. Such tensions are the lingering effects of that enmity with God in which we were born. In one of his Lenten conferences to the Duke and Duchess of Guise, the Dominican confessor explains the tension in the classical philosophical terms of reason's battle to control the appetites:

> ...*en l'homme sont comme deux moteurs qui le mouvent a chose diverses, l'ung a bien & l'autre a mal. Le premier est raison qui incline a bien, selon que dict Aristote,* **Ratio ad optima deprecatur**. *L'autre moteur tire a mal, qui est le sensuel appetit, duquel dict S. Paul:* **Video aliam legem in membris meis repugnantem, legi mentis meae**, *Rom. 7. Je voy une aultre loy en mes membres, laquelle repugne a la loy de mon esprit, c'est ce que dict en un autre epistre que la chair convoite a l'encontre de l'esprit, & l'esprit contre la chair, Galat. 5, voyla motions contraires: par ainsi apert que esmeuvent l'homme, raison & la chair a deux choses contraires: Or qui le gaignera? Il faudra en mettre deux contre ung, c'est a scavoir, l'ayde de dieu, & son mouvement, avec celuy de raison, & alors on gaignera le priz par dessus la chair, on ne la suyvra pas, ne son mouvement, ains son contraire: ce qui ne se peult faire sans l'ayde de Dieu, qui soit pour nous, & nous ayde.* [378]

Whether the tension is described in Pauline terms of the pull between flesh and spirit or in Aristotelian terms of the pull between appetites and reason, the basic problem in the struggle to live virtuously is trying to re-establish order and harmony where there is presently disorder. It is a struggle where, as Doré points out in the above citation, God's grace is absolutely essential in tipping the balance

---

[378] *La premiere partie des collations royales*, pp. 383-384.

in favor of reason or spirit over the strong and sometimes overpowering desires of the appetites or flesh.

As discussed earlier in this chapter, classical theology has always understood that, prior to the fall of Adam and Eve, humanity was gifted with the perfect ordering of the flesh under the law of the spirit, or the appetites under the rule of right reason. The two were as one and virtue came effortlessly. But with the loss of this state of original justice came a rupture in the original harmony and good-ordering of these two faculties in man, with the appetites rebelling against the rule of reason. This rebellion persists in the human experience as a result of our contamination with original sin. Doré explains the root of the problem by pointing out the very real difference between us and the Virgin Mary, who was preserved from original sin:

> *Division est par toutes autres creatures, en tant que le corps n'accorde pas avec l'esprit, il s'entrebattent comme chiens & chatz, & se sont deux, tenant deux parties, la chair demande ses plaisirs charnels, l'esprit y contredit, & demande les biens spirituels, à quoy repugne sensualité, en tels debats n'y a point d'accord & unité. Ce que n'a point esté en nostre Dame, de divine grace tant a esté prevenue, le charbon de concupiscence ne brusle point en elle, n'ayant point d'originel peché, contracté comme nous, pourquoy en elle n'a qu'unité, car en nous ceste division vient de la destitution de justice originelle.*[379]

When Doré states here that the "charcoal of concupiscence never burned in Mary," he is making a reference to the *fomes peccati* or the tinder of sin, the idea that there remains a smoldering element in the passions of the human person which can burst into flame with little provocation. Aquinas formally defines it as "nothing but inordinate though habitual desire in the sense appetite" and goes on to explain that "sensual desire is inordinate when it goes against reason, and that happens whenever it inclines towards evil or throws up a barrier to doing

---

[379] *L'image*, fol. 8v°.

good."[380] While not going into such detail, Doré simply explains that it is an effect of original sin and thus a condition which the Virgin never knew.

What of us, then, who though cleansed of original sin remain subject to its effects, in particular this burning tinder of concupiscence? How can we hope to ever gain the upper hand in the struggle to live virtuously? Such a blessed life as that of Mary would seem an absolutely impossible ideal for us to achieve. Are we doomed to the frustration of recognizing what we might be even while realizing that we are powerless to become it? Doré here sees a solution to the problem of the divided soul which continues to experience the rebellion of inordinate desire against the direction of right reason. The solution lies in love, for love by its very nature unites what is separate and divided. He reasons that the more we grow in our love of God, the less we will experience the tensions between the flesh and the spirit. As he continues to explain:

> *D'avantage division est en nous, par faute de vraye amour à Dieu, nous mettons nos pensees en divers lieux, & est nostre coeur divisé, n'ayant vie par ce moyen (comme dit Osee le Prophete). Mais amour de Dieu en la benoiste dame la rend recolligee en un, car amour est vertu unitive, selon S. Denys, comme le feu en la fornaise & fonte, ou sont divers metaux, unit tout en une masse, & tout faict en un. Par telle maniere faict charité, comparee au feu, ainsi qu'avons demonstré en nos* **Allumettes du feu Divin**, *en cest unité apparoist clerement grande beauté de ceste image, car de tant plus que l'ame est semblable à Dieu, de tant plus elle resplendist de beauté.*[381]

The reason why the Virgin Mary remained steadfast in virtue was because her mind and will were as one in the love of God. Returning to one of his favorite images, that of fire, Doré compares the melding together of different metals in the heat of a furnace to the transforming power of charity in a soul which melts all division and reveals the harmonious beauty of the divine image in us. Thus, the more we grow in the love of God, the more we will experience the healing of that division that remains in us as a result of original sin so that although the tinder of

---

[380] *Summa*, IIIa, q. 27, a. 3. See Blackfriars, 51, p. 17.
[381] *L'image*, fol. 8v°-9r°.

concupiscence will always smolder, its effects will be all but extinguished by the fire of divine love.

However, the question then arises, is growth in the love of God our work, or his? If ours, then how is it achieved given the multitude of our weaknesses which weigh us down? If his, then are we absolved of all guilt if such grace is not given to us? Doré has already more fully explained himself on these points in his earlier work, *Les allumettes du feu divin*. Here he is the first to admit that the theological virtue of charity is a gift of God which he alone can pour into our hearts. We can neither merit to have the fire of divine love lighted within us nor can we bring it into existence of our own volition. In *Les allumettes du feu divin*, our friar makes appeal to question 20 of the *prima pars* to explain that God "*...n'a pas esté provocqué premierement a nous aymer, pour le bien qui fust en nous, aincois a opposite, pourtant qu'il nous a aymez, cause, infunde, cree & produit bonté en nous & son feu de charité allume...*"[382] The context for this citation is an attempt to point out the differences between our love for other human beings and God's love for us. When we love another, it is because we perceive something in the other that is worthy of love. Not so, however, with God, who does not love us because we are in fact loveable. Doré reiterates Aquinas' point here that it is in loving us that God makes us loveable by infusing us with his own goodness and love. This infused love is the theological virtue of charity, which alone enables us to achieve the union with God for which we were created.

Yet, if God alone can light the fire of divine love within us, that is not to say that we do not have a role to play in stoking the flames and assuring that the gift does not smolder out of existence. Doré uses several images for how we keep the fire burning brightly: throwing oil on the fire as a way of increasing the intensity of the flames, re-igniting the fire with new matches, etc. The oil and the matches are metaphors for devout meditation on the life of Christ, principally his

---

[382] *Les allumettes*, fol. xxx v°.

passion, which serves to excite the faithful to a more profound appreciation of his love. As the Dominican counsels his spiritual daughter at the monastery of Poissy:

> Faictz icy ung transport de pensee, ame devote, fille de Dieu, voy ton espoux lye a la coulonne, tout nud, devant le monde, batu comme ung larron, qui est sans vice, tache ou reprehension. Regarde les verges, fouetz & escorgees, baignees en sang, & les garde hardyment pour en toy allumer le feu d'amour & devotion. Car veritablement sont allumettes a feu...[383]

So crucial is meditation to fanning the flames of divine love in one's heart that several of Doré's devotional works are in fact designed to be aids to this end. Perhaps the work which most explicitly reveals his intent in this regard is *La caeleste pensée de graces divines* (1543) where he offers his readers a specific plan of meditations for each day of the week. The plan basically corresponds to the central moments of salvation history: creation, the fall, and finally redemption in Christ Jesus. Within this general framework, the faithful are encouraged to meditate more specifically on the death and judgment which await them, on the sins they have committed by which God's love has been rejected, and on the misery of this present life. However, such meditation should not lead to despair but to a greater appreciation of God's goodness and love, for he has saved us from our sins. While *La caeleste pensée* is certainly the most developed aid to meditation in the "Doréan" corpus, it is far from being unique in its objective, for practically all of the devotional works encourage meditation as a necessary means for fanning the fire of charity which God has poured into the hearts of the faithful.

As important as meditation is to stoking the flames, it must also be accompanied by other acts on our part. Once again, Doré resorts to a metaphor to illustrate his point. A fire is preserved in two ways: by sheltering it from wind and rain which could extinguish it, and also by adding new wood as the old is consumed. Likewise, the fire of charity must both be guarded by one's careful

---

[383] Ibid., fol. xxvi rº.

avoidance of occasions of sin as well as be fed with the new wood of good works.[384] God's grace, his love in us, can be rendered ineffective by our return to the slavery of sin and by our unwillingness to exercise the virtues. For Doré, then, the virtuous life is most basically the fruition of God's grace in our lives. That fruition, however, cannot come about without our consent or our active participation. If we do not take steps to shelter the fire of divine love and fan its flames, the tinder of sin is bound to become inflamed and take its place.

Even as a person grows in virtue, Doré cautions that this does not necessarily mean that temptations will cease. In fact, they are likely to increase. As the Dominican theologian tries to explain to his readers, the experience of temptation, though disheartening to the person who is striving to be pleasing to God, is not necessarily a bad thing. It is actually a sign that we are on the path to perfection, for temptation is the devil's attempt to deter us. As Doré puts it, *"si le diable ne pensoit quelque bien estre en nous, il ne s'estudieroit pas a le desrober: c'est signe que nous sommes hors de sa puissance, puis qu'il nous tente tant, pour nous reprendre."*[385] Elsewhere he attempts, following a similar line of thought, to console those who continue to feel strongly tempted even after having received the sacrament of penance:

> *Nostre saulveur Jesus apres avoir esté baptizé est entré au desert, ou le diable l'a tenté. Comme dit sainct Jehan Crisostome, puis que l'ennemy nous tente, apres le baptesme, ou sacrement de penitence, nous debuons conjecturer qu'il y a quelque tresor en nous, qui par avant n'y estoit pas, que le larron veult desrober. Ne te trouble point chrestien, quand te sens tenté, apres ta penitence, car tu as prins de dieu armeures espirituelles, qui sont les vertus, ce n'est pas en vain que ainsi es armé de dieu, mais pour batailler & faire coups de vaillance affin que soys coroné.*[386]

As Doré sees it, temptation is not the trial of sinners, but of those walking along the path of perfection, a sign that a person possesses the treasure of grace which the devil is desperately trying to plunder. Therefore, it is not an occasion for

---

[384] See Ibid., fol. cxvii v°-cxviii r°.
[385] *La premiere partie des collations royales*, p. 305.
[386] *Le college*, fol. 94v°-95r°.

losing heart but rather for recalling the treasure within, the spiritual armor of grace that has been given us. In fact, the moment of temptation is precisely the moment where we grow in virtue by putting to good use the grace we have received. The last sentence of the above citation makes it clear—grace is given for a reason, that we might go into battle fully armed and so gain the victory of virtue over vice.

Conclusion

Obviously, the above discussion is but a thumbnail sketch of some of the principal themes encountered in Doré's devotional works. Since this study purports to be but a general overview of the Dominican's literary output, I did not want to fall into the trap of providing detailed summaries and analyses of the wide-ranging concerns addressed in these various writings. Rather, my goal was to focus instead on the broad themes which characterize his contribution in the field of devotional literature and to demonstrate how these themes complement and reinforce his overarching project of responding to Reformation theology with the solid food of orthodoxy. Although little of Doré's often biting polemics is seen in these works, he remains engaged in a battle for the minds and hearts of the faithful as he exposes for them the essence of the Christian life.

It is clear from the presentation that has preceded that for Doré, the essence of the Christian life is growth in virtue, above all the virtue of charity. From his first work, *La devise d'ung coeur assis en Pierre de vertu*, to his last, *La tourtrelle de viduité enseignant les vefves comment elles doivent vivre en leur estat*, the call to virtue is issued and amplified both with doctrinal expositions and practical counsels, the former addressing "why it is necessary" and the latter addressing "how it is achieved." Without doubt, the key work in Doré's overall presentation on the virtuous life is the lengthy *L'image de vertu*, where the Virgin

Mary is put forth as the perfect image of the virtues which all the faithful are called to cultivate. Pure and spotless from her conception, consumed with the love of God, she is, in his mind, the unquestionable prototype of what God intends for us as well through his redemptive grace.

Here it must be said that Pierre Doré has both a very realistic view of human nature with its faults and failings as well as an optimistic view of that nature as redeemed by the passion of Christ. He has no illusions concerning the often intense struggle involved in putting to death the vices of the "old man." Yet, he exudes a great confidence in the restorative power of grace which enables human beings to rediscover the harmony of a well-ordered life where the intellect is conformed to God's will and the passions are subjected to the direction of right reason. Ultimately, for the Dominican theologian, the graces of the passion of Christ communicated to the faithful in baptism and the other sacraments do more than cover over our wretchedness. These graces operate a real transformation in the depth of our being so that we may actually perform virtuous deeds which make us worthy of the eternal life made possible for us by the death and resurrection of Christ.

In light of the dignity and power for virtue which are ours through grace, Doré sets out in his devotional works to enflame the hearts of his readers with a great desire for fulfilling the marvelous vocation given us at baptism. Over and over again, he emphasizes the fact that our destiny is to be one with God in love. God himself has made our union with him possible by infusing us with the theological virtues of faith, hope and love. However, if his initiative in this regard is indispensable, so is our response. We have a definite role to play in stoking the fire of love and keeping it burning unto eternal life. It is as spiritual guide that our friar offers specific counsels as to how one might fulfill the demands of love, principally through penance for past sins and works of charity, through meditation on the passion and the cultivation of a life of prayer which leads to an increasing thirst for the Beloved who has redeemed us.

Finally, an examination of the bibliographical data reveals that the devotional category is where Doré excelled and was most appreciated by the reading public. All of his best-sellers are from this group, most notably *Les allumettes* for which there are as many as fourteen different editions. Yet, if his explicitly polemical works did not enjoy the same success, that is not to say that his project of defending orthodoxy proved a failure. On the contrary, the devotional works effectively proposed the same basic message as those which were more specifically directed to countering the Reformers' positions. In emphasizing the virtuous life as the necessary response to the grace of salvation, a response by which we merit the kingdom of heaven, Doré was clearly assaulting the cornerstone of the Reformation, the notion of justification by faith alone. It is in this sense that the devotional works were much more than instructional manuals for those inclined to piety. In fact, they formed a central element of his overall plan of attack against Reformed theology.

Conclusion

This study of Pierre Doré and his works has attempted to establish the Dominican theologian as having occupied a significant place in the Catholic response in sixteenth-century France to the influence of Reformed theology being propagated primarily through printed texts. As we have seen, his was a response directed not to the Reformers themselves in an attempt to dialogue with them or convince them of their errors but directed rather to the literate man and woman whose faith he determined to be endangered by the new ideas. By way of conclusion, a word should be said now concerning the way in which Pierre Doré fits into the larger picture of the Roman church's multifaceted response to the revolution in doctrine and discipline unleashed by Luther. In several ways, our friar's work anticipated many features of the developing Catholic "counter-Reformation," or the direct response of the Church to the reality of a religiously divided Europe.

The Council of Trent was perhaps the single most significant event of this direct response, dealing squarely with much-needed disciplinary reforms as well as providing clear teaching on the key points of debate. It unequivocally affirmed doctrines such as the necessity of Sacred Tradition in addition to the Scriptures in determining belief, the real and substantial presence of Christ in the Eucharist, the sacraments as being seven in number, and the necessity of works of charity as well as faith in the justification of the believer. Readers of Doré, however, already possessed clear teaching on these major issues several years in advance of the council's decrees. What is more, the doctrinal instruction he provided was almost always coupled with an emphasis on developing a real devotion for the mysteries of the faith. His works on the Eucharist, for example, not only explained such notions as the doctrine of transubstantiation but also sought to imbue readers with a real desire to draw closer to the Savior truly present in the sacrament. The Eucharistic-centered piety he promoted along with the encouragement to more frequent communion would in fact become hallmarks of post-Reformation Catholic spirituality in general. This linking of doctrine to piety, a centerpiece of the Dominican theologian's literary project, was crucial to addressing the legitimate spiritual aspirations of an increasingly educated laity who might otherwise have been drawn to the Christ-centered and Word-centered spirituality of the Reformers.

Since an authentic piety could only be built upon a solid doctrinal foundation, basic catechetical instruction was a necessary prerequisite. Once again, Doré proved to be a precursor, anticipating the intense efforts of the Church in the latter half of the sixteenth century to educate the laity at least in the fundamentals of the faith. Catechisms abounded in the aftermath of the Council of Trent, but the Dominican theologian had already produced a relatively popular exposition of the Catholic faith that had known six editions prior to the opening of the council in 1545. His *Dyalogue instructoire* (1538) can thus be seen as a forerunner of the popular *Summary of Christian Doctrine* by the German Jesuit Peter Canisius, first published in 1555, as well as of the official *Roman Catechism* promulgated under Pope Pius V in 1566.

While these attempts to educate or catechize were ultimately directed to all levels of society, it was the aristocratic elite who received particular attention in the period following the council. The newly formed Society of Jesus, founded in 1540 for the very general purpose of propagating the faith, soon became the driving force behind the renewal of the Church legislated by Trent. Jesuits excelled as preachers and teachers of a revitalized Catholic faith, strengthening the belief of those who remained in the fold and even winning back many who had fallen away. In their attempt to reclaim souls for the Church, they very deliberately laid great emphasis on the proper instruction and formation of those with influence in society, the rich and powerful, with the idea being that the elite could then play an active role in the re-establishment of the true faith. Here also, Pierre Doré was ahead of his time. His own program, as we have seen, was to form the upper classes in virtue and piety that they might be models of the Christian life to their subjects. He put them on guard concerning the pernicious errors of the Reformers that they might not be taken in by these wolves in sheep's clothing. Finally, he encouraged them not to tolerate heresy, indeed to extirpate it by force if necessary, for erroneous belief was a threat to the common good.

Notwithstanding Doré's endorsement of violence against unrepentant heretics, an attitude moreover which was typical of the sixteenth-century religious mindset, there are many ways in which the otherwise saintly Dominican also anticipated the best aspects of post-Tridentine Catholic spirituality as exemplified in the writings of Francis de Sales who was bishop of Geneva from 1602 to 1622. As priest and then bishop, de Sales devoted his life to successfully winning back heretics, not through force or coercion but principally through patience and charity. His efforts at evangelization in the Chablais region of Savoy resulted in a majority of the Calvinist parishes there returning peacefully to the Church of Rome. In perhaps his best known work, *Introduction to the Devout Life* (1609), he proposed to the laity the possibility of living a devout and saintly life within their station, whether they be rulers, ordinary working people, husbands and fathers or wives and mothers. No one, in his view, was exempt from the possibility of attaining to the highest degrees of charity and holiness with God's grace.

Although Doré did not quite resemble the bishop of Geneva in his pastoral approach to Protestants, his spirituality for the laity does bear a marked resemblance to that later promoted by Francis de Sales. Granted that many of the

Dominican's devotional works were dedicated to cloistered nuns, it is nevertheless quite clear that Doré considered the spiritual counsel he was offering them as applicable to all Christians desirous of growth in the spiritual life, for he writes in *Les allumettes du feu divin*, "*en mon livre n'est pas mon intention de seullement endoctriner gens de religion, voulant profiter a tous.*"[387] And judging from the publication statistics, it would seem that many of these works did indeed prove appealing to people outside of the cloister. For Doré, devotion could be practiced by the faithful in all walks of life and it was precisely toward this end that he sought to nourish religious and laity alike with scriptural meditations and commentaries on the psalms. In thus introducing them to "the devout life" his ultimate hope was that they might discover the key to personal transformation in an affective union with Christ, the source of transforming grace.

Given Pierre Doré's significance as a kind of precursor of the developing multifaceted Catholic response to the Reformation, it remains to be seen whether or not the Dominican's own strategic efforts in this regard actually succeeded. Yet it is nearly impossible now to render judgment as to how effective his personal intervention was. Did his numerous writings achieve their intended goal of keeping the ordinary faithful within the fold of the Church of Rome? Were readers of his works convinced by his doctrinal expositions that the Reformers had indeed departed from the true faith on essential points? Did his devotional works contribute to authentic reform in the Church by inspiring the faithful to strive for virtue and sanctity? These questions defy a measurable response and must unfortunately remain unanswered, at least in a definitive sense. Whereas Luther and Calvin clearly had an impact on their time and well beyond, an impact evidenced in the followers their ideas attracted as well as in the churches they established which continue in existence today, Doré can claim no such evidence as proof of the influence and success of his work. Of its very nature, his work of exposing the traditional teaching of the Church for the laity was not conducive to

---

[387] *Les allumettes*, fol. liii r°.

attracting a personal following of those convinced that the Dominican theologian spoke the truth. Anyone so convinced simply remained within the fold of the traditional faith. Thus Doré's impact on the people of his time is not as easy to determine as that of his opponents.

Lacking tangible evidence of our friar's influence on his contemporaries, we must therefore depend on the few clues available to us for arriving at some sort of judgment in this regard. First and foremost, the bibliographical evidence indicates that a good portion of his works were much appreciated by readers, with a majority having been edited at least once and six of the total thirty-five going through more than five subsequent editions. Any assessment of Doré's impact must take note of these impressive figures. They are evidence that the author managed to connect with his readers, that his thought resonated in their minds and hearts. Had Doré's works not known this popular appeal in his day, there would be little point in pursuing this present study except perhaps as an esoteric interest. However, the popular appeal is a sign that he made an impression and therefore that his thought deserves examination for coming to a better understanding of the Reformation era in France.

The fact that Doré's work was not only the first response of note to the Reformation in France by a Dominican but also the first major written response of any Catholic figure whether theologian or bishop gives him added stature as a person of influence in his time. No other Catholic writer of this period in French history produced as many volumes or achieved as many new editions as Doré. Considering the relative disinterestedness of the French hierarchy in preserving their flock from the new ideas as well as the tardy response of the Council of Trent in clarifying the Church's teaching, Doré's writings filled a serious pastoral need by offering the type of unequivocal clarity in doctrine which was lacking on the magisterial level up to that point in time. Although the Faculty of Theology, the watchdog of orthodoxy in France, did make serious attempts both to censure heresy and to positively proclaim correct doctrine with its Articles of Faith in

1543, its efforts to oppose the Reformation would have been ultimately ineffective had theologians like Doré not attempted to counter the new ideas with a fresh presentation of the traditional faith. It was not enough to repress the thought of Luther and Calvin. Their arguments demanded an appealing and intelligent response and only then might ordinary people be persuaded to reject their point of view.

In his plan of attack on the Protestant edifice, Doré took aim at the foundational principle of *sola scriptura* by attempting to demonstrate that some of the key doctrines rejected by the Reformers were solidly grounded in the Scriptures. Generally speaking, his scriptural proofs were well-founded. Yet, as this study has demonstrated, the Dominican did not always succeed in this project and at times his exegesis leaves much to be desired. Indeed, his heavy reliance on the allegorical sense of Scripture coupled with this fixation to answer the Reformers solely on their own terms rather than clearly affirming the validity of Tradition as a vehicle for transmitting the authentic faith of the Church are perhaps the greatest weakness to be found in his theological expositions.

On the other hand, his emphasis on scriptural truth was certainly commendable in that it led him to offer some significant passages of the New Testament as well as several psalms in translation and with commentary for the laity's meditation. From *Les voyes de paradis* with its exposition of the Beatitudes, to *Le cerf spirituel* with its meditative commentary on Psalm 41(42), to *Dialogue de la justification chrestienne* with its beautiful explanation of the dialogue between Jesus and the Samaritan woman at the well in John 4, Doré's lay readers were fed not only with single-verse proof-texts but with rather generous portions of the Word of God for their spiritual development.

If our friar sought to make the Scriptures more accessible to the French laity in his fight against heresy, he also introduced his readers to some more advanced theological instruction with copious citations from the Fathers and even more significantly from the great medieval doctor Aquinas. While some of his more famous confrères like Francisco de Vitoria were promoting a Thomistic renaissance in the universities of Europe, Doré sought to bring some of Aquinas' insights to bear on the lives of the ordinary faithful. His summaries and paraphrases of Thomistic determinations surely represent the first incursion of Aquinas' thought outside of the university setting in France. Here again, Doré was doing something very original and perhaps even scandalous to the intelligentsia of the Parisian Faculty of Theology. Their disapproval notwithstanding, the Dominican doctor "vulgarized" Thomas' teaching in the firm belief that his insights on grace, merit and virtue were an important antidote to the errors of the Reformers. This is why he stripped Aquinas' thought of its scholastic trappings and presented key articles of the *Summa* in a form that would be more accessible to the theologically uninitiated.

As important as Doré's innovation in this regard may have been, it is nevertheless quite certain that his readers would have appreciated less the more elevated level of theological discourse in his works than his appealing use of image and metaphor to communicate and reinforce his points. The numerous examples presented in this study have demonstrated that not all of his metaphors were equally as effective in illustrating the matter at hand. Yet by and large, the Dominican possessed a gift for instructing with analogies that were useful and very often engaging. Without doubt, this gift of being able to use an image effectively was at the heart of his success as a spiritual writer who took up the pen in defense of the traditional faith.

To return to the question raised above concerning an assessment of Doré's impact on his contemporaries, it is impossible to render a judgment based on hard statistics, for none exist. However, in consideration of his early and voluminous response to the ideas of the Reformers along with the unique elements to be found in his works and the unquestionable popularity they attained with the reading public, we can only conclude that Pierre Doré was certainly among the influential figures of his time. His life's work almost certainly had a profound impact on the lives of individual Christians seeking guidance and surety in a world of theological uncertainty. At the same time, we must admit that in the larger scheme of things, our friar had little impact on the actual course of historical events. His personal attempts to restore unity of faith in France were a failure as the nation plunged into a protracted period of civil strife near the end of his life, only to be resolved with the promulgation of the Edict of Nantes in 1598 granting certain rights to the heretics he had sought to eradicate. Yet regardless of the fact that Pierre Doré does not seem to have changed the course of history in a significant way, the lives of countless individuals were certainly affected by his theological and moral instruction in the faith. It is without doubt in the arena of the individual conscience that his life's work bore the expected fruit of helping to preserve the Catholic faith in France.

APPENDIX 1

Chronological Listing of Doré's Works and Number of Subsequent Editions

1. *La devise d'ung noble cueur* (Paris: publisher unknown, after 1525)	1
2. *Les voyes de paradis* (Lyon: François Just, 1537)	14 French; 2 Latin
3. *Les allumettes du feu divin* (Paris: Antoine Bonnemere, 1538)	12 French; 2 Latin
4. *Dyalogue instructoire des chrestiens* (Paris: Jean Réal, 1538)	6
5. *Le college de sapience* (Paris: Antoine Bonnemere, 1539)	5 French; 1 Flemish; 1 Latin
6. *L'image de vertu* (Paris: Pierre Vidoue, 1540)	6
7. *La deploration de la vie humaine* (Paris: Nicolas Barbou, 1541)	5
8. *L'arbre de vie* (Paris: Guillaume de Bossozel, 1542)	0
9. *La caeleste pensée* (Paris, Adam Saulnier, 1543)	2
10. *Paradoxa...ad profligandas haereses* (Paris: Jean de Brouilly, 1543)	0
11. *La meditation devote du bon chrestien* (Paris: René Avril, 1544)	0
12. *Le livre des divins benefices* (Paris: Jean Ruelle, 1544)	0
13. *Le cerf spirituel* (Paris: Jean Ruelle, 1544)	1
14. *L'adresse de l'esgaré pescheur* (Paris: Jean Ruelle, 1544)	1
15. *La croix de penitence* (Paris: Jean Ruelle, 1545)	2
16. *Le pasturage de la brebis humaine* (Paris: Jean de Brouilly, 1546)	1
17. *Anatomie, et mystique description* (Paris: Jean de Brouilly, 1546)	1
18. *La premiere partie des collations royales* (Paris: René Avril, 1546)	1
19. *La seconde partie des collations royales* (Paris: René Avril, 1546)	1
20. *La passe-solitaire* (Paris: Jean de Brouilly, 1547)	1
21. *La conserve de grace* (Paris: Guillaume Cavellat, 1548)	0
22. *Les triomphes du roy sans pair* (Paris: Jean de Brouilly, 1548)	0
23. *Les cantiques dechantees* (Paris: Jean Ruelle, 1549)	0
24. *L'arche de l'alliance nouvelle* (Paris: Benoît Prevost, 1549)	1
25. *Le nouveau testament d'amour* (Paris: Jean Ruelle, 1550)	1 French; 1 Flemish*
26. *La piscine de patience* (Paris: Benoît Prevost, 1550)	0
27. *Oraison panegyrique* (Paris: Jean de Brouilly, 1550)	0
28. *Anti-Calvin* (Paris: publisher unknown, 1551)	1
29. *Observance de religion chrestienne* (Reims: N. Bacquenois, 1554)	1
30. *Dialogue de la justification chrestienne* (Paris: Jean Ruelle, 1554)	0
31. *Adunatio praecipuarum materiarum* (Paris: Vincent Sertenas, 1555)	1
32. *La vie et la mort chrestiennes* (Reims: Nicolas Bacquenois, 1556)	0
33. *Le livre de la victoire* (Paris: Jean Ruelle, 1556)	4
34. *La tourtrelle de viduité* (Reims: Nicolas Bacquenois, 1557)	3
35. *Le second livre des divins benefices* (Paris: Jean Ruelle, 1569)	0

Total Number of Subsequent Editions   79

*This is a manuscript and not a printed edition.

APPENDIX 2

List of Editions of Doré's Works

1. *La devise d'ung noble cueur, assis en pierre de vertu, avec le sens moral, tant en latin que en francoys.*
--First edition is unknown, but printed in Paris sometime after 1525 [this information is based on a reference Doré makes to this small work in *Les allumettes du feu divin*. See 1538 ed., (Paris, BA—8° T 7637), fol. 31]
--1543. Paris, Adam Saulnier, 4 fol. [bound with *La caeleste pensée*]
    Amiens, BM—Les 1752 A
    Bordeaux, BM—T 7106
    London, BL—C.186.a.25

2. *Les voyes de paradis que a enseignees nostre benoist Saulveur Jesus en son evangile, pour la reduction du povre pecheur.*
--1537. Lyon, François Just (see BR, p. 139)
--1538. Paris, Antoine Bonnemere (see BR, p. 139)
--1538. No place or publisher given, no page numbers
    Amiens, BM—Rés. 143 A [bound alone; contains letter to lecteur chretien].
--1538. Paris, Etienne Caveiller, [bound with *Les allumettes du feu divin*]
    London, BL—1360.b.7
    Notre Dame, HES—BX 890 D695
--1538. Paris, François Regnault, no page numbers [bound with *Les allumettes du feu divin*]
    Aix-en-Provence, BMJ—Rés. D. 89
    Brussels, BRA—LP 481 A
    Châlons-en-Champagne, BM—Rés. Ch. 678
    Nancy, BM—Rés. 11.282
    Orléans, BM—H6572.2
    Paris, BA—8° T 7367
    Troyes, BM—G.16.4525
--1538. Paris, Etienne Caveiller, no page numbers [bound with *Les allumettes du feu divin*, dated 1539!]
    Edinburgh, UEL—De.2.2
    Paris, BSG—D 8° 6199(2) Rés. Inv. 7898
--1538. Lyon, (see BR, p. 139)
--n.d. Paris, Jean Ruelle, 67 fol. [bound with *Les allumettes du feu divin*]
    Amiens, BM—M 3468
--1540. Paris, Antoine Bonnemere, 54 fol. [bound with *Les allumettes du feu divin*]
    Ghent, BUG—Rés. 994
    Le Mans, MLA—Th. 8° 4585
    Lyon, BM—Rés. 321 726
    Paris, BMZ—49269
    Paris, BNF—Rés. D 32762
--1540. Lyon, (see BR, p. 139)
--1548. Paris, Antoine Bonnemere, (see Brunet, *Manuel*, II, p. 818)
--1548. Paris, Guillaume Thibout, [bound with *Les allumettes du feu divin*]
    Rouen, BM—Dieusy p 594
--1575. Paris, veuve de Jean Ruelle, 72 fol. [bound with *Les allumettes du feu divin*]
    Paris, BA—8° T 7368
    Paris, BNF—Rés. D 32763
--1586. Lyon, Jean Pillehotte, 103 pp. [bound with *Les allumettes du feu divin*]
    Dijon, BM—584
    Lyon, BM—813 433
--1605. Lyon, Pierre Rigaud, 133 pp. [bound with *Les allumettes du feu divin*]
    Estavayer-le-Lac, Monastère des Dominicaines—Dd 16

--1610. Rouen, Romain de Beauvais, 131 pp. [bound with *Les allumettes du feu divin*]
    Amiens, BM—Les 1742 A
    Paris, BNF—Inv. D 17410
    Paris, BS—443 E-38
    Rouen, BM—Leber 335
--1611. Cologne, Buchardus Kuickius, 83 pp. [Latin trans., *Octo viae caelum*, bound with *Scintillae divinae amoris*]
    Cambridge, CUL—Ely.e.92 (1)
    Paris, BSG—D 8° 6126 Inv. 7802(2) FA [bound with *Collegium sapientiae* (1610), not *Scintillae divinae amoris*]
--1611. Cologne, Buchardus Kuickius, 83 pp. [Latin trans., *Octo viae ad coelum*]
    Brussels, BRA—VI 5257 A 2
    Ghent, BUG—Theol. 3677(1)

3. *Les allumettes du feu divin pour faire ardre les cueurs humains en l'amour de Dieu: Où sont declairez les principaux articles et mysteres de la passion de nostre Sauveur & Redempteur Jesus Christ.*

--1538. Paris, Antoine Bonnemere (see BR, p. 139)
--1538. Paris, Etienne Caveiller, [bound with *Les voyes de paradis*]
    London, BL—1360.b.7
    Notre Dame, HES—BX 890 D695 [end page mentions that this is a new printing]
--1538. Paris, François Regnault, 146 fol. [bound with *Les voyes de paradis*]
    Aix-en-Provence, BMJ—Rés. D. 89
    Brussels, BRA—LP 481 A
    Châlons-en-Champagne, BM—Rés. Ch. 678
    Nancy, BM—Rés. 11.282
    Orléans, BM—H6572.1
    Paris, BA—8° T 7367
    Troyes, BM—G.16.4525
--n.d. Paris, Etienne Caveiller, 146 fol.
    Amiens, BM—Rés. 144 A
    Paris, BNF—Rés. 8-Z Don-594(498)
--1539. Paris, Etienne Caveiller, 146 fol. [bound with *Les voyes de paradis*, dated 1538]
    Edinburgh, UEL—De.2.2
    Paris, BSG—D 8° 6199(2) Rés. Inv. 7898
--n.d. Paris, Jean Ruelle, 169 fol. [bound with *Les voyes de paradis*]
    Amiens, BM—M 3468
--1540. Paris, Antoine Bonnemere, 162 fol. [bound with *Les voyes de paradis*]
    Ghent, BUG—Rés. 994
    Le Mans, MLA—Th. 8° 4585
    Lyon, BM—Rés. 321 726
    Paris, BMZ—49269 [end page mentions Doré as friar of Bloys]
    Paris, BNF—Rés. D 32762
--1548. Paris, Antoine Bonnemere (see Brunet, *Manuel*, II, p. 818)
--1548. Paris, Guillaume Thibout, [bound with *Les voyes de paradis*]
    Rouen, BM—Dieusy p 594
--n.d. Lyon, Pierre de Saincte Lucie, 103 fol.
    Aix-en-Provence, BMJ—Res. D. 324
    Amiens, BM—Les 1743 A
    Paris, BMZ—12580
--1575. Paris, veuve de Jean Ruelle, 183 fol. [bound with *Les voyes de paradis*]
    Paris, BA—8° T 7368
    Paris, BNF—Rés. D 32763
--1586. Lyon, Jean Pillehotte, 342 pp. [bound with *Les voyes de paradis*]
    Dijon, BM—584
    Lyon, BM—813 433

--1605. Lyon, Pierre Rigaud, 342 pp. [bound with *Les voyes de paradis*]
        Estavayer-le-Lac, Monastère des Dominicaines—Dd 16
--1610. Rouen, Romain de Beauvais, 342 pp. [bound with *Les voyes de paradis*]
        Amiens, BM—Les 1742 A
        Paris, BNF—Inv. D 17410
        Paris, BS—443 E-38
        Rouen, BM—Leber 335
--1611. Cologne, Buchardus Kuickius, 240 pp. [Latin trans., *Scintillae divini amoris*, bound with *Octo viae ad caelum*]
        Cambridge, CUL—Ely.e.92 (3)
        Paris, BNF—Inv. D 32773 [bound alone—no *Octo viae ad caelum*]
--1691. Cologne, Conradus Butgenius, (see Farge, BR, 139) [Latin trans., *Scintillae divini amoris*]

4. *Dyalogue instructoire des chrestiens en la foy, esperance, & amour en Dieu.*
    --1538. Paris, Jean Réal, 110 fol.
        Paris, BNF—Rés. D 32766 (now on microfilm m 8989)
    --1538. Lyon, Pierre de saincte-Lucie, 123 fol. [bound with *Les epistres de sainct Martial, nouvellement translatees de latin en langue vulgaire gallicane*]
        Aix-en-Provence, BMJ—C. 2196
    --1539. Paris, Antoine Bonnemere, 106 fol. [bound with *Le college de sapience*]
        Ann Arbor, UM—BV 4833 .D68
        London, BL—1360.b.7
        Lyon, BM—318 281
        Paris, BA—8° T 6955
        Paris, BMZ—49405
        Paris, BNF—Rés. R 2045
        Versailles, BM—Fonds A 8° O 46 d
        Wolfenbüttel, HAB—1028.19 Theol.
    --1542. Paris, Denis Janot, 174 fol.
        Paris, BNF—Rés. D 13571
    --1544. Paris, René Avril, 144 fol. [bound with *La meditation devote du bon chrestien*]
        Paris, BSG—D 8° 6197(2) Inv. 7892 bis FA
    --1544. Paris, Denis Janot, 95 fol.
        Orléans, BM—H6572.3
    --1545. Paris, Guillaume Thibout, 144 fol.
        Versailles, BM—Pératé A 42
        Washington, LC—BV4833, D6

5. *Le college de sapience, fondé en l'université de vertu, auquel cest rendue escolliere Magdelaine disciple et apostole de JESUS.*
    --1539. Paris, Antoine Bonnemere, 168 fol. [bound with *Dyalogue instructoire des chrestiens*]
        Ann Arbor, UM—BV 4833 .D68
        London, BL—1360.f.8
        Lyon, BM—318 281
        Paris, BA—8° T 6955
        Paris, BMZ—49405
        Paris, BNF—Rés. R 2044
        Versailles, BM—Fonds A 8° O 46 d
        Wolfenbüttel, HAB—1028.19 Theol.
    --n.d. Paris, Etienne Groulleau, 200 fol.
        Paris, BA—8° T 6956 [frontispiece missing, but is identical to Saulchoir copy]
        Paris, BS—XVI V DOR 1
    --1546. Paris, Pierre Sergent, 200 fol.
        Paris, BS—XVI V DOR 2
        Troyes, BM—G.17.4625
    --1546. Paris, Jean de Brouilly (see BR, p. 139)
    --1555. Paris, Jean Ruelle, 200 fol.
        Rouen, BM—Leber 332

--1556. Antwerp, S. Cock, 121 pp. [Flemish trans., *Die collegie der wijsheyt*]
    Brussels, BRA—II 66277 A
    Chicago, CRL—microfilm
--1598. Douai, Balthasar Bellere, 320 pp. (see Brunet, *Manuel*, II, p. 819)
--1610. Cologne, Buchardus Kuickius, 303 pp. [Latin trans., *Collegium sapientiae*]
    Brussels, BRA—VI 5257 A
    Cambridge, CUL—E* .13.37 (G)
    Ghent, BUG—Theol. 3677
    Paris, BSG—D 8° 6126 Inv. 7802(1) FA [bound with *Octo viae* (1611)]

6. *L'image de vertu demonstrant la perfection et saincte vie de la bienheuree vierge Marie, mere de dieu, par les escriptures, tant de l'ancien que du nouveau Testament.*

--1540. Paris, Pierre Vidoue, 432 fol.
    Orléans, BM—H6573
    Versailes, BM—Pératé B 34
--1540. Paris, Jérôme de Gourmont, 416 fol.
    Aix-en-Provence, BMJ—8° 844
--n.d. Paris, Jean Ruelle, 333 fol. [frontispiece says third edition; dedication to Catherine de
        Sarrebruche]
    Aix-en-Provence, BMJ—In. 8° 8276
    Paris, BS—443 E-34
    Troyes, BM—K.13.6917
--1549. Paris, Jean de Brouilly, 334 fol.
    London, BL—C.46.b.1
    Orléans, BM—H6574
--1559. Paris, Gabriel Buon, 508 fol.
    Paris, BA—8° T 7487
--1582. Lyon, Benoît Rigaud, (see BR, p. 140)
--1588. Paris, Nicolas Bonfons. 408 fol.
    Paris, BA—8° T 7488
    Paris, BNF—Inv. D 32767

7. *La deploration de la vie humaine, avec la disposition à dignement recevoir le S. Sacrement, & mourir en bon catholique.*

--1541. Paris, Nicolas Barbou, 244 fol.
    Orléans, BM—H6575
    Paris, BSG—D 8° 6428(2) Rés. Inv. 8142
--1543. Paris, Jean de Brouilly, 264 fol. [bound with *Sermon funebre, faict es exeques de feu
        messire Philippes Chabot grand Admiral de France*]
    Paris, BNF—Rés. 16-Ln27-71348
    Wolfenbüttel, HAB—1325.2 Theol.
--1548. Paris, Guillaume Thibout, [bound with *Sermon funebre*]
    Wolfenbüttel, HAB—1329.19 Theol.
--1554. Paris, Jean Ruelle, 192 fol. [bound with *Sermon funebre*]
    Paris, BNF—Rés. D 32764
--1556. Paris, Etienne Groulleau, (see BR, p. 140)
--1561. Paris, Jean Ruelle, (see BR, p. 140)

8. *L'arbre de vie appuyant les beaux lys de France, ou sont mis en lumiere les haults titres d'honneur de la croix de nostre redempteur Jesus.*

--1542. Paris, Guillaume de Bossozel, 159 fol.
    London, BL—4400.ff.53
    Marseille, BM—62753
    Munich, BSB—P.O. gall. 340/1
    Paris, BA—8° T 7415
    Paris, BNF—Rés. D 80253

9. *La caeleste pensée de graces divines arrousée ou sont declairez les sept dons du sainct esprit & la maniere de les demander à Dieu.*
 --1543. Paris, Adam Saulnier, 167 fol. [includes *La devise d'un cueur en pierre de vertu*]
   Amiens, BM—Les 1752 A
   Bordeaux, BM—T 7106
   London, BL—C.186.a.25
 --1546. Paris, Adam Saulnier, (see BR, p. 140)
 --1556. Paris, Jean Ruelle, (see Brunet, *Manuel*, II, p. 819)

10. *Paradoxa Fratris Petri Aurati, doctoris theologi, ordinis prædicatorii, ad profligandas hæreses, ex divi Pauli apostoli epistolis selecta, ineluctabilibusque sanctorum patrum firmata testimoniis.*
 --1543. Paris, Jean de Brouilly, 396 fol. [bound with *Ad philosophiae christianae candidatos, in parisiensi caenobio, exhortatio*]
   Amiens, BM—Th 6471 A
   Bordeaux—BM T 7517
   Cambridge, CUL—D*.14.10 (F)
   Le Mans, MLA—Th. 8° 4836
   Paris, BNF—Inv. D 32772
   Paris, BSG—D 8° 4193 Inv. 5221 ter FA
   Paris, IC—117 958
   Toulouse, CSTA—260 A DOR

11. *La meditation devote du bon Chrestien sus le sainct sacrifice de la Messe. Avec les hymnes de l'office du sainct sacrement translates. Et plusieurs aultres petis traictes tressalutaires.*
 --1544. Paris, René Avril, 128 fol. [bound with *Dyalogue instructoire des chrestiens*]
   Paris, BSG—D 8° 6197(1) Inv. 7892 bis FA

12. *Le livre des divins benefices, enseignant la maniere de les recongnoistre, avec l'information de bien vivre, et la consolation des affligez selon qu'il est comprins au psalme 33 de David, qui se commence, Benedicam dominum. Avec la consolation evangelique, pour les vivans & trespassez.*
 --1544. Paris, Jean Ruelle, 151 fol.
   Amiens, BM—Th 5340 A
   Le Mans, MLA—Th. 8° 4532
   Paris, BNF—Inv. D 86037

13. *Le cerf spirituel, exprimant le sainct desir de l'ame, d'estre avec son Dieu, selon qu'il est insinué au Psalme de David 41, qui se commence, Quemadmodum desiderat ceruus.*
 --1544. Paris, Jean Ruelle, [bound with *L'adresse de l'esgaré pescheur*]
   Wolfenbüttel, HAB—Yv 1492.8° Helmst
 --n.d. Paris, Jean Ruelle, 88 fol.
   Paris, BA—8° T 6943
   Paris, BA—8° T 6959
   Rouen, BM—Leber 334

14. *L'adresse de l'esgaré pescheur, contenant l'exposition du psaume penitentiel, Miserere mei Deus.*
 --1544. Paris, Jean Ruelle, [bound with *Le cerf spirituel*]
   Wolfenbüttel, HAB—Yv 1492.8° Helmst
 --1549. Paris, Jean Ruelle (see Higman, *Piety*, p. 177)

15. *La croix de penitence, enseignant la forme de soyconfesser, avec le cry du penitent, contenu au psalme penitentiel de Dauid, qui se commence, De profundis clamaui.*
 --1545. Paris, Mathurin Du Puys (see Higman, *Piety*, p. 182)
 --1548. Paris, Jean Ruelle (see Higman, *Piety*, p. 182)
 --1563. Paris, Jean Ruelle, 120 fol.
   Yale, BRBL—Mc45, D730, C87

16. *Le pasturage de la brebis humaine, selon que l'enseigne le Royal prophete David au vingtdeuxiesme Psalme.*
    --1546. Paris, Jean de Brouilly, 104 fol. [bound with *Anatomie, et mystique description de members & parties*]
        Aix-en-Provence, BMJ—C. 8976
    --1554. Paris, Jean Ruelle (see BR, p. 141)

17. *Anatomie, et mystique description de membres & parties de nostre saulveur Jesuschrist.*
    --1546. Paris, Jean de Brouilly, 92 fol. [bound with *Le pasturage de la brebis humaine*]
        Aix-en-Provence, BMJ—C. 8976
    --1554. Paris, Jean Ruelle (see BR, p. 141)

18. *La premiere partie des collations royales, contenant l'exposition de deux psalmes Davidiques, c'est a scavoir du 24 & 26. En l'ung, le chevalier errant cherche son bon chemin: en l'autre, le chevalier hardy, suyt la lumiere, qui le conduyt.*
    --1546. Paris, René Avril, 428 pp.
        Paris, BA—8° T 869
        Paris, BS—XVI V DOR 3 (1)
        Troyes, BM—K.15.7287
    --1546. Paris, René Avril, 428 pp. [bound with *La seconde partie des collations* and a letter of Doré to Pope Paul III, April 1546]
        Amiens, BM—Th 603 A
        Paris, BNF—Inv. A 6838

19. *La seconde partie des collations royales, contenant le trespas du roy des chevaliers chrestiens, mort au lict d'honneur, en la croix: selon que David l'enseigne, au psalme 21. Avec ung nouvel office, de la desponsation de la B. vierge Marie.*
    --1546. Paris, René Avril, 273 pp. [bound with *Officium in festo desponsationis beatae Mariae virginis* and letter of Doré to Pope Paul III]
        Paris, BS—XVI V DOR 3 (2)
    --1546. Paris, René Avril, 273 pp. [bound with *La premiere partie des collations, Officium* and letter of Doré to Pope Paul III, April 1546]
        Amiens, BM—Th 603 A
        Paris, BNF—Inv. A 6838

20. *La passe-solitaire à tous amateurs de Dieu, & vie spirituelle, ou contemplative, donnée pour instruction. Avec l'exposition du psalme Davidique 123, qui se commence, Nisi quia dominus erat in nobis.*
    --1547. Paris, Jean de Brouilly, 126 fol. [also contains *Sermon de Sainct Cecile Cyprian, intitulé de Mortalité. Enseignant comment on ne craindra la Mort*]
        Amiens, BM—Les 1772 A
        Paris, BA—8° T 6957
        Washington, FSL—166-860q
    --1549. Paris (see BR, p. 141)

21. *La conserve de grace requise par le prophete David au psaume XV, Conserva me Domine: Avec un doux chant consolatif de l'ame fidele extrait de l'escripture sainte.*
    --1548. Paris, Guillaume Cavellat (see BR, p. 141)

22. *Les triomphes du roy sans pair, avec l'excellence de l'Eglise, son espouse, et leur noble lignage, selon que David l'enseigne au Psalme XLIV.*
    --1548. Paris, Jean de Brouilly (see BR, p. 141)

23. *Les cantiques, dechantees à l'entrée du Treschrestien Roy Henry second de ce nom, & de la royne de France en la ville de Paris, & le jour de la procession celebre, faicte par eulx en ladicte ville.*
    --1548. Paris, Jean Ruelle (see Brunet, *Manuel*, II, p. 820)
        This must be an error because the procession occurred in 1549!
    --1549. Paris, Jean Ruelle, 44 fol.
        Versailles, BM—Goujet in-12 U 1
        Washington, LC—PQ 1628 .L24A67

24. *L'arche de l'alliance nouvelle, et testament de nostre Saulveur Jesus Christ, contenant la manne de son precieux corps, contre tous sacramentaires heretiques.*
--1549. Paris, Benoît Prevost. 233 fol.
Ghent, BUG—Theol. 1697
Marseille, BM—63552
Paris, BNF—Inv. D 21877
--1556. Paris, Jean Ruelle. 233 fol.
Le Mans, MLA—Th. 8° 3448
Orléans, BM—H6576

25. *Le Nouveau Testament d'amour de nostre pere Jesuchrist, signé de son sang. Autrement son dernier sermon, faict apres la cene, avec sa passion, ou sont confutées plusieurs heresies.*
--1550. Paris, Jean Ruelle, 328 fol.
Munich, BSB—Asc. 1488
Toulouse, BM—Rés. D XVI 1156
--1557. Paris, Jean Ruelle, 327 fol.
Neuchâtel, BPU --NP ZQ 889
Orléans, BM—H6577
Paris, BNF—Rés. D 32768
Paris, BSG—A 8° 757 Rés. Inv. 908
--1585. Manuscript, Flemish translation of 1550 edition, 316 fol.
Paris, BA—ms 8227

26. *La piscine de patience, avec le miroir de patience, veu & corrigé par le mesme autheur.*
--1550. Paris, Benoît Prevost et Jean Ruelle, 78 fol.
Paris, BA—8° T 6959

27. *Oraison panegyrique pleine de consolation, pour hault et puissant prince, Claude de Lorraine, Duc de Guyse, per de France, decedé ceste presente année, 1550.*
--1550. Paris, Jean de Brouilly, 128 fol. [bound with *La douce musique Davidique, ouye au cantique 125, qui se commence, In convertendo dominus* and with *Un remede salutaire contre les scrupules de conscience*]
Châlons-en-Champagne, BM—AF 17856
Le Mans, MLA—B.L. 8° 1098
Nancy, BM—Rés. 11.218; Rés. 10.956
Paris, BA—8° BL 3258
Paris, BNF—Rés. Ln27. 9400

28. *Anti-Calvin, contenant deux defenses catholiques de la verité du sainct Sacrement, & digne sacrifice de l'Autel, contre certains faulx escrits, sortiz de la boutique des Sacramentaires, Calvinistes, Heretiques: mis au vent, & semez par certains lieux de ce Royaume, au scandale des fideles et pusilles. Avec un traicté de nature et grace, fait par maniere de dialogue, pour appaiser la conscience paoureuse à la mort.*
--1551. Paris, publisher unknown, (see BR, p. 142)
--1568. Paris, Sébastien Nivelle, 93 fol.
Geneva, BPU—Bc 3515

29. *Observance de religion chrestienne, contenant l'exposé du Psalme XXXVIII.*
--1554. Reims, Nicolas Bacquenois (see BR, p. 142)
--1556. Reims, Nicolas Bacquenois (see BR, p. 142)

30. *Dialogue de la justification chrestienne entre nostre saulveur Jesus & la Samaritaine.*
--1554. Paris, Jean Ruelle, 56 fol.
Paris, BA—8° T 6959
Paris, BNF—Rés. D 32765
Rouen, BM—Leber 331

31. *Adunatio praecipuarum materiarum sparsim contentarum in diversis locis epistolarum divi Pauli.*
--1555. Paris, Vincent Sertenas, (see QE, II, p. 204)
--1557. Paris, Antoine Bonnemere, (see QE, II, p. 204)

32. *La vie & la mort chrestiennes, des epistres de S. Paul, extraicte.*
--1556. Reims, Nicolas Bacquenois, 445 pp.
Troyes, BM—H.12.4699

33. *Le livre de la victoire de toutes tribulations: traduict de Latin en Francoys par F. P. Doré docteur en theologie.*
- --1556. Paris, Jean Ruelle, 71 fol.
  - Paris, BNF—Rés. D 80389
  - Paris, BSG—D 8° 11.170(2) Rés.
- --1557. Antwerp, Christophe Plantin, 71 pp.
  - Brussels, BRA—II 19633 A
- --1558. Reims, Nicolas Bacquenois (see BR, p. 142)
- --1558. Paris, Sébastien Nivelle (see BR, p. 142)
- --1558. Antwerp (see BR, p. 142)

34. *La tourtrelle de viduité enseignant les vefves comment elles doivent vivre en leur estat, & consolant en leurs adversitez, aussi les orphelins.*
- --1557. Reims, Nicolas Bacquenois, 212 pp.
  - Rouen, BM—Leber 333
- --1574. Paris, veuve de Jean Ruelle, 83 fol.
  - Washington, FSL—BV4908 D6 1547 Cage
- --1605. Arras, Guillaume de la Rivière, 186 pp.
  - Cambridge, HOU—FC5 D7302 557tc
- --1605. Arras, Guillaume de la Rivière, 174 fol.
  - Amiens, BM—Les 5153

35. *Le second livre des divins benefices, declarant les grandes misericordes de Dieu, ou est contenue l'enarration du doux psalme davidique 102, qui se commence Benedic anima mea domino.*
- --1569. Paris, Jean Ruelle, 216 fol.
  - Paris, BS—443 E-32

Unpublished works

1. *La fin du bon catholique monstrant comme on luy doibt ayder a la mort.*
- n.d.   Paris, BSG—Ms 2875

Addendum

1. *Les soupirs de l'ame fidele.*
- n.d.   Paris (see QE, II, p. 205)

2. *L'esperance assurée.*
- n.d.   Paris (see QE, II, p. 205)

3. *L'oraison du profete David extraite du psalme LXXXVI.*
- n.d.   (see QE, II, p. 205)

4. *Oeuvres de penitence.*
- n.d.   (see QE, II, p. 205)

APPENDIX 3

Editions of Doré's Works Arranged according to Library

Aix-en-Provence, Bibliothèque Méjanes
Dyalogue instructoire des chrestiens
   --1538. Lyon, Pierre de Saincte Lucie.   C. 2196
Le pasturage de la brebis humaine
   --1546. Paris, Jean de Brouilly.   C. 8976
Les allumettes du feu divin
   --1538. Paris, François Regnault.   Rés. D. 89
   --n.d.   Lyon, Pierre de Saincte Lucie.   Rés. D. 324
Les voyes de paradis
   --1538. Paris, François Regnault   Rés. D. 89
L'image de vertu
   --1540. Paris, Jérôme de Gourmont.   In. 8° 8448
   --n.d.   Paris, Jean Ruelle.   In. 8° 8276

Amiens, Bibliothèque Municipale
La caeleste pensée
   --1543. Paris, Jean André.   Les 1752 A
La passe solitaire
   --1547. Paris, Jean de Brouilly.   Les 1772 A
La premiere partie des collations royales
   --1546. Paris, Jean Ruelle.   Th 603 A
La seconde partie des collations royales
   --1546. Paris, Jean Ruelle.   Th 603 A
La tourtrelle de viduité
   --1605. Arras, Guillaume de la Rivière.   Les 5153 A
Le livre des divins benefices
   --1544. Paris, Jean Ruelle.   Th 5340 A
Les allumettes du feu divin
   --n.d.   Paris, Etienne Caveiller.   Res 144 A
   --n.d.   Paris, Jean Ruelle.   M 3468
   --n.d.   Lyon, Pierre de Saincte Lucie.   Les 1743 A
   --1610. Rouen, Romain de Beauvais.   Les 1742 A
Les voyes de paradis
   --n.d.   Paris, Jean Ruelle.   M 3468
   --1538. no place or publisher given.   Rés. 143 A
   --1610. Rouen, Romain de Beauvais.   Les 1742 A
Paradoxa...ad profligandas haereses
   --1543. Paris, Jean de Brouilly.   Th 6471 A

Ann Arbor, University of Michigan Library
Dyalogue instructoire des chrestiens
   --1539. Paris, Antoine Bonnemere.   BV 4833 .D68
Le college de sapience
   --1539. Paris, Antoine Bonnemere.   BV 4833 .D68

Bordeaux, Bibliothèque Municipale
La caeleste pensée
  --1543. Paris, Adam Saulnier.   T 7106
Paradoxa...ad profligandas haereses
  --1543. Paris, Jean de Brouilly.   T 7517

Brussels, Bibliothèque Royale Albert Ier
Le college de sapience
  --1556. Antwerp, S. Cock.   II 66277 A
    (Flemish ed., *De collegie der wijsheyt*)
  --1610. Cologne, Buchardus Kuickius.   VI 5257 A
    (Latin ed., *Collegium sapientiae*)
Le livre de la victoire
  --1557. Antwerp, Christophe Plantin.   II 19633 A
Les allumettes du feu divin
  --1538. Paris, Etienne Caveiller.   LP 481 A
Les voyes de paradis
  --1538. Paris, Etienne Caveiller.   LP 481 A
  --1611. Cologne, Buchardus Kuickius.   VI 5257 A 2
    (Latin ed., *Octo viae ad caelum*)

Cambridge (England), Cambridge University Library
Le college de sapience
  --1610. Cologne, Buchardus Kuickius.   E*.13.37 (G)
    (Latin ed., *Collegium sapientiae*)
Les allumettes du feu divin
  --1611. Cologne, Conradus Butgenius.   Ely.e.92 (3)
    (Latin ed., *Scintillae divini amoris*)
Les voyes de paradis
  --1611. Cologne, Buchardus Kuickius.   Ely.e.92 (1)
    (Latin ed., *Octo viae caelum*)
Paradoxa...ad profligandas haereses
  --1543. Paris, Jean de Brouilly.   D*.14.10 (F)

Cambridge (Massachusetts), Houghton Library (Harvard University)
La tourtrelle de viduité
  --1605. Arras, Guillaume de la Rivière.   F65 D7302 557tc

Châlons-en-Champagne, Bibliothèque Municipale
Les allumettes du feu divin
  --1538. Paris, François Regnault.   Rés. Ch. 678
Les voyes de paradis
  --1538. Paris, François Regnault.   Rés. Ch. 678
Oraison panegyrique
  --1550. Paris, Jean de Brouilly.   AF 17856

Chicago, Center for Research Libraries
Le college de sapience
 --1556. Thantwerpen, S. Cock.   microfilm
  (Flemish ed., *De collegie der wijsheyt*)

Dijon, Bibliothèque Municipale
Les allumettes du feu divin
 --1586. Lyon, Jean Pillehotte.   584
Les voyes de paradis
 --1586. Lyon, Jean Pillehotte.   584

Edinburgh, University of Edinburgh Library
Les allumettes du feu divin
 --1539. Paris, Etienne Caveiller.   De.2.2
Les voyes de paradis
 --1538. Paris, Etienne Caveiller.   De.2.2

Estavayer-le-Lac (Switzerland), Monastère des Dominicaines
Les allumettes du feu divin
 --1605. Lyon, Pierre Rigaud.   Dd 16
Les voyes de paradis
 --1605. Lyon, Pierre Rigaud.   Dd 16

Geneva, Bibliothèque Publique et Universitaire
Anti-Calvin
 --1568. Paris, Sébastien Nivelle.   Bc 3515

Ghent, Bibliothèque de l'Université de Gand
Le college de sapience
 --1610. Cologne, Buchardus Kuikius.   Theol. 3677
  (Latin ed., *Collegium sapientiae*)
L'arche de l'alliance nouvelle
 --1549. Paris, Benoît Prevost.   Theol. 1697
Les allumettes du feu divin
 --1540. Paris, Antoine Bonnemere.   Rés. 994
Les voyes de paradis
 --1540. Paris, Antoine Bonnemere.   Rés. 994
 --1611. Cologne, Buchardus Kuickius.   Theol. 3677(1)
  (Latin ed., *Octo viae caelum*)

Le Mans, Médiathèque Louis Aragon
L'arche de l'alliance nouvelle
 --1556. Paris, Jean Ruelle.   Th. 8° 3448
Le livre des divins benefices
 --1544. Paris, Jean Ruelle.   Th. 8° 4532
Les allumettes du feu divin
 --1540. Paris, Antoine Bonnemere.   Th. 8° 4585

LeMans (cont.)
   Les voyes de paradis
      --1540. Paris, Antoine Bonnemere.   Th. 8° 4585
   Paradoxa...ad profligandas haereses
      --1543. Paris, Jean de Brouilly.   Th. 8° 4836
   Oraison panegyrique
      --1550. Paris, Jean de Brouilly.   B.L. 8° 1098

London, British Library
   Dyalogue instructoire des chrestiens
      --1539. Paris, Antoine Bonnemere.   1360.f.8
   La caeleste pensée
      --1543. Adam Saulnier.   C.186.a.25
   L'arbre de vie
      --1542. Paris, Guillaume de Bossozel.   4400.ff.53
   Le college de sapience
      --1539. Paris, Antoine Bonnemere.   1360.f.8
   Les allumettes du feu divin
      --1538. Paris, Etienne Caveiller.   1360.b.7
   Les voyes de paradis
      --1538. Paris, Etienne Caveiller.   1360.b.7
   L'image de vertu
      --1549. Paris, Jean de Brouilly.   C.46.b.1

Lyon, Bibliothèque Municipale
   Dyalogue instructoire des chrestiens
      --1539. Paris, Antoine Bonnemere.   318 281
   Le college de sapience
      --1539. Paris, Antoine Bonnemere.   318 281
   Les allumettes du feu divin
      --1540. Paris, Antoine Bonnemere.   Rés. 321 726
      --1586. Lyon, Jean Pillehotte.   813 433
   Les voyes de paradis
      --1540. Paris, Antoine Bonnemere.   Rés. 321 726
      --1586. Lyon, Jean Pillehotte.   813 433

Marseille, Bibliothèque Municipale
   L'arbre de vie
      --1542. Paris, Guillaume de Bossozel.   62753
   L'arche de l'alliance nouvelle
      --1549. Paris, Benoît Prevost.   63552

Munich, Bayerische Staats Bibliothek*
   L'arbre de vie
      --1542. Paris, Guillaume de Bossozel.   P.O. gall. 340/1
   Le nouveau testament d'amour
      --1550. Paris, Jean Ruelle.   Asc. 1488

Nancy, Bibliothèque Municipale
   Les allumettes du feu divin
      --1538. Paris, François Regnault.   Rés. 11.282
   Les voyes de paradis
      --1538. Paris, François Regnault.   Rés. 11.282
   Oraison panegyrique
      --1550. Paris, Jean de Brouilly.   Rés. 11.218; Rés. 10.956
        (two copies)

Neuchâtel, Bibliothèque Publique et Universitaire
   Le nouveau testament d'amour
      --1557. Paris, Jean Ruelle.   NP ZQ 889

New Haven, Connecticut, Beinecke Rare Book Library (Yale)
   La croix de penitence
      --1563. Paris, Jean Ruelle.   Me45, D730, C87

Notre Dame, Indiana, Theodore Hesburgh Library (University of Notre Dame)
   Les allumettes du feu divin
      --1538. Paris, Etienne Caveiller.   BX 890 D695
   Les voyes de paradis
      --1538. Paris, Etienne Caveiller.   BX 890 D695

Orléans, Bibliothèque Municipale
   Dyalogue instructoire des chrestiens
      --1544. Paris, Denis Janot.   H6572.3
   La deploration de la vie humaine
      --1541. Paris, Nicolas Barbou.   H6575
   L'arche de l'alliance
      --1556. Paris, Jean Ruelle.   H6576
   Le nouveau testament d'amour
      --1557. Paris, Jean Ruelle.   H6577
   Les allumettes du feu divin
      --1538. Paris, François Regnault.   H6572.1
   Les voyes de paradis
      --1538. Paris, François Regnault.   H6572.2
   L'image de vertu
      --1540. Paris, Pierre Vidoue.   H6573
      --1549. Paris, Jean de Brouilly.   H6574

Paris, Bibliothèque de l'Arsenal
   Dialogue de la justification chrestienne
      --1554. Paris, Jean Ruelle.   8° T 6959
   Dyalogue instructoire des chrestiens
      --1539. Paris, Antoine Bonnemere   8° T 6955
   L'arbre de vie
      --1542. Paris, Guillaume de Bossozel.   8° T 7415

Paris, l'Arsenal (cont.)
 La passe-solitaire
  --1547. Paris, Jean de Brouilly.   8° T 6957
 La piscine de patience
  --1550. Paris, Benoît Prevost et Jean Ruelle.   8° T 6959
 La premiere partie des collations royales
  --1546. Paris, René Avril.   8° T 869
 Le cerf spirituel
  --n.d. Paris, Jean Ruelle.   8° T 6943
  --n.d. Paris, Jean Ruelle.   8° T 6959
 Le college de sapience
  --1539. Paris, Antoine Bonnemere.   8° T 6955
  --frontispiece missing.   8° T 6956
 Le nouveau testament d'amour
  --1585. Manuscript—Flemish translation.   ms 8227
 Les allumettes du feu divin
  --1538. Paris, François Regnault.   8° T 7367
  --1575. Paris, veuve de Jean Ruelle.[388]   8° T 7368
 Les voyes de paradis
  --1538. Paris, François Regnault.   8° T 7367
  --1575. Paris, veuve de Jean Ruelle.   8° T 7368
 L'image de vertu
  --1559. Paris, Gabriel Buon.   8° T 7487
  --1588. Paris, Nicolas Bonfons.   8° T 7488
 Oraison panegyrique
  --1550. Paris, Jean de Brouilly.   8° BL 3258

Paris, Bibliothèque Mazarine
 Dyalogue instructoire des chrestiens
  --1539. Paris, Antoine Bonnemere   49405
 Le college de sapience
  --1539. Paris, Antoine Bonnemere.   49405
 Les allumettes du feu divin
  --1540. Paris, Antoine Bonnemere.   49269
  --n.d. Lyon, Pierre de Saincte Lucie.   12580
 Les voyes de paradis
  --1540. Paris, Antoine Bonnemere.   49269

Paris, Bibliothèque Nationale de France
 Dialogue de la justification chrestienne
  --1554. Paris, Jean Ruelle.   Rés. D 32765

---

[388] Geneviève Boisset (from 1571-1613). See Philippe Renouard, *Les marques typographiques Parisiennes des XVe et XVIe siècles* (Paris: Librairie Ancienne Honoré Champion, 1926), p. 330.

Paris, Nationale (cont.)
Dyalogue instructoire des chrestiens
--1538. Paris, Jean Ruelle.   Rés. D 32766 (microfilm m 8989)
--1539. Paris, Antoine Bonnemere.   Rés. R 2045
--1542. Paris, Denis Janot.   Rés. D 13571
L'arbre de vie
--1542. Paris, Guillaume de Bossozel.   Rés. D 80253
L'arche de l'alliance nouvelle
--1549. Paris, Benoît Prevost.   Inv. D 21877
La deploration de la vie humaine
--1543. Paris, Jean de Brouilly.   Rés. 16-Ln27-71348
--1554. Paris, Jean Ruelle.   Rés. D 32764
La premiere partie des collations royales
--1546. Paris, René Avril.   Inv. A 6838
La seconde partie des collations royales
--1546. Paris, René Avril.   Inv. A 6838
Le college de sapience
--1539. Paris, Antoine Bonnemere.   Rés. R 2044
Le livre de la victoire
--1556. Paris, Jean Ruelle.   Rés. D 80389
Le livre des divins benefices
--1544. Paris, Jean Ruelle.   Inv. D 86037
Le nouveau testament d'amour
--1557. Paris, Jean Ruelle.   Rés. D 32768
Les allumettes du feu divin
--n.d.   Paris, Etienne Caveiller.   Rés. 8-Z Don-594(458)
--1540. Paris, Antoine Bonnemere.   Rés. D 32762
--1575. Paris, veuve de Jean Ruelle.   Rés. D 32763
--1610. Rouen, Romain de Beauvais.   Inv. D 17410
--1611. Cologne, Conradus Butgenius.   Inv. D 32773
    (Latin ed., *Scintillae divini amoris*)
Les voyes de paradis
--1540. Paris, Antoine Bonnemere.   Rés. D 32762
--1575. Paris, veuve de Jean Ruelle.   Rés. D 32763
--1610. Rouen, Romain de Beauvais.   Inv. D 17410
L'image de vertu
--date illegible. Paris, Nicolas Bonfons.   Inv. D 32767
    (most probably 1588; see BA—8° T 7488)
Oraison panegyrique
--1550. Paris, Jean de Brouilly.   Rés. Ln27.9400
Paradoxa...ad profligandas haereses
--1543. Paris, Jean de Brouilly.   Inv. D 32772

Paris, Bibliothèque Sainte-Geneviève
Dyalogue instructoire des chrestiens
--1544. Paris, René Avril.   D 8° 6197(2) Inv. 7892 bis FA

La deploration de la vie humaine
--1541. Paris, Nicolas Barbou.   D 8° 6428(2) Rés. Inv. 8142

Paris, Sainte-Geneviève (cont.)
La fin du bon catholique
   --n.d.   Manuscript.   Ms 2875
La meditation devote du bon Chrestien
   --1544. Paris, Jean Ruelle.   D 8° 6197(1) Inv. 7892 bis FA
Le college de sapience
   --1610. Cologne, Buchardus Kuickius.   D 8° 6126 Inv. 7802(1) FA
       (Latin ed., *Collegium sapientiae*)
Le livre de la victoire de toutes tribulations
   --1556. Paris, Jean Ruelle.   D 8° 11.170(2) Rés.
Le nouveau teastament d'amour
   --1557. Paris, Jean Ruelle.   A 8° 757 Rés. Inv. 908
Les allumettes du feu divin
   --1539. Paris, Etienne Caveiller.   D 8° 6199(2) Rés. Inv. 7898
Les voyes de paradis
   --1538. Paris, Etienne Caveiller.   D 8° 6199(2) Rés. Inv. 7898
   --1611. Cologne, Buchardus Kuickius.   D 8° 6126 Inv. 7802(1) FA
       (Latin ed., *Octo viae caelum*)
Paradoxa...ad profligandas haereses
   --1543. Paris, Jean de Brouilly.   D 8° 4193 Inv. 5221 ter FA

Paris, Bibliothèque du Saulchoir
La premiere partie des collations royales
   --1546. Paris, René Avril.   XVI V DOR 3 (1)
La seconde partie des collations royales
   --1546. Paris, René Avril.   XVI V DOR 3 (2)
Le college de sapience
   --n.d.   Paris, Etienne Groulleau.   XVI V DOR 1
   --1546. Paris, Pierre Sergent.   XVI V DOR 2
Le second livre des divins benefices
   --1569. Paris, Jean Ruelle.   443 E-32
Les allumettes du feu divin
   --1610. Rouen, Romain de Beauvais.   443 E-38
Les voyes de paradis
   --1610. Rouen, Romain de Beauvais.   443 E-38
L'image de vertu
   --n.d.   Paris, Jean Ruelle.   443 E-34

Paris, Institut Catholique
Paradoxa...ad profligandas haereses
   --1543. Paris, Jean de Brouilly.   117 958

Rouen, Bibliothèque Municipale
Dialogue de la justification chrestienne
    --1554. Paris, Jean Ruelle.   Leber 331
La tourtrelle de viduite
    --1557. Reims, Nicolas Bacquenois.   Leber 333
Le cerf spirituel
    --n.d.   Paris, Jean Ruelle.   Leber 334
Le college de sapience
    --1555. Paris, Jean Ruelle.   Leber 332
Les allumettes du feu divin
    --1548. Paris, Guillaume Thibout.   Dieusy p 594
    --1610. Rouen, Romain de Beauvais.   Leber 335
Les voyes de paradis
    --1548. Paris, Guillaume Thibout.   Dieusy p 594
    --1610. Rouen, Romain de Beauvais.   Leber 335

Toulouse, Bibliothèque du Couvent Saint-Thomas d'Aquin
Paradoxa...ad profligandas haereses
    --1543. (frontispiece missing)   260 A DOR

Toulouse, Bibliothèque Municipale
Le nouveau testament d'amour
    --1550. Paris, Jean Ruelle.   Rés. D XVI 1156

Troyes, Bibliothèque Municipale
La premiere partie des collations royales
    --1546. Paris, René Avril.   K.15.7287
La vie et la mort chrestiennes
    --1556. Reims, Nicolas Bacquenois.   H.12.4699
Le college de sapience
    --1546. Paris, Pierre Sergent.   G.17.4625
Les allumettes du feu divin
    --frontispiece missing   G.16.4525
      (probably 1538. Paris, François Regnault)
Les voyes de paradis
    --1538. Paris, François Regnault.   G.16.4525
L'image de vertu
    --frontispiece missing.   K.13.6917

Versailles, Bibliothèque Municipale
Dyalogue instructoire des chrestiens
    --1539. Paris, Antoine Bonnemere.   Fonds A 8° O 46 d
    --1545. Paris, Guillaume Thibout.   Pératé A 42
Le college de sapience
    --1539. Paris, Antoine Bonnemere.   Fonds A 8° O 46 d
L'image de vertu
    --1540. Paris, Pierre Vidoue.   Pératé B 34
Les cantiques dechantees
    --1549. Paris, Jean Ruelle.   Goujet in-12 U 1

Washington, District of Columbia, Folger Shakespeare Library
    La passe solitaire
        --1547. Paris, Jean de Brouilly.   166-860q
    La tourtrelle de viduite
        --1574. Paris, veuve de Jean Ruelle.   BV4908 D6 1574 Cage

Washington, District of Columbia, Library of Congress
    Dyalogue instructoire des chrestiens
        --1545. Paris, Guillaume Thibout.   BV4833, D6
    Les cantiques dechantees
        --1549. Paris, Jean Ruelle.   PQ 1628 .L24A67

Wolfenbüttel, Herzog-August-Bibliothek*
    Dyalogue instructoire des chrestiens
        --1539. Paris, Antoine Bonnemere.   1028.19 Theol.
    La deploration de la vie humaine
        --1543. Paris, Jean de Brouilly.   1325.2 Theol.
        --1548. Paris, Guillaume Thibout.   1329.19 Theol.
    Le cerf spirituel
        --1544. Paris, Jean Ruelle.   Yv 1492.8° Helmst
    Le college de sapience
        --1539. Paris, Antoine Bonnemere.   1028.19 Theol.

*I am indebted to Higman's *Piety and the People* for the information on the Munich and Wolfenbüttel libraries.

APPENDIX 4

List of Dedications

Les voyes de paradis	Françoise de Bouchet, countess of Montfort
Les allumettes du feu	an unnamed religious of the monastery of Poissy
Dyalogue instructoire	all true Christians
Le college de sapience	a humble widow of Blois
L'image de vertu	the reader (first two editions) Catherine de Sarrebruche, Countess of Rossy (later editions)
La deploration de la vie	Louise de Bourbon, Abbess of Fontevraulx
L'arbre de vie	King Francis I
La caeleste pensée	Princess Marguerite, daughter of Francis I
Paradoxa...ad profligandas	François Cardinal de Tournon
La meditation devote	Pierre Lambert, Dominican of the priory at Blois
Le livre des divins benefices	a devout Parisian noblewoman
Le cerf spirituel	Renée de Lorraine, daughter of Claude de Lorraine and Abbess of monastery of S. Pierre at Reims
L'adresse de l'esgaré pescheur	
La croix de penitence	Doré's only sister, Marguerite
Le pasturage de la brebis	spiritual daughter and disciple living in Paris (same woman as *Le livre des divins benefices*)
Anatomie et mystique description	same woman as *Le livre des divins benefices*
La premiere partie des collations	Claude de Lorraine, Duke of Guise
La seconde partie des collations	Antoinette de Bourbon, Duchess of Guise
La passe solitaire	Charlotte de Genly, religious
Les cantiques dechantees	
La conserve de grace	

Les triomphes du roy	
L'arche de l'alliance	King Henry II
Le nouveau testament d'amour	Queen Catherine de Medici, wife of Henry II
La piscine de patience	Antoinette de Bourbon, Duchess of Guise
Oraison panegyrique	Antoinette de Bourbon, Duchess of Guise
Anti-Calvin	none
L'observance de religion	
Dialogue de la justification	the Christian reader
Adunatio praecipuarum	
La vie et la mort chrestiennes	Antoinette de Bourbon, Duchess of Guise
Le livre de la victoire	Renée de Lorraine (this dedication is made by the editor, Nicolas Bacquenois of Reims)
La tourtrelle de viduité	none
Le second livre des divins benefices	all faithful readers

BIBLIOGRAPHY

Manuscript Sources

Archivio Generale Ordinis Praedicatorum, Rome.
    IV. 25.   Registrum litterarum et actorum fr. Augustini Recuperati, Procuratoris et Vic. Gen. Ordinis, deinde Mag. Gen. O.P., pro annis 1538-40, raro 1541.

    IV. 30.   Registrum litterarum et actorum fr. Francisci Romei de Castiglione, Mag. Gen. O.P. 1550 Sept. 1 - 1552 Jul. 15.

Bibliothèque Nationale de France, Paris.
    N Acq Fr 6537, fol. 279

Primary Sources

Aquinas, Thomas. *Scriptum Super Libro Sententiarum.* Edited by P. Mandonnet. Paris: P. Lethielleux, 1929.

_____. *Summa Theologiae.* Edited by Blackfriars. New York: McGraw-Hill Book Company, 1969.

Backus, Irena and Claire Chimelli, eds. *La Vraie Piété: Divers traités de Jean Calvin et Confession de foi de Guillaume Farel.* Geneva: Labor et Fides, 1986.

Calvin, John. *Institutes of the Christian Religion*, vol. 1-2. Edited by John T. McNeill. Philadelphia: The Westminster Press, 1967.

_____. *Institution de la religion chrestienne.* Critical edition by J.-D. Benoît. Paris: Librairie Philosophique J. Vrin, 1957.

Coyecque, Ernest, ed. *Recueil d'actes notariés relatifs à l'histoire de Paris et de ses environs au XVIe siècle*, vol. 1. Paris: Imprimerie Nationale, 1905.

D. Martin Luthers Werke, Kritische Gesamtausgabe. Weimar: Hermann Böhlaus Nachfolger, 1883.

Denzinger, Heinrich. *Enchiridion symbolorum definitionum et declarationum de rebus fidei et morum.* Freiburg im Breisgau: Herder, 1991.

Divi Thomae Aquinatis Doctoris Angelici Ordinis Praedicatorum Opera, vol. 8. Venice: 1775.

DuPuy, Pierre, ed. *Preuves des libertez de l'église gallicane* (2nd ed.), vol. 2. Paris: Sébastien Cramoisy, 1651.

Guérin, Paul, ed. *Registres des délibérations du Bureau de la ville de Paris*, vol. 3. Paris: Imprimerie Nationale, 1886.

Luther, Martin. *Luther's Works.* Edited by Hilton Oswald. *Lectures on Romans—Glosses and Scholia*, vol. 25. Saint Louis: Concordia Publishing House, 1972.

_____. *Luther's Works.* Edited by Abdel Ross Wentz. *Word and Sacrament*, vol. 36. Philadelphia: Fortress Press, 1959.

Mansi, J.D. *Sacrorum conciliorum nova et amplissima collectio.* Paris: H. Welter, 1904.

Reichert, Benedictus Maria, ed. *Monumenta ordinis fratrum praedicatorum historica*, vol. 9. Rome: 1901.

Tanner, Norman P., ed. *Decrees of the Ecumenical Councils* (vol. 2, Trent to Vatican II). Washington: Georgetown University Press, 1990.

Secondary Sources Which Mention Doré

Antonio Senensi. *Chronicum Fratrum Ordinis Praedicatorum.* Paris: Nicolas Nivelle, 1585.

Aubert, R. and E. van Cauwenbergh. *Dictionnaire d'histoire et de géographie ecclésiastiques.* Paris: Letouzey et Ané, 1960. S.v. "Doré, Pierre," by R. Aubert.

Baudrier, Julien. *Bibliographie lyonnaise—Recherches sur les imprimeurs, libraires, relieurs et fondeurs de lettres de Lyon au XVIe siècle*, vol. 2-3. Lyon: Auguste Brun, 1895.

Bedouelle, Guy and Bernard Roussel. *Le temps des réformes et la Bible*. Paris: Éditions Beauchesne, 1989.

Brunet, Jacques-Charles. *Manuel du libraire et de l'amateur des livres*, vol. 2. Geneva: Slatkine Reprints, 1990.

Bure, Guillaume-François de. *Bibliographie instructive: ou Traité de la connoissance des livres rares et singuliers*. Paris: Guillaume-François de Bure, 1763.

Cioranescu, Alexandre. *Bibliographie de la littérature française du seizième siècle*. Paris: Klincksieck, 1959.

Chenu, Marie-Dominique. "L'humanisme et la réforme au collège de Saint-Jacques de Paris," *Archives d'histoire dominicaine*, 1 (1946): 130-154.

Crouzet, Denis. *Les guerriers de Dieu: La violence au temps des troubles de religion (vers 1525-vers 1610)*, vol. 1. Seyssel: Champ Vallon, 1990.

D'Amat, Roman and R. Limouzin-Lamothe. *Dictionnaire de biographie française*. Paris: Letouzey et Ané, 1967. S.v. "Doré," by R. Limouzin-Lamothe.

Dictionnaire bibliographique, historique et critique des livres rares. Paris: Cailleau et fils, 1791.

Droz, Eugénie. *Les chemins de l'hérésie—textes et documents*, vol. 1. Geneva: Slatkine Reprints, 1970.

Farge, James K. *Biographical Register of Paris Doctors of Theology 1500-1536*. Toronto: Pontifical Institute of Mediaeval Studies, 1980.

_____. "Les Dominicains et la Faculté de Théologie." *Mémoire Dominicaine*, 12 (1998/1): 21-38.

_____. *Orthodoxy and Reform in Early Reformation France: The Faculty of Theology of Paris, 1500-1543*. Leiden: E. J. Brill, 1985.

_____. *Registre des conclusions de la faculté de théologie de l'université de Paris*. Paris: Klincksieck, 1994.

_____. *Registre des procès-verbaux de la faculté de théologie de l'université de Paris (de janvier 1524 à novembre 1533)*. Paris: Aux Amateurs de Livres, 1990.

Féret, Pierre. *La faculté de théologie de Paris et ses docteurs les plus célèbres— Époque moderne*, vol. 2. Paris: Alphonse Picard et fils, 1901.

Febvre, Lucien and Henri-Jean Martin. *L'apparition du livre*. Paris: Éditions Albin Michel, 1971.

Fragonard, Marie-Madeleine. "Les publications des dominicains, entre innovation et réaction (1500-1560)." In *Changements religieux, genèse de l'État moderne et transformations sociales. Place, fonction et images des clercs, France et Empire (1500-1650)*, Actes du Colloque de Göttingen, March 1992. Publication forthcoming.

_____. "Pierre Doré: Une stratégie de la reconquête." In *Calvin et ses contemporains*, ed. Olivier Millet, 179-194. Geneva: Droz, 1998.

Graesse, J.G. Théodore. *Trésor de livres rares et précieux*, vol. 2. Geneva: Slatkine Reprints, 1993.

Grente, Georges. *Dictionnaire des lettres françaises, le seizième siècle*. Paris: Arthème Fayard, 1951.

Herbermann, Charles G. *The Catholic Encyclopedia*. New York: Encyclopedia Press, 1913. S.v. "Doré, Pierre," by Thomas Schwertner.

Higman, Francis. "'Il seroit trop plus decent respondre en latin': les controversistes catholiques du XVIe siècle face aux écrits réformés." In *Langues et Nations au temps de la Renaissance*, ed. Marie-Thérèse Jones-Davies, 189-212. Paris: Klincksieck, 1991.

_____. "La réfutation par Pierre Doré du catéchisme de Megander." In *Aux origines du catéchisme en France*, ed. Pierre Colin, 55-66. Paris: Desclée, 1989.

_____. "Le domaine français." In *La réforme et le livre--l'Europe de l'imprimé (1517-v. 1570)*, ed. Jean-François Gilmont, 105-154. Paris: Éditions du Cerf, 1990.

_____. *Lire et Découvrir: La circulation des idées au temps de la Réforme*. Geneva: Droz, 1998.

_____. *Piety and the People, Religious Printing in French, 1511-1551*. Aldershot: Scolar Press, 1996.

_____. "Premières réponses catholiques aux écrits de la Réforme en France, 1525-c.1540." In *Le Livre dans l'Europe de la Renaissance*, Actes du XXVIIIe colloque international d'études humanistes de Tours sous direction de Pierre Aquilon et Henri-Jean Martin, 361-377. Promodis: Éditions du Cercle de la Librairie, 1988.

Hoefer. *Nouvelle biographie générale depuis les temps les plus reculés jusqu'à 1850-60, avec les renseignements bibliographiques*, vol. 13-14. Copenhagen: Rosenkilde et Bagger, 1965.

Juvigny, Rigoley de. *Les bibliothèques françoises de La Croix du Maine et de Du Verdier*, vol. 2. Paris: Saillant & Nyon, 1772.

Langlois, John. "Pierre Doré—Écrivain spirituel et théologien des laïcs." *Mémoire Dominicaine*, 12 (1998/1): 39-48.

Levesque, J. D. "Le couvent des frères prêcheurs de Blois." *Documents pour servir à l'histoire de l'ordre de Saint-Dominique en France*, 28 (1er trimestre 1993): 3-28.

Mallet, Antoine. *Histoire des saincts, papes, cardinaux, patriarches, archevesques, evesques, docteurs de toutes facultez de l'Université de Paris, & autres hommes illustres, qui furent superieurs, ou religieux du couvent de S. Jacques de l'Ordre des FF. Prescheurs à Paris*, vol. 2. Paris: Jean Branchu, 1645.

Mortier, D.A. *Histoire abrégée de l'ordre de Saint-Dominique en France*. Tours: Maison Alfred Mame et fils, 1920.

_____. *Histoire des maîtres généraux de l'ordre des frères prêcheurs* (vol. 5: 1487-1589). Paris: Alphonse Picard et fils, 1911.

Polman, Pontien. *L'élément historique dans la controverse religieuse du XVIe siècle*. Gembloux: Imprimerie J. Duculot, 1932.

Quétif, J. and J. Échard. *Scriptores ordinis praedicatorum*, vol. 2. 1721.

Sauzet, Robert. *Les reguliers mendiants--Acteurs du changement religieux dans le royaume de France (1480-1560)*. Tours: Publications de l'Université de Tours, 1994.

Viller, Marcel. *Dictionnaire de spiritualité*. Paris: Gabriel Beauchesne et fils, 1937. S.v. "Doré, Pierre," by André Duval.

Walz, Angelus. *Compendium Historiae Ordinis Praedicatorum*. Rome: Pontificium Athenaeum "Angelicum," 1948.

Other Secondary Sources

Bagchi, David. *Luther's Earliest Opponents: Catholic Controversialists, 1518-1525*. Minneapolis: Fortress Press, 1991.

Baumgartner, Frederic J. *Change and Continuity in the French Episcopate: The Bishops and the Wars of Religion, 1547-1610*. Durham: Duke University Press, 1986.

_____. *France in the Sixteenth Century*. New York: St. Martin's Press, 1995.

Bedouelle, Guy. "Guillaume Petit, humaniste, théologien et politique." *Mémoire Dominicaine*, 12 (1998/1): 63-74.

_____. *Lefèvre d'Étaples et l'intelligence des Écritures*. Geneva: Droz, 1976.

Birely, Robert. *The Refashioning of Catholicism, 1450-1700*. London: MacMillan, 1999.

Bynum, Caroline Walker. *Jesus as Mother—Studies in the Spirituality of the High Middle Ages*. Berkeley: University of California Press, 1984.

Cessario, Romanus. *Le thomisme et les thomistes*. Paris: Éditions du Cerf, 1999.

De Bujanda, J.M., ed. *Index des livres interdits*, vol. 1. Geneva: Droz, 1985.

De Meyer, Albert. *La Congrégation de Hollande ou La réforme dominicaine en territoire bourguignon, 1465-1515*. Liège: Imprimerie Soledi, 1946.

Ellington, Donna Spivey. *From Sacred Body to Angelic Soul: Understanding Mary in Late Medieval and Early Modern Europe*. Washington: The Catholic University of America Press, 2001.

Farge, James K. *Le parti conservateur au XVIe siècle--Université et Parlement de Paris à l'époque de la renaissance et de la réforme*. Collège de France, 1992.

Febvre, Lucien. "Les origines de la réforme française et le problème des causes de la réforme" in *Au coeur religieux du XVIe siècle*. Paris: SEVPEN, 1957.

Fragonard, Marie-Madeleine. "Guillaume Pépin" *Mémoire Dominicaine*, 12 (1998/1): 49-62.

Gaboriau, Florent. *Ecriture seule?* Paris: FAC-éditions, 1997.

Gadoffre, Gilbert. *La révolution culturelle dans la France des humanistes*. Geneva: Droz, 1997.

Ganoczy, Alexandre. *Calvin, théologien de l'église et du ministère*. Paris: Éditions du Cerf, 1964.

Gilmont, Jean-François, ed. *La Réforme et le livre: L'Europe de l'imprimé (1517-v. 1570)*. Paris: Éditions du Cerf, 1990.

Graef, Hilda. *Mary: A History of Doctrine and Devotion*, 2 vols. New York: Sheed and Ward, 1964.

Hefele, Charles-Joseph. *Histoire des Conciles d'après les documents originaux*. Translated by H. Leclercq. Paris: Letouzey et Ané, 1916.

Higman, Francis. *Censorship and the Sorbonne*. Geneva: Droz, 1979.

_____. *La diffusion de la réforme en France (1520-1565)*. Geneva: Labor et Fides, 1992.

_____. "Luther et la piété de l'église gallicane: *Le Livre de vraye et parfaicte oraison*," in *Revue d'histoire et de philosophie religieuses*, 63 (1983): 91-111.

Holt, Mack P. *The French Wars of Religion, 1562-1629*. Cambridge: Cambridge University Press, 1995.

Imbart de la Tour, Pierre. *Les origines de la réforme*, vol. 1-4. Paris: Librairie Hachette, 1905-1914.

Isambert, Decrusy and Armet. *Recueil général des anciennes lois françaises*, vol. 12. Paris: Belin-Leprieur, 1828.

Laurent, M.H. "Autour de la controverse luthérienne en France," in *Revue d'histoire écclésiastique*, 35 (1939): 283-290.

Lestringant, Frank. *Une Sainte Horreur ou le voyage en Eucharistie, XVIe -XVIIIe siècle*. Paris: Presses Universitaires de France, 1996.

McDonnell, Killian. *John Calvin, the Church, and the Eucharist*. Princeton: Princeton University Press, 1967.

McGrath, Alister E. *Reformation Thought—An Introduction*. Oxford: Blackwell, 1996.

Minnich, Nelson. *The Catholic Reformation: Council, Churchmen, Controversies*. Brookfield, VT.: Variorum, 1993.

Mollat du Jourdin, Michel and André Vauchez, eds. *Histoire du Christianisme des origines à nos jours*, vol. 6. Paris: Desclée-Fayard, 1990.

Montagnes, Bernard. "La Congrégation de France (1497-1569)," in *Archivum Fratrum Praedicatorum*, LV (1985): 67-114.

Moreau-Rendu, S. *Le couvent Saint-Jacques--evocation de l'histoire des dominicains de Paris*. Paris: Éditions du Cerf, 1961.

Mulchahey, M. Michèle. *"First the Bow is Bent in Study"—Dominican Education before 1350*. Toronto: Pontifical Institute of Mediaeval Studies, 1998.

Mullaney, T.U. "Mary Immaculate in the Writings of St Thomas," in *The Thomist*, XVII 4 (1954): 433-68.

Niesel, Wilhem. *The Theology of Calvin*. Philadelphia: Westminster Press, 1957.

Olin, John. *Catholic Reform—From Cardinal Ximenes to the Council of Trent, 1495-1563*. New York: Fordham University Press, 1990.

Pelikan, Jaroslav. *Mary Through the Centuries: Her Place in the History of Culture*. New Haven: Yale University Press, 1996.

_____. *The Christian Tradition: A History of the Development of Doctrine*, vol. 4, *Reformation of Church and Dogma (1300-1700)*. Chicago: University of Chicago Press, 1984.

Pernot, Michel. *Les guerres de religion en France 1559-1598*. Paris: Sedes, 1987.

Péronnet, Michel. "Les évêques français et le livre au XVIe siècle: auteurs, éditeurs et censeurs." In *Le Livre dans l'Europe de la Renaissance*, Actes du XXVIIIe colloque international d'études humanistes de Tours sous direction de Pierre Aquilon et Henri-Jean Martin, 159-169. Promodis: Éditions du Cercle de la Librairie, 1988.

Peter, M. Rodolphe and M. Bertrand Roussel. *Le livre et la réforme*. Bordeaux: Société des Bibliophiles de Guyenne, 1987.

Peter, Rodolphe. "La réception de Luther en France au XVIe siècle," in *Revue d'histoire et de philosophie religieuses*, 63 (1983): 67-89.

Renaudet, Augustin. *Préréforme et humanisme à Paris pendant les premières guerres d'Italie (1494-1517)*. Geneva: Slatkine Reprints, 1981.

Renouard, Philippe. *Imprimeurs & libraires parisiens du XVIe siècle*, vol. 1. Paris: 1964.

Romier, Lucien. *Le royaume de Catherine de Médicis: La France à la veille des guerres de religion*. Geneva: Slatkine Reprints, 1978.

Rummel, Erika. *Erasmus and his Catholic Critics*. Nieuwkoop: De Graff, 1989.

_____. *The humanist-scholastic debate in the Renaissance & Reformation*. Cambridge, MA: Harvard University Press, 1995.

_____. "The Importance of being a Doctor: The Quarrel over Competency between Humanists and Theologians in the Renaissance," *The Catholic Historical Review*, 82 (1996): 187-203.

Salmon, J.H.M. *Society in Crisis—France in the Sixteenth Century*. New York: St. Martin's Press, 1975.

Steinmetz, David. *Calvin in Context*. New York: Oxford University Press, 1995.

_____. *Luther in Context*. Bloomington: Indiana University Press, 1986.

Strehle, Stephen. *The Catholic Roots of the Protestant Gospel—Encounter between the Middle Ages and the Reformation*. Leiden: E. J. Brill, 1995.

Swiezawski, Stefan. "Le thomisme à la fin du Moyen Age." In *San Tommaso, fonti e riflessi del suo pensiero*. Studi Tomistici 1, 225-248. Rome: Città Nuova Editrice, 1974.

Tallon, Alain. *La France et le Concile de Trente (1518-1563)*. Rome: École Française de Rome, 1997.

Taylor, Larissa. *Heresy and Orthodoxy in Sixteenth-Century Paris: François Le Picart and the Beginnings of the Catholic Reformation*. Leiden: E. J. Brill, 1999.

_____. *Soldiers of Christ—Preaching in Late Medieval and Reformation France*. New York: Oxford University Press, 1992.

_____. "The Influence of Humanism on Post-Reformation Catholic Preachers in France," *Renaissance Quarterly*, 50 (1997): 119-135.

Thompson, Bard. *Humanists and Reformers—A History of the Renaissance and Reformation*. Grand Rapids: Eerdmans, 1996.

Touron, A. *Histoire des hommes illustres de l'ordre de Saint Dominique*, vol. 4. Paris: Babuty and Quillau, 1747.

Veissière, Michel. *L'évêque Guillaume Briçonnet, 1470-1534*. Provins: Société d'histoire et d'archéologie, 1986.

Villoslada, Ricardo G. *La Universidad de Paris durante los estudios de Francisco de Vitoria, O.P. (1507-1522)*. Series Facultatis Hist. Ecclesiasticae, vol. 14. Rome: Aedes Universitatis Gregorianae, 1938.

Wendel, François. *Calvin, sources et évolution de sa pensée religieuse*. Geneva: Labor et Fides, 1985.

INDEX

Aaron, 196
Abel, 195
Abraham, 142-145, 162, 195-196
absenteeism, 26
absolution, 213
abstinence, 69, 213
Acts of the Apostles, 103
Adam, 216, 242, 247, 251
  and Eve, 181, 217-218, 231, 237-238, 247, 253
adoptive sonship, 124, 216
affaire des placards, 32, 36, 49
affective union with Christ, 132, 226, 228, 264
Alan de Rupe, 233
Albert the Great, St., 109
allegorical interpretation of Scripture. *See* Scripture
Ambrose, St., 109
Anselm, St., 109, 231
Antoinette de Bourbon, duchess of Guise, 56, 79, 90, 289-290
apostles, 102, 118-119, 198-200, 204
Apostles' Creed, 67
apostolic succession, 101
appetites, 214, 232, 252-253
Aquinas, Thomas, St., 47-49, 60, 99, 109-112, 140-141, 149, 153, 157, 162-163, 169, 185-186, 208, 216, 234-235, 239-246, 250, 253, 255, 266-267
Arande, Michel d', 31
aristocracy (French), 27, 34, 39, 53, 92-94, 119
Aristotle, 68
Arius, 53
Articles of Faith, 30, 32-33, 38, 50, 52-53, 265
Augustine, St., 99, 109, 135, 160, 219, 231
Augustinian Hermits, 41, 134

Babylonian Captivity of the Church, 175, 193
Badet, Arnaud, 64
Bandelli, Vincent, 42-43
baptism, 194, 232, 252, 259
Baumgartner, Frederic, 26

beatitude, 138, 148-149, 168, 241
Beatitudes, 83, 107, 111, 137, 147-150, 153, 155, 162, 266
Beda, Noël, 31
Bedouelle, Guy, 24, 66
Bellarmine, Robert, St., 105
Bernard of Clairvaux, St., 109, 121, 250
Berquin, Louis de, 31
bishop
  French episcopate, 2, 21-22, 25-27, 31, 35-36, 53, 66-67, 265
  office of, 33, 119, 194, 200
breasts of Christ, 121
Briçonnet, Guillaume, 22-23, 25-26
Brunet, J.C., 9-10
Bucer, Martin, 69
Bynum, Carolyn, 121

Cajetan (Thomas de Vio), 44, 56, 60
Calvin, John, 1-2, 17, 19, 53, 86, 91, 122, 125-129, 131-132, 135-136, 147, 167, 170-171, 176-177, 183-187, 189-192, 194-196, 202, 208, 212-213, 220, 222, 234, 264, 266
Calvinism, 62, 69, 122
Campester, Lambert, 63
Canisius, Peter, St., 262
cardinal virtues, 229
Carmelites, 71
Caroli, Pierre, 28
catechism, 20, 64-65, 67-68, 72, 84-85, 103, 125, 138-139, 162, 169, 198, 226, 262
Catherine de Medici, 90, 290
Catherine of Siena, St., 41
Catholic League, 53
censorship, 27-30, 34, 37, 49-50, 69, 86, 265
Chabot, Philippe de, 52, 87, 116
Chamier, Daniel, 105-106
charity, 67, 96, 132, 136, 139-146, 153, 160, 162, 210, 217, 222, 227-230, 254-256, 258-259, 261, 263
Charles IX, 39
Charles V, 32
Charles de Lorraine, 26, 35, 53, 55, 57
Charronelle, Gilles, 47
chastity, 206-207

Chenu, M.D., 47
Christian humanism. *See* humanism
Cicero, 115
circle of Meaux, 22-25, 28, 31
circumcision, 145
Cistercians, 58
Claude de Lorraine, duke of Guise, 53-57, 79, 88-90, 125, 144-145, 289
Clement of Alexandria, St., 121
Clérée, Jean, 43, 46
Clichtove, Josse, 13
Cochlaeus, Johann, 105
College of Montaigu, 47
Commentary on the Books of the Sentences, 110
communion. *See* Eucharist
conciliarism, 56, 239
Concordat of Bologna, 27, 33
concupiscence, 221, 253-255
confession of sins, 213
Congregation of France, 44
Congregation of Holland, 43-44
conscience, 4, 17, 53, 94, 134, 176, 205, 268
consubstantiation, 173-174, 183-184
contemplation, 84, 97, 107, 118, 251
contrition, 158-159, 206-208, 213, 219, 230, 249
Corinthians, first letter to, 107, 132, 136-137, 139, 141, 147, 162, 176-177, 205, 207
Corpus Christi, feast of, 169
Council of Basel, 56, 237-238, 243, 246
Council of Constance, 56
Council of Ferrara-Florence, 237-238
Council of Trent, 2, 27, 30, 55-56, 102, 105, 156, 159, 165-166, 209, 212, 215, 261-262, 265
Counter-Reformation, 27, 261
Covenant
  New, 107, 195-197, 200-201
  Old, 126, 179, 191, 196-197, 200
creation, 247, 251, 256
Crockaert, Pieter, 47-48, 60, 68, 71
Croso, Bernard de, 63
cross, 105-106, 176, 194-195
Crouzet, Denis, 3, 14-16
Cyril of Alexandria, St., 109

damnation, 138
death, 15, 84, 134, 148, 153, 168, 170, 172, 180, 210, 218, 232, 248, 256, 259
deification, 165, 182, 215-216, 218-221

despair, 143, 249, 256
devil. *See* Satan
Dietenberger, Johann, 62
divine image. *See* image of God
divinity of Christ, 165, 188
divinization. *See* deification
Divolé, Pierre, 72
doctors of the Church, 109
Dominican Order, 3, 6, 41-42, 44, 60, 71, 75, 104, 234, 239, 243, 246
  English Dominicans, 62-63
  French Dominicans, 39-40, 51, 60-61, 63-64, 68, 70-73
  German Dominicans, 62-63
Du Prat, Antoine, 26
Duval, André, 12-13, 39, 58-59

Ebner, Margaret, 121
Échard, J., 8-10, 39-40, 44, 58, 76-79
Eck, Johann, 105
Edict of Chateaubriant, 30
Edict of Nantes, 81, 268
Elijah, 178-179, 203-204
Ephesians, letter to the, 177
Erasmus, 19, 100, 112-115, 201
Esau, 178, 180
eternal life, 123, 136, 138, 144, 148, 150-155, 162, 168, 181, 212, 218, 228-229, 259
  See also beatitude
Eucharist, 15-16, 32-33, 36, 49, 84, 88, 116, 119, 121-122, 131-132, 165-199, 202-223, 227, 261-262
  adoration of, 167
  Calvinist understanding, 176-177, 183-187, 194-195
  conditions for worthy reception, 169, 206-207, 209
  frequent reception, 209-216, 222, 262
  as Holy Communion, 15-16, 97, 165, 168, 177, 181-182, 184, 191, 207, 210, 216, 218-219, 222-223, 227
  Lutheran understanding, 173-175, 192-193, 195
  real presence, 15, 32-33, 122, 132, 166, 171, 173-174, 177, 180-183, 189, 202, 208, 211, 215, 222-223, 261
  as sacrifice, 84-85, 166-168, 188, 190-195, 198-202
  as thanksgiving, 191
Eugenius IV, 237-238
évangélisme, 22-23

Eve, 181, 216, 218, 231, 237, 247-248, 251, 253
   See also Adam and Eve
Exodus, book of, 206

Fabry, Jean, 51
Faculty of Theology (University of Paris), 10, 13, 21, 23-25, 27-34, 36-38, 44-45, 49-50, 52-53, 56, 58-59, 66, 69, 75, 90, 96, 113, 119, 233, 238-239, 265, 267
faith, virtue of, 67-68, 84, 93, 131-147, 150-151, 158, 160, 162-163, 191, 208, 220, 225, 230, 260
fall of man, 217, 231-232, 237, 253, 256
Farel, Guillaume, 22-23, 67
Farge, James, 3, 12-13, 27-28, 30, 39, 49, 71, 76-80, 82-83
fasting, 69
Fathers of the Church, 20, 99, 104, 109
Febvre, Lucien, 233
Féret, Pierre, 10-11
First Book of the Sentences, 45, 47-48, 243, 245
fomes peccati, 253
forgiveness of sin, 192, 200, 221-222, 250
fortitude, 229
Fourth Lateran Council, 170, 172, 210
Fragonard, Marie-Madeleine, 3, 16-18, 63, 69, 72, 86
Francis I, 22, 27, 31-33, 36, 49, 51-52, 55, 90-91, 93, 113, 289
Francis II, king, 55
François I, duke of Guise, 55
Francis de Sales, St., 1, 209, 263
free will, 131, 136-137, 146-147, 157, 159-160
French Dominicans. *See* Dominican Order
French humanists, 22-26, 28, 31-33, 49, 66, 112
   See also humanism
friendship with God, 143

Galatians, letter to the, 15, 133, 145, 219
Gallican Congregation, 43-44, 46, 51, 55
General Chapters of the Dominican Order
   (1523) Valladolid, 61-62, 64, 73
   (1525) Rome, 45, 61, 64, 73
   (1530) Rome, 61, 64, 73
   (1553) Rome, 57
Genesis, book of, 142, 178, 180, 247
Gervais, Henri, 51

good works, 133-135, 139-140, 144, 151, 153-154, 162, 230, 257
grace, 85, 118-119, 121, 131-133, 135-136, 146, 148, 150, 152-155, 157-163, 181, 209, 211, 213, 215-216, 218, 220-221, 223, 228, 230-232, 235, 237, 242, 244, 246-252, 257-260, 263-264, 267
   as perfecting nature, 135, 182, 216, 228, 235, 251, 259, 263, 264
   cooperation with, 133, 136, 155, 157-159, 161, 249
   primacy of, 133, 153-155, 160
   See also *sola gratia*
Great Western Schism, 60
Gregory the Great, St., 109
Guerric of Igny, 121
Guise, house of, 7-8, 11-12, 14-15, 26, 33, 36, 40, 53-57, 87-90, 144-145, 154, 252, 289

Hail Mary, the, 243, 245
Hapsburgs, 32-33, 56
Hebrews, letter to the, 105, 195-197
Henri, third duke of Guise, 53, 57
Henry II (Valois), 30, 36-37, 39, 55, 90-91, 290
Henry VIII of England, 62
heresy, 2, 12, 14, 18, 21, 25-28, 30-34, 36-37, 40, 49, 54, 60-64, 66-68, 70, 85, 87, 91-92, 131, 147-148, 163, 202, 225, 237, 263, 265-266
hierarchical nature of the Church, 34
Higman, Francis, 3, 19-20, 29, 38, 65-67, 125, 225-226
holiness, 218, 223, 263
Holofernes, 247-248
Holy Communion. *See* Eucharist
Holy Orders. *See* priesthood
Holy Roman Empire, 62
Holy Spirit, 93, 102, 119, 124, 146, 153, 179, 218, 235
   gifts of, 84
Homer, 115-116
hope, 38, 67, 126, 132, 139-141, 143-145, 148, 160-161, 236, 248, 254, 259
humanism, 13, 22-26, 28, 31-33, 49, 66, 100, 112-115, 117, 201
   See also French humanists
humanity of Christ, 183, 187-190, 241
human nature. *See* nature
hypostatic union, 188-189

image of God (*imago Dei*), 216, 235-237, 247, 249, 251, 254
Imbart de la Tour, Pierre, 23-24
Immaculate Conception, 233-243, 245-246
immortality, 217
impurity, 208, 249-250
imputation of righteousness, 135
Incarnation, 185
Index of Prohibited Books, 56
indulgences, 41, 63, 101, 134
Innocent III, 188
inquisition, 37
Institutes of the Christian Religion, 86, 91, 126, 128, 147, 183, 186, 234
Introduction to the Devout Life, 263
Isaac, 143, 178, 180-181, 195

Jacob, 105-106, 178, 180
Jacobin friars. *See* French Dominicans
James V, 53
James, letter of, 133, 135-137, 139
Jeremiah, 88
Jerome, St., 109, 113
Jesuits. *See* Society of Jesus
John the Baptist, St., 205
John Chrysostom, St., 109
John of the Cross, St., 1
John, gospel of, 123, 137, 145, 147, 151, 154-155, 159-161, 174-175, 199, 206
Josiah, 88
Judas, 208
Judith, 247-248
Julius III, 165
justice, 93, 144, 151, 153, 155, 229, 250
See also original justice
justification, 56, 84, 131, 133-138, 141, 146, 150, 155-159, 223, 230, 249, 261
by faith alone, 68, 137, 144, 191, 260
See also *sola fide*
Catholic understanding of, 85, 99, 143, 156, 159-163
Justiniani, Vincent, 11

Kings, first book of, 178-179, 203
Köllin, Conrad, 62

Lambert, Pierre, 90-92, 103, 289
Langmann, Adelheid, 121
Lateran Council IV. *See* Fourth Lateran Council

Laurent, Thomas, 70
Le Picart, François, 38
Lefèvre d'Etaples, Jacques, 22-24, 31, 108
Leo X, 27, 49
levitical priesthood. *See* priesthood
Lievin, Valentin, 70
liturgy. *See* Mass
Louis XII, 39, 43
Louis, cardinal de Guise, 53, 57
love, 38, 84, 108, 132-134, 137-147, 214, 217, 222, 227, 229-230, 251, 254-257, 259
See also charity
Luke, gospel of, 97, 143, 209, 235
Luther, Martin, 2, 19, 23-27, 29, 31-32, 41, 53, 55, 61, 63-68, 70, 101, 122, 125, 131-134, 136, 150-151, 171, 173-175, 192-196, 202-204, 216, 220, 222, 225, 261, 264, 266
Lutheranism, 25, 28, 61, 66, 69, 72, 86, 122, 190

magisterium, 23, 56, 156, 240
Maigret, Aimé, 28, 68-69, 71
Mair, John, 13
Malachi, book of, 187
Mallet, Antoine, 7-8, 11
manna, 175, 187, 203-204
Marguerite de Navarre, 31, 50
Marguerite, daughter of Francis I, 90, 93, 289
Marian devotion, 72, 233, 250
Marie de Guise, 53
marriage, 159, 177, 217
Marshall, Richard, 62
Mary. *See* Virgin Mary
Mary Magdalene, 51, 83, 118, 144
Mary Stuart, 53, 55
Mass, 166-168, 187, 190-195, 202-203, 210, 223
Massacre of Wassy, 53
Matthew, gospel of, 102, 105, 111, 137, 147-148, 150, 182, 185, 218
Mazurier, Martial, 28
Meaux. *See* circle of Meaux
meditation, 93, 109, 120, 168, 207, 218, 255-256, 259, 264, 266
Megander, Gaspard, 20, 85, 125
Melchizedek, 195-196
Mensing, Johann, 62
mercy, 143-144, 149, 151, 249
merit, 85, 131, 137, 147-155, 161-163, 221, 228, 240, 255, 260, 267

ministerial priesthood. *See* priesthood
Miroir de l'âme pécheresse, 50
monarchy (French), 21-22, 31, 33, 36-37, 49, 51, 90
Moriae Encomium, 112
Morin, Nicolas, 63
Mortier, D.A., 11-12, 14, 44, 62
mortification, 206
Mosaic Law, 88, 133, 143, 195-196
Moses, 107, 175, 196
Mother of God. *See* Virgin Mary
Mulchahey, Michelle, 48
Muses, 116
mysticism, 14-16, 109, 120-121, 215, 223, 227

nature, human, 132, 136, 216, 228, 231-232, 259
New Covenant. *See* Covenant
New Testament. *See* Scripture
Novum Instrumentum, 113
Novum Testamentum, 113-114

observant movement, 41-43, 60
Old Covenant. *See* Covenant
Old Testament. *See* Scripture
Order of Preachers. *See* Dominican Order
ordination, 6, 193-194
original justice, 231-232, 237, 247, 253
original sin. *See* sin
orthodoxy, 2, 23, 25, 28, 30-31, 33, 36, 50, 54, 61, 72, 93-94, 98, 119, 128-129, 132, 135-136, 167, 177, 258, 260, 265
Ory, Matthieu, 5, 49, 70
Our Father, the, 67

Pantagruel, 5-6, 11
papacy, 2, 56, 62, 101, 238
papal authority, 239
Paris, Etienne, 72
Parlement of Paris, 29-31, 43, 46, 51
paschal lamb, 206
passion of Christ, 79, 85, 134, 153-154, 170, 172, 194, 202, 207, 221, 256, 259
passions, 231, 253, 259
Passover, 179, 206
Paul, St., 15-16, 53, 84, 107, 112, 114-115, 132-134, 136-139, 141-143, 145, 147, 162, 176-177, 199, 205, 207, 219, 232, 247, 252

Pelagianism, 148, 154, 191, 249
Pelagius, 53, 160
Peloponnesian War, 116
penance, 134, 148, 158, 206, 259
  sacrament of, 84, 200, 257
Pépin, Guillaume, 69, 71-72
Pericles, 116
Peter, first letter of, 194
Peter, St., 102-103, 138-139, 152-153, 171, 198-199, 220
Peter Canisius. *See* Canisius, Peter, St.
Peter Lombard, 45, 47-48, 243, 245
Peter Martyr (of Verona), St., 58-60
Petit, Guillaume, 25-26, 64-68, 70, 72, 112
Petit traicté de la Saincte Cène, 126, 128, 167, 171, 177, 212-213
Pius IX, 240
Pius V, St., 262
Plato, 115
pluralism, 26
poverty of spirit, 149
prayers on behalf of the dead, 28, 104
priesthood, 115, 190-204, 223
  of believers, 193-194
  of Christ, 195-198, 203
  levitical, 196-197
  ministerial, 101, 114-115, 167, 190-191, 194-195, 198-200, 202-204
  royal, 194
printing press, 2, 25, 70, 89
Protestantism, 2, 11, 18, 21, 55, 122
  See also Calvinism, Lutheranism
providence, 217-218
Province of France, 43
prudence, 200, 229, 231
psalms, 83, 95, 117, 154, 264, 266
purgatory, 101
purity, 149, 151, 206-207, 219, 245, 248

Quétif, J., 8-10, 39-40, 44, 58, 76-79

Rabelais, 5-6, 11, 19, 26
Raymond of Capua, 41
real presence. *See* Eucharist
reason, 173, 188, 232, 237, 252-254, 259
Rebecca, 178
redemption, 133, 233, 239, 247, 256
Reformation, 1-3, 11, 15-17, 19, 21-28, 30, 32-34, 37-38, 40-41, 49, 53, 55, 60-61, 63, 67-68, 72-73, 82, 91, 94, 98, 101, 106, 122, 124-125, 129, 131-133, 144, 181,

204, 209, 215, 225-228, 233-234, 258, 260-262, 264-266
Reformed theology, 2, 21, 27, 32, 67, 70, 98, 100-101, 122, 129, 131-133, 148, 150, 156, 158, 165, 204, 215-216, 225, 228, 258, 260-261
regeneration, 135, 216
relics, 101
Renaissance, 22, 26, 31, 49, 112
Renée de Lorraine, 90, 289-290
resurrection, 259
revelation, 99, 101-102, 111, 175
righteousness, 134-135, 142-143, 150, 191, 218
Roman Catechism, 262
Romans, letter to the, 133-134, 142-143, 150, 232
rosary, 72, 233, 239
Rotier, Esprit, 62, 70, 72
Roussel, Gérard, 31, 50
royal priesthood. *See* priesthood

S. Jacques, 7, 40, 42-43, 45-48, 51, 56-58, 60, 68, 78, 99, 110, 163, 228
sacra doctrina, 110
sacraments, 84, 101, 103, 105, 165, 194, 199, 220, 223, 259, 261
sacrifice, 115, 143, 151, 176, 179, 190-196, 198, 200, 202
See also Eucharist
Saint-Germain-des-Près, 22
saints, prayers to the, 28, 101, 234
salvation, 17, 65, 67-69, 123, 126, 128, 134, 139-141, 143-144, 147-148, 153-154, 161, 193, 223, 230, 249-250, 260
salvation history, 195, 256
Salve Regina, 239
Samaritan woman, 85, 137, 144, 157, 159, 161, 266
sanctification, 250
Satan, 118, 127, 166-167, 171, 180-181, 217, 247-248, 257
satisfaction, 148, 194
Sauzet, Robert, 63, 68, 70
scholastic method, 71, 99-100, 111
scholastic theology, 49, 100, 112, 136, 141, 163, 267
Scriptores Ordinis Praedicatorum, 7-9, 12, 39, 76, 78
Scripture, 23, 25, 29, 45, 101, 107-110, 112-114, 117-118, 133, 162-163, 172, 266
allegorical interpretation of, 104-106, 266

New Testatment, 102, 108, 113, 121, 133-134, 137, 178, 204-205, 266
Old Testament, 108, 121, 178-180, 187
primacy of, 98, 101-109
translation into vernacular, 100, 106-108, 112, 114, 266
unity of Scripture and Tradition, 102, 106, 160, 204, 261
See also *sola scriptura*
scrupulosity, 134, 213
Seneca, 115
Senensi, Antonio, 6
Sentences. See *First Book of the Sentences*
simul justus et peccator, 150-151, 216
sin, 15, 92, 103, 135, 144-145, 150-151, 154, 157-161, 166-167, 176, 192-194, 196, 198-200, 206-207, 213-214, 216-217, 219, 222-223, 228-229, 231, 235-236, 242, 244, 246-250, 253, 256-257, 259
grave, 120, 213
original, 218, 231-232, 234, 237-240, 242, 244-248, 252-254
Sixtus IV, 233
Society of Jesus (Jesuits), 262
sola fide, 132-134, 136-137, 142, 144-145, 148-149, 161-163, 223, 228
sola gratia, 133, 148-149, 228
sola scriptura, 99, 101-102, 133, 170, 173, 192, 204, 266
Song of Songs, 104, 109, 242, 246
Summa Theologiae, 47-48, 110-111, 140-141, 149, 157, 163, 189, 239-241, 243, 246, 254, 267

Taylor, Larissa, 38, 71
temperance, 229
Temple, 102, 200
temporal punishment, 103
temptation, 118, 180, 213-214, 216, 218, 222, 252, 257-258
Ten Commandments, 67, 153
Teresa of Avila, St., 1
Tessaradecas Consolatoria, 125
theological virtues, 67, 132, 139-141, 160, 259
Theotokos, 237
Thomas Aquinas. *See* Aquinas
Thomas de Vio. *See* Cajetan
Thomism, 112
Thucydides, 116
Timothy, first letter to, 114-115

Timothy, St., 199-200
Titus, St., 199-200
Tournon, François de, 26, 90-91, 289
Tradition, 99, 101-102, 104, 106, 133, 135, 160, 191, 199, 202, 204, 242, 261, 266
transubstantiation, 165, 167, 169-174, 176-177, 179-180, 182-187, 189-190, 205, 209-210, 212, 215, 222, 225, 262
Trinity, 236

University of Paris, 1, 5, 21, 40, 46-47, 113

veneration of relics. *See* relics
Villoslada, Ricardo, 47, 49
Virgil, 115-116
Virgin Mary
  as image of virtue, 83, 104, 225, 232-233, 235-238, 241, 247, 249, 251, 254, 259
  as intercessor, 234, 248-250
  as model of discipleship, 235
  Mother of God, 104, 232-233, 235, 237, 241, 245, 251
  as new Eve, 247-248, 251
  See also Immaculate Conception
virginity, 214
virtue, 83, 93-95, 104, 111, 116, 118, 120, 132-133, 137-141, 144, 147, 149-150, 154, 216, 218, 221, 226-233, 235-236, 241-242, 246-247, 249, 251-255, 257-259, 263-264, 267
virtuous life, 98, 132, 148, 225, 230, 232, 235-236, 246, 248, 252, 257-258, 260
Vitoria, Francisco de, 48-49, 60, 68, 71, 110, 267
vows, 69
Vulgate, 106, 113-115, 154

wars of religion, 14, 53, 55, 81, 268
widowhood, 81, 84, 214
women, role of, 18, 89-90, 94-95, 97-98, 110, 227
works-righteousness, 135, 191

Zwingli, Ulrich, 122

ROMAN CATHOLIC STUDIES

1. L. Thomas Snyderwine (ed.), **Researching the Development of Lay Leadership in the Catholic Church Since Vatican II: Bibliographical Abstracts**
2. Frank Przetacznik, **The Catholic Concept of Genuine and Just Peace as a Basic Collective Human Right**
3. Andrew Cuschieri, **Introductory Readings in Canon**
4. Ernest Skublics, **How Eastern Orthodoxy Can Contribute to Roman Catholic Renewal: A Theological and Pastoral Proposition**
5. Robert J. Kaslyn, **"Communion with the Church" and the Code of Canon Law: An Analysis of the Foundation and Implications of the Canonical Obligation to Maintain Communion with the Catholic Church**
6. Patricia Voydanoff and Thomas M. Martin (eds.), **Using a Family Perspective in Catholic Social Justice and Family Ministries**
7. Michael Sundermeier and Robert Churchill (eds.), **The Literary and Educational Effects of the Thought of John Henry Newman**
8. Ross A. Shecterle, **The Theology of Revelation of Avery Dulles, 1980-1994: Symbolic Mediation**
9. Filippo Maria Toscano, **El Universalismo Del Pensamiento Cristiano De Don Luigi Sturzo**
10. James L. MacNeil, **A Study of Gaudium et Spes 19-22, The Second Vatican Council Response to Contemporary Atheism**
11. David B. Perrin, **The Sacrament of Reconciliation: An Existential Approach**
12. Stephen R. Duncan, **A Genre in Hindusthani Music (Bhajans) as Used in the Roman Catholic Church**
13. Maria G. McClelland, **The Sisters of Mercy, Popular Politics and the Growth of the Roman Catholic Community in Hull, 1855-1930**
14. Robert Berchmans, **A Study of Lonergan's Self-Transcending Subject and Kegan's Evolving Self: A Framework for Christian Anthropology**
15. Larry Hostetter, **The Ecclesial Dimension of Personal and Social Reform in the Writings of Isaac Thomas Hecker**
16. Patricia Smith**, Theoretical and Practical Understanding of the Integral Reordering of Canon Law**
17. Kevin E. Schmiesing, **American Catholic Intellectuals and the Dilemma of Dual Identities, 1895-1955**
18. John Langlois, **A Catholic Response in Sixteenth-Century France to Reformation Theology–The Works of Pierre Doré**